RIT PRESS

The Comics Scare Returns: The Contemporary Resurgence of Horror Comics

RIT PRESS

The Comics Scare Returns: The Contemporary Resurgence of Horror Comics

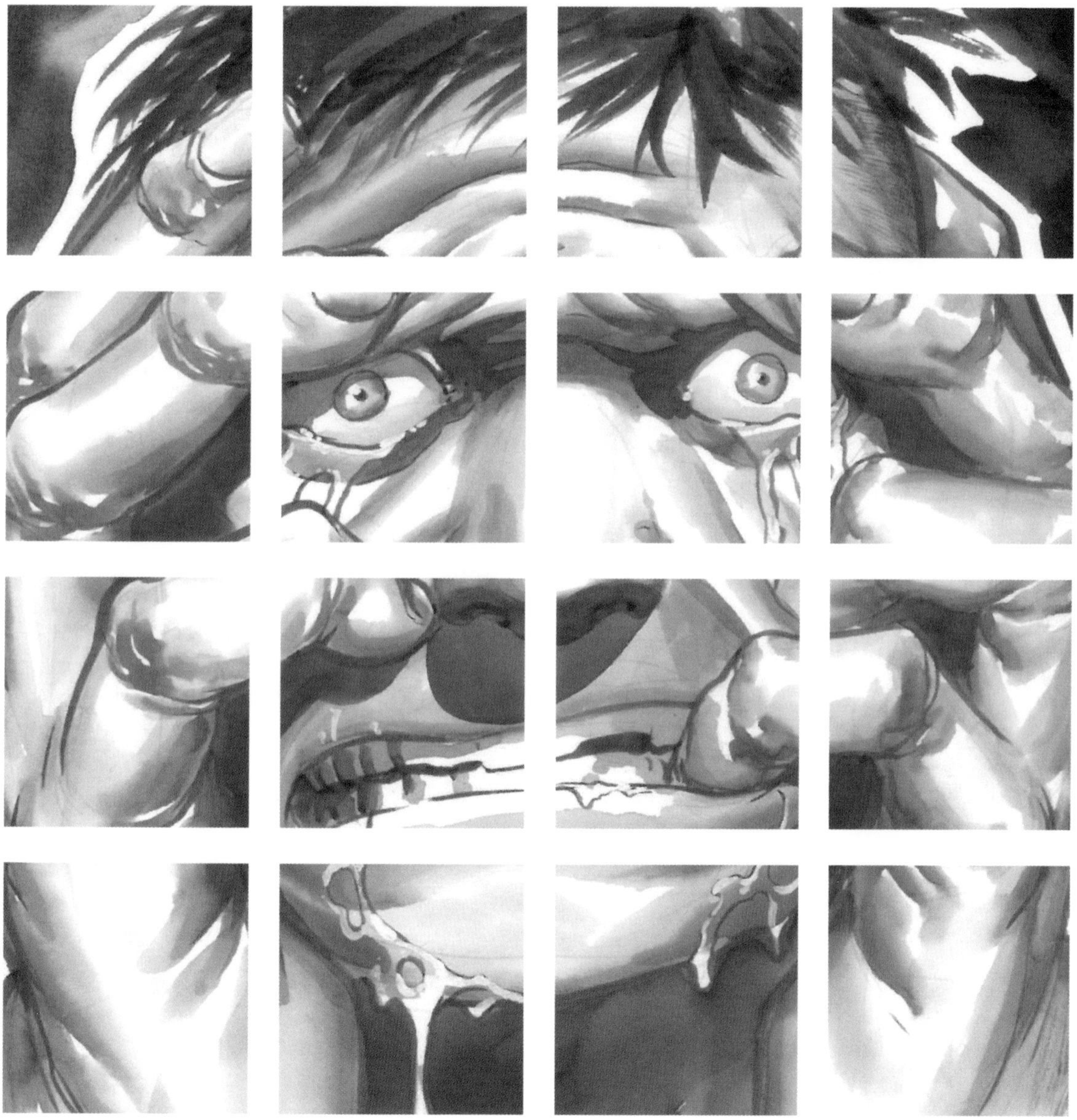

Terrence R. Wandtke

The Comics Scare Returns:
The Contemporary Resurgence of Horror Comics

RIT Press
90 Lomb Memorial Drive
Rochester, New York 14623-5604
http://ritpress.rit.edu

ISBN 978-1-939125-51-4 (print)
ISBN 978-1-939125-56-9 (e-book)

Library of Congress Cataloging-in-Publication Data

Wandtke, Terrence R., author.
The Comics Scare Returns:
The Contemporary Resurgence of Horror Comics /
Terrence R. Wandtke.
Rochester, New York: RIT Press, [2018]
pages cm. – (Comics Studies Monograph Series)
Includes bibliographical references and index.
LCCN 2017054162 ISBN 978-1-939125-51-4 (print (softcover): alk. paper)
ISBN 978-1-9399125-56-9 (e-book)
LCSH: Horror comic books, strips, etc. – History and criticism.
Comic books, strips, etc. – United States – History and criticism.
LCC PN6725.W295 2018 DDC 741.5/973–dc23
LC record available at https://lccn.loc.gov/2017054162

For educators in my life such as Mary Ann Noe, Cole Woodcox, and Georgia Johnston:
At one time I regarded the rigor of my educational requirements with horror, but now I realize how fulfilling your expectations provided me with the means to fulfill my own desires.

Comics Studies Monograph Series
Gary Hoppenstand, Series Editor

Narrative Structure in Comics: Making Sense of Fragments
Barbara Postema

Superheroes in Crisis: Adjusting to Social Change in the 1960s and 1970s
Jeffrey K. Johnson

The Dark Night Returns: The Contemporary Resurgence of Crime Comics
Terrence R. Wandtke

The Comics Scare Returns: The Contemporary Resurgence of Horror Comics
Terrence R. Wandtke

CONTENTS

CONTENTS

FOREWORD BY DOUG JONES

"What are you watching in there?" my mother would yell from the next room anytime she heard foreboding music or screams coming from the television. Likewise, if a darker comic book was lying about that wasn't *Superman* or *Archie*, our protective mother would question again where it came from and how to rid our house of it. And who could blame this good Christian woman for wanting to shelter her children from monsters and demons? Little did she know that her youngest son would grow up to play many of those monsters in film and television.

When I was offered the role of Abe Sapien in the first *Hellboy* movie, it came with a script and a short stack of the source material, graphic novels by the brilliant Mike Mignola. At first I thought my mother would disown me if I played in a movie with a demon as the hero. But after reading the script and those exciting comics, it was my conversation with director Guillermo del Toro that clinched the deal for me. I asked him how it could be possible that as a Christian, I was not in the least bit offended by this material. His answer summed it up for me, "It's not meant to offend you, my friend. It is an exploration of the baggage and the past we all carry around and the choice we have to keep dragging it or to cut it loose. And who better to embody this notion than a reformed demon from hell?" I was sold.

I have learned over my thirty-year career that to tell the story of a hero, someone has to be the bad guy. The more grotesque and imposing that bad guy is, the more glorious the triumph. I know for me, personally, when I read a comic or watch a movie in which the hero is devising ways to wrestle and conquer some hideous demon, it only empowers me to return to my own life and do the same with whatever demons might be plaguing me.

Terry Wandtke is an author of moral fiber who understands entertainment with this right kind of grit. And as it turned out, before she left this Earth in 2014, my dear mother understood this, too, as she would share my film credits with anyone who would listen.

Biography

Doug Jones is a versatile actor who has performed several comic book-related roles, including Abe Sapien in *Hellboy* and *Hellboy II: Rise of the Golden Army* and the Silver Surfer in *Fantastic Four: Rise of the Silver Surfer*. His horror resume is extensive and also includes roles as monsters on film and television in *Hocus Pokus, Buffy the Vampire Slayer, Pan's Labyrinth, The Strain,* and *The Shape of Water.* In a rare appearance without extensive prosthetics, Jones performed in one of his favorite projects, *The Butterfly Circus*, a short film about the beauty and integrity found in a community of circus freaks. And as someone who regularly lives inside horror stories, he is one of the nicest people on the planet–something that works in opposition to the assumptions made by people who burned horror comic books in the 1950s.

PREFACE

The Monstrous Crime: The Horror of Writing Books

Searchers after horror haunt strange, far places.
H.P. Lovecraft[1]

This book is a companion to my previous work, *The Dark Night Returns: The Contemporary Resurgence in Crime Comics*, though I didn't have a companion piece in mind when I wrote *The Dark Night*. But books are like monsters who sometimes demand a companion. And those companions often stand on their own and have a life quite different from the last work of madness. While referencing the desire of Frankenstein's creature for a mate might seem an overly cute opening for a book on horror comics, I take my similes quite seriously. Consequently, I want to elaborate a bit in order to explain the force that drove me to write this volume.

Like most scholars, I regularly venture into the void (not always the black pit void of horror stories but a perceived void nonetheless). And then I end up writing about those things not previously considered or at least about those things previously considered but in need of a different and perhaps fuller perspective. In the case of *The Dark Night Returns*, much work had already been written that dealt with crime comics of the 1950s that caused so much controversy and in part led to the deeply prohibitive Comics Code. In addition, some notable work had been done on selected writer/artists such as the often-mentioned Frank Miller. However, no substantial and coherent study of increasingly popular contemporary crime comics had been written that systematically tied those comics back to the infamous comics scare of the 1950s.

As I was writing and completing that book, I recognized another void calling out to me. Of course, the 1950s crusade of Fredric Wertham and others like him was concerned with horror comics as well as crime comics despite Wertham's adherence to "crime comics" as an all-encompassing label. That blurred line should be of interest to anyone interested in genre studies of comics (or literature, radio, film, or television). While horror comics are necessarily that other half of the story, I was drawn to the study of horror comics due to the curious distinctions from crime comics that emerged in the history and resurgence of horror comics.

In The Dark Night Returns, my point of departure was the mainstream cultural reactions to what was then called a mass medium, starting with the Red Scare fervor over juvenile delinquency that led to politician Estes Kefauver's hearings on comics. However, in the process of writing, the new focus that emerged in relation to horror comics was much more on the industry-specific cultural reactions and the creation of a Comics Code that explicitly prohibited horror.

While the industry should be understood as a microcosm of mainstream culture, it was also an institutional consciousness that would continue to be resisted in an aggressive way by the unconscious forces of horror. The resistance of these forces would be seen subsequent to the 1950s comics scare in the continued publication of horror comics (technically speaking horror magazines) in the 1960s and 1970s, a two-decade time frame when less directly targeted crime comics were almost completely absent. Working with the idea that this is an essential counterpart to my monstrous undertaking in *The Dark Night Returns*, this volume describes how "contemporary" horror comics deal even more directly with an industry hostile to creators and the personal ownership of ideas. And those horror comics demonstrate that ideas born in the unconscious have a life of their own that resists restrictions with nightmarish intensity and unforeseen consequences.

As known by every good stand-up comic (a different kind of comic), every pun that pokes fun at two different meanings of the same thing is serious (just like a simile). The title of this chapter (like other titles and subtitles to come) represents a serious attempt to open up possibilities: "the monster" could be EC, Fredric Wertham, the Comics Code, or me and other scholars like me—and that's just the start of a long and perhaps never-ending list. While good scholarship introduces specific facts and well-defined insights that illuminate the void, good scholarship also acknowledges that the void is vast and open to interpretation: a situation that is potentially frightening (perhaps even monstrous). And while thinking ahead to the means by which the contours of this void might be illuminated, it seems worth mentioning how this book will be similar and different from its companion.

Like *The Dark Night Returns*, this volume acknowledges that American comics exist in connection to the overlapping worlds of literature, radio, film, and television, all of which exist within the larger framework of American history. Building on the work of others, this volume begins with an overview of the 1950s comics controversy that led to the creation of the Comics Code. It then moves into an extended study of subsequent major works in contemporary horror comics. More particularly, this preface is immediately followed by

Dr. Gary Hoppenstand's introduction, a pre-history to modern horror and the horror comics craze of the 1950s. Unless one is willing to work with Wertham's definition of crime, which includes almost all things objectionable, it must be stated that the origin of crime as a genre is much more discrete than horror, which has origins based in oral culture. The first chapter will identify some of the same basic contours of 1950s history but intentionally explores material not covered in my previous book and reorients the focus toward issues more clearly tied to horror comics history. The second chapter will address 1960s and 1970s, grappling with the ways that horror comics survive in a somewhat underground context in a way that crime comics did not. And so the introduction and the first two chapters serve as a more extensive history, required to understand the chapters focusing on the major horror comics of the late twentieth and early twenty-first century.

In addition, this volume considers some comics writers that have been "darlings" of comics scholarship for decades: Alan Moore with *Swamp Thing* and *From Hell,* Neil Gaiman with *Sandman*, and Robert Kirkman with *The Walking Dead.* And while this is something of a distinction from *The Dark Night Returns* (with the exception of Frank Miller with *Sin City*), the approach will be similar, using rich context to reposition these creators and their comics within the current body of comics scholarship. Last but not least is the genre itself, which varies so much in its exact expression that I will only make generalizations about horror when necessary or useful. Right now, the generalization of horror as more fantastic and abstract than crime is useful in justifying this volume's more theoretical approach to the genre. In the end, this monster is not freakishly different than the monster that preceded it but still a freak living on its own terms.

In *The Comics Scare Returns: The Resurgence in Contemporary Horror Comics*, I assert that horror comics challenge comics culture and the Comics Code in notable ways (simultaneously thriving in an industry devoted to broad popularity and presenting subversive material that keeps comics on the margin). The focus on the resurgence of horror comics will examine the shift in culture and industry toward creator rights that begins with the modifications to the Code in the 1970s and eventually leads to the abandonment of the Code in the 2000s. Challenging the multimedia superhero industry, these comics represent the autonomy and artistic experimentation that sustains the industry beyond the speculator bust of the 1990s and on to a growing multimedia phenomenon directly inspiring literature, film, and television. And along those lines, the volume will examine changes in the industry and the culture it serves, as the subversive content of horror comics makes a more concerted and less contested move into the mainstream.

I have one last difference to note in the transition from the last volume to this one. Unlike *The Dark Night Returns*, the title *The Comics Scare Returns* doesn't directly reference a particular comic book within the genre. While it is certainly designed to refer back to the last volume, it also is meant to elicit an open interpretation. After all, while the "comics scare" is often used to refer to the cultural reaction against comics in the 1950s, this volume also deals with scary comics. However, I'd also like to broaden the terms in the phrase so that a few questions come to mind: What is the comics scare in historical, political, and artistic terms? When exactly did it take place? How did it return (and did it ever really go away)? These are questions that I hope will generate some answers—only some of which I will be able to address along the way. With this in mind, I invite you to start your list of questions (and answers)—ones that start within the confines of this volume but go far beyond. And together we can peer into the void...

Preface Notes

1 H.P. Lovecraft, "The Picture in the House," *The Complete Fiction of H.P. Lovecraft* (New York: Chartwell, 2014), 103.

ACKNOWLEDGMENTS

I would like to thank all those who helped with this project in large and small ways. In general, I'll state that you know who you are (thereby covering myself in case I forget any of the major players). I'll thank those who enabled my research (especially Randall Scott at Michigan State University and Sarah Baumeister at Judson University), gave me encouragement (especially Gary Hoppenstand and Anna Wandtke), and provided me with a place to write (especially the Blue Box Café and the Gail Borden Public Library). And in particular, I'll thank Sean Phillips and Dean Motter for the wonderful cover art from the interior of *The Heart of the Beast* and Bruce Ian Meader for the meticulous design work that makes this book look exactly the way it should.

EDITOR'S INTRODUCTION

Graphic Frights

The impulse to frighten ourselves is as old as the human condition. Before we could put pen to paper, we told our scary stories around campfires, tales that may have had a practical purpose in cautioning our ancestors to beware of things that "go bump in the night," because the night is dark, dangerous, stalked by predators, and generally unknowable.

With the advent of the printing press, and later the Industrial Revolution, in Europe and America, horror became commodified and packaged as commercial entertainment. In fact, much of the popular culture entertainments we enjoy today had their origin in the horror story. As popular fiction, Horace Walpole's short Gothic novel *The Castle of Otranto* (1764), for example, heralded the beginning of popular fiction within the frame of the horror narrative. From Gothic horror, the love romance, as found in the Brontë sisters' novels, established itself in the nineteenth century, as did the science fiction story in Mary Shelley's novel *Frankenstein*; *or, The Modern Prometheus* (1818). Even the detective story crawled out from the clutching skeletal fingers of the hoary Gothic tale, as seen in Edgar Allan Poe's "The Murders in the Rue Morgue" (1841). Horror continues to thrive today in the hybrid literary genre known as urban fantasy as well as in its more traditional expressions.

During the twentieth century, our entertaining frights became visual. Film took to horror in a significant way during the Great Depression in America, as seen in the Universal Studios' monster-movie franchises such as Frankenstein and Dracula. These films helped Americans cope with the horrors of economic depression by distracting them with horrors of the imagination, all for the mere price of a cheap movie ticket. Following the invention of television, this medium also explored entertaining frights mid-century with such now-classic shows as *The Twilight Zone* (1959–1964) and *The Outer Limits* (1963–1965), televised stories that not only chilled the blood of their audiences but also explored the complex metaphors of the human soul.

One of the most significant forms of horror escapism came to be found in that uniquely American invention called the comics, not the strips that were published in newspapers, but the book-like pamphlets, and later the even more book-like graphic novels. Both as artifacts of popular culture and as a unique form of visual narrative entertainment, comics and graphic novels can offer a fascinating look at the text and sub-text of our culture and of our imagination. Terrence Wandtke's excellent monograph *The Comics Scare Returns: The Contemporary Resurgence of Horror Comics* offers an informative historical and cultural survey of the horror story, its origins in folklore, and its subsequent manifestation in comic books of the 1950s, 1960s, and 1970s. His first-rate critique provides a conversant understanding of the dynamic relationship between our entertaining diversions and our social reality. His examination of the contemporary horror comics scene is equally expansive, covering some of the most successful popular cultural expressions found today, such as *The Walking Dead*. I envy you your imminent pleasure in exploring Wandtke's discerning and entertaining analysis of our collective, allegorical "heart of darkness," as depicted in the illustrated pages and panels of that ubiquitous medium known as comics.

Gary Hoppenstand, Ph.D.
Series Editor

VARNEY, THE VAMPYRE;

OR,

THE FEAST OF BLOOD

A Romance.

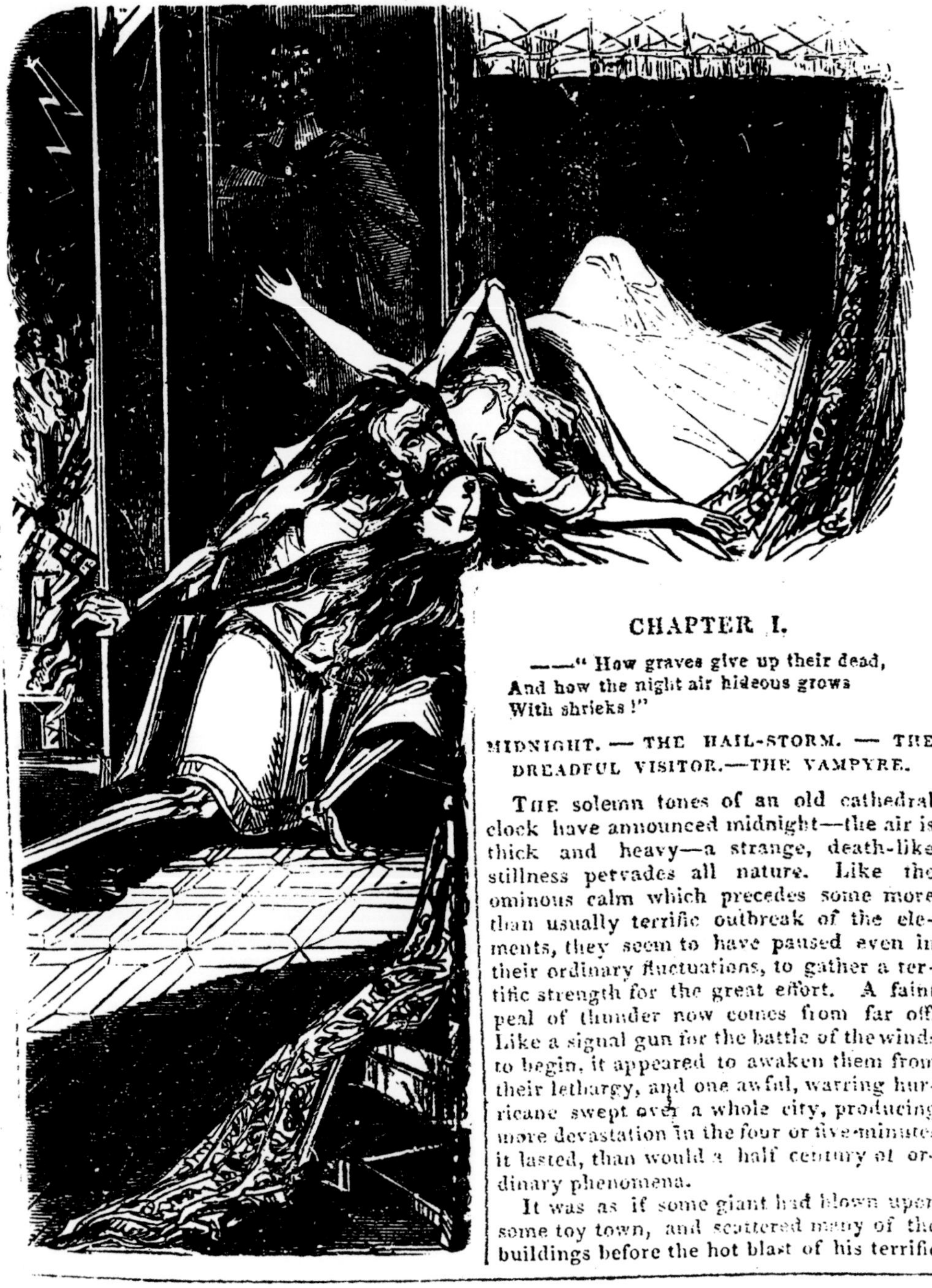

CHAPTER I.

——"How graves give up their dead,
And how the night air hideous grows
With shrieks!"

MIDNIGHT. — THE HAIL-STORM. — THE DREADFUL VISITOR.—THE VAMPYRE.

THE solemn tones of an old cathedral clock have announced midnight—the air is thick and heavy—a strange, death-like stillness pervades all nature. Like the ominous calm which precedes some more than usually terrific outbreak of the elements, they seem to have paused even in their ordinary fluctuations, to gather a terrific strength for the great effort. A faint peal of thunder now comes from far off. Like a signal gun for the battle of the winds to begin, it appeared to awaken them from their lethargy, and one awful, warring hurricane swept over a whole city, producing more devastation in the four or five minutes it lasted, than would a half century of ordinary phenomena.

It was as if some giant had blown upon some toy town, and scattered many of the buildings before the hot blast of his terrific

INTRODUCTION

The Monstrous Glint in the Eye: From Folktales to the Horror Industry

Fig. Intro 1
Varney the Vampire
Horrifying images are paired with horrifying words in the penny dreadful *Varney the Vampire*, a clear predecessor of the horror comic.

Monsters come in all shapes and sizes. Some of them are things people are scared of. Some of them are things that look like things people used to be scared of a long time ago. Sometimes monsters are things people should be scared of, but they aren't.
Neil Gaiman[1]

An Overview of Horror Fiction: Something Goes Bump in the Dark Night

TALE NO. 1

After years of conquest, a warlord establishes a haven in which all his people may enjoy his spoils only to see it attacked by a man-eating beast spawned from a race of giants; after a decade-long siege, an unknown hero from afar kills the monster but does not end the horror, inciting the revenge of the monster's formerly unknown mother.

TALE NO. 2

Motivated by bloodlust and a desire for capital gain, the vampire, Sir Francis Varney, brings woe to an aristocratic family reeling from the death of its patriarch; although clearly monstrous in his intentions, Varney's story becomes more sympathetic with the revelation that his vampiric condition is the consequence of actions that he now regrets–the accidental murder of his son.

TALE NO. 3

After a difficult birth, a mother becomes convinced that her child is a murderer, and as the son grows, so does that conviction as she finds more reasons to fear her time alone with her infant. After her concern is initially dismissed by her husband, she trips over their son's toy and falls down the stairs to her death causing the husband to then share her paranoia[2] (something likewise discredited by the family doctor until the husband dies from gas inhalation while alone in his house with his still-surviving young son).

Taken respectively from an oral epic (a portion of *Beowulf*), a penny dreadful (*Varney the Vampire*), and a comic book story ("The Small Assassin"[3] in Shock SuspenStories No. 7), these tales represent the story structure of a genre known as horror. Even though a descendent of many traditions including not only the oral epic but also the fairy tale and adventure novel, the horror story has less to do with the triumph of a hero who represents civilization and more to do with civilization's discovery of the monster and the resiliency of that monstrous threat. Stories of the horrible have deep roots in human history, and the fear-inducing conventions of those stories are well known and often revisited. And whether they portray fundamentally evil demons or sympathetic vampires, horror stories reveal the anxieties of the ages in which they are produced. Consequently, the ghosts that once haunted castles in the Gothic settings of European Romanticism now haunt high-rise penthouses in the pseudo-Gothic settings of American postmodernism. In twentieth- and twenty-first-century America, the long-standing basis for the horror story is seen in many different media forms such as the novel, the film, and quite significantly, the comic book.

Even though the pre-history of the modern horror story will be profiled in this chapter and the history of horror comics in the next, it is important to start with a note on the twentieth- and twenty-first-century horror story as both a product of and a threat to society and its industries. Within the horror story, the monstrous things portrayed are often separated from the heroic characteristics of civilization only as much as they are connected to those very same characteristics. And that makes the horror story, ironically beloved by so many thoroughly civilized people, uniquely qualified to threaten the status quo of those currently in power. Following on the heels of the triumphant rise of crime comics to popularity in the 1940s, horror comics would dominate spaces devoted to comic books on newsstands in the early 1950s. Of course, that would only last until comics protests led to congressional hearings, which in turn encouraged the development of the highly restrictive Comics Code.

However, unlike the crime comics that almost completely disappeared in the later 1950s, 1960s, and 1970s, horror comics proved to be remarkably resilient in the face of a Code that targeted horror much more specifically than crime. Since the construction of the Comics Code was a result of cooperation of major forces within the industry, this meant some of their vested interests lay not only in the survival of the medium but also in the prohibition of horror. While the Code meant the near-extinction of certain publishers (most famously EC), the survival of horror comics suggests other forces existed that readily overcame the will of the Comics Magazine Association of America. These forces led to magazine publications like *Creepy* in the 1960s and the more direct challenge from mainstream publishers like Marvel with *Tomb of Dracula* in the 1970s.

And like the crime comics that returned with a vengeance in the 1980s and grew exponentially in the 1990s and beyond, horror comics didn't just succeed in the environment provided by the relaxed Code; they flourished in the Code-free world of the direct market, bookstores, and online markets, environments seemingly far removed from newsstands and drug stores. This contemporary resurgence contained titles that offered the nuanced treatment of abstract themes as well as the excessive presentation of formerly prohibited content (in terms of sex and especially violence). With a broader readership built on many interests in mainstream popular culture, these horror comics helped to sustain the comics industry when the superhero collector's market fell apart in the 1990s. Moreover, following a lead established by infamous horror hosts from classic horror comics, these comics may have buoyed industry sales but only while also critiquing mainstream culture and its industrial standards.

TALE NO. 4

Living on a planet originally running with rivers of blood, a race of "vampires" who now face a planet-threatening blood-drought investigate the crash landing of an Earth spaceship; when an irresistibly attractive planetary representative is attacked by the astronauts, she kills them for their blood, travels to Earth and ultimately fights other supernatural monsters.

TALE NO. 5

After a falling away from his religious calling, a preacher is inhabited by a force known as Genesis, the spawn of a demon-angel pairing that drove God from heaven to wander the earth. As a result, the now vastly powerful preacher unintentionally slaughters his congregation and assembles a rag-tag group (including a vampire) to force God to take responsibility for a world filled with horrors.

Fig. Intro 2
Preacher No. 7
DC Comics, 1995
© DC Comics
Jesse Custer inhabits a world made horrifying by everyone who hides the vast emptiness behind conventional morality.

TALE NO. 6

Kyle Barnes grows up plagued by the demonic possession of those around him and as an adult begins to investigate the arc of his life with the aid of a clergyman. In the process, they discover the presence of demons is far more pervasive and that the demons have complex motivations and work in the service of an antagonist who might be the devil (or something else in a Godless world).

Taken from various horror comic books (respectively *Vampirella*, *Preacher*, and *Outcast*), these stories represent the union of camp excess and sophisticated artistry that keeps horror on the margins of respectability. Moreover, these comic book stories, presented in brief form and only in words, clearly work in the same terms as the first three exemplars: as representations of the monstrous things that threaten our world but with which we readily identify. And furthering the tradition established by EC horror comics, these stories strike at the sanctity of the American dream by not only making the monster into the protagonist but also taking God from his sacred place in heaven, where he confers his approval of all things American.

In the 1970s, Alan Moore gave up an office job in Northampton to return to his countercultural roots and work on one of his first loves: comic strips for alternative magazines and fanzines. Focusing on parody as well as subversive takes on science fiction, Moore was eventually hired by to contribute strips to *Tharg's Future Shocks* in the anthology *2000 AD*[4] Subsequently bouncing between publishers and generally unsatisfied by the limitation of the short story format, Moore started two continuing series to the anthology *Warrior: Marvelman*, a story undermining standard superheroic morality as with his revision of a classic superhero, and *V for Vendetta*, a story undermining mainstream British politics with his anarchic terrorist hero. Unfortunately for Moore, the magazine was cancelled long before the completion of these more ambitious works.

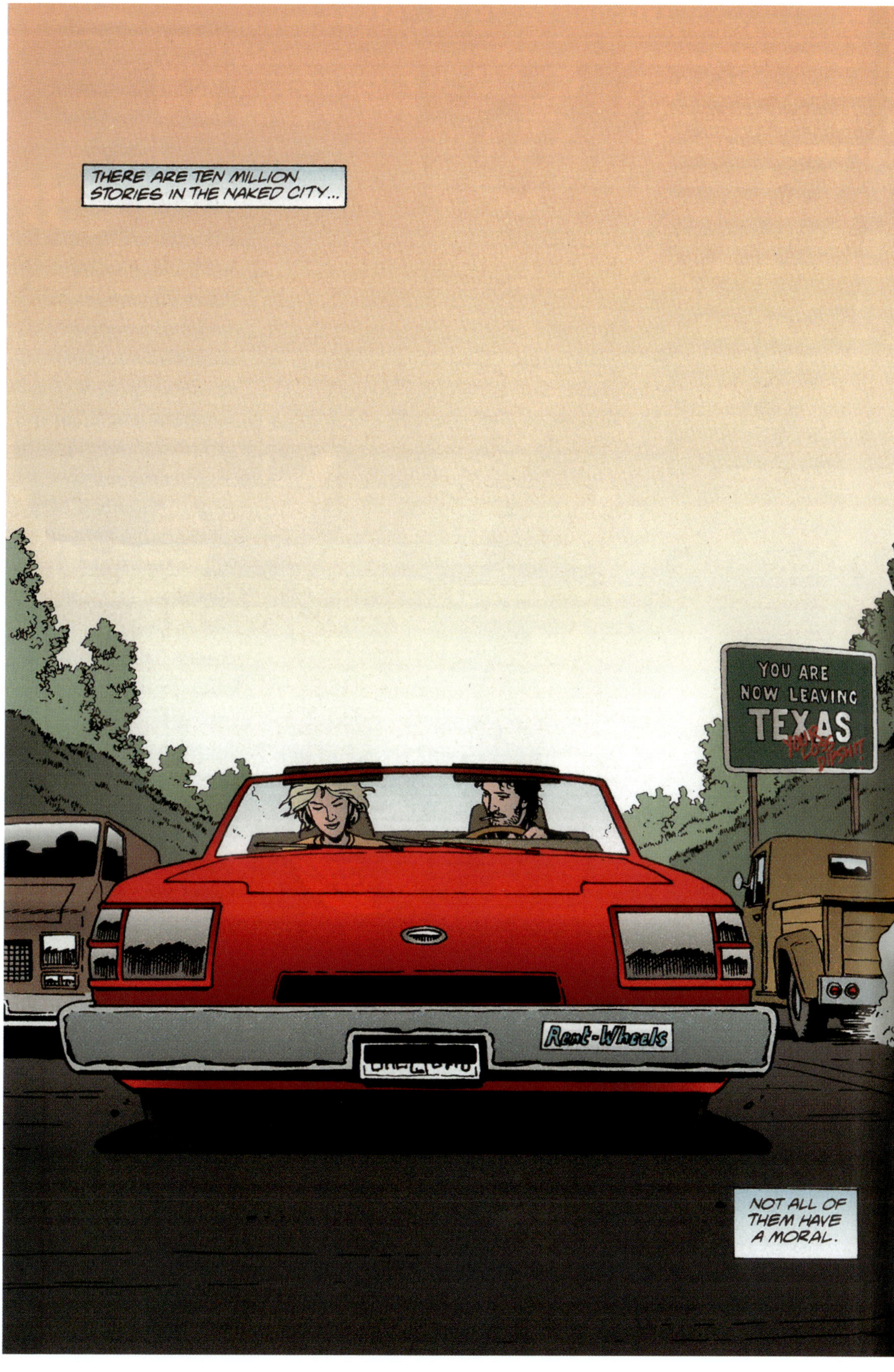
THERE ARE TEN MILLION STORIES IN THE NAKED CITY...
YOU ARE NOW LEAVING TEXAS
YOUR LOSS DIPSHIT!
Rent-Wheels
NOT ALL OF THEM HAVE A MORAL.

With this pedigree, Moore seems an unlikely candidate to make a lasting impact on the comics industry or even to be of remote interest to the superhero-dominated mainstream American comic book industry. However, his work with *Future Shocks* and *2000 AD* was seen by DC editor Len Wein, and he hired Moore in 1983 to write the flagging horror series *Swamp Thing* (which Wein had co-created). Beginning with a story that fundamentally revised the Swamp Thing's origin story, Moore quickly developed the title into one of the most popular series at DC at that time; with freedom to explore philosophic notions of horror, he wrote for a new audience that supported *Swamp Thing*'s move to direct market publication (where it became the first comic book in the 1980s to be regularly published without Comics Code approval).

Years later after the publication of his other game-changing horror title *From Hell*, Moore would ruminate on his influence on the comics, on his readers, and on ideas in general: "[F]or the number of people who read my work and get something out of it, I'm already having an untoward effect upon their minds and thoughts. Which I must admit I quite enjoy, in a kind of a spooky, creepy way." Subsequently, Moore moves on from this self-described (albeit tongue-in-cheek) "creepy" influence to discuss his preference for magic over religion, his worship of a second-century Roman snake god, and his desire that people approach life in an anarchic way: "All I would be urging people to do... is to explore... using whatever system they happen to feel comfortable with, whether that be Christianity, or paganism, or Hinduism, or anything else... It doesn't really matter which way you use, or which system you adopt.... To point out that territory to other people is something I feel happy about doing. To erect a huge church there and officiate over rituals, is not."[5]

In contrast to the Red Scare era that would give birth to the Comics Code in America, Moore's ideas radically separate him from Americans who burned comic books in the 1950s. Since Moore would spearhead the contemporary boom in comic book genre that refused to die, he must be seen not only as a representative of a continuing philosophy of the underground but also as an emergent spokesperson of an increasingly influential comics culture. Nevertheless, in an era in which graphic novels are regularly sold at Amazon.com and reviewed in *Entertainment Weekly*, Moore's words still position this well-regarded comics writer outside the comfortable place of general approval by the culture-at-large.

Due in part to the comic book's enduring dubious respectability with the general public, the horror story has emerged in a greater degree, realizing much of the subversive potential only suggested in its early twentieth-century origins; it seems to have subsequently achieved its great potential as a monstrous threat with narratives noted for their excess and radically offensive content in literal and ideological terms. This book will explore the meaning of this monstrosity known as horror comics and its growing appeal to creators and consumers both inside and outside the comic book industry that once took up the "heroic" cause to destroy it. In short, it will take a hard look at why we've come so far in our appreciation of those things that go bump in the night and more importantly, reject all that we supposedly hold dear.

The Pre-History of the Modern Horror Story: The Monstrous Life of Common Folk

As is always the case at the beginning of a long interpretive work, it is important to establish definitions that will provide a framework for subsequent analyses. However, unlike the crime story (its companion in the controversy that led to the Comics Code), the horror story has a longer history as a distinctive genre in folktales and popular entertainment. Establishing definitions in *The Dark Night Returns* was a bit easier because much of the critical writing on crime fiction coincided with its rather discrete appearance in the nineteenth and twentieth centuries. While that time frame will again be the significant starting point in a history of horror comics, it must be acknowledged that horror stories have a lengthier history extending back beyond the ages of literary criticism and even of literacy with folktales.

This is a worthwhile starting point, as the tension between literate culture and the oral basis of the folktale can be seen in a similar way between high-minded cultural critics and the popular nature of horror comics. And the connection between folktales, pulp fiction, and comic books will be developed further in the remainder of the book. This connection is the result of horror comic books carrying on the counter-cultural tradition integral to horror stories. With all of this in mind, I'll begin with a pre-history of horror comics and then develop a working definition of horror.

Since the exact definition is forthcoming, it is necessary to begin with a general definition of horror stories in order to distinguish certain folktales from others and to identify certain aspects of folktales. Although somewhat simplistic, horror stories are regularly assumed to be stories of the supernatural in which conflict results in large or small part due to an encounter with monsters.[6]

In reference to the ancient origins of these types of stories, history scholar W. Scott Poole claims, "Humanity emerged from the Stone Age dreaming of monsters."[7] With references to cave paintings of evil shapeshifters and monsters as points of contrast to people and their gods in religious myths, Poole argues that horror stories are narratives that represent basic human psychology.

And certainly, stories of supernatural worlds and the monsters that inhabit them have existed for millennia. Stories of now classic monster types like the shape-shifting werewolf have been tied back to the Greek myth of Lycaon who tested Zeus and was punished with his transformation into a wolf. And while undead creatures like vampires, ghouls, and zombie-like creatures were less distinct in ancient times, stories of blood-drinking and flesh-eating creatures are part of folktales of ancient Mesopotamia, medieval Europe, and far beyond (in terms of time and place). Of course, the details of monsters will always vary from place to place and time to time depending on the needs of the culture as cogently argued by Nina Auerbach in *Our Vampires, Ourselves*. Many classic monsters can be seen in works more readily identified as heroic epics or adventure stories than as horror stories (such as Polyphemus, the Cyclops in Homer's *Odyssey*). Poole's argument about monsters presented in religious discourse is along the same lines as horrific visions of the inferno in Dante's *Divine Comedy*.[8]

But even these more well-known supernatural monster stories readily accessible in written form were inspired by orally transmitted folktales held in common by all the people within a culture. This type of oral transmission has been widely studied by scholars such as Milman Parry, Albert Lord, and Walter Ong, who identify the ways that the conventions of the tales grew from the oral transmission and sociology of oral culture. For instance, Ong claims that, among other things, the oral tale is 1) close to the human lifeworld, 2) aggregative rather than analytic, and 3) participatory rather than objectively distanced.[9] Although more concerned with the oral epic than folktale (and not at all with the contemporary horror story), Ong identifies characteristics of the oral tale that have interesting implications to the typical low culture status of the horror story; the oral tale can be recognized for its 1) literalness (including the most gruesome details), 2) unconscious repetitions (rather than deeper meanings), and 3) emotional identification (rather than objective study).

However, as noted, these scholars are primarily concerned with the construction of the oral epic; something that combines constituent elements of folktales and often becomes part of literate culture beyond what is held in common by all the people.

And as Ong notes, the refined version of the oral epic tends to serve conservative needs[10] with a "heavy" hero[11] who conquers monsters and builds a nation. Without moving too deeply into monster theory, it is worth mentioning that English scholar Jeffrey Cohen describes the monster in its most basic form as "an uncertain cultural body... [that allows] the past its eternal return. The monster *haunts*...."[12] Even in an adventure story like the *Odyssey* (often identified as representative of Greek cultural values), a well-drawn monster is never completely vanquished by the hero. Polyphemus, the physically and morally monstrous son to Poseidon, still lives after his encounter with Odysseus and shares much in common with the cultural vanguard represented by Penelope's suitors.

Moving beyond the limitations imposed by the prescriptive notions of the heroic epic, folktales less refined by song traditions include those now commonly known as fairy tales. Although identified by Hans Christian Andersen as moral tales for children, stories of *Little Red Riding Hood*, *Hansel and Gretel*, *Beauty and the Beast*, and *Bluebeard* have elements that tie them to the horror story as we've thus far identified it (something seen especially by purveyors of fairy tales such as Angela Carter). In addition to usually being supernatural tales of monsters, these fairy tales focus on literal, sometimes gruesome details, have an unconscious connection and repetitive structure, and encourage emotional identification with characters placed in fearful situations.

While the least supernatural of the examples listed above, *Bluebeard* certainly provides access to the horror of Bluebeard's penchant for murdering his wives in horrible ways. Even if the current wife survives, she does so by doing something fraught with anxiety because it is strictly forbidden by the authority figure in her life (opening the door she is told not to open). Folklore scholar Max Lüthi suggests that the happy ending of the fairy tale is arrived at in a haphazard and almost unintentional way: "As if led by an invisible force and with the confidence of a sleepwalker, he follows the right course. He is isolated and at the same time in touch with things."[13] The willful resolution of a moral problem is less likely the goal than the depiction of frustration that common people feel with overwhelming forces around them. Describing the problem with the moral didacticism of the tales of Hans Christian Anderse`n and Oscar Wilde, folklore scholar Maria Tartar states, "What both Andersen and Wilde seem to have forgotten is that the folktale thrives on conflict and contrast, not sentiment and pathos."[14]

Even more to the point of horror in its folktale origins is the example of *Faust* (later *Dr. Faustus*), originally a folktale but famously adapted by Christopher Marlowe and later by Johann Wolfgang von Goethe. Supposedly based on the life of an egotistical, roaming academic in Germany, the story of Faust is one of a rich, learned man who sells his soul to the devil for knowledge and power. After living a life of increasing debauchery in which his moral bankruptcy becomes evident, demons appear at the appointed time and drag him screaming to hell. Eventually written down as a German chapter book in 1587, the story would be famously retold by Marlowe in 1604 as a myth of Renaissance humanism.

However, before it took shape with the help of classical dramatic construction and humanist philosophical preoccupations, it represented concerns of the peasantry. As an oral tale, it cast aspersions on the written contract as a tool of the devil by which he secures Faust's soul. With a protagonist rich and book-smart but without enough common sense to *not* sell his soul to the devil, it criticized the upper class as layers of Faust's subsequent debauchery were added to the tale. And with an ending that reveled in the excessive pain of Faust being carried off by demons, it operated in moral terms that were predicated not so much on justice as the gratuity of excess so readily associated with the genre of horror.

While horror comics draw most directly on the content of nineteenth- and twentieth-century literature for inspiration, this folktale tradition gives rise to that literature. And the folk origins of the horror story are based on the concerns of a general population and not just the wealthy, educated, and powerful few who seek to moralize and thereby consolidate power. Derided since ancient times by patriarchy as domestic (wives' tales) and therefore artless,[15] folktales persist within cultures where literacy is widespread and provide narratives that compete with and sometimes supplant those provided by the powerful minority. Bram Stoker identified Transylvania as Dracula's point of origin due to the widespread belief in vampires that existed in Eastern Europe in the eighteenth century but also led to official investigations and scholarly books.[16]

With eighteenth-century writers such as William Wordsworth and Samuel Taylor Coleridge, the Romantic movement challenged the rationalism of the age and approximated the voice of the common people. Consequently, it should not be surprising that Coleridge produced "The Rime of the Ancient Mariner," and Romanticism gave birth to Gothic novels such as *The Castle of Otranto*. And to some degree, the folktale has a persistent corollary with urban legends such as vanishing hitchhiker tales as well as more recent Internet-based *Slenderman* and *Killer Clowns* stories.

As folklore scholars Martin Hallett and Barbara Karasek claim, "Although the urban legend is much more localized and anecdotal than the folktale and is characterized by sensationalism and black humor, it too has its origins in aspects of life that provoke anxiety and insecurity, such as our ambivalence with technology or our suspicion that beneath the veneer of normalcy lurk chaos and madness."[17]

Last but certainly not least in regard to this origin point is that common links exist between comics and folktales, as both forms' original intended audience is mass culture. As I've argued elsewhere, mostly notably in *The Meaning of Superhero Comics*, many characteristics of the comic book experience link it to the orally transmitted story experience despite the visual basis for comics and the printing press technology responsible for its reproduction.[18] For instance, the ephemeral nature of sound experience or oral tales that necessitates retelling can be connected to the presumed disposability of comics, which encourages one to pass them along.[19] And just as the tale tellers can gauge and almost immediately respond to an audience and alter content, comic book publishers relied heavily on public opinion to determine content, something very quickly gathered via sales figures and readers' responses in letters and surveys.

In Maria Tatar's introduction to the fairy tale, she describes ideas central to literate culture and indicates that orally transmitted tales are not in line with those ideas: "Fairy tales, Angela Carter tells us, are not 'unique one-offs,' and their narrators are neither 'original' nor 'godlike' nor 'inspired.' To the contrary, these stories circulate in multiple versions, reconfigured by each telling to form kaleidoscopic variations with distinctly different effects."[20] With this claim in mind, it is important to note that while many criticized specific aspects of comic book content in the 1940s and '50s, many others criticized general patterns of comic book production during the same time period; critics found fault with comic books as being derivative and repetitive stuff produced by workmanlike hacks. These are charges that wouldn't be made within an oral culture and often were not made within the context of a workmanlike culture that readily consumed inexpensively produced entertainment for the masses. The characterization of comic books as low culture comes largely from those who are well-educated and fully committed to a high culture paradigm of literacy.[21]

Comic books should consequently be understood as 1) a communication mode that works by different aesthetic standards, 2) a narrative representation of the desires of a broad swathe of "blue collar" or "common" people, and 3) a potential threat to the ideas of a dominant minority that maintains power through the deployment of carefully organized rhetoric.

This understanding can be easily applied to crime comics but perhaps even more readily to horror comics that more often veer toward content that offends the sensibilities associated with the "polite" part of a stratified society. Widespread popularity of anything does necessarily lead to respectability in the short run, but that was especially the case with horror comics during the comics scare of the 1950s.

And with the government relying heavily on its respectability as a force supposedly fighting juvenile delinquency and Communism, horror comics publishers would lose even their low ground of popularity; other comics publishers sought the respect of a fearful culture no longer certain of what it feared and developed the Comics Code to eliminate horror comics (as if comics were the things to be feared rather than the representations of the things to be feared). But this is a story for the next chapter, a story that begins with the Gothic novel and horror classics such as *Frankenstein*, *Dr. Jekyll and Mr. Hyde*, and *Dracula* (as well as horror conveyances such as the penny dreadfuls, radio shows, and early twentieth-century films).

A More Exact Definition of Horror (or A Monster for His Time)

In this introduction, the horror story has been defined simply as a tale of the supernatural fundamentally focused on the threats posed by one or more monsters. By identifying its roots in the folktale, several more things were added: these stories are literal (including gruesome details), unintentionally repetitive (returning to persistent unconscious threats), and emotionally riveting (most notably creating an almost unbearable, fearful situation). Furthermore, these tales represent the widespread anxieties of common people in ways that are sometimes gratuitous and often resistant to the authority of the powers-that-be. Together, these ideas effectively set up an overview of a few selected key texts in the history of horror criticism.

But this is not meant to be a definitive overview of horror scholarship that results in an authoritative definition of horror. Instead, it is meant to account for that field of studies in a way that effectively accounts for and anticipates where horror comic books take the genre. Since horror is a genre that continues to have a dubious reputation in aesthetic terms, the length of study in history is certainly notable. Part of the reason for its academic roots dating back to the nineteenth century in English language traditions has to do with the burgeoning interest in the occult with figures such as Madame Blavatsky (a counter-current to Enlightenment rationalism). Thematic studies like Edith Birkhead's *The Tale of Terror* would appear in the early twentieth century, and historical surveys of folk beliefs would proliferate at the same time with authors such as Montague Summers.

While much of the interest eventually focused on the setting of the Gothic novel, some of the best early studies came from practitioners such as H.P. Lovecraft with "Supernatural Horror in Literature." This long essay carefully catalogues the essential history of horror literature and takes a tone that is scholarly and somewhat snobbish; Lovecraft's tone effectively removes horror stories from the category of unsophisticated tales designed only to build to big scares like jokes that build to big punch lines. The essay is able to do so primarily because Lovecraft builds a case for the necessary role of fear in the human psyche and the supernatural horror story as a means to explore the mind (clearly questioning rationalism as a dominant mode of understanding).

Acknowledging that fear held a more practical place in primitive cultures (enabling survival in a more dangerous environment), Lovecraft argues that "Against [the weirdly horrible tale] are discharged all the shafts of materialistic sophistication which clings to frequently felt emotions and external events, and of a naively insipid idealism which depreciates the aesthetic move and calls a didactic literature to uplift the reader toward a suitable degree of smirking optimism. But in spite of all this opposition the weird tale has survived."[22] In addition to identifying the "weird tale" as a countercurrent, he suggests that it is closer to the truth of things than other runs of information from the mainstream. Moreover, while he suggests the supernatural activates the imagination, an antidote to the false optimism of society, Lovecraft makes the experience of fear a central part of that definition of supernatural. Rather than focus on the supernatural happenings within the works, he marveled at the way good horror literature could access a different type of thought prohibited by the overgrown super-ego of society: "much of the choicest weird work is unconscious" to both the writer and the reader.[23]

Further along these lines and much further along in history,[24] Tzvetan Todorov's definition of the fantastic has often been used in horror studies despite also being rejected by many for the limitations that the term "fantastic" might place on horror. Regardless, Todorov's claims about the fantastic can be quite helpful if the term is understood as liberally and abstractly as Lovecraft understands the term supernatural when Lovecraft extolls the virtues of E.A. Poe's stories that lack any markers of the traditionally supernatural. Todorov suggests the fantastic, a world associated with devils and vampires, always contains a contradiction wherein the devils and vampires are both real and illusory.[25] This lack of certainty provokes a deep level of unease within the conscious mind that wants to follow the ordinances of a rational world. Consequently, this anxious feeling that rational society lacks a full explanation puts everyone who experiences horror in a position of wariness in relation to that society.

The most radical way we are put in this position is articulated by Julia Kristeva in *Powers of Horror*, a work often cited in horror studies. With this extended study of the abject (that which we find disgusting, like smeared feces or a rotten corpse), Kristeva argues that the disgusting is what we fear most because "it [is] a border; abjection is above all ambiguity."[26] This becomes centrally important in her study, because she claims this ambiguity is "opposed to I"[27] as it is delineated by a supposed sensible and unified culture. Consequently, Kristeva makes the disgusting, an often lowly esteemed part of horror, a significant experience that fundamentally opposes the self and society by exposing an unwanted truth. She uses terms that unintentionally but nicely connect the abject to the horror film tropes: "abjection…is immoral, sinister, scheming, and shady: a terror that dissembles, a hatred that smiles, … a friend who stabs you."[28] And her overview of abjection describes those who experience it as "its fascinated victims–if not its submissive and willing ones": a perfect description of those who encounter the horror story (hating what they see but unable to turn away).

Finally, since the common definition of horror includes the monster, but not all monsters are easily identified by a disgusting (abject) appearance, it is worth mentioning another cultural theory that has become important in horror studies. With examinations of the authorship of *Frankenstein* and the sources of the Golem legend, Marie-Hélène Huet's work *Monstrous Imagination* seems more clearly to be a genre study than Todorov's and Kristeva's. In some ways that is true, but it is also more concerned with the monstrous at a conceptual level than with the literal manifestations of the monster. Within that framework, Huet embarks on a historical survey beginning with classicism that identifies the monstrous as that which deviates from culture's norm (including something as basic as woman as a deviation from man). Analyzing the fear and power endowed on the deviant, the work identifies the widespread experience of abjection (not a term she uses but appropriate, nonetheless). The example of the deformed child (a horrible freak of nature) as a supposed product of a woman's imagination may put blame on the woman but also recognizes in that woman the power to subvert the authority of the father and patriarchal culture.

As indicated earlier, these ideas are meant to more effectively set up this study of horror comics, but with that in mind, I should mention a unique aspect of horror comics as they were identified in the 1950s. Fredric Wertham's inability or unwillingness to separate horror comics from his larger category of crime comics should not be seen as a great symptom of the flaw in his argument. After all, EC in particular would make these generic distinctions less clear with anthology series such as *Crime SuspenStories* and *Shock SuspenStories*. Intended to feature stories from several genres (such as crime, horror, science fiction, etc.), the distinctions were often unclear, demonstrating an important link between crime and horror especially in the twentieth century.

This situation is mentioned mainly to demonstrate that the definition of horror comics is largely the result of a self-conscious balancing act. Moving beyond the common definition of the horror story as a tale of the supernatural fundamentally focused on threats posed by one or more monsters, twentieth- and twenty-first-century comics horror represents the widespread anxieties of common people in ways that are excessive, sometimes gratuitous, and often resistant to the authority of the powers-that-be. More particularly, this end is accomplished through the experiences of fear and disgust achieved through contact with the monstrous that forces the individual to lose a sense of distance between the self and the tale, having closer contact with both the individual and cultural unconscious.

The phenomenon of horror comics works in a way that is similar to the crime comics as a seat for cultural criticism (something often associated with EC as a target of Wertham's ire). However, horror comics are also different with their longer inherited history and its use of more abstract means of generating fear (something both expressed and apprehended as a threat at a less conscious level). The threat of the monstrous part of our culture and therefore ourselves is something that can be associated with a creator like Alan Moore, who is central to the resurgence that brings horror comics back to the mainstream. However, he is a figure mentioned before not because he's necessarily the great genius of contemporary comics as many suggest, but because he responds so effectively to cultural cross-currents.

So far outside the mainstream of the 1950s in terms of ideas and temperament, Moore could still be seen as a monster for his time, and perhaps as a consequence, articulates the monstrous in effective ways:

> Something wanting to kill us… often a really ugly and monstrous something… has been our constant companion since the Palaeolithic. Much more alarming, in my estimation, is the entity of which we haven't the faintest idea what it wants; the dancing dwarf in Twin Peaks as opposed to the shuffling and brain-seeking cadavers of our zombie movies. This posited unknowable entity doesn't even have to mean you any harm or be aware of your existence in order to terrify. The very fact of its irresolvable and unfathomable nature is enough to haunt and obsess us forever after, to the point where we might end up wishing that we'd encountered a nice, down-to-earth, uncomplicated rampaging sasquatch instead.[29]

Horror pokes holes in the cultural system of post-industrial society in a way that is fundamentally different than crime fiction, which features interesting and sympathetic criminals; horror (and horror comics in particular) creates free-floating anxiety with the monstrous that cannot be tied to a clearly defined outlier. This blurring of categorical distinctions in what threatens the world we know brings us back to a few of the previously mentioned examples. *Vampirella* does what horror hosts have done well from the start, she blurs the boundaries between reader, narrator, and character that keep the reader safe; moreover, as a character in her own story, her campy sex appeal has the potential to make the reader love that which should be feared and desire the threatening void of female sexuality.

Preacher depicts Jesse Custer as the ultimate end of the Western's implicit fear of American expansion with the hero as an earnest believer who destroys that in which he believes; in addition to depicting the preacher on friendly terms with a vampire, the series provides a vision of post-religious society in which the most sacred course is to fight the authority of God. And while *Outcast* is designed to offer some conventional scares associated with the horror genre, the most frightening aspect of the series is that safe notions of good and evil are lost; the hero moves into nebulous territory that potentially makes demons sympathetic, possession an act of mercy, and God a participant in evil in a grander and more ambiguous sense.

In addition to identifying the trends that implicitly characterize horror comics as a threat to political and industry leaders in the 1950s, this book will demonstrate how those trends shape the creators central to the production of classic horror comics. In the process, this book may knock EC horror a bit from its pedestal but will also show how many forces still conspire to keep EC in its revered place. Ultimately, the goal is to better contextualize and thereby appreciate the classic image of a severed head on the cover of *Shock SuspenStories* No. 22 (and Bill Gaines's congressional testimony) as a harbinger for contemporary horror comics–conjoining bad taste with good, and cheap and shocking entertainment with radical and emerging art.

In order to survey comics horror effectively in the six chapters of this book, I have worked in a way similar to that of *The Dark Night Returns*, balancing depth and breadth. I will demonstrate comics horror as a part of a medium-crossing tradition begun in the late nineteenth century, and this will form the foundation for a focus on the aesthetic approaches of some of the foremost practitioners of horror comics, storytellers and artists alike. In turn, I will determine how they deploy the conventions of classic horror comics in extreme and self-conscious ways to critique the history of horror, American culture, and the American comics industry in particular.

In Chapter 1, I scrutinize the boom in the horror comics of the 1950s and the controversy that accompanied it. In addition to EC, I will examine other horror comics from this era in order to identify significant trends with particular attention paid to significance of the horror hosts. And with special emphasis on Bill Gaines's faulty defense of comics and the Comics Code designed to eliminate horror comics, this chapter provides a framework for much of what follows.

Chapter 2 is a chapter that was not needed for crime comics in *The Dark Night Returns* but in this case of horror comics, the early history needs an extended overview and analysis. Even though more directly targeted by the Comics Code, horror proved more resilient than crime, moving into the comics magazines of the 1960s and blended with superhero universes of the 1970s (whereas crime comics almost completely disappeared).

In Chapter 3, I examine selected works of Alan Moore, beginning with the *Saga of the Swamp Thing*, as horror comics return in the era of the "graphic novel." With John Totleben, Steve Bissette, and Rick Veitch, Moore would reinvent the muck-encrusted monster from the 1970s with lasting effects on the comics industry in both aesthetics and creators' rights. And subsequently, Moore would produce *From Hell* with Eddie Campbell, synthesizing and reinventing the conventions of crime and horror in one of his greatest works.

In Chapter 4, I analyze *Sandman* by Neil Gaiman with Dave McKean, Sam Keith, and others as a pivotal work that would advance changes seen with Moore's *Swamp Thing*. With critical acclaim not usually associated with the genre or medium, this horror comic led to other titles in DC's "adult" imprint Vertigo, like *Hellblazer* and *Preacher*, robustly outliving the loss of the 1990s collector's markets and dealing with issues formerly off-limits in the highly regulated comics industry.

In Chapter 5, I focus on Mike Mignola's *Hellboy* and Eric Powell's *The Goon*, representing them as works that take a very different approach from works by Moore and Gaiman, rejecting conventional acclaim and more fully embracing the folk and pulp origins of comics. Extolling the virtues of slapdash craftsmanship produced by supposedly bad taste, both series craft a transgressive aesthetic that laughs at critics and engages the void.

And in Chapter 6, I discuss *The Walking Dead* by Robert Kirkman, Tony Moore, and Charlie Aldrad as the behemoth phenomenon within the resurgence of horror comics. Using the zombie–post-modernity's favorite monster–the series clearly establishes the widespread experience of monstrosity at a social level, something that is only indirectly connected to the supernatural presence of zombies.

The order of chapters is roughly but not strictly chronological in that several of the chapters overlap in time with their focus on particular publishers, series, and/or comics creators. However, these chapters are designed specifically as useful groupings that describe the aesthetics, worldview, and impact of these various publishers, series, and/or comics creators. And the conclusion will make sense of these various groupings as a whole, discussing whether the "irresolvable and unfathomable nature" of so many horror comics can remain truly threatening in a culture so happy to buy into things terrifying and grotesque.

Introduction Notes

1 Neil Gaiman, *The Ocean at the End of the Lane* (New York: William Morrow, 2013), 112.

2 The structure of this book in some ways mirrors that of *The Dark Night Returns* (which opened with stories representing various points in the history of the genre of crime). I am changing the terminology from "case" to "tale" to represent a difference in the genre and its history. While case is more clinical and effectively relates to the investigation of crime, tale identifies the longer history of horror as an oral story and alludes to famous horror comics anthologies like *Tales from the Crypt*.

3 This is one of many EC stories based on the work of Ray Bradbury which began as a playfully contentious relationship but became a mutually beneficial arrangement in monetary and artistic terms.

4 *Future Shocks* was a companion to the more well-known *2000 AD*.

5 Tasha Robinson, "Interview: Alan Moore," The Onion A.V. Club, last modified Oct. 24, 2001 http://www.avclub.com/article/alan-moore-13740.

6 J.M.S. Tompkins, *The Popular Novel in England* (London: Methuen, 1973), 245.

7 W. Scott Poole, *Monsters in America: Our Historical Obsession with the Hideous and the Haunting* (Waco: Baylor UP, 2011), 5.

8 Wheeler Winston Dixon, A History of Horror (New Brunswick: Rutgers UP, 2010), 1.

9 Walter Ong, *Orality and Literacy* (London: Routledge, 2002), 38–46.

10 Ibid., 41–42.

11 Ibid., 69–70.

12 Jeffrey Jerome Cohen, *Monster Theory: Reading Culture* (Minneapolis: U of Minnesota P, 1996), ix.

13 Max Luthi, "The Fairy Tale Hero: The Image of the Man in the Fairy Tale," *Folk and Fairy Tales*, ed., Martin Hallett and Barbara Karasek (Petersborough, Ontario: Broadview, 2009), 321.

14 Maria Tartar, "Introduction," *The Classic Fairy Tales*, ed., Maria Tartar (New York: W.W. Norton, 1999), xv.

15 Ibid., x.

16 Paul Barber, *Vampires, Burial, and Death: Folklore and Reality* (New Haven: Yale UP, 1988), 2–4.

17 Martin Hallett, Martin and Barbara Karasek, "Introduction," *Folk and Fairy Tales* (Peterborough, Ontario: Broadview, 2009), 17.

18 The new technology that enables comic book production can be understood as a stepping stone to other technologies related to the Internet. As argued by John Miles Foley with his *Pathways Project*, the Internet reactivates sensibilities associated with oral culture. For more on this, see Andrew J. Friedenthal's *The Retcon Game* (Jackson: UP of Mississippi, 2017), connecting traditions in folktale practices to the comic book retcons to Internet conventions.

19 Many of the same things can be said about other mass media produced at the time, including penny dreadfuls, dime novels, pulp fiction, radio shows, and films. While I more fully argue that comic books deserve the comparisons in *The Meaning of Superhero Comic Books*, these other media permutations will be mentioned in Chapter 1.

20 Maria Tartar, "Introduction," ix.

21 Amy Nyberg makes reference to Fredric Wertham's uniform rejection of a suggestion like this: "Wertham also shared some of the cultural elitism of the Frankfurt School in his rejection of the suggestion that comic books were a form of children's culture that could be likened to fairy tales or figures from folklore" (Amy Nyberg, *Seal of Approval: The History of the Comics Code* [Jackson, UP of Mississippi, 1998], 94). See also Bart Beatty, *Fredric Wertham and the Critique of Mass Culture* (Jackson: UP of Mississippi, 2005), 142.

22 H. P. Lovecraft, "Supernatural Horror in Literature," *The H.P. Lovecraft Archive*, last modified Oct. 20, 2009, http://www.hplovecraft.com/writings/texts/essays/shil.aspx.

23 Ibid. Despite his protest against psychoanalysis, Lovecraft is quite Freudian in his formulations.

24 While this represents a jump from 1927 to 1975, Timothy Jones makes this claim about Lovecraft's essay: "First published in the 1920s, the essay suggests a continuity not considered by the academy until the late 1970s" (Timothy Jones, *The Gothic and the Carnivalesque in American Culture* [Chicago: U of Chicago P, 2015], 72).

25 Tzvetan Todorov, "Definition of the Fantastic." *The Horror Reader*, ed., Ken Gelder (London: Routledge, 2000), 14–15.

26 Julia Kristeva, *Powers of Horror: An Essay on Abjection*, translated by Leon S. Roudiez (New York: Columbia UP, 1982), 9.

27 Ibid., 1.

28 Ibid., 4.

29 Alan Moore, "Ask the Author: Alan Moore," *Good Reads*, last modified Oct. 30, 2015, https://www.goodreads.com/author/3961.Alan_Moore/questions.

CHAPTER 1

The Birth of the Monster and the Specter of Communism: Horror Comics and the Comics Scare of the 1950s

None of the captions said anything like
"If you are unhappy with your step mother, shoot her."
Bill Gaines[1]

The Origins of Horror Comics in Gothic Novels: A Dark Spot in the Enlightenment

Classic horror comics of the 1940s and '50s find their most discrete point of origin in the tales of terror published in pulp fiction magazines and aired in radio shows. However, it is difficult to discuss these other tales without discussing the Gothic traditions firmly established in the nineteenth century. As mentioned in the introduction, stories of the monstrous have deep roots in human history, and the fear-inducing conventions of such stories are well known. Within the literate age of English Romanticism, those conventions took new shape in the Gothic novel and would be refined by now well-known authors such as Mary Shelley, Robert Louis Stevenson, and Bram Stoker. And whether they portray demons or vampires, horror stories cause a backward look while revealing the anxieties of the age in which they are told. It is important to chart the course that led to classic horror comics, acknowledging that the horror story takes various shapes and sympathies. Contemporary horror begins as a disruption of the strict rationalism of Enlightenment era ideals in ways that still disgust purveyors of the status quo in visceral, aesthetic, and moral terms.

Nevertheless, it is also important to acknowledge the exponential growth of horror as a genre in the early twentieth century through the synergy between comic books and other forms of media including not only literature but also other emerging forms such as film, radio, and television. And with new forms of expression like comic books, horror develops immediacy and a visceral impact by creating a sensory experience that seems especially threatening.

In *Horror Comics: The Illustrated History*, Mike Benton makes the claim that horror comics are the most threatening of the new media forms by allowing the reader a greater amount of participation with the content:

> Pictures of werewolves and zombies and children-eating witches, frozen in time on each comic book page, daring us to look at them, to read their stories, to turn the next page. Because, unlike monster movies where you can hide your eyes or duck your head at the really scary parts, there is no escape from a horror comic book. Reading a horror comic story is like driving slowly past a bloody car accident–you have to look and linger and absorb and remember the horror of the moment.[2]

While Benton's comparison of comics to other media forms could be disputed, he uses the idea of comic book reader participation popularized by Will Eisner and Scott McCloud. With little objective distance, there is less rational thought to distance the reader from horror and the fear it induces (and our fascination with the irrational is something that he implies motivates our everyday actions). Even if comics do have an extraordinary ability to engage the reader in this way, comics do not stand alone in their attempt to actualize the experience of horror (what Skywald comics publications would call the "horror mood"). Although sometimes obscured by history, a generally agreed-upon literary starting point in this regard can be found with the Gothic stylizations of Horace Walpole's *The Castle of Otranto*.

Walpole was fascinated by medieval history, or at least the medievalism of authors like Sir Walter Scott, and went so far as to construct his Strawberry Hill House in 1749 in a faux Gothic style. This sort of stylization would be characteristic of his novel *The Castle of Otranto*, which Walpole claimed was inspired by the ghost story of Hamlet (but bears only a superficial resemblance). Nevertheless, this orientation toward the past would fundamentally influence the plot and operate in opposition to the future-looking gaze of Enlightenment culture. Jerrold Hogle describes the four central elements in Gothic texts to be an antiquated space, a hidden secret from the past, a haunting, and a movement between literal reality and the supernatural[3]– characteristics linking the past to the supernatural movement of the plot.

Focused on Lord Manfred's family, *The Castle of Otranto* opens with his son's death, crushed under a giant helmet that falls from the sky on his son's wedding day. As the sinister Manfred schemes to eliminate his own wife and marry his son's intended bride, Isabella, in order to cement an alliance, the peasant Theodore aids Isabella's escape.

Due to Manfred's evil schemes, the supernatural testifies against his fitness to rule the castle not only in the form of an ancient prophecy but also as the ghost of his grandfather (and the surprising appearance of giant disembodied hands and feet). When Manfred unintentionally kills his own daughter, Theodore is identified as the rightful heir of the castle, and the sins of the father fundamentally shape the present.

Although the story is often mentioned for its somewhat absurd elements, Walpole combines an older style of the supernatural portrayed in medieval Romanticism with a newer style that was more realistic. The horror was consequently linked more to Manfred and the mood he created within his gloomy castle than to the giant monster roaming its halls. In fact, this Gothic horror had very little to do with visceral scares, using devices to distance the reader from the experience; most notably, they include the framing device of a translator's note that identifies the novel as a translation of a 1529 Italian text. This distance implies that horror is less the result of the sudden fright and more the result of the dread of the inevitable.[4] Moreover, this device has another effect by setting up tension. While there is safety in the idea that the events took place long ago in a faraway place, it also portrays those *supernatural* events as truths verified by an authentic text in print. The novel thereby creates a timeless sense of the supernatural as hyperreal. As W. Scott Poole notes in *Monsters in America*, the Enlightenment experience is more complex than implied by its hyper-logical caricature in most history textbooks: "The eighteenth-century rationalists did not easily relinquish mythical and fantastic beliefs, even as they attempted to wedge themselves into the new, naturalistic paradigm."[5]

Other notable Gothic novels would follow (like Ann Radcliffe's *Mysteries of Udolpho*) but Mary Shelley's *Frankenstein; or The Modern Prometheus*, first published in 1818, is the most notable early Gothic bridge between the older traditions concerning the fantastic and more modern notions of the scientific (as indicated by its title). The now-archetypal horror tale depicts Victor Frankenstein's desire to realize the ultimate end of medical science: to bring life to the dead (in this case, with a creature assembled from the body parts of lifeless cadavers). After the doctor turns from his work as horrific, the creature ultimately reacts to further rejection from society with violent actions guided by his desire for revenge against Dr. Frankenstein. In consequence, the experience of the monstrous is something that is not only located within the reanimated creature but is also traced back to the human being who refuses responsibility for his actions.

Famously the product of a ghost story contest between Romantic writers (including Lord Byron, Percy Bysshe Shelley, and John Polidori), Mary Shelley's story deploys the resources of folktales about alchemists and visions of the future offered by her famous rationalist parents, William Godwin and Mary Wollstonecraft. The sense of doom that results from past sins infects the hopeful future built on the supposed progress of science and technology in contemporary civilization.

These concerns would be echoed nearly seventy years later in Robert Louis Stevenson's *The Strange Case of Dr. Jekyll and Mr. Hyde* in which the protagonist tries to solve with chemistry the problem of his evil desires. The result was the manifestation of another personality, more primal and destructive, leading eventually to the extinction of the doctor's presumed self. Both texts work to engage the reader with frames that imply access to the real story, but in each case require a certain amount of discernment to mitigate the skewed perspective of the storyteller. In *Frankenstein*, the frame is the journal of the explorer Robert Walton, who comes across a dying Frankenstein in the harsh climate of the North Pole. The authority implied by a written account of facts is subverted because Frankenstein's story is presented to Walton through the scientist's potentially questionable point of view (utilizing the novel's innovative form of first-person narrative).

Moreover, the larger part of the story of *Dr. Jekyll and Mr. Hyde* is told from the limited perspective of a lawyer not privy to the transformation of Dr. Jekyll into Mr. Hyde. This is something fully confirmed only by a posthumous record left by Dr. Jekyll that explains the string of violent events committed by him as Mr. Hyde and disturbingly ending with Jekyll's abrupt end in narration (only to be "finished" by the previously implied dominance of Mr. Hyde). With reference to the responsibility placed on readers to fill in the gaps, this horror technique serves as a point of transition to Bram Stoker's 1897 novel *Dracula*.

This vampire classic was preceded by prominent dissertations on demonology that discussed vampirism as actual phenomena and notable fictions like John Polidori's *The Vampyre* (a product of the same contest that led to Frankenstein). While Polidori presents his vampire as a Byronic "figure of heterosexual erotic desire,"[6] Stoker makes Dracula more uniformly evil; "Stoker broke radically with the seductive, Byronic image of vampirism that had already been popularized."[7] Nevertheless, this vampire is represented not as a mindless undead creature of folktales; instead, he is a sophisticated foreigner who begins to infiltrate English society through his ability to purchase property and establish his place in society.

Based not only on previous horror stories but also on contemporary fears of powerful foreign influences, Dracula becomes an archetypal representation of the society's fear of the seductive Other. But most important in terms of the recurrent formal motif of Gothic horror is the novel's design as an epistolary tale. Composed of personal letters as well as journal entries and ship's logs, *Dracula* requires the reader to participate in this assembly-required format, and individual entries seemingly corroborate one another and add credence to the supernatural events. The reader's central role in the construction of the story personalizes the horror and results in radically different interpretations of *Dracula*.[8]

All of the above-mentioned novels enjoyed a degree of popular success and in some cases even critical approval, including reviews that acknowledge a history of horror and identify *Dracula* as superior to that of *Frankenstein* and Edgar Allan Poe's short stories. As horror made its mark as a genre, it spread to a media form that preceded but resembled comic books in its physical form and its lack of respectability: the penny dreadful. A derogatory term used interchangeably with other terms like penny awful or penny blood, penny dreadful was meant to describe the low quality and sensational content of these serially published stories. Focusing on adventure and crime as well as horror stories and including series such as George Reynolds's *Wagner, the Wehr-Wolf*, penny dreadfuls were produced in the mid-nineteenth century at the intersection of the rise of literacy and publication technology that produced low-cost reading material for the rapidly growing middle class audience.[9] While *Dracula* had many predecessors other than those already mentioned above, one of the most famous predecessors followed more closely in Polidori's narrative footsteps: James Malcolm Rymer's *Varney the Vampire*.

When held to the standards of a novel like *Frankenstein*, *Varney the Vampire* is far from great literature. As David Skal states, "Stuffed with prose that transcends the merely purple in a quest for the ultraviolet,... [t]he plot is endlessly convoluted... [but] Varney nonetheless strengthened the image of the bloodsucking fiend... and its depiction of an un-dead Eastern European aristocrat."[10] While inconsistent and digressive, *Varney the Vampire* presents a vampire that is more clearly sympathetic and reluctant in his evil-doing[11] even as it describes his evil deeds. *Varney* and the penny dreadful in general demonstrate the growing appetite for sensational ultraviolet *and ultraviolent* tales that regularly exposed the Victorian reader to content considered inappropriate at the time.

And with woodcut illustrations, the penny dreadful anticipates the horror comic in several important ways: 1) description that focuses on literal details of the human world, 2) narration by a chatty persona that gives the reader access to characters' thoughts and feelings, and 3) seriality that continues a story without a clear tie to classical rules of storytelling. Although the penny dreadful would soon be replaced by other low-cost publications, it provides a direct link to serial narratives driven by technology across the big pond.

Dime Novels Become a Penny Dreadful(ler) in Pulp and Radio Horror

Even though haunted castles seemed quite separate from the new world, H.P. Lovecraft would make the connection between the Gothic tradition and the horror story in America. After all, castles are the most superficial part of the Gothic, as demonstrated by one of Lovecraft's most prominent examples, Edgar Allan Poe's "The Fall of the House of Usher." As Graham Clarke notes in his introduction to *Edgar Allen Poe: Critical Assessments*, many of his nineteenth-century contemporaries regarded his work with reluctance because it is supposedly without moral principle but energized by a powerful imagination–"aspects of Poe's work which, paradoxically make it so significant for a twentieth-century reader. In an extreme sense Poe's writing seems to be the embodiment of what we recognize as the quintessential modern condition; a world defined through its concern with doubt, fear, and anxiety."[12] Well known as a critic and regarded more highly for his poetry than his fiction, Poe made a living with his writing (even though the quality of that living and writing varied). In retrospect, he is now considered to be a master of the short story and of the horror genre. While Bill Gaines often refers to the ending of EC stories as having a O. Henry twist, they were more informed by the macabre turns of Poe's stories with their emphasis on the monster that lives in all people.

"The Pit and the Pendulum" plays with the proximity to horror that is developed by first-person narration, something that, in this story, reveals the narrator's survival of the very torture he relates. However, the tale of a victim of the Spanish Inquisition still has the power to disturb the reader due to the psychological realism of the all-encompassing narrative experience. First-person narrative brings the reader even closer to the monstrous in Poe tales in which an unreliable narrator has committed a crime, such as "The Tell-Tale Heart" and "The Black Cat." Rather than putting the reader in the place of a person who is shaped by fear (a general strategy of horror stories), Poe puts the reader in the place of a person who is guilty of a crime, initially unrepentant, and ultimately disturbed.

The subterranean forces of the human mind create the excessive punishments often associated with horror stories; in the case of "The Tell-Tale Heart," this would be the deafening heartbeat of the man whom the narrator murdered for having a filmy "vulture eye." Although writing at roughly the same time as authors of classic Gothic novels, Poe seems to anticipate the turn toward modern Gothic described by English scholar Fred Botting: away from external forces to be overpowered and toward internal forces such as the ungovernable feelings of guilt and despair.[13] Of course, Poe is often credited with inventing the mystery or crime story with "Murders in the Rue Morgue," establishing a connection between the starkly realistic crime story and the less supernatural horror story of the twentieth century (so characteristic of EC comics).

As Walter Ong has noted, the detective story can be considered the embodiment of literacy,[14] and it could be argued that the Enlightenment era in the nineteenth century is the pinnacle of literacy. However, Ong makes a distinction between the detective story and the mystery, "which does not have so tidy a closed organization."[15] While the English parlor room mystery serves well as the embodiment of Ong's detective story, American stories of the hard-boiled detective serve well as the embodiment of Ong's mystery (often leaving aspects of the cases unresolved). While "Murders in the Rue Morgue" is not necessarily a predecessor of the hard-boiled detective story, it resists the tidiness of the Enlightenment world's clockwork universe in two ways: 1) the excessive violence of the murders themselves, and 2) the bizarre culprit found in the orangutan, which is at odds with the conventional search for motive.[16]
The nineteenth century may be the height of the Enlightenment, with the Industrial Revolution providing the technological embodiments of progress and orderly civilization. However, it is also a time when the problems of such progress become more apparent through workers' rights abuses, industrial waste products, and the widespread production of increasingly destructive weapons. Within the Enlightenment utopia was a dystopia, and "The Murders in the Rue Morgue" represents that tension through horror elements that expose the cultural unconscious.

As one of the first American authors to make a living through his writing, Poe struggled to have his work featured in respectable publications. The opportunities for publication were numerous at the time and became more numerous with advances in print technology. As technology marched forward, for better or worse, it created new ways to produce old media as well as facilitating the development of new media forms. And in nineteenth- and twentieth-century America, the appetite for the genre of horror grew among the common people and the discontents of civilization in the forms of dime novels, pulp fiction, radio shows, films, and of course, comic books.[17]

The twentieth-century American descendent of the penny dreadful would be the pulp fiction magazine, a replacement for the dime novel that was known more for plucky adventure heroes and working-class women defending virtue and finding romance. Like the dime novel, pulp fiction magazines like the pioneering *Argosy* appealed to a working class readership with its low cost and sensational content. More than the dime novel, pulp fiction magazines became specialized with anthology formats featuring short stories devoted to emerging genres such as mystery, science fiction, or horror. While generally held in low critical esteem, the magazines were wildly popular and provided a home for fiction by early masters of horror such as H.P. Lovecraft. Among many others such as *Terror Tales*, *Ghost Stories*, and *Horror Stories*, one of the first and most notable of these publications is *Weird Tales*. Publishing horror (as well as some fantasy and science fiction) stories, the series debuted in 1923 and remained extremely profitable for the next fifteen years.[18] Of course, its debut coincided with the widespread feeling of dread produced by the aftermath of the World War that challenged the Enlightenment notion of civilization's march toward perfection.

Filled with stories of witches, vampires, and mad scientists in neo-Gothic settings, the authors of *Weird Tales* connect with a history of horror as a sensational genre as well as a counter-cultural narrative. With painted covers that often featured images of scantily clad women making pacts with the devil, the interior content only sometimes lived up to that provocative promise. Authors as varied as H.P. Lovecraft, Seabury Quinn, and Robert E. Howard provided gratuitous scares and titillations mixed with sophisticated suspense. Moving beyond the typical criticisms lobbed against pulp fiction, English scholar Timothy Jones begins his overview of the magazine with a reader's estimation of the stories produced by "brilliant writers." With the exception of Lovecraft, who is now highly regarded, this estimation might seem far too generous unless one acknowledges that horror provides access to the forbidden: something prohibited by high culture but desired by the common reader. As Jones argues, horror readers have a different aesthetic framework for their appreciation, a need "to experience 'delicious shudders,'"[19] the unpleasant that is deeply pleasurable.

With "The Call of Cthulhu" first appearing in 1928, Lovecraft deepens the experience of dread in a genre that confronts a civilization unwilling to acknowledge the forces lurking beneath the surface. Based on the second-hand and questionable account of the protagonist's grandnephew, the story follows the course of an archaeological dig leading to the unintended release of an ancient extraterrestrial monster.

In addition, the monster has an ancient order of worshippers who threaten all who might reveal its presence before the creature's so-called appointed time. With its lack of resolution, the story evokes a paranoia that is characteristic of other tales of participatory horror, suggesting that evil is not a figure to be overcome but the inevitable end of the human world. Jones describes Lovecraft and the writers of *Weird Tales* as an essential link in American horror history: "The procedures sketched by Poe in his stories of the 1830s and 1840s were substantially developed by this group in the 1920s and 1930s, and would be taken up by later writers who looked towards Lovecraft as a touchstone as the twentieth century progressed."[20]

Although pulp fiction was the mass market publication that paved the way for comic books as a medium, an even more direct point of inspiration for horror comics content would be found elsewhere: "the horror radio shows of the 1930s and 1940s, with their short story formats, surprise endings, and emphasis on breathless dialogue."[21] Comics historian Mike Benton quotes Al Feldstein, writer and editor of EC horror comics, who identifies radio shows such as *Inner Sanctum* and *Lights Out* as providing a template for his horror comics.[22] In fact, in years to come, many radio shows such as *The Mysterious Traveler* would become horror anthology comics.[23] With Stephen King as his source, Richard Hand describes the power of horror radio in *Terror on the Air!*: "[I]n radio drama such dilemmas and perils are redundant because 'you made the monster in your mind… it was a perfect monster.'"[24] In this way, the monster could then be said to engage the audience and bridge the gap between its literal representation and the subterranean fear that gave birth to it.

While Benton's above-mentioned list of characteristics for horror radio shows is fairly complete (highlighting characteristics regularly identified with the EC horror story), it leaves off one of the most important parts of the shows and of horror comics: the host.[25] In addition to reactivating the oral experience of the folktale that gives rise to the horror story, the host creates for the recipient a complex relationship with the horror story. To begin, the host serves practical functions such as suggesting a common link between different stories in an anthology series as well as providing an introduction and exposition for each story. While these functions might seem to distance the recipient from the story, the host can also bring the recipient nearer (as in the case of the first-person narration in horror, with literary frameworks and the stories themselves).[26] In radio series, the host speaks directly to listeners in a way described by media scholar Richard Hand, "a self-reflexive and self-conscious stance on itself as a 30-minute 'show' which… can range from being deadly earnest to frivolously ironic."[27]

Deadly earnestness can exponentially increase the drama when the show presents a first-person account: "the intimacy of radio is [exploited by] the type of play that puts us inside the head of the lunatic."[28] Frivolous irony might seem to do the opposite, but in fact exposes, acclimates, and normalizes the experience of horror for the recipient as part of the "real" world. Moreover, Old Nancy, the witch of Salem, served as the host of *The Witch's Tale* (along with her cat, Satan) but also became a character in her own right, breaking down the discursive boundaries between the "real" and fictive elements: "the boundary between fiction and fact is consciously blurred."[29]

Influences on Horror Comics: The Universal Experience of Horror

While these storytelling precedents provide a narrative, conceptual, and thematic basis for horror comics, visuals serve as a key determinant of the experience created by them. Those visuals would be drawn in part from a long history that includes paintings like Henri Fuseli's *The Nightmare* and illustrations like Gustave Doré's series for "Rime of the Ancient Mariner." However, painting would move in wildly different directions in the twentieth century, with movements specifically devoted to the uncanny, like expressionism and surrealism, and illustration would become much more widespread and genre-oriented with the advent of newspapers, magazines, and pulp fiction. In addition, the advent of film would provide another way to experience horror in one of the most influential representations of horror in a visually-driven narrative form. With precedents set in the politically contentious Jacobean period with plays like *The Duchess of Malfi*, Paris's Grand Guignol theater presented sensationally violent horror productions,[30] a template for future horror films and comics.[31]

Reaching a wider audience, film took the spurting blood of stage productions one step further with many other effects developed through the benefit of models, stop action, and other tricks of cinematography. One of the first American producers to take advantage of these film possibilities and satisfy the audience's desire for such horror was Thomas Edison.[32] He was the first to bring the story of Frankenstein to the screen, with special effects that depicted the creature's assembly from a vat of chemicals. As Dixon argues, this production doesn't stand in isolation in Edison's catalogue of films: "Thomas Edison, that most exploitational of entrepreneurs, produced the first filmic version of *Frankenstein*... but that film was preceded by a series of equally bloodthirsty entertainments, including the bizarre *Electrocuting an Elephant* (1903) and *The Execution of Mary, Queen of Scots* (1895), the first an authentic 'snuff film'... and the latter a lip-smacking vignette depicting Mary Stuart's death by the ax."[32]

Although not necessarily a bloodthirsty entertainment, *Frankenstein* set a precedent for horror as a film genre, notably something also seen in other early national film traditions such as German Expressionism. With films like Robert Wiene's *The Cabinet of Dr. Caligari* disorienting audiences and causing controversy in the United States,[34] German Expressionism eventually produced *Nosferatu*, an unofficial adaptation of Dracula well known for its grotesque depiction of the Count.

However, cinematic styles like German Expressionism would only influence American comic book artists in limited degrees (with the possible exception of Basil Wolverton), much more oriented by the American film industry toward moody realism. As Benton claims, "The Universal monster series… and all their many sequels and imitators of the 1930s and 1940s gave comic book artists the visual language they needed to draw 'horribly.'"[35] Beginning with the successes of *The Hunchback of Notre Dame* and *The Phantom of the Opera* (both featuring grotesque visuals of Lon Chaney in heavy makeup), Universal was committed to the horror film. With their famous production of *Dracula* starring Bela Lugosi, director Tod Browning would combine the haunting effect of Expressionism's long shadows with more realistic settings and naturalistic performances. In this way, Universal started to develop a visual language that could bridge the gap between the supernatural and the real world, a bridge made famous in literature by the Gothic novel.

While Lugosi's distinctive, heavily accented performance struck a chord with audiences, Universal's *Frankenstein* permanently established the tropes of Universal's horror films with its monster as both sympathetic and uncanny to modern audiences. Although Shelley's story was liberally adapted, the film maintained that the monstrous could be found with the creator as readily (if not more so) than with the creature. Cultural historian David Skal describes the cultural resonance of Boris Karloff's version of the creature: "Untold millions had been left with the feeling that modern life—and death—was nothing but an anonymous, crushing assembly line. Whale's film depicted a monster squarely in the grip of this confusion, a pathetic figure caught, as it were, on the barbed wire between humanism and mechanism."[36] With an art design that mixes past and present, *Frankenstein* makes Gothic horror relevant again (as do later Universal films such as *The Wolf Man*, by placing the classic monster type in a contemporary setting). And the film also redeploys the frame device common to past and present horror narratives with a host who warns the audience about the impending horror of the film. Consequently, folktale monsters became the basis for mass media myths and provided a starting point for horror creators to work in popular narrative and visual forms.

For the all the power of Universal Studios' horror, the films had limitations based in finite budgets for sets and costumes and in conservative studio expectations that led to B-list casting. And the films' larger-than-life performances have been found alternately praise-worthy and laughable due in part to the new medium's transition from the excessive pantomime of the silent film to the neo-realism of the talkie.[37] Moreover, the films represent how easily a genre founded on excess can be overwrought and therefore, primed for parody. In the history of horror, the excessiveness of the Gothic world has regularly led to this in unintentional ways with something like the absurdity of death by giant helmet in *The Castle of Otranto*. However, when those artistic choices that walk the borderline between horror and humor are intentionally made (as was the case with the overacting associated with Old Nancy, the host of the radio show *The Witch's Tale*), we have the phenomenon of camp. And this effectively describes the hosts of horror comics soon to come, perhaps the largest problem for emissaries of high culture and critics of horror comics who do not find them funny in the least.

The Foundation of the Comics Scare: Newspaper Strips, Comic Books, and Other Crimes

Cheaply printed for the masses, the newspaper was the home for the wildly successful comic strip that led to the comic book. With its commercial importance represented by the Pulitzer/Hearst fight over Outcault's "Yellow Kid," the series' strips were eventually collected in the first comic book, the unexpectedly successful *Famous Funnies*. This book is mentioned not only as part of comics history but also because the person partly responsible for *Famous Funnies* was Max Gaines.[38] In addition to being the first to collect *Dick Tracy* (an important origin for crime comics), Gaines would found EC: the future home of so many popular and reviled horror comics. Of course, *Dick Tracy* was one among many strips that Gaines collected (also including comedy, romance, and adventure), and originally EC stood for Educational Comics. Publisher of comic book Bible stories, EC eventually fell on financial hard times,[39] and it was Gaines's son, William "Bill" Gaines, who solved those financial problems with the help of crime and horror comics.

Regardless, the story of comics starts with collections of comics strips, anthologies of new comic book material, and the amazing breakthrough of the mythic and commercial entity known as the superhero. Although highly profitable for a short time, the dominance of the superhero story looked to be short lived, initiated with *Superman*'s debut in Action Comics No. 1 in 1938 but quickly waning after the end of World War II.

Other genres vied for the attention of the comic readers, and the next smash hit would be the crime story, particularly represented by Charles Biro's *Crime Does Not Pay* (which began its run in 1942). Taking a lead from the formula of the murder mystery, the crime story left behind the mysterious and the detective in order to focus on crime and the criminal. Coinciding with the fear and romanticism simultaneously associated with real gangsters, *Crime Does Not Pay* lived up to the title only in the slightest way, with the criminal caught in the last few panels. The stories mostly represented a fascination with the life associated with violent crime depicted by a gratuitous panorama of violence on almost every cover of *Crime Does Not Pay*.

In general, crime comics questioned the American dream, representing figures who sought and achieved it as law-breakers breaking free from the industrial grind of a bleak post-Depression-era society. With an increasingly older readership for comic books in the 1940s, crime comics proliferated, as other titles emphasized sensational content and barely made the cursory and tenuous claim that "crime does not pay." With this emphasis on the monstrous criminal without the clear counterbalance of a virtuous law enforcer, the groundwork was laid for the advent of the horror story. Mike Benton claims, "[T]he crime comics of the later 1940s, with their stories of terror and blood, pave the way for the arrival of horror comic books in the early 1950s.... After the crime comic reading boom peaked in 1948, comic book publishers began adding elements of horror and terror to the crime comics in an effort to keep their readership."[40]

This statement can easily be understood too simplistically, as if horror comics are just crime comics plus elements of extreme terror (something no more true than stating crime comics are superhero comics plus elements of criminal misconduct). Nevertheless, it is worth exploring the overlap between these three genres popular in the early years of comic book publication, starting with superheroes and horror in particular reference to supervillains and some of the heroes who contend with them. In "The Horror Narrative and the Graphic Novel," Lance Eaton states, "[I]t was Batman, whose identity was subsumed by horror and whose costume struck fear in villains, where many horror-inspired characters appeared."[41] And by debuting in *Detective Comics*, Batman represents a critical nexus between the conventions of superheroes, crime, and horror.[42] For instance, "Batman Versus the Vampire" in *Detective Comics* No. 31 and No. 32 features the superhero not only investigating a vampire adversary but also confronting a somnambulist and a giant gorilla, as well as making references to werewolves in Eastern Europe.[43]

In addition, the 1950s boom in horror comics coincides with the emergence of other media forms and the growth of certain cultural anxieties as Benton describes: "The horror comic book, like television and rock and roll, is really a child of the 1950s, born in the Coldest days of the Cold War and at the height of our nuclear age paranoia."[44] In *Tales from the Crypt: The Official Archives*, researcher Digby Diehl describes the connection between classic horror stories' critique of the industrial age and 1950s horror comics' portrayal of modern terrors: "*Frankenstein*, *Dracula*, and *The Phantom of the Opera* had sprung from the nightmare conditions of the early days of the Industrial Revolution. Horror comics of the 1950s appealed to teens and young adults who were trying to cope with the aftermath of even greater terrors–Nazi death camps and the explosions of bombs at Hiroshima and Nagasaki."[45] In *The Horror! The Horror!: Comic Books the Government Didn't Want You to Read*, Jim Trombetta is even more particular:

> The prominence of horror comics exactly parallels the emergence of the United States as a military and economic superpower nonpareil: The nation had defeated two evil empires, and its productive capacities were intact; it possessed not only ultimate weapons (for a while, exclusively) but also the moral high ground over its potential enemies. At the same time, however, American citizens still carried the scars from the Great Depression and the Second World War, which had gone nuclear. Pretty soon the threat of destruction hung over the planet like an eternal winter... [and] the fifties establishment wanted to suppress terror, or at least control it.[46]

Transitioning between what the nation wanted to be at a conscious level and what it feared it was at an unconscious level, the 1950s was a time in which the cultural unconscious emerged in a dramatic way.

As a result, horror comic books increased in popular interest and concomitantly in prominence on the newsstands. Unlike superhero and crime stories, horror had few precedents or corollaries in the newspaper strips, something that may have made this genre more threatening to a mass audience in its comic book form. The very first horror comics were adaptations of literature–*Classic Comics: Dr. Jekyll and Mr. Hyde* in No. 13 (1943), *Frankenstein* in No. 26 (1945), and *Mysteries by Edgar Alan Poe* in No, 40 (1947) (more accurately horror stories than mysteries). As adaptations of "classic" literature, *Classic Comics* were somewhat insulated from the criticism that later plagued horror comics, but the covers clearly indicated their horror content, with Mr. Hyde as a fanged werewolf and "The Pit and the Pendulum"'s narrator about to be severed by a giant blade.

In addition to these digest-style publications, horror made its way into the more traditional pamphlet-style anthologies in *Yellowjacket Comics* (a superhero series) with an installment called "Tales of Terror." Debuting in 1944, the first issue of the first comic from Charlton Press adapted Poe's "The Black Cat," a tale hosted by an old witch. Followed by "The Pit and the Pendulum" in issue No. 3, this horror tale, somewhat interesting in its panel arrangement, demonstrates the potential challenges of visually adapting a textual account of psychologically based fear. The protagonist's fears are literally rendered as a mix of devils, skulls, disembodied eyes, and totemic masks floating in the air, nearly laughable due to the variety of styles used from one figure to the next.

Working with the idea that crime comics peaked in 1948, the appearance of horror anthologies is only as significant as the transformation of anthologies formerly devoted to superheroes and crime. Avon Comics released *Eerie*, the first horror-only title in 1947 (lasting only one issue), and American Comics' *Adventures into the Unknown* became the first ongoing horror anthology comic in 1948 devoted to the most obvious horror motifs—"ghosts, werewolves, and frightened women in Gothic castles."[47] Marvel's failing title *Captain America* became *Captain America's Weird Tales* in 1947,[48] and *Marvel Mystery Comics* became *Marvel Tales* (a horror comic) in 1949. And most significantly, as many publishers leaned in this direction, the EC line of comics, rejuvenated by Bill Gaines's choice to produce superhero and crime comics, experimented with horror tales like "Zombie Terror" in *Moon Girl* No. 5 (1948) and "Return from the Grave!," a Crypt-Keeper story, in *Crime Patrol* No. 15 (1949).

The Danse Macabre, Monster Mash, and O. Henry Twist in Horror Comics

Following the pattern established by *Adventures into the Unknown*, many early horror comics included traditional and clearly expected content such as monsters in contemporary Gothic settings depicted in Universal horror films. As indicated by the above EC story titles, stories of reanimated corpses were favorites but ran parallel to stories of ghosts, witches, and werewolves. For instance, *Adventures into the Unknown* No. 10 featured "The Boy Who Cried Wolf," the story of Jimmy Rogers, a young man prone to telling tall tales. Trying to impress the locals in Pendleton, he invents a story about his battle with a ghost in Pendleton manor where Josiah Pendle burned to death 100 years ago. After others laugh at his story and see through Jimmy's feeble ruse to prove the existence of Pendle's ghost, Jimmy is summoned to the house by the actual ghost.

Angered by the scoffing laughter of the others, Pendle's ghost works to destroy the town by bending Jimmy to his will and using him to open a dam that will flood the town. However, Jimmy resists, runs back to Pendleton manor, and sets fire to the house, thereby destroying the ghost. And as news of the manor's destruction spreads, he refuses to tell the story to the townies, who expect him to spin yet another unfounded tale. Providing a contemporary variation on the folktale "The Boy Who Cried Wolf," the story also becomes a tale of the supernatural: not only a moral tale but also a redemptive adventure.

Edvard Moritz provides elegant line work for "The Boy Who Cried Wolf" with a style that exists somewhere between *Archie* comics and a starker realism. While experimenting with panel arrangement in interesting but unmotivated ways, the story effectively utilizes the conventional presentation of a ghostly figure in conventional terms (white and transparent). Rendered as a realistic figure, Josiah Pendle is frightening due to choices in perspective that begins with the initial view: an extreme close up of Pendle's face, old, green-eyed, and hysterical. After the next view establishes Pendle's ghost as physically larger than Jimmy, the following panel forces the reader into Jimmy's low-angle perspective, looking up at the angry ghost hovering near a cracked, red ceiling. And this creative use of perspective works well in other places to create a general atmosphere, such as the beginning of the story where one of the townies baits Jimmy to tell another laughable story. When he says, "Oh c'mon, Jimmy! I bet that was nothing compared to some of your other adventures! Tell us more!,"[49] he looks directly at the reader and winks (implicating us as part of the group that laughs at Jimmy). The subsequent transition from the seat of power with those who belittle Jimmy to the position of powerlessness with a terrified Jimmy controlled by a ghostly spirit represents an important and uncanny turn in a horror narrative. However, with all of this stated, there are plenty of hackneyed aspects of the story that reduce the overall effect ranging from a text box accompanied by a skull unrelated to the story content to a future headline representing Jimmy's fears and referring to Jimmy as a "crazed boy." In addition, readers are subjected to the supernatural inconsistency of a ghost that wanders freely from his haunted manor with Jimmy and yet is destroyed within his burning home.

Similar early stories represent creators still working out the narrative conventions and visual tropes of the comic book horror story as is the case in "The Civic Spirit," another story in the same issue in which the ghosts are distinctly Casper-like and unfrightening. However, in Cornell's *Suspense* No. 5, "Mark of the Witch" demonstrates an early maturity, portraying the Lord Mayor of a sixteenth-century English town as a witch-hunting zealot prone to torture and seizing the property his victims.

His paranoid fervor extends to the townspeople who recognize him as a self-serving murderer but also label him with the same terms he uses against others: devil-worshiper, demon, monster. The story opens with him on the run from the townspeople and relating his story to the kindly woman who shelters him; and in the end, the woman reveals herself as a haggard witch with fearsome claws who strangles him to death. With the "Bang! Bang!" of the angry townspeople at the door (echoing the "Bang! Bang!" of the Lord Mayor knocking on the kindly woman's door at the start), Russ Heath's nicely drawn final panel positions us near the floor, allowing us to see the Lord Mayor's upturned dead face.

In addition to providing a critique of witch-hunting, the story moves beyond conventional justice and provides justice through the clawed hands of a supernatural threat. The twist ending that would so famously become associated with horror comics (and especially with EC horror) provides moral lessons–but those moral lessons depend on excessive punishment and often on the continued existence of "evil" in the world. Also, while the Lord Mayor did not clearly kill actual witches, the story provides a different perspective on the witch at the end as a product of culture (or at least connected to the mechanics of culture). *Suspense* was one of many comics connected to productions in another media form (in this case a radio show), and the title applies equally well to crime and horror tales (with the comic and radio series often connecting the two). In this case, even though the supernatural plays a part in the story, it deals as much if not more with the psychology of the criminal on the run and the surprise twist at the end.

Even though the supernatural is important to many of the famous EC stories at the forefront of the horror comics boom, the twist ending associated with suspense was the EC trademark. For instance, in EC's *The Vault of Horror* No. 14,[50] Harry Harrison produced such a story (building to what Bill Gaines famously called the O. Henry twist)–"Werewolf" about mountain climbers in the Carpathian Mountains. Although a bit heavy-handed in the exposition of the characters, the story showcases Harrison's clean style and creative choices. As the characters are introduced, two long images of the climbers are subdivided into five panels. Four of those panels facilitate the introductions, while the last and the largest foreshadows the attacks upon, suspicions between, and dire ends of the climbers. And panel five, the largest of seven on the first page (though still relatively small), is the only indicator of its supernatural content with the title of the story, "Werewolf," superimposed on the mountain.

Set within a typical arc for a suspense story, the grizzled mountain guide tries to convince the young American newlywed of his suspicions that a Transylvanian climber (in this particular case, a werewolf) is a threat to their lives. As a man of the modern world, the American resists the seemingly baseless notions of the guide's superstitions until the newlywed's wife is found dead. While the remaining climbers succeed in killing the werewolf, all but the formerly doubting American has been bitten or scratched. As might be expected, the last page reveals that they all are now "Werewolves!" Even though it is not the most ironic twist in horror history, the ending works, like the best of EC's twists, to disrupt closure in a dramatic way distinctly based in comic book conventions. The last page is a splash page featuring the werewolves partially transformed and about to attack the protagonist, whose back is turned toward the reader (again placing the reader in the terrifying position of the protagonist). As opposed to the first page of the story, which is designed more like an interior page, the final page is designed more like a traditional single-panel first page (with its much larger pluralization of the title), demonstrating that the horror provoked by the twist is the point of the story; the threat of horror is not resolved (even in an excessive, disturbing way) and consequently persists beyond the end of the story.

Fig. 1.1
The Vault of Horror No. 14, EC, 1950, © William M. Gaines Agent, Inc.
The splash page layout ends rather than opens "Werewolf" with a visual and narrative twist that is punctuated by a change to the title.

Even when EC stories utilized supernatural monsters, they worked to evoke a dread that necessarily accompanied these plot twists influenced as much by Edgar Allan Poe and O. Henry. That sense of continued haunting would be the basis for many 1950s horror comic stories (not only EC) but especially in regard to EC's implicit cultural commentary. The most popular horror comic stories of the time were more realistic and sophisticated, focusing less on Universal's monsters and more on the human monster tied to cultural anxieties (predating a radical reinvention of the horror genre with a movie like *Psycho* by nearly two decades). EC horror titles like *The Vault of Horror* and *Tales from the Crypt* portrayed suburban life as the horror that gave rise to deranged wives and psychopathic husbands.

Before looking more at EC and some other major horror comics publishers in the years leading to 1954, it is important to establish how much horror grew in popularity in just a few years. In comparison to some of the still profitable superhero comics, Benton identifies that horror comics outsold *Superman* and *Batman* comics in the 1950s four to one.[51] In *The Ten Cent Plague: The Great Comic-Book Scare and How It Changed America*, David Hajdu adds, "By the end of 1952, nearly one-third of all the comics on the newsstands were devoted to the macabre."[52]

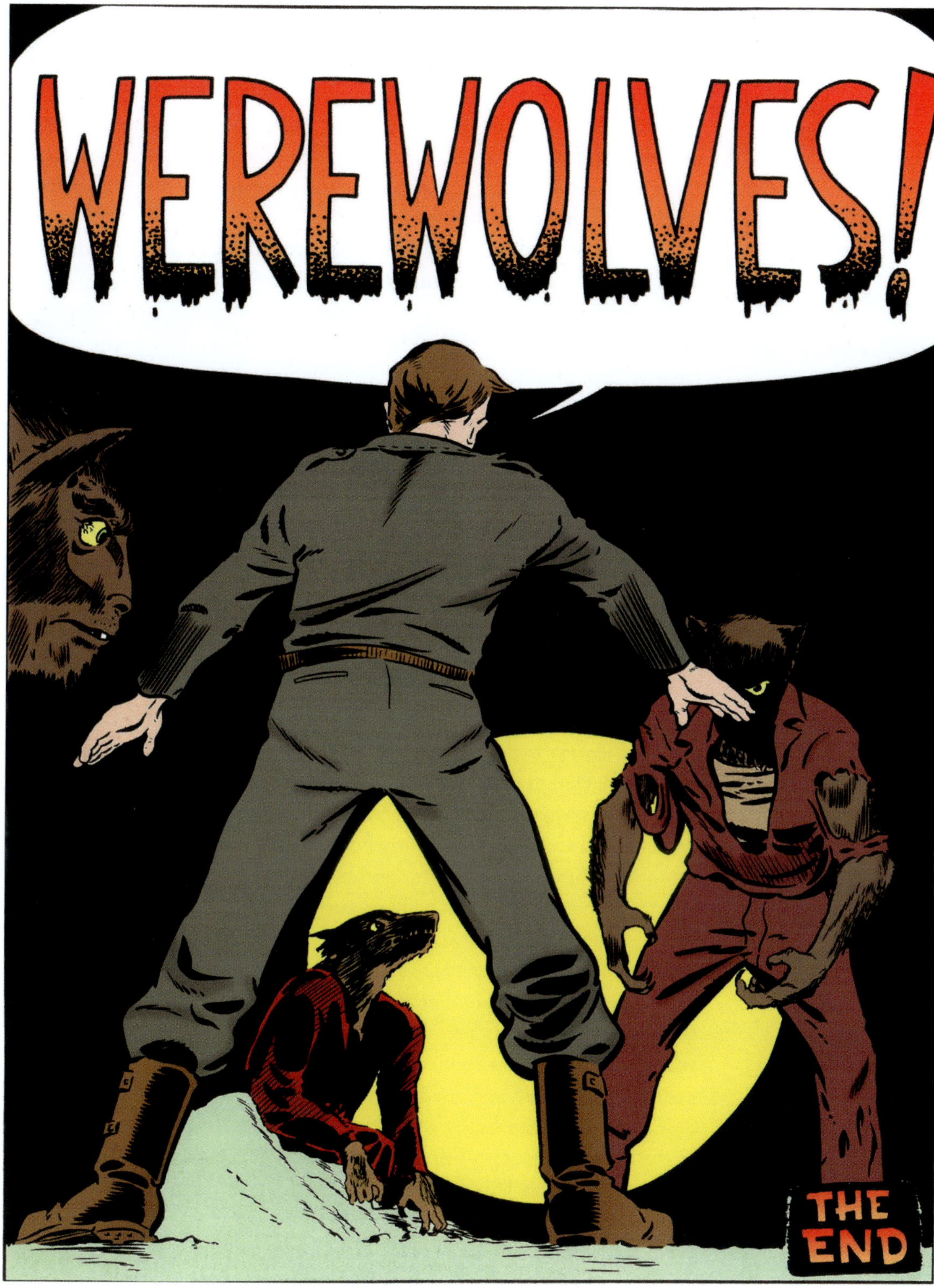

WEREWOLVES!
THE END

While it doesn't verify the growing adult readership that EC claimed at that time, Diehl clearly shows the widespread appeal of the genre with horror comics outselling *Reader's Digest* and *The Saturday Evening Post*.[53] And as the demand for horror comics grew at a nearly exponential rate, most other comic book publishers contributed to this explosion, with EC only representing three percent of the horror comic books published in the 1950s.[54]

Since horror in comics didn't start with EC, and EC produced a small number of the overall titles, it is important to mention the reasons for the seemingly disproportionate place EC occupies in comics scholarship. There is a tendency to regard EC as the one creative font amidst a glut of opportunistic horror comics publishers and to make Bill Gaines the champion of creators' rights, the hero valiantly fighting for art and the First Amendment against a self-serving congressional committee and the forces of censorship.[55] In fact, there are grains of truth to this characterization beyond this intentionally inflated description, but EC's comic book output should certainly be placed alongside other horror comics published at the time. In addition, other factors that contribute to EC's iconic status must be analyzed, including the phenomena of EC fan culture and ironically, the spectacular failure of Gaines's muddled congressional testimony.

EC Horror in the American Commonplace: From Domestic Bliss to Domestic Blasphemy

When Max Gaines died in 1947, Bill Gaines inherited Educational Comics, a company economically floundering with his father's hopes to sell comic books about history, science, and the Bible. Renaming the company Entertaining Comics and with no particular expertise or interest in the business, Bill set about producing comic books more in line with other then-popular comic book genres: romance, crime, science fiction, and war stories. In short order, Gaines proved himself a shrewd businessman and adapted to a business model that relied upon a quick reaction to your audience by employing "road men" to visit newsstands and track sales.[56] Crime did well, but Gaines was even more excited that the sales of the crime titles with horror installments sold extremely well. While horror may have been an outlet needed by a 1950s "button-down America… punctuated by outbursts of paranoia," Gaines had been long drawn to horror at a more instinctual level. After receiving positive responses from horror stories in various EC superhero and crime comics,[57] Gaines moved enthusiastically in that direction with *The Crypt of Terror* (later *Tales from the Crypt*) and *The Vault of Horror* replacing two crime comics, and *The Haunt of Fear* replacing a Western comic.

Horror stories also continued in *Crime SuspenStories* and later appeared in the even more diverse anthology *Shock SuspenStories*, serving with the other three fundamentally connected titles as the collective cornerstone of EC horror.

As already mentioned, the comic book horror story generally moves away from Universal's monster retreads with EC Comics famously taking the lead in the exploration of the human monster in the 1950s. This move is represented effectively in the very first issue of *The Crypt of Terror* with the Johnny Craig story "Curse of the Full Moon!" While the cover teases an attack on an unsuspecting woman by a Lon Chaney-like wolfman, the story itself is primarily concerned with the bizarre paranoia of a man who suspects he is a werewolf responsible for a killing spree. When the ending reveals he is not a werewolf, but his confidante is, there is no physical transformation and readers are left wondering whether the real killer is just as deluded as the story's protagonist. The horror of the human mind has always been part of the horror story, but the hideous appearance of the monster always insulated people from their unconscious awareness that the monstrous is really inside them.[58] The narrative depiction of losing one's sense of a virtuous self in America and its cultural institutions like marriage is represented in the crime/horror synthesis "Horror Under the Big Top!", a story of circus performers in *Crime SuspenStories* No. 7. When a husband rightly suspects his wife of cheating, she and her lover advance the timetable of their plans for murdering him. In a barely believable and clumsily poetic way, they cause the husband's flying cannonball act to malfunction and he drops from an extreme height only to kill his wife in the fall. And when the ringmaster insists that the show must go on and the lover begins his trapeze act, he discovers that the husband cut his rope, and he falls to his death as well.

While not EC's most sophisticated tale, this story by Albert Feldstein–Gaines's most significant writer and his partner in crime (and horror)–represents the most prevalent components of EC horror very well. The characters in this story are not motivated by the absolute evil that is regularly associated with a monster like Dracula; instead, they are motivated by venal self-interest, and there is no implication that anything more noble thrived in them before that self-interest was put in place. Although in a more conventional setting, this story is characteristic of almost all domestic dramas in EC horror, influenced less by medieval notions of original sin than modern frustrations with everyday routine. In *The Ten Cent Plague*, Hajdu describes this focus in EC horror: "EC made a specialty of intimate, domestic terror.... Married people, especially wives, were invariably duplicitous, conniving, abusive, and often murderous....

In EC's horror paradigm, the true graveyard was the living room of the American home."[59]

While this domestic horror is regularly associated with EC, these stories could be seen elsewhere (especially as EC's popularity grew) in stories such as "Happy Anniversary" in Harvey's *Chamber of Chills* No. 19. Reminiscing as she prepares her husband's drink to celebrate their ten-year anniversary, Charlotte recounts the way that he once resented her controlling ways and became a philanderer. However, she's very happy that his infidelities eventually came to an end and things have been so consistent since then (the final panel depicts her bringing the drink to her husband's propped-up corpse). Inside the quintessential dream home of the 1950s, she raises her glass in that panel with tears in her eyes revealing the psychosis that lies right beneath the surface of the "perfect" marriage.[60] And the horror of the domestic scene is effectively encapsulated in the issue's cover by Lee Elias and Warren Kremer–a skeletal hand toasts a beautiful woman whose face is seen in part through the upraised wine glass as the skull beneath the skin.

Fig. 1.2
© *Chamber of Chills* No. 19, Harvey Comics, 1953
In classic horror comics, a "Happy Anniversary" ends with a corpse, a subliminal desire within every superficially perfect marriage.

With EC's trademark twist endings,[61] EC and their imitators develop a horror aesthetic based not on the fear of the unexpected but rather the dread that comes from knowing something horrible will inevitably happen. Eaton describes the contrast between these two approaches: "The two significant ways of playing with visuals in comic books is either by providing as graphic an illustration as possible, thereby emphasizing gore or disgust. However comic books also play with visuals by denying the reader the ability to see what is horrific. Readers are often left to wonder why a protagonist's face is stricken with fear, or what the monster looks like that is casting such a strange shadow."[62] With this in mind, Johnny Craig's EC covers serve as an embodiment of this aesthetic with scenes separate from the interior stories but evoking a fear of what would follow. They encourage the reader to imagine the subsequent event, thus making the reader "an equal partner in crime." In the background of the cover to *Crime SuspenStories* No. 7, a woman watches a television news report about a "maniacal ax-killer," and in the foreground, a male hand reaches toward an ax on the desk. In addition to participating in the crime to come, the drama created by the cover design suggests the ax-murderer was someone living in the woman's home.[63]

By playing with perspective, the visual dynamics of the comic book form implicated the reader within crime and horror, especially significant as they relate to an unfolding narrative. Famously used by Wertham to reveal the dangers of comics, "The Orphan" in *Shock SuspenStories* No. 14, is told by a child trapped in an abusive home.

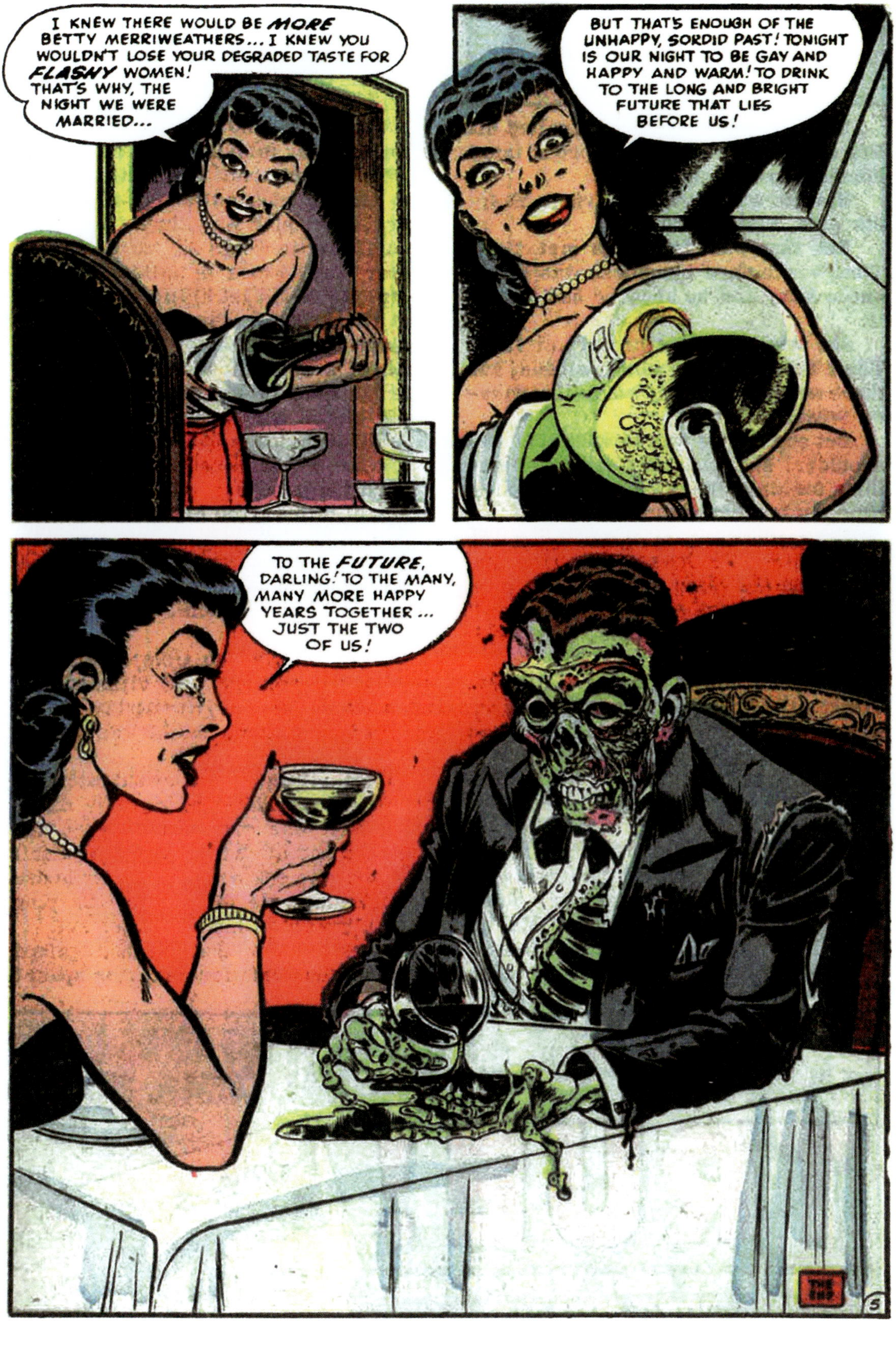
I KNEW THERE WOULD BE MORE BETTY MERRIWEATHERS... I KNEW YOU WOULDN'T LOSE YOUR DEGRADED TASTE FOR FLASHY WOMEN! THAT'S WHY, THE NIGHT WE WERE MARRIED...
BUT THAT'S ENOUGH OF THE UNHAPPY, SORDID PAST! TONIGHT IS OUR NIGHT TO BE GAY AND HAPPY AND WARM! TO DRINK TO THE LONG AND BRIGHT FUTURE THAT LIES BEFORE US!
TO THE FUTURE, DARLING! TO THE MANY, MANY MORE HAPPY YEARS TOGETHER ... JUST THE TWO OF US!
THE END
5

After cheating on the child's drunken father, the mother tries to leave the house with her lover. When the father confronts them, a shot rings out and the father falls, the mother faints, and her lover runs away. Because the police find the father shot to death and the mother with a gun in her hand, the mother and her lover are tried and executed for planning the murder. In the last two panels, the child turns to the reader and with a wink, breaks the fourth wall (her narration in a speech balloon rather than narrative box as it had been): "[This] is just the way I'd hoped it would work out when I shot daddy from the front bedroom... and put the gun in mommy's hand."[64] As her confidante, we know the real mechanism by which the abusive parents met their punishment, encountering another EC tale of domestic terror[65] and strange, subversive morality described by Skal in *The Monster Show*: "If the rigid moralism of the core stories was not recognized by their (equally moralistic) critics, it was perhaps because the stories swung wildly between—and sometimes mixed together—moralism, sadism, and outright nihilism. In the horror comics view of America, morality was a state of grace attainable only by the living dead and the murderous insane."[66]

If some sort of justice was realized in horror comics, that justice is determined less by the rigid moralism of the hero–villain dynamic and more by the slippery psychology of the perpetrator–victim dynamic. Johnny Craig would often put the reader in the victim's place, the other undesirable position in horror comics (as already demonstrated, a position not mutually exclusive from that of the perpetrator). For instance, the cover of *Crime SuspenStories* No. 16 depicts a lunatic slashing the outstretched hands of the "reader," activating fear and threatening the psychological integrity of the subject. This interactive, unstable, and disconcerting position of the reader causes comics historian Bradford Wright to state, "Into a self-satisfied culture of abundance and moral certitudes, EC injected a dose of sober revisionism and liberating anarchy."[67] While sometimes very specific in their political commentary,[68] horror comics at this time were meant to be broadly disturbing, as indicated by the EC Comics "help wanted" ad in *Writer's Digest*: "You should know this about our horror books... we relish the *contes cruels* (tales of sadism). Virtue doesn't always have to triumph."[69] Destabilizing the sacred is a thrilling, if perverse, end in itself as represented by the killer Santa story "...And All Through the House..." in *The Vault of Horror* No. 35. Although Bill Gaines and Al Feldstein claimed to be writing for adults,[70] and some statistics indicate a large adult readership, this gleefully unnerving take on culture was popular not only with adult readers but teenage and youth readers as well.[71]

The boundary-crossing enticed a broad demographic group at least in part with the promise of participating in something horrifying and perhaps even forbidden. And the most significant boundary-crossing between the horror comic and security of the reader's mind came in the form of the horror hosts.

The Real History of the Perceived Threat from the Imaginary World of Horror Hosts

Boundary-crossing has long been an integral part of horror, ranging from the hypertextuality of Angela Carter's "The Bloody Chamber" as a variation on "Bluebeard" to the metatextuality of Mary Shelley's *Frankenstein* with Captain Walton's journal as a "real world" commentary on Victor Frankenstein's spoken narrative. Through 3D film technology, André de Toth's *The House of Wax* in 1953 and Jack Arnold's *Creature from the Black Lagoon* in 1954 crossed a boundary between the screen and theater-goer that was less literary and more literal. Comic books would try to copy that experience in 1953 with St. John's *The House of Terror*, which was sold with red and blue 3D glasses for a whopping 25 cents.[72] While this type of boundary-crossing is not exclusive to horror, it is an approach preferred by many horror creators who use formal aspects of a medium to threaten the supposed separation between the content and its consumer.[73] Horror hosts are at the forefront with comics in this regard and begin most discretely with Mr. Crime in *Crime Does Not Pay*.

Despite the bias toward realism in this pioneering crime comic, Mr. Crime clearly had an unexplained connection to supernatural horror via his fangs and the ghostly nature of his general appearance (his white transparency and flowing sheet-like robes). As sinister as he might initially look, his appearance was also obvious and comical in its design, with the word "crime" emblazoned on his top hat. Serving the typical role as a radio host might, Mr. Crime introduces stories with a disturbing wit as in the case of "The Kill-Crazy Fleagle Brothers" in *Crime Does Not Pay* No. 50. On the first page, Mr. Crime leans into the full-page panel, invisible to the Fleagle brothers, who shoot a bound and blindfolded doctor in the back. Looking directly at and speaking to the reader, Mr. Crime says, "Think that's an odd way to pay the doctor bills—with a bullet? Then you don't know the Fleagle brothers!"[74] As the story proceeds, Mr. Crime continues to serve as the only narrative voice, alternating between looking at the action and looking at the reader, between occupying the same space as the Fleagle brothers and existing independently (i.e., as a disembodied head alongside the face of other people the brothers have killed).

In addition to serving as narrator, he plays a role as an evil influencer of events indicated by his closing words as he looks at the hanging Fleagle brothers: "Good pupils, too, tsk, tsk! I try hard but none of my pupils ever gets away with murder!"[75]

In addition to introducing and concluding the tales, this sinister character with a blue collar vernacular exists inside as well as outside and the diegetic space of the story. In a way more profound than the interloping host of the radio show *The Witch's Tale*, the space Mr. Crime occupies is literal, as he moves about the story as a visual presence, but also conceptual, as he doesn't necessarily obey the rules of spatial representation within the story. In addition, the breaking of the fourth wall becomes more threatening, because he is not limited by the story in traditional ways after he establishes a connection to the reader.[76] Mr. Crime makes the reader not only a part of the violence when on the inside but also a part of the gleefully sardonic commentary on the violence when on the outside. While it is always briefly implied that "crime does not pay," Mr. Crime's perspective (and therefore, the reader's perspective) is one that takes excessive satisfaction in the unsavory. Referred to as black humor in André Breton's *Anthology of Black Humor*, this specific form of parody encourages the reader to trivialize suffering and laugh like a victimizer. And this gallows humor would be that encouraged by the consistently wise-cracking EC horror hosts who exhibited a glee in the forbidden territory covered in most horror comics.

In horror comics, the EC hosts were definitely not the first, but few realized the subversive potential of the horror host as well. For instance, in an early radio tie-in in 1948, Steve Ditko presents the Mysterious Traveler as a host for the one-shot anthology unsurprisingly titled *Mysterious Traveler*. The rather innocuous train-riding, fedora-wearing host with a shadowed face has much more discrete boundaries than Mr. Crime: always visually presented in a context separate from the story and primarily serving as a neutral omniscient narrative voice.[77] Although similarly constrained as introducers and narrators of tales, other early horror comics hosts at least drew more clearly on radio's Old Nancy as a frightening presence, including the Witch in *Hit Comics* from Quality Comics and the Black Witch in *Blue Ribbon Comics* from MLJ comics (later Archie Comics). However, the Man in Black, debuting in Harvey's one-shot *Front Page Comic Book* in 1945, not only sports a Dracula-like costume and horn-like hairstyle but also has his own distinct story and agenda, working to shape the events of the stories he hosts.[78]

Regardless, the standards for horror hosts would undeniably be the hosts of the EC trilogy of horror tales: the Crypt-Keeper, the Vault-Keeper, and the Old Witch.

While each were associated with specific EC titles (*Tales from the Crypt*, *The Vault of Horror*, and *The Haunt of Fear* respectively), each appeared in all three comics on a monthly basis, and their approach was very similar. Alliterative, pun-filled, and delivered by seemingly fully formed ghouls, the introductions and conclusions to EC stories represent the hosts' glee at presenting gruesome tales of depravity, an embrace of horror's excess, extending the black humor pleasure principle at work with Mr. Crime. And in the wake of the success of EC horror comics, horror hosts in that same vein would then proliferate with Ace's Fate, Fawcett's Dr. Death, Stanmore's Mister Mystery, and others.

Often imitated by other horror hosts, a standard introduction delivered by the Crypt-Keeper opens "Dead Right!" in *Tales from the Crypt* No. 37, with his painfully alliterative and often abusive style: "This is the Crypt-Keeper... your host in howls, master of scare-a-monies, and A-1 tale-teller... ready to reveal another revolting recitation from my library of loathsome literature. This spine-tingling scream-story will be told by Dr. Carl Winston, in his own whimpering words. Dr. Winston... if you please... go ahead with the yelp-yarn."[79] Moving beyond the horror host's vernacular style, this introduction does more than introduce; it establishes a tone and more notably portrays the host as a character who interacts with another narrator. This textual layering is complemented in unconventional visual terms, as a seemingly giant Crypt-Keeper gestures to a miniature version of Winston (both of whom face the audience).

Concomitantly, border-crossings between EC stories were commonplace as horror hosts worked with an awareness of one another; for instance, in *Tales from the Crypt* No. 24, the Crypt Keeper informs the reader that he will turn the narrative reigns over to "that bag, the Old Witch."[80] On the next page, in a separate panel, the Old Witch responds with "Hmmph! Now that you have been duly bored by the Crypt-Keeper's fairy tale, I'll tell you a horror story!"[81] In *Gothic and the Carnivalesque in American Culture*, Timothy Jones argues, "The tales the hosts told were located within a 'real' of some sort... However, the hosts themselves inhabit another place, composed mainly of dungeon rooms and mausoleums, illuminated by candlelight."[82] By constructing a comic book space that doesn't keep anthology stories separate from one another, the reality of that space becomes less separate from the reader's world. And by connecting the dungeon "rooms" that represent the story, storyteller, and the audience, this strange comic book space activates an up-ending carnivalesque attitude of the American Gothic tradition.

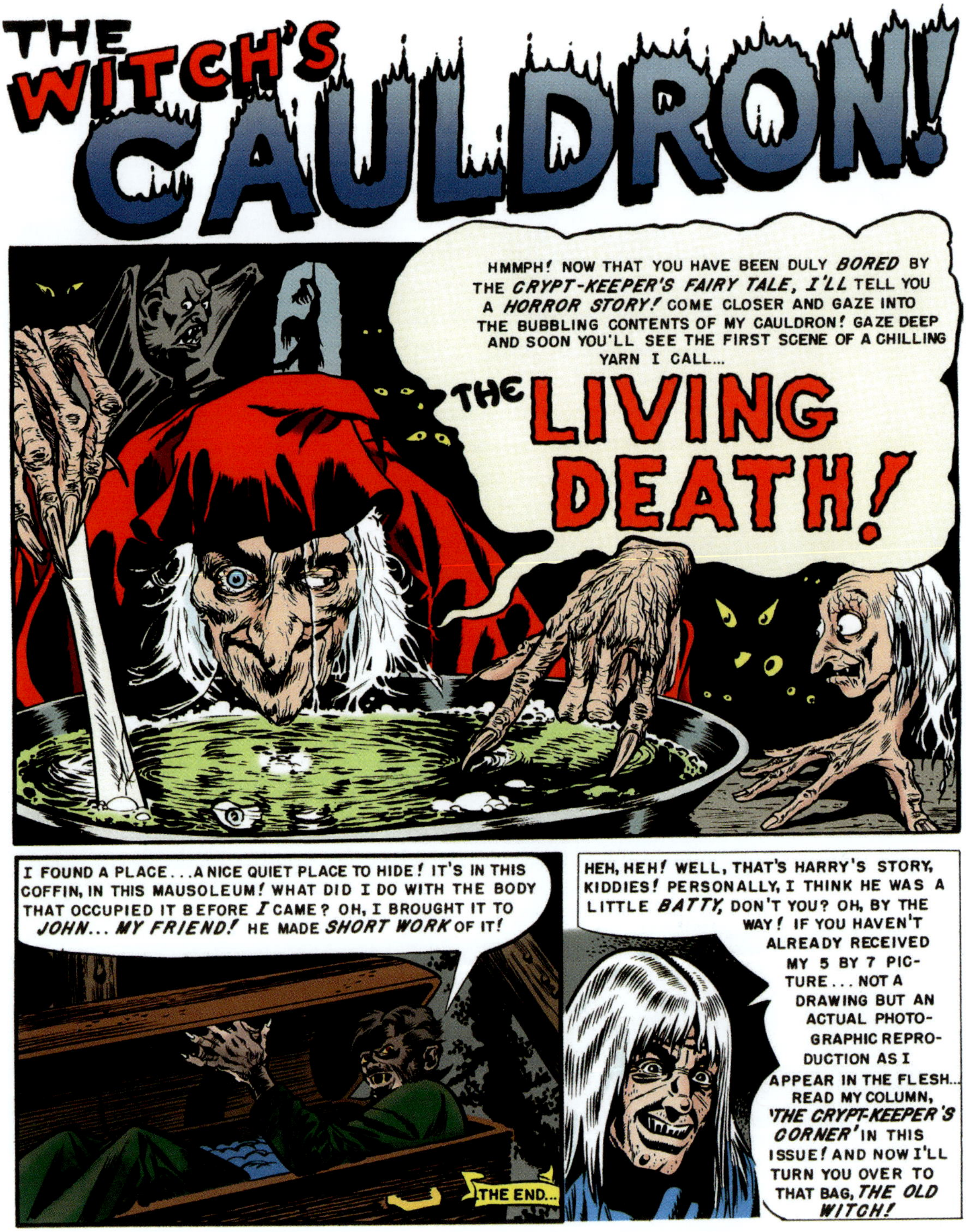
THE WITCH'S CAULDRON!
HMMPH! NOW THAT YOU HAVE BEEN DULY BORED BY THE CRYPT-KEEPER'S FAIRY TALE, I'LL TELL YOU A HORROR STORY! COME CLOSER AND GAZE INTO THE BUBBLING CONTENTS OF MY CAULDRON! GAZE DEEP AND SOON YOU'LL SEE THE FIRST SCENE OF A CHILLING YARN I CALL...
THE LIVING DEATH!
I FOUND A PLACE...A NICE QUIET PLACE TO HIDE! IT'S IN THIS COFFIN, IN THIS MAUSOLEUM! WHAT DID I DO WITH THE BODY THAT OCCUPIED IT BEFORE I CAME? OH, I BROUGHT IT TO JOHN... MY FRIEND! HE MADE SHORT WORK OF IT!
THE END...
HEH, HEH! WELL, THAT'S HARRY'S STORY, KIDDIES! PERSONALLY, I THINK HE WAS A LITTLE BATTY, DON'T YOU? OH, BY THE WAY! IF YOU HAVEN'T ALREADY RECEIVED MY 5 BY 7 PICTURE... NOT A DRAWING BUT AN ACTUAL PHOTOGRAPHIC REPRODUCTION AS I APPEAR IN THE FLESH... READ MY COLUMN, 'THE CRYPT-KEEPER'S CORNER' IN THIS ISSUE! AND NOW I'LL TURN YOU OVER TO THAT BAG, THE OLD WITCH!

These narrative and visual reorientations are suitably connected to the hosts' (and by extension, the readers') gleefully inappropriate reaction to horror stories that present the supposedly disgusting in physical, psychological, and/or spiritual terms. On EC's letters page, fans are encouraged to write in and directly interact not with the comics creators but with the horror hosts who are just as sardonic as in the stories. In reference to their bleak opinions readily shared with the reader, Jones analyzes the hosts' reaction to "Midnight Snack!" in *Tales from the Crypt* No. 24, a story of an unruly mob chasing a sympathetic man who eventually realizes his blackouts have been hiding his life as a corpse-eating psychotic. The moral from the Vault-Keeper is, "He who eats and runs away will live to eat another day!" and Jones explains the effect of this claim: "[A] moral is offered, spoofing the well-known proverb... The 'moral' of the story is effectively evacuated of any meaningful value it might hold."[83] The notion that tales should have a moral is readily associated with the standards applied to the nineteenth-century literary appropriation and redemption of fairy tales by Charles Perrault. Further along the lines of how the horror hosts resist those standards and work against any conventional redemptive value for their tales can be found in "Lower Berth" in *Tales from the Crypt* No. 33, the Crypt-Keeper's own story.

Fig. 1.3
Tales from the Crypt No. 24, EC, 1951, © William M. Gaines Agent, Inc.
EC's horror hosts do more than break the fourth wall and interact with the reader; the ending is never-ending and boundaries between stories are porous.

"Lower Berth" depicts a love story between the reanimated corpses of two circus freaks (a mummy and a two-headed man) who subsequently produce an offspring, the Crypt-Keeper, abandoned and left "crying for its parents." While the story encourages the reader's disgust with the Crypt-Keeper's freakish forebears, it also reorients the horror by making them victims of the greedy carnival owner who puts them on exhibit. And while the abandonment of the baby Crypt-Keeper evokes a certain level of pathos, the adult Crypt-Keeper's calloused commentary avoids a moral and prevents the reader from feeling too much sympathy, encouraging the reader to laugh at the horror: "I understand that there's a carnival today... that still exhibits a mummy and a two-headed corpse! If any of you see them... write me! I want to send a card! It's their anniversary next month!"[84] These narrative reorientations don't allow the reader to settle comfortably on a single interpretation of the events beyond a countercultural apprehension of monstrosity as commonplace.[85]

How Bill Gaines Became the Horror Host of the Comics Scare

Other horror comic book publishers explored the porous boundary between the horror in fictive and real worlds as well but demonstrated more anxiety about the movement between those worlds. Hosted by the robed, faceless, and strangely squat Nameless One, Trojan's *Beware* No. 11 features a cover that represents what would become one of the foremost concerns of the critics who protested horror comics. On the verge of attacking an artist drawing a horror comic, one of the monsters implies the artist worked with evil forces that he did not understand: "You summoned us from the dreadful realm beyond the grave. You didn't think we existed, eh?" This scene effectively depicts a notion that became increasingly prevalent as horror comics' content grew more graphic in a very short time in its depictions of sexuality and violence. As Benton succinctly states, "With over 200 horror stories every month, there were bound to be efforts that were boring, offensive, bizarre, and maybe even kinky."[86] Certainly, the quick pace of production meant material was often substandard, derivative, and confused. Stories were often a strained mix of motifs trying to generate interest by presenting the bizarre such as the truly awful "The Vampire Puppet" in Avon's *Witchcraft* No. 2. However, in the long run, the larger problem would be stories that excessively plumbed the forbidden.

Following in the footsteps of pulp magazines such as *Weird Tales* with its almost complete female nudity, horror comics featured scantily clad women on the covers from the very start with Avon's *Eerie* in 1947.[87] And horror comics were quick to push the envelope, leading to stories like "Grave Rehearsal" in Farrell's *Strange Fantasy* No. 7 (as described by Benton): "Humiliation, domination, [and] sadomasochism… fill up most of the story, which ends with the [protagonist] buried alive in wet cement."[88] The connection between the sexual and not only the violent but also the macabre is dramatically shown on the cover of *Chamber of Chills* No. 23, featuring a woman, horrified but nevertheless engaged in an open-mouth kiss with a skeleton. Due especially to the visual basis of the medium, these depictions of sexuality and especially of violence would not go unnoticed by critics who considered themselves to be the country's moral guardians.

As early as 1948 in an article called "Puddles of Blood," *Time* covered the symposium "The Psychopathology of Comic Books" and gave prominent space to the complaints of comics critics like Fredric Wertham. Ignoring earlier critics' charges that comic books fostered illiteracy, Wertham was much more narrow, suggesting that comics violence caused juvenile delinquency.

Nevertheless, most publishers were emboldened by Wertham's inability to gain traction for his argument in the courts at a state level and escalated the violent content that translated to strong sales.[89] Among the most notorious stories in the EC catalogue is "Foul Play" in the *Haunt of Fear* No. 19 in which deranged baseball players dismember an opponent and play baseball with his body parts. Another infamous tale, "Wish You Were Here" in *The Haunt of Fear* No. 22, has a literary precedent in W.W. Jacobs's "The Monkey's Paw"; but the bereaved wife of "Wish You Were Here," who wishes her husband back to life, must hack him to pieces to end the pain of his life as an embalmed corpse. The ending is not only more disturbing than that of "The Monkey's Paw," but it is also vividly portrayed through graphic visuals. Many of the other major horror publishers, like Avon and Harvey, would present equal levels of violence in terms that made even less sense.[90]

Benton characterizes the popularity that gave rise to competition and increasingly extreme content: "By 1954 over forty horror comics came out every month and occasionally ten or more new horror comics would appear on the same day."[91] As horror peaked in popularity, EC consistently outsold other publishers (especially those publishers who did not produce horror or horror publishers who did not push the boundaries like EC). For better or worse, EC's success insulated Bill Gaines from the growing mainstream criticism of the horror comics that he loved, and this insulation increased with the development of a "new direction" in EC's work culture. EC was part of a slowly emerging trend in the 1950s; their artists were paid more,[92] artwork was preserved,[93] and individual style (not house style) was encouraged.[94] With artists like Johnny Craig, Wally Wood, Jack Davis, and others profiled in each issue, EC had a star system in place, with Gaines working like a Hollywood producer[95] to realize "the genius of the system."[96]

While this model worked well to foster pride and artistry,[97] it put EC at odds with the big business factory model used by most of the comic book publishers at that time. By revising practices that devalued workers and viewed their product as sub-standard, EC had unprecedented creator support not only in pursuing ever more sensational content but also in confronting social issues in the service of a progressive social agenda. At the same time, Gaines made another business-smart community-building move by being the first publisher to self-consciously craft a comics fan culture with the EC "fan addict club."[98]

More important than the special benefits that came with purchased memberships was the feeling that fans were now undeniably part of the EC creator community (something already implied by the personal tone of the letters pages and creator profiles).

In fact, familiarity with the EC creator community was encouraged in a self-effacing way seen in a story written for EC insiders in EC's parody comic *Mad*. The story portrayed the EC staff as beings from Venus sent to warn humankind about Martians. In *Comics Culture*, comics scholar Matthew Pustz comments on the letters page and this story as a strategy: "This insiderism—making readers feel like they were part of an exclusive group—typified EC's relationship to its readers."[99] EC fans were "the strongest fan following that the industry had yet seen" (more than 25,000 paying members),[100] starting the trend of fan magazines that in future years would be long associated with comics fan culture.[101] As a consequence, these devoted groups would give Gaines an unclear sense of the temperament of culture at large as comics critics gained the support of politicians who swayed the public.

Returning to the folk culture and folktales as metaphor to loosely describe the changing nature of twentieth-century mass media culture, it is important to note that comic books, particularly horror comics, often represent the voice of the common people in opposition to centralized authority. Like film and pulp fiction, comics were not only inexpensive for consumers and marketed to a society at large but were also derided by cultural critics who advocated for art forms produced by and only available to members of an educated upper class. However, as Antonio Gramsci and Louis Althusser suggest, culture is a complex system subject to manipulation that can lead to the majority working against itself. And while common people may be closer to Fredric Jameson's cultural unconscious, they can be horrified by a culture industry's negative portrayal of ideas generally held but not fully understood (as long as those ideas are associated with the right monstrosity).

While comics had come under fire in the 1940s as illiterate, fascist, and sexist, none of these charges had a lasting impact (initially also including Fredric Wertham's claims about comics as a cause of juvenile delinquency in 1948). Since comics publishers were not oblivious to these concerns, National and All-American Comics put together an advisory board with the help of Max Gaines in 1941 "to mollify parents and preempt critics….[But] it was a phantom board."[102] And even though he approached comics content with a different attitude than his father, Bill Gaines was part of a small group of publishers that formed the Association of Comics Magazine Publishers, developing a set of comics decency standards in 1948.[103] Regardless, due to the rapidly increasing popularity of the medium, Bill Gaines wasn't the only publisher who felt insulated; with 425 titles published in 1948, 592 in 1949, and 696 in 1952,[104] these standards were never applied.[105]

This sense of uninhibited independence would change when Wertham's anti-comics *Seduction of the Innocent*[106] gained attention thanks in large part to Estes Kefauver, head of the Senate Subcommittee on Juvenile Delinquency. Identified as an anti-crime crusader, Kefauver picked comics as his new cause in a paranoid culture ready to believe that comics-fed juvenile delinquency would lead to the spread of Communism.[107]

As the tide turned against the comics industry at a political level, some publishers recognized this danger while others continued on the same course (effectively represented by the gratuitous covers of Home Comics' *Black Cat* in 1954).[108] But eventually even Bill Gaines acknowledged the situation as a serious threat and "would try to use this [EC fan] sense of identification with the company when the controversy over comic books heated up."[109] Unrealistically believing their fan community could mobilize and reverse this political momentum, EC would put their famous "Are You a Red Dupe?" editorial in their titles. Claiming that "the group most anxious to destroy comics are the communists," EC crafted their own propaganda war with patriotism as the basis for a pro-comic, not anti-comic, position.

Although unlikely to reach anyone not already devoted to horror comics, some comics creators reached out to fans in subtler ways. In Dick Briefer's "Three-Fold Horror and Revenge" in Feature's *The Monster of Frankenstein* No. 31,[110] three brothers (a painter, a singer, and a conductor) act as champions of high art and they rob the monster of his sight, hearing, and speech in order to rid the world of the ugliness he produces. After the monster is restored by a witch (another cultural outsider), he enacts his revenge on the brothers by taking away their sight, hearing, and speech (making them simultaneously unable to see, hear, or speak evil and unable to perform as artists). In Carl Wessler and Graham Ingels's "The Prude" in EC's *Haunt of Fear* No. 28, an adulterous man copes with his guilt over his mistress's suicide by campaigning against public affection, resulting in separate cemeteries for men in women. However, the dead "good women" rise to rebury themselves next to their husbands, and his mistress forces him to join her in her grave[111]. With one story on the destruction of all art and the other on the problem of misguided piety, both stories decry the anti-comics campaign that comics publishers cannot practically oppose.

As has been noted, Bill Gaines would be looking not to capitulate but to fight, and his controversial testimony at the 1954 congressional hearings on comic books would be a major factor leading to the industry's plan to self-regulate. Following the case made by Fredric Wertham in which he portrayed crime and horror comics as a cause of juvenile delinquency, Gaines mounted a case that mostly missed what made Wertham so appealing to people who feared juvenile delinquency and Communism. Beginning with his father's legacy as a wholesome entertainer, Gaines defended comics on the basis of the First Amendment freedoms, the ability to trust the judgment of our children, and inaccuracy of some of Wertham's readings.

While his points were fairly persuasive on their own terms, they did not assuage general fears or prove his claim that horror stories provided "nothing more nor less… [than] harmless thrills."[112] Even worse, questions forced Gaines to deal with whether he thought the cover of *Crime SuspenStories* No. 22 (featuring the severed head of a woman) was in good taste, and he famously replied, "Yes, sir, I do, for the cover of a horror comic."[113] The line of questioning that led to this point exposed the contradiction in Gaines's argument that horror comics were both art, a form of protected speech with meaning intended for sophisticated readers, and entertainment, a matter of taste with no real meaning intended for children. While his argument did effectively represent the crossroads of horror comics and comics in general at that time, it would prove disastrous for EC and other horror publishers.

The Design of the Comics Code: Ending Horror and Curing Werewolfism

The popular success of horror comics suddenly ended thanks to the comics scare and the comics publishers' reaction to it, a reaction that took shape as the Comics Code. With the film production code already in existence, publishers had a model for designing something that would address the violent and sexual content[114] that concerned Wertham and others. However, while the Code certainly did address those content issues in comics in general, it would be designed to target horror comics in particular. While the Code dealt with the presentation of violence, sexuality, profanity, and the punishment of criminals, the Code also stated, "no comics magazine will use the words 'horror' or 'terror' in its title." In addition, due to the fear of a one-to-one relationship between reading comics and performing acts of juvenile delinquency, there was a literalness to the Code based on the idea that comics taught criminal behavior.[115]

That makes the prohibition against "scenes or instruments associated with walking dead, torture, ghouls, cannibalism, or werewolfism" more perplexing—as if the unreal threats of the walking dead, ghouls, and werewolves belong in the same category as the real specters of torture and cannibalism.

In *The Horror! The Horror! Comics Books the Government Didn't Want You to Read*, Jim Trombetta notes, "The Comics Code is a genuinely strange, neo-medieval document that puts the witch back in witch hunt.... The coinage of werewolfism suggests that there was a genuinely clinical condition or practice that produced the transformation; similarly, the prohibition of 'instruments' implies that, in the manner associated with crime comics, the reader could acquire the devices and imitate the procedures of supernatural horror stories. In other words, you might be able to raise the dead and produce obedient zombies in your garage."[116] In a curious turn, the slippage between the real and the fictitious encouraged by EC hosts seems to have been readily accepted as an unavoidable consequence of horror comics by Code writers seeking to prohibit them. Designed to promote stories with a happy ending that suited the vision of culture set forth by Estes Kefauver, the Comics Code justified the role played by politicians like him and also maintained the traditional model for big business control by eliminating horror comics—or more to the point, the alternative business model of EC.

The Code moved attention away from the medium of comics and on to horror comics, famously represented by Bill Gaines, who said what many thought to be all the wrong things at a nationally televised congressional hearing. The newly formed Comics Magazine Association responsible for the Code had excluded Gaines and made it possible for only publishers who produced lines less exclusively devoted to horror (and more exclusively devoted to wholesome values) to succeed. As Diehl argues, "Rivalry in the comic book industry had always been fierce.... While Gaines and EC were taking a pounding in the media, the other comic book publishers sat on their hands, happy to see a rival brought down."[117]

The president of the CMAA would be John Goldwater, the man behind the very wholesome *Archie Comics*, famous for its teen comedy titles that underperformed in an era dominated by horror comics.[118] The subversive humor of EC's horror hosts found more specific outlets with the parody magazine *Mad*, and they included Archie in the *Mad* magazine No. 12, published during the comics scare in June of 1954. With *Mad*'s deconstructive flair, the "Starchie" feature moved far beyond a typical Archie story to expose the dysfunction under the surface in the form of teenage, crime, lust, and debauchery.

With this in mind, the Code should be understood at least as indirectly targeting Gaines and EC for the public ways in which they undermined the idea of comics as being safe for children.[119]

Surprisingly and unfortunately for the future of EC, Gaines maintained what Jones refers to as his "carnival Gothic"[120] attitude at the congressional hearing where he stated, "It would be just as difficult to explain the harmless thrill of a horror story to a Dr. Wertham… as it would be to explain the sublimity of love to a frigid old maid."[121] The Senate Subcommittee didn't see the humor in Gaines's sarcastic jab at Wertham, and Gaines's anger and defensiveness subsequently turned to sadness and capitulation. With the "In Memoriam" statement soon thereafter printed in the final issues of EC's cancelled horror titles, a chapter in history seemed closed for EC comics, horror comics, and comics in general. Horror titles from other publishers like Harvey would also be cancelled, while horror titles from still other publishers like Marvel would continue in variations that erased the horror from those titles. It is ironic that part of what separates EC from many other publishers is the defiant end of its horror titles in the wake of the Comics Code.

Wertham initially became the hero who vanquished the villainy of Gaines and the immorality of EC, but Gaines retrospectively became the hero who was overcome by the villainy of Wertham and censorship of the Cold War. That slowly emerging retrospective view led to a critical reevaluation and collector culture that grew around EC horror comics, but in fact, neither hero-villain interpretation of the situation is correct. A more accurate characterization can be found in the circular relationship between victim and victimizer often seen in good horror comics in which the identity of the true monster long remains a question. And the complexity of the monstrous is revealed through the complicit role of culture in general and the comics industry in particular in the downfall of horror comics.

The remainder of the book will examine the evolution of this relationship between culture and industry relative to horror comics. Unlike the criminal of a crime story that disappears and resurfaces later, horror comics are like the monster of a horror story that moves further underground but continues to disturb. When horror comics continue in black-and-white magazines, the comic book worlds of superheroes can't hold back the grotesque excess that represents the culture's unacknowledged and incoherent identity.

Chapter 1 Notes

1 "Testimony of William M. Gaines, Publisher, Entertaining Comics Group, New York, NY," *TheComicbooks.Com*, last modified 2016, http://www.thecomicbooks.com/gaines.html.

2 Mike Benton, *Horror Comics: The Illustrated History* (Dallas: Taylor Publishing, 1991), 3.

3 Julia Round, *Gothic in Comics and Graphic Novels* (Jefferson, NC: McFarland, 2014), 17.

4 This is something discussed at various points in Slavoj Žižek's *Everything You Wanted to Know about Lacan… but Were Afraid to Ask Hitchcock* (New York: Verso, 1992).

5 W. Scott Poole, *Monsters in America: Our Historical Obsession with the Hideous and the Haunting* (Waco: Baylor UP, 2011), 10.

6 Wheeler Winston Dixon, *A History of Horror* (New Brunswick: Rutgers UP, 2010), 2.

7 David J. Skal, *The Monster Show: A Cultural History* (New York: Farrar, Straus, and Giroux, 1993), 83.

8 This variety of critical opinions is noted by David J. Skal in *Hollywood Gothic: The Tangled Web of Dracula from Novel to Stage to Screen* (New York: Farrar, Straus, and Giroux, 2004), 38–39.

9 Michael Anglo, *Penny Dreadfuls and Other Victorian Horrors* (London: Jupiter, 1977) 18–19.

10 David J. Skal, *Hollywood Gothic: The Tangled Web of Dracula from Novel to Stage to Screen*, 19–20.

11 The text describes the bony appearance of the vampire, and this relates to the Fritz Lang film *Nosferatu*; the woodcuts depict the vampire in aristocratic garb and wearing a cape, and this relates to the stage and film productions of *Dracula*. In terms of motivation, the vampire is a reluctant evil-doer, and this may relate to the novel *The Vampyre* and definitely relates to the Anne Rice novel *Interview with the Vampire*.

12 Graham Clarke, "Introduction," *Edgar Allen Poe: Critical Assessments*, ed., Graham Clarke (East Sussex: Helm Information, 1991), 1.

13 Fred Botting, *Gothic* (London: Routledge, 2013), 10.

14 Walter Ong, *Orality and Literacy* (London: Routledge, 2002), 146–47.

15 Ibid., 146.

16 At the same time, I don't want to downplay the way the detective, C. Auguste Dupin, serves as a prototype for the brilliant sleuth who solves impossible puzzles; this aspect of the character is more apparent in other stories such as "The Mystery of Marie Roget" and "The Purloined Letter."

17 Amy Nyberg, *Seal of Approval: The History of the Comics Code* (Jackson, UP of Mississippi, 1998), 1.

18 The magazine was published through 1954, but its later years represent its decline in terms of quality and profitability.

19 Timothy Jones, T*he Gothic and the Carnivalesque in American Culture* (Chicago: U of Chicago P, 2015), 72.

20 Ibid., 97.

21 Mike Benton, *Horror Comics: The Illustrated History*, 7.

22 Ibid., 7–8.

23 This type of cross-media pollination was seen officially and unofficially with the simultaneous run of the *Witch's Tale* radio show and pulp magazine (in the 1930s) and the *Witches Tales* comic book (in the 1950s)–seemingly titled to connect to past horror entertainments (Richard J. Hand, *Terror on the Air! Horror Radio in America*, 1931–1952 (Jefferson, NC: McFarland, 2006), 81).

24 Ibid., 14.

25 Old Nancy from *Witch's Tale* is mentioned as an inspiration for EC's "GhoulLunatics" by Mike Benton (*Horror Comics: The Illustrated History*, 21) and Digby Diehl (*Tales from the Crypt: The Official Archives* [New York: St. Martin's Press, 1996], 23).

26 "Although radio could simultaneously reach an audience in the multi-millions, its localized effect was through an infiltration of domestic lives and environments, and is therefore an intensely intimate form" (Richard J. Hand, *Terror on the Air! Horror Radio in America*, 46).

27 Ibid., 23.

28 Ibid., 31.

29 Ibid., 43.

30 Wheeler Winston Dixon, *A History of Horror*, 22–24.

31 Due to the large audience for film and comic books, alarmist critics of horror would identify the visuals in film and comic books as a new level of depravity but really such visual conventions were far from new.

32 The film, often called "Edison's *Frankenstein*," was produced by Edison Studios, but it is unclear whether Edison himself had any direct involvement.

33 Wheeler Winston Dixon, *A History of Horror*, 3.

34 For more on the virulent American reaction to *The Cabinet of Dr. Caligari*, see David J. Skal, *The Monster Show: A Cultural History*, 38–39, 46.

35 Mike Benton, *Horror Comics: The Illustrated History*, 8.

36 David J. Skal, *The Monster Show: A Cultural History*, 135.

37 In the case of Bela Lugosi in *Dracula*, it is a transition of stage acting to film acting.

38 Max Gaines was part of the initial boom in comics with *Famous Funnies* from Dell and *Popular Comics* featuring the first comic book appearance of Dick Tracy (as well as Little Orphan Annie) (Digby Diehl, *Tales from the Crypt: The Official Archives*, 14).

39 Digby Diehl, *Tales from the Crypt: The Official Archives*, 39.

40 Mike Benton, *Horror Comics: The Illustrated History*, 9.

41 Lance Eaton, "The Horror Narrative and the Graphic Novel," *Critical Insights: The Graphic Novel*, ed., Gary Hoppenstand (Armenia, NY: Salem Press, 2014), 19.

42 DC, home of Superman and Batman, was named after Detective Comics a flagship title of National Allied Publications; the series was an anthology featuring detective stories and crime fiction but became most famous for introducing Batman. Although the publishers quickly embraced the superhero, Batman is an interesting exception to some of the superhero tropes quickly established. DC's horror titles were quite tame before the Code, but not uninteresting after the Code (something described more fully in Chapter 2).

43 Other figures are worth mentioning as well such as Jerry Siegel's supernatural avenger, the Spectre (debuting in 1940), and the Werewolf Hunter (debuting in 1943); although uncostumed and balding, the Werewolf Hunter was in the vein of superheroic adventure more than horror, dealing also with strange science villains.

44 Mike Benton, *Horror Comics: The Illustrated History*, 7.

45 Digby Diehl, *Tales from the Crypt: The Official Archives*, 28.

46 Jim Trombetta, *The Horror! The Horror!: Comic Books the Government Didn't Want You to Read* (New York: Harry N. Abrams, 2010), 23.

47 Mike Benton, *Horror Comics: The Illustrated History*, 11.

48 *Captain America* became *Captain America's Weird Tales* with issue No. 74, featuring supernatural tales with Captain America (and including a back-from-hell Red Skull). The very next issue featured Captain America in title only and it became a straightforward horror anthology.

49 Edvard Moritz, "The Boy Who Cried Wolf," *Adventures into the Unknown* 10, American Comics Group (April-May 1950), 2.

50 *War on Crime* ended with No. 11, and the series was retitled *The Vault of Horror* with No. 12 so that EC could save money on second-class postage permits.

51 Mike Benton, *Horror Comics: The Illustrated History*, 5.

52 David Hajdu, *The Ten Cent Plague: The Great Comic-Book Scare and How It Changed America* (New York: Farrar, Straus, and Giroux, 2008), 189.

53 Digby Diehl, *Tales from the Crypt: The Official Archives*, 76.
54 Mike Benton, *Horror Comics: The Illustrated History*, 23.
55 Bart Beatty argues that in retrospect Fredric Wertham has been demonized while Bill Gaines has been deified (*Fredric Wertham and the Critique of Mass Culture* (Jackson: UP of Mississippi, 2005), 203–204).
56 Digby Diehl, *Tales from the Crypt: The Official Archives*, 24.
57 EC Comics presents its first horror story ("Zombie Terror") in *Moon Girl* No. 5. Horror begins to supplant other genres, most notably crime. The last two issues of *Crime Patrol* featured "an illustrated SuspenStory from the Vault of Horror."
58 This is part of Jeffrey Cohen's argument in "Monster Culture (Seven Theses)." *Monster Theory: Reading Culture* (Minneapolis: U of Minnesota P, 1996), 3–25.
59 David Hajdu, *The Ten Cent Plague: The Great Comic-Book Scare and How It Changed America*, 179.
60 This is a microcosmic representation of larger cultural anxieties that made horror comics relevant to so many readers: "[Y]ou can't trust anyone in a horror comic. That was part of the delicious paranoia that ran throughout the early 1950s horror comics. With government officials, Hollywood entertainers, and sometimes your next-door neighbors under suspicion for being Communist sympathizers, it was only natural that the horror comics played upon those natural fears of mistrust and betrayal" (Mike Benton, *Horror Comics: The Illustrated History*, 30).
61 EC was well known for twist endings in part because Gaines mentioned so often that they were inspired by O. Henry's short fiction; however, twists hardly made EC unique as such endings were part of most horror comics at that time. A very self-conscious use of O. Henry's twist ending is "The Rift of the Magis" in *Harvey's Tomb of Terror* No. 11; a parody of O. Henry's "Gift of the Magi," it features homicidal spouses giving one another lethal gifts.
62 Lance Eaton, "The Horror Narrative and the Graphic Novel," 17.
63 Benton comments on Johnny Craig's choice to present clean-cut characters in horror contexts: "If [Jack] Davis' characters looked like they hadn't seen a barber shop or bathtub in months, the people in a Johnny Craig EC story were freshly scrubbed and laundered advertisements for the All-American Family. The clean and wholesome look that Craig gave his horror stories made them all the more terrifying" (Mike Benton, *Horror Comics: The Illustrated History*, 15).
64 Al Feldstein, Jack Kamen, Marie Severin, and Jim Wroten, "The Orphan," *Shock SuspenStories* 14, EC (April–May 1954), 8.

65 Another bad seed story worth mentioning is "Grounds… for Horror!" in *Tales from the Crypt* No. 29; Artie's abusive step-father punishes him by locking him in the closet. However, Artie meets a friend who lives in the closet and the new friend suggests ways to deal with the step-father.

66 David J. Skal, *The Monster Show: A Cultural History*, 231.

67 Bradford Wright, *Comic Book Nation: The Transformation of Youth Culture in America* (Baltimore: Johns Hopkins UP, 2001), 136.

68 A few examples include "The Rug" in *Shock SuspenStories* No. 1 (against hunting and animal cruelty) and "The Whipping" in *Shock SuspenStories* No. 14 (against racism and violence).

69 Mike Benton, *Horror Comics: The Illustrated History*, 23.

70 Ibid., 36, David Hajdu, *The Ten Cent Plague: The Great Comic-Book Scare and How It Changed America*, 239.

71 Mike Benton, *Horror Comics: The Illustrated History*, 36–37.

72 Other publishers experimented with this short-lived craze, including two issues of a *Three-Dimensional Tales from the Crypt* in 1954 with past stories redrawn to create the 3D effect.

73 In reference to *Witch's Tale*, Hand traces the horror host tradition back even further: "The most synonymous horror comics of the 1950s–the EC titles–featured three hosts in their horror titles… the Old Witch… is clearly a homage to Old Nancy… Of course, the witch had been a familiar icon of supernatural and horror culture long before the invention of radio, even in a 'host' role. Indeed, we could even consider the Three Witches in Shakespeare's *Macbeth* as precursors. Although Shakespeare's 'weird sisters' are an important part of the action and plot, they function as an equivalent to the familiar 'Prologue' character of the Renaissance stage" (Richard J. Hand, *Terror on the Air! Horror Radio in America, 1931–1952*, 83).

74 George Tuska, "The Kill-Crazy Fleagle Brothers," *Crime Does Not Pay* 50 (Lev Gleason Publications, March 1947), 1.

75 Ibid., 14.

76 Comics seem inclined to breaking the fourth wall with interaction between reader and characters (who serve as both characters and narrators) dating back to classic comic strips like *The Yellow Kid*, *Krazy Kat*, and *Little Nemo in Slumberland* (Jesus A. Gonzalez, "'Living in the Funnies': Metafiction in American Comic Strips," *The Journal of Popular Culture* 47 [August 2014]: 838).

77 He looks like Timely's Witness (debuting in *The Witness* No. 1 in 1948) who had more influence on the comic book stories.

78 The Man in Black received his own (short-lived) series in the post-Code era (1957–1958).

79 Al Feldstein, Jack Davis, Marie Severin, and Jim Wroten, "Dead Right!" *Tales from the Crypt* 37, EC (August–September 1953), 1.

80 Al Feldstein, Jack Davis, Marie Severin, and Jim Wroten, "Bats in My Belfry!" *Tales from the Crypt* 24, EC (June–July 1951), 8.

81 Al Feldstein, Graham Ingels, Marie Severin, and Jim Wroten, "The Living Death!" *Tales from the Crypt* 24, EC (June–July 1951,), 1.

82 Timothy *Jones, The Gothic and the Carnivalesque in American Culture*, 128.

83 Ibid., 129.

84 Al Feldstein, Jack David, and Jim Wroten, "Lower Berth!" *Tales from the Crypt* 33, EC (December 1952–January 1953), 8.

85 This is an idea central to the then-suppressed film *Freaks* by *Dracula* director, Todd Browning.

86 Mike Benton, *Horror Comics: The Illustrated History*, 26.

87 While EC wasn't necessarily above this (see the covers of *Tales from the Crypt* No. 32 and *Crime SuspenStories* No. 2), the scantily clad nature of the women is more readily explained by story mechanics.

88 Mike Benton, *Horror Comics: The Illustrated History*, 27.

89 Ibid., 37 and Digby Diehl, *Tales from the Crypt: The Official Archives*, 77.

90 The bizarre cover of Master's *Dark Mysteries* No. 13 features a dismembered leg in chains and a prison guard who states, "It's Tom's leg… but he was executed last night." Trombetta discusses the unintended but threatening meaning of this combination of horror motifs: "The image invokes several horror myths–crime and punishment, dismemberment, cannibalism, and the living dead–without establishing any real relationship between them. It is super-saturated with dream imagery that refuses to fit together… Story beats that were often repetitious, senseless, even contradictory, and that were often conceived in haste, still created a public, communal dream (or nightmare)" (Jim Trombetta, *The Horror! The Horror!: Comic Books the Government Didn't Want You to Read*, 43–44). Although not quite as absurd as the cover of *Dark Mysteries* No. 13, the cover of American Comics Group's *Forbidden Worlds* No. 15 works in similar ways. A man is attacked by a woman in an evening gown, identified as a "vampire cat" with hairy arms reaching for his throat. He says, "My strength's–failing! I can't fight off this demon–any longer–" making the illustration a strange dream-like mix of attack and seduction by a vampire cat/demon/femme fatale/wo(man).

91 Mike Benton, *Horror Comics: The Illustrated History*, 25.
92 "The EC Comics of the 1950s were consistently well drawn and painstakingly crafted. Part of the reason was that Gaines paid his artists above-average rates, but it was also the free-flowing creative environment" (Mike Benton, *Horror Comics: The Illustrated History*, 14).
93 Digby Diehl, *Tales from the Crypt: The Official Archives*, 73.
94 Ibid., 52. In a few scant places, this can be seen with other publishers and sometimes featuring artists with dramatically different styles (like the expressionist/surrealist style of the incomparable Basil Wolverton).
95 "Gaines and Feldstein wrote stories geared to the particular styles of the artists, who always signed their work, and so fostered the comic book industry's first 'star system'" (Bradford Wright, *Comic Book Nation: The Transformation of Youth Culture in America*, 136). This is also mentioned in Digby Diehl, *Tales from the Crypt: The Official Archives*, 47.
96 Thomas Schatz uses this term to describe how Hollywood's factory model was conducive to the creation of great film art in *The Genius of the System: Hollywood Filmmaking in the Studio Era* (Minneapolis: U of Minnesota P, 2010).
97 Skal examines the classical precedents in visual art for EC compositions (David J. Skal, *The Monster Show: A Cultural History*, 231).
98 Mike Benton, *Horror Comics: The Illustrated History*, 22.
99 Matthew J. Pustz, *Comic Book Culture: Fanboys and True Believers* (Jackson: UP of Mississippi, 1999), 39.
100 Mike Benton, *Horror Comics: The Illustrated History*, 22.
101 Randy Duncan and Matthew J. Smith, *The Power of Comics: History, Form, and Culture* (New York: Bloomsbury, 2009), 38–39.
102 David Hajdu, *The Ten Cent Plague: The Great Comic-Book Scare and How It Changed America*, 46.
103 Ibid., 128–29.
104 Randy Duncan and Matthew J. Smith, *The Power of Comics: History, Form, and Culture*, 37.
105 Gaines did occasionally revise content to limit gratuity; he replaced a cleaver in the head of a zombie with a light effect on the cover of *The Vault of Horror* No. 32 (Jim Trombetta, *The Horror! The Horror!: Comic Books the Government Didn't Want You to Read*, 81; David Hajdu, *The Ten Cent Plague: The Great Comic-Book Scare and How It Changed America*, 45). However, the standards that guided him were just as often aesthetic as moral.

106 There are various theories about *Seduction of the Innocent* in relation to Wertham's earlier work *Dark Legend* as a reaction formation (Digby Diehl, *Tales from the Crypt: The Official Archives*, 85) or a clear conflict (Bart Beatty, *Fredric Wertham and the Critique of Mass Culture*, 152).

107 Amy Nyberg, *Seal of Approval: The History of the Comics Code*, 19. This shift to general concerns would make less relevant the specialized positions that were more effectively argued and reflected more favorably on comic books; this includes Marilyn Graalfs' 1954 report on the impact of horror comics on children for the Washington State Council for Children and Youth (Mike Benton, *Horror Comics: The Illustrated History*, 35–36).

108 *Black Cat* is a good example of a title that heedlessly pursued trends, also known as *Black Cat Mystery, Black Cat Western, Black Cat Western Mystery, Black Cat Mystic*, and more.

109 Matthew J. Pustz, *Comic Book Culture: Fanboys and True Believers*, 39.

110 Issue numbering is complicated with this series; this issue is also known as No. 3 of volume 5.

111 It is important to note this would be the last issue after the debut of the Comics Code and included EC's famous "In Memoriam" statement for their horror comics. Of course, the lead-time needed to produce the story means the story itself predates the debut of the Code.

112 David Hajdu, *The Ten Cent Plague: The Great Comic-Book Scare and How It Changed America*, 267.

113 Ibid., 270.

114 Amy Nyberg, *Seal of Approval: The History of the Comics Code*, 23; David Hajdu, *The Ten Cent Plague: The Great Comic-Book Scare and How It Changed America*, 127–28.

115 Amy Nyberg, *Seal of Approval: The History of the Comics Code*, 45.

116 Jim Trombetta, *The Horror! The Horror!: Comic Books the Government Didn't Want You to Read*, 91.

117 Digby Diehl, *Tales from the Crypt: The Official Archives*, 88.

118 Horror comics were part of the lineup for the publishing house that would later be known as Archie comics (but they were never as popular as the EC titles).

119 In reference to *Mad*'s Starchie, Les Daniels states, "Goldwater was presumably not amused. This much is clear: the Comics Code Authority which he headed inspired marketing pressure which drove certain comic books out of business" (COMIX: A History of Comic Books in America [New York: Outerbridge and Dienstfrey, 1971], 85).

120 Timothy Jones, *The Gothic and the Carnivalesque in American Culture*, 124.

121 Ibid., 126.

CHAPTER 2

The Monster vs. the Superhero: Horror "Magazines" and the Comics Industry of the 1960s and '70s

The single most unrealistic thing I've ever read in comics is when some group of characters calls themselves the Brotherhood of Evil or the Masters of Evil. I don't believe any character believes their goals to be truly evil.... [Y]ou won't find a truly evil monster in the [Swamp Thing] bunch.
Len Wein[1]

The New Focus for Horror Comics: Time Travel and Trips to the Service Station

The psychologist Fredric Wertham and the politician Estes Kefauver were the prime movers with regard to the hearings that led to the Comics Code. Regardless of how faulty his research,[2] Wertham was a true believer in the evil influence of crime comics on juveniles and ultimately was unsatisfied with industry self-regulation. Deeply invested in the Cold War fears of juvenile delinquency, he questioned comic books in general as a medium sold to juveniles, which graphically represented his personal anxieties (sex and violence in particular).[3] And regardless of how questionable his political motivations were, Kefauver was a true believer in the need to fight Communism and ultimately felt the Code represented a good faith solution on the part of American industry. Although deeply invested in the Cold War fears of corruption within, he believed in the American system with an industrial culture tied to the ends of capitalism (market freedom within governmental authority in particular). Regardless of Wertham's and Kefauver's different perspectives on the Comics Code, there is no doubt that a specter had been haunting America in the form of Communism; and despite the fact that various powers were in a holy alliance to exorcise this specter, the ghost would continue to haunt and possess.[4]

After 1954, the politics of the paranoia that fueled the Red Scare backfired, and the so-called "witch hunts" of Senator Joseph McCarthy caused some people to question the American political establishment. While neither Wertham or Kefauver faded from view in either of their fields, they became associated with more politically liberal issues such as racial integration and consumer protection.

The Comics Code was eventually revealed as a superficial fix for a superficial problem with loopholes that could be exploited by those people who loved horror comics and the general idea of comics for adults. Like Communism, the specter of horror comics was unsuccessfully exorcised and its threat lived on especially in the form of black-and-white magazines of the 1960s, like *Creepy*.

However, the road to *Creepy* is long and twisted, because the effects of the congressional hearings and the Code on comics were far from negligible. As mentioned by Code historian David Hajdu, the 1955 radio show *Confidential File* alerts the public to the dangers of crime and horror comics—as if action had not already been taken. In addition to being the product of lazy journalism and the continued fear of juvenile delinquency, this show is also likely a testament to the inability of comic burnings and the Code to erase horror comics from the cultural memory. Comics were well known for their pass-along value, and the Code had the unintended consequence of making horror comics, especially those produced by EC, objects of fascination and collector's items.

But the slow redevelopment of EC fan culture can be seen only in relief to the apparent success of the Code in its early years and the "death" of EC comics represented by Gaines's "In Memoriam" statement in final issues of EC's cancelled horror and crime titles. After questioning whether these issues will ever reach the newsstands, Gaines defaults to pointed humor: "Naturally, with comic magazine censorship now a fact, we at EC look forward to an immediate drop in the crime and juvenile delinquency rate of the United States."[5] After thanking the readers and moving onto a preview of publications to come, the only financial good thing in the immediate future of EC would be the continued success of parody magazines like *Mad*.

Based on the freedom allowed to *Mad*, with its classification as a magazine (rather than a comic book), Gaines tried to develop a "new direction" for EC horror in magazine "picto-fictions."[6] Picture books for adults, these magazines quickly failed: perhaps because the form was not what was wanted by the remaining horror comic fans[7] or perhaps because the EC logo on the cover represented a brand now anathema to the general reading public.[8] However, *Mad* magazine served EC creators well as a means to vent frustration with parodies such as the 1957 piece "Baseball Is Ruining Our Children" by Frederick Werthless, "citing specific examples of the values that children were supposed to be learning from the game: pitchers teach deceptive practices, batters encourage the use of force, [and] arguing with the umpire leads to lack of respect for authority."[9]

With other publishers, the superhero genre was quickly sanitized to fit the confines established by the Code, and some horror titles continued to be published with radically revised content. Trying to whitewash their past publishing a horror comic, American Comics Group featured an introduction to *Adventures into the Unknown* No. 60 (the issue published in November–December 1954 in the wake of Code pronouncements)—after identifying their comics as good, clean entertainment, they made several claims: "Never have we made a policy of outright sensationalism; of horror for horror's sake. Instead, we have published such stories as our fathers and grandfathers before us have thrilled to."[10] This claim would be hard to substantiate, but invoking the patriarchal authority of fathers and grandfathers effectively sets up the tame stories that follow. While some initial stories include ghosts, the supernatural serves only as an agent of justice, and these stories are quickly replaced by science fiction stories like "There's a New Star Tonight" (in which an egotistical astrophysicist schemes to launch himself into space).[11]

In former horror comics titles, new favorite tropes include the time travel story seen in "One Exciting Knight" in ACG's *Forbidden Worlds* No. 37 and parallel worlds seen in "Escape to Nowhere" in Marvel's *Journey into Unknown Worlds* No. 39. In terms of the way the old order of horror is overthrown, "When Sorcerer's Meet" in Marvel's *Strange Tales* No. 47 is more pointed. Already doubting his choice of profession, a stage magician meets actual sorcerers; the sorcerers' morally questionable ideas cause him to give up even stage magic and commit to making a more conventional good living for himself and his wife. Even better in regard to the post-Code triumph of the American dream is the cover of Charlton's *This Is Suspense* No. 25 (formerly *Strange Suspense Stories*). With a clear view of a stereotypical couple in their respectable sedan (she with her rosy cheeks and pearls, he with his clean-shaven face and tie), she says, "Gosh, look at this hill—I'm glad you had the brakes fixed!" and he responds with horror, "The brakes??" Judging by this standard, the new height of comics horror in the 1950s post-Code era is the all-American man forgetting to take his car to the service station.

Another notable switch in focus in this era would be with Harvey. Previously well-known for their gory horror comics (often less sophisticated than those of EC), Harvey became more exclusively focused on comedy titles like *Richie Rich*. Already publishing comics based on the animated character Casper the Friendly Ghost in 1952, Harvey would purchase the rights to the character outright in 1959, indicating a decisive turn for ghost stories. While most humor comics like *Archie* proudly displayed the Comics Code seal of approval, Dell did not, with its funny animal comics so wholesome that the publisher deemed the seal unnecessary.

In an interesting exception to these trends, *Classics Illustrated* also ran without the seal (due to its association with classic literature) and became gorier post-Code,[12] apparently filling a void left by pre-Code horror comics.

Monsters Become More Respectable and Get a Home on Main Street

The consumer appetite for horror didn't abate and would be filled by other media forms less constrained by industry regulations. After the collapse of the Universal monster film tradition due to weak sequels (culminating in parody films like *Abbot and Costello Meet Frankenstein* in 1948),[13] horror would move in new directions with novels like Richard Matheson's *I Am Legend* (1954)—a post-apocalyptic lone man story that depicts vampirism as a disease (a forerunner of the zombie stories of the 1960s and 1970s). With comparisons to Henry James's *The Turn of the Screw*, Shirley Jackson's *The Haunting of Hill House* (1959) became a finalist for the National Book Award, focusing on mysterious happenings as a metaphor for psychological disturbance. And within a few years, Ray Bradbury (a favorite author for former EC comic adaptations) produced a similarly clever, popular, and well-reviewed horror novel with *Something Wicked This Way Comes*.

With authors like Patricia Highsmith (*Strangers on a Train* in 1950), Jim Thompson (*The Killer Inside Me* in 1952), and Robert Bloch (*Psycho* in 1959), the human monster (associated with EC) continued to be explored in pulp fiction works later regarded as classics. And in what Wheeler Winston Dixon identifies as a rebirth of Hollywood horror,[14] Warner Bros. worked within the confines of the Hollywood production code and remade M*ystery of the Wax Museum* as the *House of Wax* in 1953. While showcasing the 3D film experience, the film worked well as a thriller based on psychological aberrance and paved the way for a film for Vincent Price's career based on the portrayal of the monstrous in the human mind.

With William Castle's *House on Haunted Hill* (1959), a critique typically seen in EC horror comics could also be seen in film (here described by David J. Skal): "A striking characteristic of fifties horror is its ambivalence about the good life, the tenuous nature of material security and social identity."[15] However, this is not to suggest that horror in other media forms shifted completely to the sophisticated vein of some pre-Code horror comics. While other media forms were less constrained than comics, the horror culture of the 1950s was built by a culture industry shaped like the Comics Code: by the paranoia of the Red Scare and a faith in the American dream. As a consequence, horror camp was also prevalent, working in ways that were funny—subversive but also safe and not too challenging to cultural identity.

With the broadcast of the Kefauver comic book hearings, television was a mass medium that played a role in the downfall of horror comics but later also provided another means by which the genre might be encountered. Although governed by the Federal Communications Commission and the self-regulation of the National Association of Broadcasters, horror found its way onto the television airwaves in an unusual way: *The Vampira Show*. With television a showcase for now less-frightening classic horror films, *The Vampira Show* features a horror host who tentatively follows in the footsteps of radio and comics horror. As the hostess, actress Mailia Nurmi was inspired by Morticia Addams, the *Addams Family* character that Charles Addams first created in 1938 for a New Yorker cartoon. That classic cartoon simultaneously spoofs domestic life and Universal horror by putting a door-to-door vacuum salesman next to a witchy woman.

Skal would characterize this strange, yet short-lived, merger of the aberrant and the ordinary with Vampira this way, "Death and sensuality had always had a deep affinity, but never before had they been so pointedly merged in a popular icon."[16] Later with a starring role in Ed Wood's bizarre and laughable sci fi horror movie *Plan 9 from Outer Space* (also featuring Bela Lugosi), Vampira would pave the way for the terribly familiar monster to be part of popular culture. In years to come, this would be best exemplified by the 1960s television show *The Munsters*, featuring a family composed of Universal monster lookalikes, interestingly contained within the patriarchal limitations of a family comedy.

Likewise occupying this middle ground between the subversive and the conservative would be the giant monster movies of the 1950s.[17] While *Them!* and the imported Godzilla movies offered commentaries on atomic radiation and wartime devastation in 1954, the commentaries were superficial and special effects so weak that these obviously fake monsters were deemed entertaining for the whole family. Comics consequently embraced this trend as a way to present horror stories that were acceptable within the parameters of the Comics Code and far from a threatening expression of excess barely contained within the cultural unconscious. Utilizing talents like Stan Lee and Jack Kirby, Zenith's *Tales to Astonish* showcases giant monster stories, and the clearest connection to more threatening horror stories of the recent past is the giant mummies in issues No. 8 and No. 31.

While giant monsters present a serious threat to people within the literal confines of a story, these monsters were incredibly safe to people outside the story and within 1950s mainstream culture.

Into this mix came a magazine specifically designed for horror fans to celebrate true horror as well as the nostalgic love of movie monsters, *Famous Monsters of Filmland*. First published in 1958, the magazine was designed by James Warren to be a one-shot publication to capitalize on the success of old horror movies flooding the syndicated television market. But with its unexpected success, Warren saw the promise of publishing success that he had been seeking, something that led directly to the comics magazines *Creepy* and *Eerie*.

Famous Monsters Become Less Respectable and More Creepy

Famous Monsters of Filmland, the forerunner for horror magazines like *Fangoria*, was not a fan publication but a publication for fans and did not lack enthusiasm. With articles on and photographs of classic monster movies, and with authors who wrote like comics horror hosts, *Famous Monsters* spares neither puns nor exclamation marks.[18] However, its tone is a bit softer and clearly nostalgic as the monsters are not considered horrible but rather funny and a quaint throwback to past times. For instance, the first issue's cover features a beautiful woman in eveningwear affectionately staring backward at her date, and a man attired in an equally formal style, except for the fact he wears a Boris Karloff Frankenstein mask.

In short order, Warren featured original painted covers of classic monster movie characters by Basil Gogos, which directly led to increased sales. While Warren had and would venture into other publications including *After Hours* (a men's magazine like *Playboy*), *Help!* (a comedy magazine like *Mad*),[19] and *Famous Westerns of Filmland*,[20] none were as successful as *Famous Monsters*. And while it initially focused on horror that had been tamed through commodification, it eventually featured more recent, startling, and controversial horror (featuring Vincent Price on the cover of issue No. 9).

In addition to fanzines produced by EC fans who eventually attend conventions, *Famous Monsters* is identified by Robert Michael Cotter in *The Great Monster Magazines* as a crucial publication in the development of fan culture. "FM created a rallying point for fans which in turn led to horror-film criticism.... FM not only perpetuated the genre, but became its leading exponent."[21] Most significant to the return of true horror comics would be the short 1964 run of the magazine in which the title became *Monster World* and featured horror comics (initially a reprint of a *Mummy* adaptation by Russ Jones and Wally Wood).

The success of *Famous Monsters* was followed by *Creepy* (first published in 1964), Warren's great contribution to the world of horror comics in which conventional horror comics were prohibited by the Comics Code. Initially edited by Russ Jones but soon edited by its primary writer Archie Goodwin (a former EC fan-addict), the black-and-white magazine was a horror comics anthology inspired by fan investment in *Famous Monsters*. With Goodwin at the helm, the comics magazine would be less influenced by monster movie nostalgia and more by EC horror (and tangentially connected to the only other horror anthologies of the time, the television shows *The Twilight Zone* and *The Outer Limits*).[22]

Like radio, the mass media expression of television had the potential to enact the dynamics and represent the content of the ancient folktale (especially with *The Twilight Zone*'s Rod Serling, whose hosting serves, as media scholars Lorna Jowett and Stacey Abbott suggest, as an omniscient voice of fate).[23] Serling often drew from classic stories,[24] revising them to implicitly comment on contemporary politics[25] and moving those stories from simple scares to places more unsettling and uncanny.[26]

With conflicts in Korea and then Vietnam challenging the national consciousness and the counter-culture in its early stages of development, horror comics artist and historian Stephen Bissette comments on the significance of history to horror comics creators of the time: "We were living in a cruel new decade of civil rights protests and violence, the escalation of the Vietnam War and rumblings from a new youth movement that seemed positively tribal in nature."[27] *Creepy* bridged the gaps between familiar monsters of folktales, famous monsters of filmland, horror buried within EC comics in the 1950s, and anxiety tied to contemporary history; and in the process, Archie Goodwin would produce stories that horrified his readers.

What scholar Richard J. Arndt describes as "playing it safe"[28] (not controversial but appealing to Warren's fan base), the cover of *Creepy* No. 1 featured its horror host reading from the magazine to a collection of monsters (primarily classic monster types like the vampire and werewolf favored by fans of *Famous Monsters*). As Mike Benton claims, "[S]tories in *Creepy* and *Eerie* tended to be more gothic. The 1930s Universal horror movies often provided the settings and characters for many of the earlier stories."[29] However, as a magazine publication, *Creepy* was insulated from the criticism leveled a decade earlier, and in many ways, picked up where horror comics left off in 1954.

Uncle Creepy is an ugly host who introduces tales with less verbosity and fewer puns but with a sense of humor similar to that of EC's "ghoulunatic" hosts; but even more to the point is the introduction to the magazine in which Uncle Creepy draws a direct line between pre-Code horror comics and this horror magazine: "Welcome to the comic world's newest, most exciting, and most imaginative magazine in 10 years!... *Creepy* is different! *Creepy* is expensive!–But *Creepy* is the start of a great (gasp!) new wonderful world of repulsive entertainment."[30] In addition to creating a discrete timeline and exercising Uncle Creepy's self-effacing humor regarding the "expensive" format, the introduction clearly identifies the magazine as entertainment and not art with redeeming value: a classification that may have pleased fans but troubled critics who found repulsive stories contrary to the goals of high culture.

Fig. 2.1
Creepy No. 4, Warren, 1965, © New Comic Company LLC

Subtler as a narrative but more pointed as a reference to EC is the story of Uncle Creepy called "Monster Rally" in *Creepy* No. 4. Featuring a mad scientist motivated by Dr. Frankenstein's notebooks, the story depicts his hunchback servant collecting monsters his master might use (including a vampire, werewolf, ghoul, and witch). When villagers burn down the scientist's castle, only one product of his experiments escapes: a baby that will grow up to be Uncle Creepy. Within this story populated with standard horror characters and tropes, the last image is almost exactly that of the baby Crypt-Keeper at the end of his origin story, "Lower Berth." That panel is accompanied by a caption identifying the Uncle Creepy baby as "something born of Dr. Habeas's strange experiments and the fodder of his monsters' remains... and somehow destined to keep the tradition very much alive!" In the final panel, the adult Uncle Creepy breaks the fourth wall, speaks directly to the reader, and claims, "Luckily I was able to clean up ol' Habeas's dungeon and turn it into a going concern again... only instead of monsters, I have (choke!) comic artists!"[31]

Fig. 2.2
Tales from the Crypt No. 33, EC, 1952–1953, © William M. Gaines Agent, Inc.
Creepy made many allusions to EC comics including an image of Uncle Creepy in a "Monster Rally" that alludes to the Crypt-Keeper in "Lower Berth."

With this crossover between the story of Uncle Creepy and his current profession as host of Creepy magazine, the narrative playfully moves between different registers. Like the mad scientist Habeas, horror comics creators seek out the bodies of knowledge associated with a long history of monsters. Like the villagers, the U.S. public and the comics industry destroy horror comics and its experiments—and yet, EC comics continues to live in Creepy. And with the help of more self-effacing humor, Uncle Creepy identifies the supposed inadequacy of comics creators to do so with his stifled sob ("choke!").

With EC horror hosts and twist endings as precedents, Goodwin's scripts would often self-consciously honor and subvert horror story and monster movie material from the past.

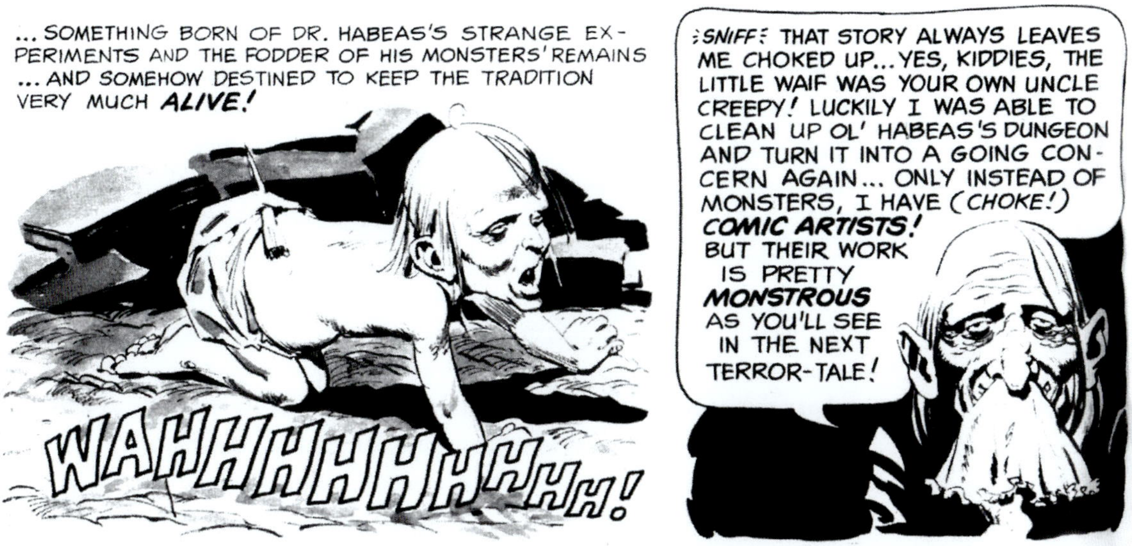

... SOMETHING BORN OF DR. HABEAS'S STRANGE EXPERIMENTS AND THE FODDER OF HIS MONSTERS' REMAINS ... AND SOMEHOW DESTINED TO KEEP THE TRADITION VERY MUCH ALIVE!
WAHHHHHHHHHHH!
:SNIFF: THAT STORY ALWAYS LEAVES ME CHOKED UP... YES, KIDDIES, THE LITTLE WAIF WAS YOUR OWN UNCLE CREEPY! LUCKILY I WAS ABLE TO CLEAN UP OL' HABEAS'S DUNGEON AND TURN IT INTO A GOING CONCERN AGAIN... ONLY INSTEAD OF MONSTERS, I HAVE (CHOKE!) COMIC ARTISTS! BUT THEIR WORK IS PRETTY MONSTROUS AS YOU'LL SEE IN THE NEXT TERROR-TALE!

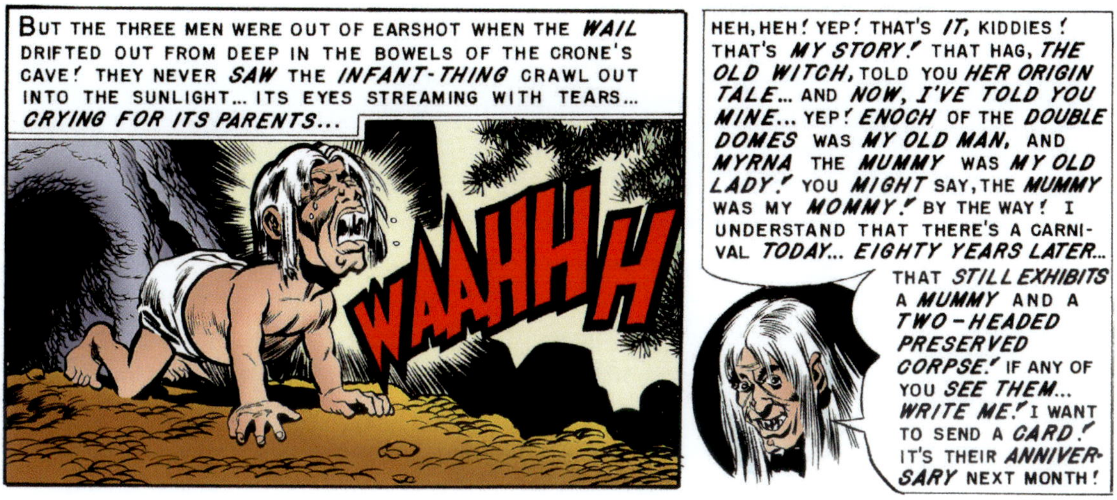

BUT THE THREE MEN WERE OUT OF EARSHOT WHEN THE WAIL DRIFTED OUT FROM DEEP IN THE BOWELS OF THE CRONE'S CAVE! THEY NEVER SAW THE INFANT-THING CRAWL OUT INTO THE SUNLIGHT... ITS EYES STREAMING WITH TEARS... CRYING FOR ITS PARENTS...
WAAHHH
HEH, HEH! YEP! THAT'S IT, KIDDIES! THAT'S MY STORY! THAT HAG, THE OLD WITCH, TOLD YOU HER ORIGIN TALE... AND NOW, I'VE TOLD YOU MINE... YEP! ENOCH OF THE DOUBLE DOMES WAS MY OLD MAN, AND MYRNA THE MUMMY WAS MY OLD LADY! YOU MIGHT SAY, THE MUMMY WAS MY MOMMY! BY THE WAY! I UNDERSTAND THAT THERE'S A CARNIVAL TODAY... EIGHTY YEARS LATER...
THAT STILL EXHIBITS A MUMMY AND A TWO-HEADED PRESERVED CORPSE! IF ANY OF YOU SEE THEM... WRITE ME! I WANT TO SEND A CARD! IT'S THEIR ANNIVERSARY NEXT MONTH!

Beginning with issue No. 2, Goodwin would regularly offer "Loathsome Lore" on familiar monsters like vampires and werewolves that blur the line between fact and fiction (and complicate familiar monster stories). In connection, "Vampires Fly at Dusk" begins with a series of vampire-like killings that started shortly after Count Orsini came to reside in the Old Villa. After the Count enforces a nighttime-only waking life for his wife and servants, his wife begins to suspect that he is the vampire (as does the reader who knows the basic rules of vampirism). However, when she throws open the curtains that block them from the sunlight, she dies, and he reveals that he had been secretly feeding her blood to keep her from the hidden truth that she was a vampire. Although a bit long on explanation at the end, the twist reveals a human in love to be the perpetrator of monstrous acts, someone who acts quite separate from a bloodlust easily associated with his vampire wife. Consequently, "Loathsome Lore" works like similar history segments of 1950s horror comics, but in this case, intentionally sets up the reader with false expectations. "Vampires Fly at Dusk" works like EC's macabre "Grim Fairy Tales" to undermine those expectations and redefine the monstrous.

Likewise in *Creepy* No. 7, Bill Pearson directly addresses the ideas that folktales have no clear moral imperative and primarily serve as a representation of anxiety in "Image of Bluebeard!" When a woman reads the legend and becomes suspicious of her husband's actions, she identifies him as Bluebeard, kills him to protect herself, and then learns that he was innocent. In a similar way in *Eerie* No. 13 (a companion magazine introduced in 1966), Archie Goodwin depicts the terrifying power of stories as embodiments of horror in "Tell Tale Heart!" With an added frame set in an asylum, Goodwin tells Poe's story through the voice of an inmate, the killer, who throws himself to his death upon discovering his eye has been injured and now resembles the "vulture eye" of his victim.

Creepy (and *Eerie*) Art: Black and White and Read

The sinister power of Poe's stories also had been well-established in the late 1960s by Roger Corman's films featuring Vincent Price, and *Creepy* and *Eerie*, together with the Hammer horror film imports, were part of a phenomenon that found classic monsters threatening again. For instance, Terrence Fisher's *Dracula* (1958) establishes Dracula as a genuinely seductive presence, but along with his sexual desirability comes his monstrous invasions of body and moral space.[32]

In his essay "Horror Is My Business," Terrence Fisher comments, "We're not as materialistic or income-tax conscious as we think. At the moment our superstitions are tucked away, but they come out sometimes in strange ways—sex crimes, black masses. Sometimes they're the results of genuine lunacy but usually they're an attempt to escape from society which is too well ordered. So well ordered that as soon as someone like Hitler rebels against it, out come all the hidden hatreds and fears."[33] This sophisticated analysis of horror effectively identifies the way the unconscious breaks through in the form of supposedly disgusting desires, revealing something fundamental about our culture's barely constrained self.

Bloch's *Psycho* would famously take shape in Alfred Hitchcock's hands as a 1960 film radically innovative in narrative and visual terms. Although much can be said about it, film critic Raymond Durgnat wisely focuses on the audience's reaction to the central character, the killer, Norman Bates: "The audience's moral purity is being outflanked at both ends—by morbid, slightly pornographic fascination, and by pity for the charming Norman."[34] This claim demonstrates the link between Fisher's supernatural story of *Dracula* and Hitchcock's realistic story of *Psycho*, with both uncovering monstrosity in the human mind.

Creepy and *Eerie* didn't abandon traditional monsters as fully as EC titles, but domestic strife still provided the impetus for breakdown and homicide in many tales. In *Eerie* No. 4, "Hatchet Man" is a such a story, evoking the split personality anxieties not only of *Psycho* but also of *Dr. Jekyll and Mr. Hyde*. After depicting an attack by a "maniac hatchet killer," the next panel sequence moves to a married couple discussing the newspaper report of the crime. Feeling oppressed by his wife's constant disapproval, Harvey schemes to kill his wife in the same manner as the hatchet killer. After committing the crime, he disposes of the hatchet and returns home to find the police (as he expected). However, the police have found another hatchet in his home, and when they accuse him of the murder spree, a separate personality manifests itself in Harvey (revealing that Harvey's personality known to the reader imitated crimes committed by his other personality).

Suggesting that the mundane experience of a typical marriage drives people to moral failure and crime, this story connects contemporary blue collar life to an experience of dread. Dehumanized to a degree much greater than Harvey is consciously aware of, he encounters the horror of his other personality already experienced by the reader in the first few panels depicting the hatchet attacks. In that prologue, Gene Colan focuses on the perspective of the woman attacked (and later on Harvey's wife).

In addition, the gutters are blackened, and neat ninety degree right angles of panels are abandoned during the attacks, emphasizing the victim's experience in a way not seen in EC comics. But the depth of depravity with *Eerie*'s host, Cousin Eerie, is seen in spectacular EC fashion as he appears and jokes about the content of the second page: a splash page reveal of the hatchet killer about to kill his victim.

While *Creepy* and *Eerie* would feature former EC artists and partly develop that visual association,[35] its black-and-white format would become one of its most distinctive features, encouraging work unique to the comic book form at that time. In addition to having greater freedom in content free from threats of censorship, the black-and-white format, seemingly a limitation, encouraged experimentation. The color palate of early comics was severely limited by print technology and is rightly associated with garish primary colors of superhero costumes; there was little variation available in darker colors, especially within the grayscale that many would associate with the visual aesthetic of horror.

Fig. 2.3
Eerie No. 4,
Warren, 1966,
© New Comic Company LLC
With black gutters skewed at unconventional angles, "Hatchet Man" positions the reader within the psychological experience of the victim.

In addition, color served as something of a crutch to fill in the large spaces within the minimalist line drawings of comics (minimalist most often due not to artistic choice but to time constraints). In order to work with the black-and-white space in a way that didn't leave large parts of the visual field empty, artists used cross-hatching and shading techniques to create different degrees of darkness. The consequential style was more illustrative with a classical sense of depth: more like a charcoal drawing but allowing for a divergence in individual style not seen in comics of the 1960s. As Richard Arndt argues in *Horror Comics in Black and White*, "Unlike DC, Marvel, Dell, or Gold Key,... Warren had no house style for the artists to conform to.... Without color, the line work gained prominence, enabling fine line artists such as Al Williamson, Reed Crandall, and Angelo Torres to really shine. The superior artwork from all the EC vets pushed other artists to bring their own "A" game to the Warren table."[36]

Further, Warren horror scripts were much less text heavy[37] than typical EC horror scripts, and the images served more as the vehicle for the horror experience. In *Creepy* No. 1, Goodwin called attention to the importance of the images (and the artistic style in *Creepy*) in "The Success Story," a self-reflexive story about a comic book producer who employed other artists and took credit for their work. The break-down of labor in the factory model employed by the comic book industry made them unaware that he contributed nothing to the comic books. When they discover the truth, he kills them all with years of their work still to publish. But after they return from the dead to exact their revenge, all that is left behind of him is an illustration of their reanimated corpses attacking the comic book cheat.

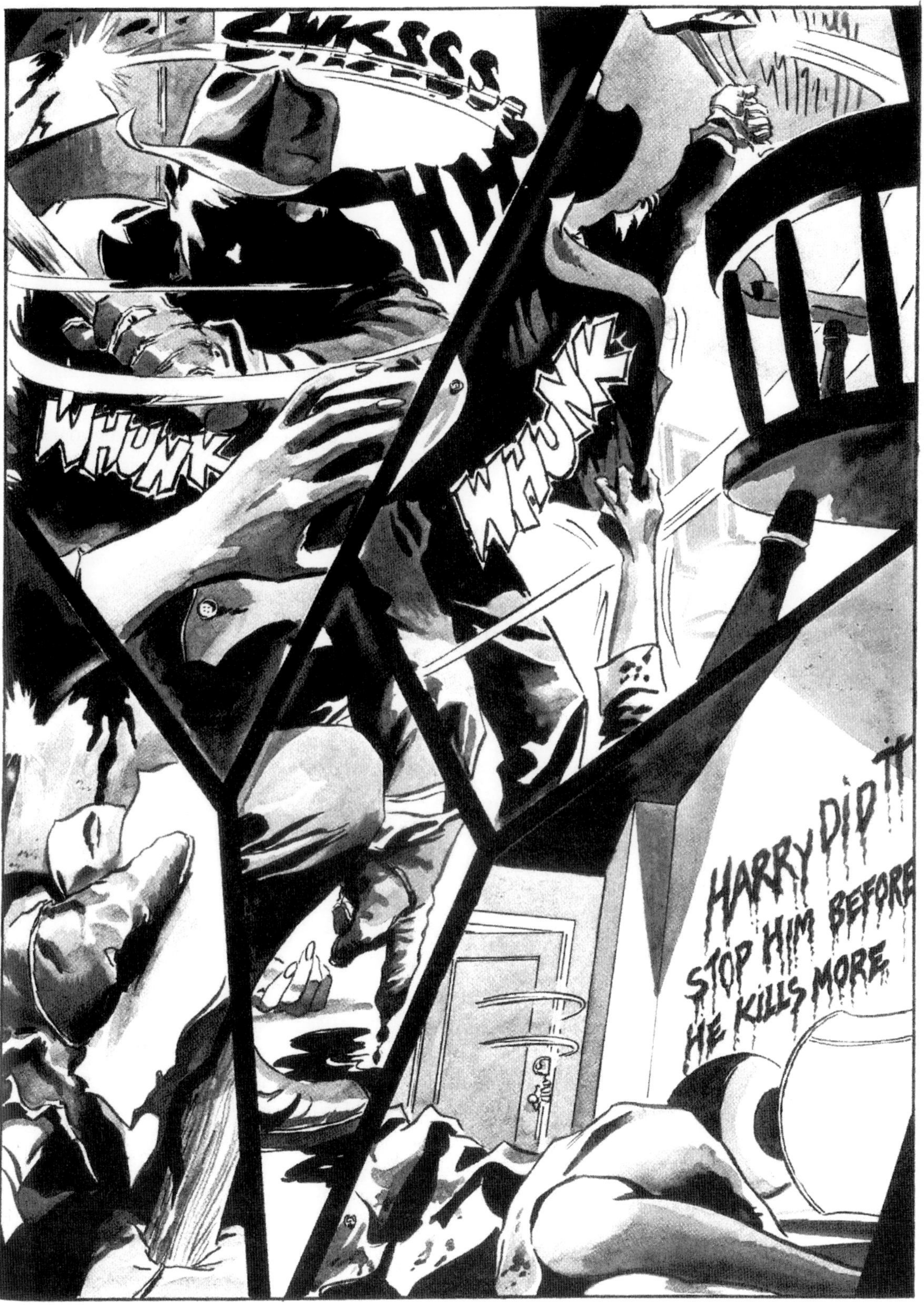
WHUNK
WHUNK
HARRY DID IT
STOP HIM BEFORE
HE KILLS MORE

In addition to critiquing standard industry practices, the story is drawn by Al Williamson in a style somewhat more typical of 1950s comics until the corpses appear in an illustrative style different from the rest of the story. The illustration of the attack is found on the floor and serves as the final panel likewise rendered in an illustrative style (and according to the publisher, colored with blood). Of course, the reader can't see the red of the blood but can see the difference in style, similar to that which generally would come to dominate *Creepy* and *Eerie*. Thereby, this story gives a generous touch of the abject to the illustration via the idea that the style is a consequence of the blood that can't be seen in black-and-white magazines.

Fig. 2.4
Creepy No. 1,
Warren, 1964,
© New Comic Company LLC
Commenting on the magazine's black and white illustrative style, the story contrasts traditional comic book line drawing with an illustrative style "colored [in] blood!"

Departing from the house style model reasserted in the post-Code era, talented artists like Alex Toth and Neal Adams were allowed to interpret the scripts and develop their own pacing, panel arrangement, and style. Often resulting in exciting experiments in the visual presentation of horror, this artistic freedom would also distinguish *Creepy* and *Eerie* from the precedents set in most 1950s horror comics. Former EC artist Frank Frazetta illustrated his last comic book story in *Creepy* No. 1 and would later become a painter for the covers of *Creepy*, *Eerie*, and *Blazing Combat* (Warren's other comic magazine).[38] His covers became stylistic trademarks of the magazines and charted territory outside the relative safety of the aforementioned cover of *Creepy* No. 1. They regularly featured voluptuous, scantily clad women who were sometimes warriors and sometimes bound by their demon lovers, connecting Warren publications with pulp fiction and horror comic traditions. And Warren would offer more explicit sexual content in years to come, navigating less successful years in the late 1960s and early 1970s by appealing to their male audience base.

Vamping It Up: Creepy Monsters Become Even Less Respectable and More Sexy

Although occasionally editing, writing stories, and providing a background for the popular character of Vampirella, Goodwin departed Warren as an editor in 1967. Without his creative guidance, the magazines regularly turned to more sensational content in the wake of copycat magazines that offered more violence and especially more nudity. Ever since the Kinsey report had shocked the nation, the culture worked to accommodate those new ideas about sexuality and yet maintain the parochial morality of a patriarchal society. The middle ground came in the form of Hugh Hefner's male-centric playboy philosophy and magazine (and quite notably, one of James Warren's first forays into publishing was with the *Playboy* imitation *After Hours*).

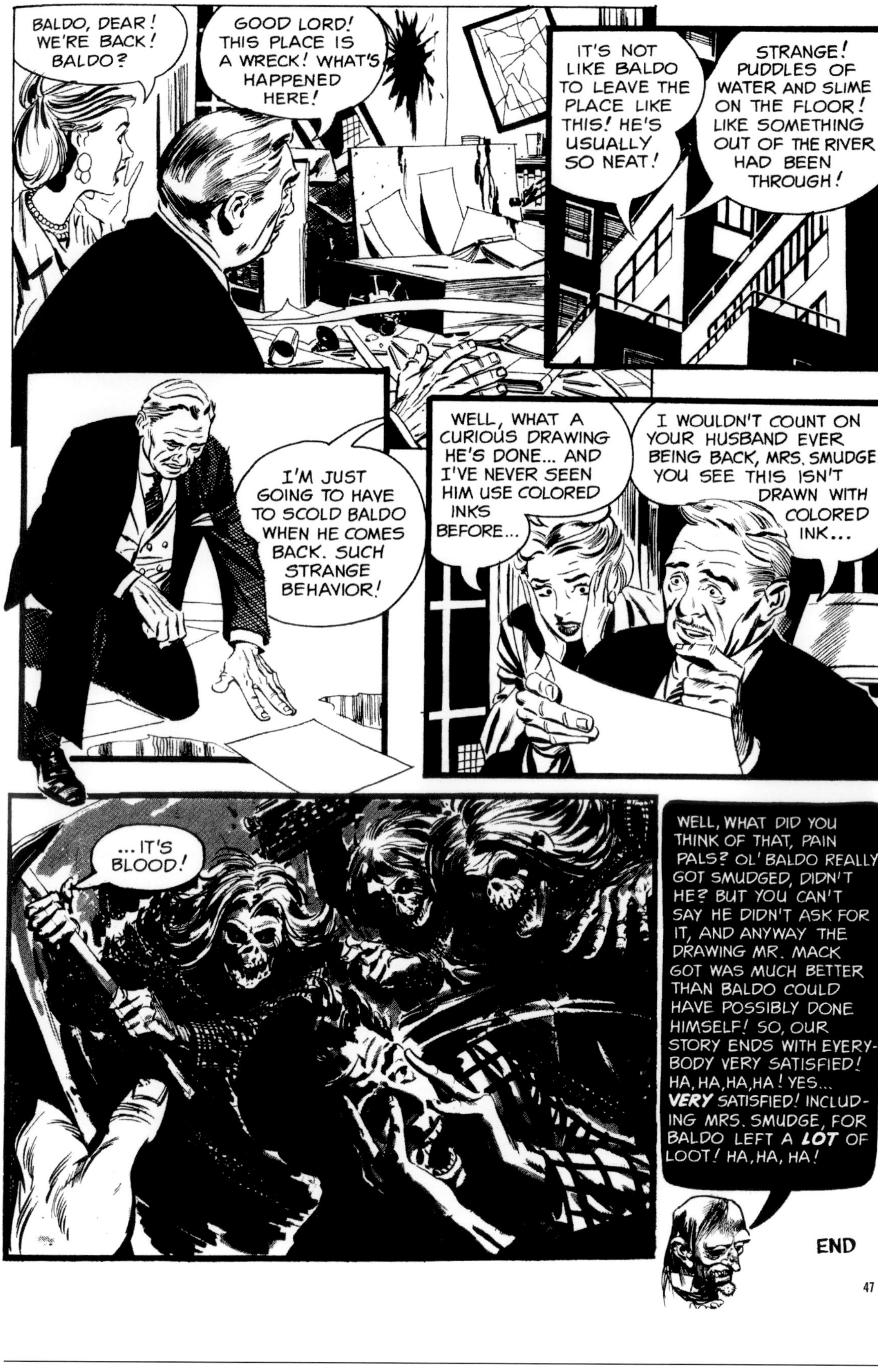
BALDO, DEAR! WE'RE BACK! BALDO?
GOOD LORD! THIS PLACE IS A WRECK! WHAT'S HAPPENED HERE!
IT'S NOT LIKE BALDO TO LEAVE THE PLACE LIKE THIS! HE'S USUALLY SO NEAT!
STRANGE! PUDDLES OF WATER AND SLIME ON THE FLOOR! LIKE SOMETHING OUT OF THE RIVER HAD BEEN THROUGH!
I'M JUST GOING TO HAVE TO SCOLD BALDO WHEN HE COMES BACK. SUCH STRANGE BEHAVIOR!
WELL, WHAT A CURIOUS DRAWING HE'S DONE... AND I'VE NEVER SEEN HIM USE COLORED INKS BEFORE...
I WOULDN'T COUNT ON YOUR HUSBAND EVER BEING BACK, MRS. SMUDGE. YOU SEE THIS ISN'T DRAWN WITH COLORED INK...
...IT'S BLOOD!
WELL, WHAT DID YOU THINK OF THAT, PAIN PALS? OL' BALDO REALLY GOT SMUDGED, DIDN'T HE? BUT YOU CAN'T SAY HE DIDN'T ASK FOR IT, AND ANYWAY THE DRAWING MR. MACK GOT WAS MUCH BETTER THAN BALDO COULD HAVE POSSIBLY DONE HIMSELF! SO, OUR STORY ENDS WITH EVERYBODY VERY SATISFIED! HA, HA, HA, HA! YES... VERY SATISFIED! INCLUDING MRS. SMUDGE, FOR BALDO LEFT A LOT OF LOOT! HA, HA, HA!
END
47

With the sexually explicit French comic book *Barbarella* serving as the basis for the science fiction film starring Jane Fonda in 1968, the general interest in the film indicated an appetite for such genre material.[39] And as described by W. Scott Poole in *Monsters in America*, horror stories would react to these changes: "Changes in sexual attitudes and cultural images of male sexual aggression found expression in American monster lore of all kinds."[40] Within this climate, Warren debuted *Vampirella* in 1969.

Warren dealt with financial woes in the post-Goodwin era that resulted from over-expansion and the decline in the quality of its flagship magazines. Launching a new series was consequently a strange and perhaps bold choice, but it ultimately paid off.[41] *Vampirella* joined *Creepy* and *Eerie* to complete Warren's triad of popular horror titles. Once again the magazine was hosted by the title character. Vampirella was unlike the ugly and disagreeable Uncle Creepy or Cousin Eerie—she was a sexy vampire in a barely there swimsuit-like costume with high-heeled boots.

Precedents for Vampirella included Drusilla, an attractive assistant who joined the Vault-Keeper in the final issues of EC's *Vault of Horror*, and Vampira, the television show host who drew inspiration from the *Addams Family*, vampire stories, and S&M fashion.[42] While this seems an obvious and superficial means to secure a male audience also attracted to Frazetta's cover paintings of women, Vampirella's presence in her own magazine became more substantive with her a character in her own continuing story.

In "Who Serves the Cult of Chaos?" in *Vampirella* No. 8, Archie Goodwin provided essential background and clear motivation for the main character but also began the story in a way essential to her—scantily clad and in a snowstorm (and neither cold nor self-conscious). On a planet of vampires suffering a drought that dried up its blood rivers, Vampirella travels to Earth to save her race but finds only blood-filled creatures to satisfy her needs. However, Vampirella mostly wants to do good, essentially a superhero with powers tied to her monstrous nature. Most of the story consequently is spent with her working against a monster-worshipping cult (often in states of undress and bondage).

Initially illustrated by Tom Sutton in a style much more indicative of superhero comic books, Vampirella serves as a bridge between the good girl superheroes of the past and the bad girl superheroes of the 1990s (overly sexualized and hyper-violent like Lady Death, Angela, and Witchblade). While informed by superhero tropes, stories often served as props for presenting Vampirella as a sex object. Although initially fighting other horror figures such as Dracula, the overall picaresque arc of Vampirella becomes increasingly strained and she wears less and less clothing.

Vampirella does have advocates who admire her "innocent" sexuality,[43] and Vampirella's costume designer, Trina Robbins, defended her as one of the most proactive female characters in comics at the time.[44] Even by ignoring the number of times Vampirella finds herself in chains, it is hard to accept a characterization of Vampirella as a proto-feminist figure in comics. While the artwork in her series eventually achieves some level of illustrative beauty as well as titillation thanks to Jose Gonzalez,[45] her depiction as a hostess of stories consistently places her in sexualized positions. And yet while this sexist portrayal isn't unique in comic books or horror stories, Vampirella is in fact worth mentioning as more than a link between the good girl and bad girl art.

Like the femme fatale of film noir, Vampirella's power comes from her sexuality (in a vampire story, represented by her desire for the life-blood of others). *Vampirella* represents that simultaneous movement often seen in crime and horror stories: to express forbidden desires, and to contain those desires within a familiar framework (in this case, the framework provided by patriarchy). The vampire's desire predictably activates desire in others, but something else happens in *Vampirella* that extends her story in at least one interesting way. Although visually she is limited as a sex object and her stories are partly designed to support that visual presentation, her role as a femme fatale with desires of her own never comes to an end.

In film noir, men give into the sexual abyss of the femme fatale, but that woman is inevitably punished or killed in the end; in addition, the femme fatale is usually set in opposition to the virtuous good girl, who is revealed as the better choice for the story's doomed hero. However, Vampirella is never killed, and there is no good girl who is preferable to Vampirella, a situation best represented by another story in the anthology. In *Vampirella* No. 16, "Purification" presents a humorous story of a sexy witch about to be burned at the stake. Illustrated by Joan Nebot in a cartoonish style that accentuates the witch's sexual appeal, the villagers tear her clothes off to prepare her for execution. However, the village, comprised completely of men, is captivated, and they happily walk away with her as her executioners burn in the background.[46] This absurdist fantasy of the sexy witch reveals the interesting underbelly of Vampirella's story: that things traditionally described as disgusting by culture are not only desirable but also preferable to culture itself.

This argument does not excuse *Vampirella* for its overtly and increasingly sexist portrayal of women, and unfortunately more of this would be seen in other black-and-white horror magazines.

With former Warren writer Alan Hewston as editor, Skywald Publications entered the fray in 1970 with *Nightmare*, *Psycho*, and *Scream*, and a survey determined that the readers of this magazine type were ninety percent male and mostly between thirteen and sixteen years.[47] While the accuracy of the survey cannot be determined, Skywald certainly seemed to believe it, catering to the interests of teenage boys with gratuitous violence and sexuality that goes far beyond the excesses of horror comics in 1954.

In general, Skywald's approach was much more impressionistic than Warren's, working with themes rather than with stories carefully constructed in their own terms. The resulting collections of stories embraced excess as an aesthetic and created a interesting nightmarish experience described by Arndt: "Skywald tales were a feverish concoction of stories that sometimes barely made sense but each story both built on and fed upon each horror tale that appeared before and after them in a single issue."[48] As Cotter claims, the Comics Code prohibitions served as a to-do list for Skywald, as one of their foremost priorities was resisting authority.[49] Although this might not fully explain all of Skywald's artistic choices, an approach largely motivated by such an ideal would necessarily have a limited lifespan.

In 1968, Eerie Publications had tried to do something similar (with no connection to Warren even though they used the catchphrase "Eerie," or to EC even though they published a magazine called *Tales from the Crypt* until Bill Gaines stopped them). However, their stories, focused almost solely on gore[50], were less innovative than the scatological Skywald tales and were drawn in a rushed style reminiscent of the earliest comic books. As Warren continued to produce horror in the 1970s, they began to walk an uncomfortable line between parodying their work and taking it too seriously. The cover of *Eerie* No. 81 features a giant naked woman who, like King Kong, stands atop the Empire State Building and fights off biplanes.[51] Frazetta pays homage to a classic giant monster movie and playfully acknowledges the leanings of all Warren magazines at that time (featuring more diverse, less horrific, stories with more nudity[52]). However, the interior stories use the painting as a point of inspiration and every one tells a tale of a giant woman (although not all lead to the top of the Empire State Building).

Some later entries in the Warren magazines were truly innovative though, such as work produced by Richard Corben. The inserts devoted to his stories often showcased his innovative color design such as that of "Bless Us Father..." in *Creepy* No. 59 (a killer Santa story by Bill DuBay that is literate, emotional, and experimental with a touch of macabre humor).

However, while often well-drawn, that self-aware humor is largely missing in later issues of magazines past their prime as changes paved the way for the return of horror to conventional comic book formats.[53]

More or Less Horrific: DC Develops Self-Awareness of Biblical Proportions

In this time period, the American film industry went through changes that would relate to the changes that were to come in American comics industry. Challenged by more innovative foreign and independent films, Hollywood studios confronted problems with the film production code that prohibited certain content central to the narrative of "issue" films (like nudity in the 1964 Holocaust film *The Pawnbroker*). After major studios like MGM produced films without code approval, the move toward a ratings system was underway, opening the door for the exhibition of previously prohibited content. Tangentially, as Hollywood studios found themselves in financial crisis, the risky solution of the high concept blockbuster was embraced in the 1970s. With mainstream theaters screening big-budget Hollywood films, art house theaters showcasing low-budget independent films, and drive-ins becoming a new home for quickly made "exploitation" films,[54] the horror genre found itself uniquely suited to provide content for all of these film types.

Studio efforts like *The Exorcist* (1973) were critically acclaimed, low-budget independents like *Night of the Living Dead* (1968) were financially successful, and controversial slasher films like *The Texas Chainsaw Massacre* (1974) were primed to generate cult followings. Moreover, all of these films were considered disgusting by many, stretching the boundaries of good taste. However, when *The Exorcist* was nominated for an Academy Award, it became clear that taste, the weapon used against Bill Gaines, was changing. With America proclaiming its status as a superpower while facing domestic challenges from new ideas about race, sex, and class identity, the country became a repository of surplus repression.[55] That surplus needed a release, and horror was a release valve accepted to different degrees (but nevertheless more than it had been in the 1950s).

The widespread success of horror author Stephen King clearly demonstrated that the literary form of the genre no longer lived in pulp fiction type publications. In terms of leaving behind those supposedly tawdry origins, horror was moving from shorter form fiction (e.g., short stories in anthology magazines and comics) to longer form fiction (e.g., novels).[56] Outside of the world of novels, the most notable move toward longer form fiction can be found in the transition from television anthology shows such as *The Twilight Zone* to television serials like *Dark Shadows*.

With its soap opera format, *Dark Shadows* was a pioneer more characteristic of what would eventually be known as TV2 (self-contained stories in continuing shows like *The Night Stalker*) and TV3 (long arc stories in continuing series like *True Blood*).

The sympathetic vampire Barnabas Collins led to higher ratings for *Dark Shadows*,[57] a show that also featured werewolves, witches, and even a parallel universe. Jowett and Abbott argue that the soap opera format prevents closure and provides only continuous disruption[58]–exposure to a horrifying wound that will never heal. Horror comics had experimented with seriality much earlier with the Werewolf Hunter in *Rangers Comics*, the Heap in *Air Fighter's Comics*, and Dick Briefer's *Frankenstein*. Nevertheless, the dominant form of horror stories in comics was the short story until the late 1960s with Vampirella and a few other recurring characters in Warren titles: Dr. Archaeus, The Spook, Adam Link, robot detective, Dax, the warrior, and others.[59] The era of long arc stories was dawning in mainstream comics, especially in the superhero comics at Marvel, a company that would soon dominate the horror comics market in both magazines and traditional comic books. DC Comics would also be part of this change and initiate the return of real horror to the comic book format with its new horror hosts and the part it played in the 1971 revision of the Comics Code.

While it would be too simple to say seriality in horror entertainments led to the end of the horror hosts in comics, the horror host definitely evolved at this time. The host became even more of a character within a story (as seen with Vampirella) and moved even further beyond typical duties as a host. In regard to major comic book publishers, DC returned to horror more gradually and Marvel more suddenly. DC and Marvel were part of the 1950s horror boom and scare (Marvel was then known as Atlas). DC generally played it safe with content before the implementation of the Comics Code, and Atlas quickly backpedaled from more controversial content after the implementation of the Comics Code. As a result, DC's *House of Mystery*, although not the most popular horror title of the 1950s, had more staying power in the Code era because it did not revise its content as radically. But the title did shift to some more science fiction monster stories and then to some superhero stories (including the those of the Martian Manhunter).

Coinciding with the success of horror comics magazines, *House of Mystery* would move back to its focus on horror in 1968 with issue No. 174 and would introduce Cain, a new horror host, in No. 175.

As Julia Round notes in "Embedded Metafiction: Cain and Abel in DC Comics," Cain follows in the footsteps of previous horror hosts with his dark humor and punning (even referring to himself as an "able caretaker" before his brother Abel[60] appeared as host of the companion title *House of Secrets*[61]). In addition to breaking the fourth wall, Cain (and later Abel) would function in extradiegetic and intradigetic ways (working outside and also within their storyworlds).[62] Their movement between the two worlds would disrupt the conventional storytelling associated with comic books in visual and narrative terms.

The visual experimentation in Warren horror stories is also seen in these titles (especially with the cross-over of Warren artists such as Alex Toth) but is more directly connected to the hosts. As the literal house of Cain changes its shape with various artists who represent it differently,[63] *House of Mystery* allows the destabilization of visual elements to become an essential part of the comic. In "The Devil's Doorway" in No. 182, Cain introduces the story as part of a frame composed of horrific images, but the frame contains a comic panel that contains an arched doorway that then contains the title of the story. After already mixing frame elements with the literal story elements (e.g., a doorway) with extradiegetic elements (e.g., a title), the first page also features Cain's fingers draped over the panel with the "smoke" that surround's Toth's signature on the frame wafting over the title.

Immediately thereafter, the second page features the main character reacting to a demonic image in the doorway, something disconnected from the story that begins on that page in two panels inserted at a rough angle. By leaning back into the page, those two panels defy the conventional comic book space of a grid with ninety-degree angles, and yet it is therein that the story finds its chronological start. The image of the main character's reaction to the demon dominates the page, even though it serves as a gutter for the two more conventional panels (that his body in part obscures). This dynamic fits into Julia Round's notion of gutter as crypt in *Gothic in Comics and Graphic Novels* where the gutter serves as space that disrupts temporality: an only partially sealed space associated with the unconscious experience of horror. In addition to serving as characters in stories as Cain does in "Boom!" (No. 185), the hosts move more freely in the comic book space. Due to the violation of comic book form, the resulting disorientation subtly provokes an abject response, something usually only associated with content prohibited by the Comic Code.

In the first issue of *House of Secrets* featuring Abel as host, he assumes his role at the auspices of the "reality agent," someone revealed as a story figment in angular panels that break away from the ninety-degree angles of panels thus far presented. In addition, "His Name Is... Kane" (with "Cain" crossed out) features Gil Kane as a frustrated artist producing horror comics. Harkening back to motifs in 1950s horror comics, Kane is literally sucked into his work in which reality and fiction are inseparable and Cain frames Kane's artwork in order to trap him inside. The final issue of *House of Mystery* in 1983 (No. 321) would pick up on this intertextual thread and reverse the power dynamic in a way that is more playful but still somewhat threatening; Cain's house is about to be demolished because Karen Berger, DC editor (who becomes a character in the long frame story) has cancelled the series. While this story is not as significant to horror comics history as others in the series, it is notable as a continued self-conscious appropriation of poststructural technique pioneered in horror comics.[64]

The Code Is No Cure of Werewolfism: The Wandering Wolfman and Marvel

In comics, the idea that the external world also lives within the pages of the comic leads to a fairly pointed anecdote famously related to *House of Secrets* No. 83 (1969). Within Abel's introduction, he identifies the story as one told to him by "a wandering wolfman," something the Comics Code Authority indicated must be omitted (just like any mention of monsters like vampires, ghouls, etc.). However, the writer of the story was in fact Marv Wolfman, and the reference was allowed in the Code-approved book as long as Wolfman received story credit.

While humorously exposing some of the absurdity in the Code's prohibitions, this anecdote does indicate the times were changing in connection to the Code and other issues. Despite the indirect nature of the challenge made by the "wandering wolfman" reference, the challenge implies the Code was considered worth challenging by DC creators (even with DC long being one of the most conservative comics publishers). And in the wake of this publication, other comics creators also wanted credit, showing that related issues (like creators' rights) were beginning to develop in germinal ways.

More famous in Code history, the Spider-Man drug-abuse story in *The Amazing Spider-Man* No. 96 to No. 98 (1971) was rejected by the Comics Code Authority (particularly by Archie president John Goldwater).[65] Considering the story's anti-drug message, the problems with Code were readily apparent, and the Code was revised in that year not only to allow similar stories, but also to eliminate prohibitions against monsters and horror comics.

The caveat was that vampires, ghouls, and werewolves would be allowed "when handled in the classic tradition such as Frankenstein, Dracula, and other high caliber literary works written by Edgar Allan Poe, Saki, Conan Doyle, and other respected authors whose works are read in schools around the world."[66] While the caveat tied the presentation to classics tested by time and taught in the classroom, it nevertheless acknowledged the changing opinion of the genre.[67]

In a time when superheroes were dominant but understood as likely to fade from popularity, little more was needed to encourage Marvel to join the fray. While Marvel would not be as formally adventurous as DC in their return to horror, Marvel would be adventurous in other ways: 1) committing to on-going stories of horror characters (in some cases with series devoted to a single character), 2) adopting an increasingly illustrative style that was modeled on work in black-and-white horror magazines, and 3) moving into the horror comics magazine market as well as the traditional horror comics market. With these strategic choices, Marvel would be fairly successfully with their titles and bring the monster horror aesthetic into Marvel's shared superhero universe.

Thanks to changes made to the Code, Morbius, "the Living Vampire," was appropriately introduced in the title generally credited with those changes: *The Amazing Spider-Man* (No. 101). While researching a cure for his own blood disease, Dr. Michael Morbius acquires his vampirism, becoming a tragic and therefore sympathetic antagonist for Spider-Man. As Randy Duncan and Matthew Smith claim in *The Power of Comics*, "When changes to the Code came, they also helped to foment changes in the perception of the horrific creatures, as creators began to adopt a view as somewhat sympathetic protagonists instead of misery inducing antagonists."[68] While Morbius eventually wears a costume more typical of superheroes or supervillains, his visage is pale and skull-like, creating the experience for horror as well as sympathy with this "supervillain." Morbius would be followed by other similarly antiheroic protagonists and antagonists such as Ghost Rider, Man-Wolf, and Son of Satan;[69] but more importantly, Marvel would create comic book series for monsters formerly prohibited by the Comics Code in the form of *Werewolf by Night*, *Frankenstein Monster*, and *Tomb of Dracula*.

All the titles brought these classic monsters into a contemporary context and a universe shared by Marvel superheroes; the most significant, popular, and long-running was also the most traditionally horror-based: Marv Wolfman and Gene Colan's *Tomb of Dracula*. While the other two monsters generated sympathy and fought against villains, Dracula is the one most tied to literary roots and therefore most conventionally evil.

After quickly moving through several writers including Archie Goodwin,[70] Marvel settled on Marv Wolfman and his more traditional interpretation of Dracula: "Wolfman admitted that he had never even seen a Dracula movie, nor any vampire movie for that matter, before he wrote the comic book series. As a result, the comic book retains some of the pacing and literate self-reflection of the original work."[71] While Wolfman's Dracula had been brought back to life in contemporary times, the comic was notably separate from the Marvel universe despite featuring a wholly new vampire hunter, Blade, relying as much upon opponents who were descendants of characters in Stoker's novel.

Compared to Marvel's superhero titles, the pace is slower, the presentation is moodier, and the experience of horror is a result of the subtle way in which Dracula's evil acts were depicted by the painterly style of Gene Colan. Even though the series demonstrates the weaknesses of the limited color palate in comics at that time, Colan produces work that rivals what he did with Warren. In *Tomb of Dracula* No. 27, as panels work cinematically to zoom into Dracula's face and eyes, the titular character summons an undead army and consequently, the panel structure breaks down. Various aspects of the individual panels serve to simultaneously divide and connect images of the progress being made by his "vampire legions."

Although Wolfman tended to narrate much more than Goodwin and to crowd the page with words, he used this novelistic approach to create horror with ideas of what might happen. Even with a newly invented tragic origin, Wolfman made Dracula self-consciously evil, and this tended to make the implications of the story more interesting, as Dracula would never die—as long as the comic series continued. Instead, Dracula's antagonists (the heroes) might succeed in frustrating his plans, but the story encouraged the reader to root for the success of the monster. In the case of the series, evil would persist and the heroes were as likely to be killed as Dracula's evil counterparts.

With the success of their monster comic books, Marvel made a more direct assault upon black-and-white horror magazines with their own black-and-white magazine titles in 1973: *Dracula Lives!*, *Monsters Unleashed*, *Tales of the Zombie*[72], and *Vampire Tales*.[73] All were anthology titles, but like the traditional horror comics that Marvel produced, all were largely devoted to providing installments of continuing stories.[74] Probably emboldened by both the magazine format and the changes to the Comics Code, Roy Thomas wrote an editorial for *Monsters Unleashed* No. 1, describing monsters as an essential, trans-historical outgrowth of mythology:

> Slithering, shambling–gibbering madly or writhing obscenely–they have been ever lurking, just outside the door or around the corner or beneath the paper-thin top layer of consciousness.... We'll run the full gauntlet of familiar haunts and nameless, unglimpsed things that have clawed at the mind of man since he first came cautiously down from night-shadowed trees. And maybe–just maybe, mind you–someone among us will spawn a new kind of monster or two along the way.[75]

Although the move toward seriality coincides with the disappearance of the horror host, this editorial nevertheless serves one of the same functions as the horror host. After identifying monsters as the things that break through from the subterranean parts of the human psyche, the "someone" that might bring forth "a new kind of monster or two" is left ambiguous, potentially conflating the comics creators and the reader. With the monster embraced rather than eschewed, and categorical distinctions blurred, Marvel moved into the magazine business more fully with some great triumphs like this issue's adaptation of Robert Bloch's "The Man Who Cried Werewolf!" with beautiful art by Pablo Markos.

However, beauty is probably not the highest priority in any horror story. While Markos provides richly textured backgrounds and fantastic depth through careful attention to the light source, his significant innovation is the creative use of the color blue in his mostly black-and-white illustrations to dramatically represent moonlight, mood, and significant text elements. For the most part, Marvel magazines offer soft R-rated content (using the standards of the new movie rating system) but not much in the way of profoundly transgressive material. While Stan Lee may have styled Marvel comics as a new wave for more adult readers,[76] the company was developing a more conservative corporate structure looking to reach a wide audience.[77]

Along these lines, Arndt argues, "If Skywald's approach was seat-of-the-pants publishing and Warren's was stay-small-but-be-the-best-at-what-you-do, then Marvel's take on the B&W field was that of a corporate model."[78] As the popularity of superheroes faded again in the early '70s, other genres such as horror seemed a good bet to maintain their market hold.[79] With fairly good revenue streams already in place and solid lines of distribution, Marvel would reach slightly older readers with their slate of black-and-white magazines and effectively compete with the other comics horror magazines. While their horror innovations were less bold than those of Warren or Skywald, the basic impulse was nevertheless to produce quality horror (as evidenced by Thomas's editorial).

Marvel took earnest renditions of monsters as well as earnest examinations of the monstrous to a larger audience.[80] And with the strong horror stories produced by various corporate sources in the forms of novels and films, the notion that good horror only exists completely outside the industrial system is too simple. As has been noted, *The House of Mystery* and *The House of Secrets* from DC (a company thoroughly invested in conservative corporate culture) contained horror and presented taboo content via their radical form. Seemingly, the corporate model of modern capitalism doesn't completely prevent the production of horror that represents the mass unconscious.

A Slimy Trail Leads to a Muck-Encrusted Monster (and the Resurgence of Horror Comics)

In reference to DC, it is important to mention their move toward seriality in horror fiction, something that builds a bridge to work profiled in the next chapter, which discusses the beginning of the contemporary resurgence in horror comics. *The House of Mystery* moved toward serial stories with "I... Vampire" in the early 1980s (the story's title eventually became larger than the comic's title on the cover). However, more significant as a story and character that spun off into its own series would be Len Wein and Bernie Wrightson's "Swamp Thing" in *House of Secrets* No. 92 (1971).

Told in part from the perspective of Alex Olsen, the story follows a man transformed into a swamp monster by a chemical explosion engineered by the murderous friend who covets Alex's wife, Linda. As the paranoid murderer begins to fear that Linda will learn of his crime, he plans to kill her as well. Although Olsen is able to kill his false friend before he acts, Linda reacts to the "swamp thing" in horror. When she screams, the monster, unable to speak, thinks, "The tortured, shattered look in her once-sparkling eyes is more than I can endure–I turn my face away from her–and I start to go home... Only the swamp is kind to me now–It is only the swamp that cares."[81]

While a variation on other comic swamp monsters like the Heap and Marvel's Man-Thing, "Swamp Thing" finds its edge as a horribly tragic love story that ends in isolation. The panels that the "swamp thing" narrate are framed in a black border that seems to separate his experience from all else. Wrightson creates a Gothic mood in his timeless settings and a skillful use of shadows that make the monster's body into negative space needing to be filled. Built largely on familiar but compelling tropes, the story and its execution generated a strong response and resulted in a self-titled series.

With an origin re-written to position the character now called Alec Holland (no longer Alex Olsen) more as a tragic science hero in the DC superhero universe, the series maintains the outsider status and horror roots of the now well-muscled and super-strong monster. Although early stories read like anthology stories connected by a recurring character, they regularly question the value of the "normal" life Holland longs to have again as he encounters mad scientists, alien creatures, and other monstrous freaks.

Moreover, *Swamp Thing*'s continued exploration of monstrosity took DC somewhat beyond simplistic notions of good and evil in their revised Code superhero universe. And eventually, this title paved the way for Alan Moore's version of the *Saga of the Swamp Thing*–a direct market title produced without Comics Code approval that led the resurgence of horror comics in the 1980s.[82] In any case, *Swamp Thing* was to be part of the move toward a lengthening of the horror story in the 1970s, and toward an on-going experience of survival horror far beyond the seriality of the penny dreadful. In essence, these on-going comics stories suggest that genuine horror doesn't end at dawn; instead, they argue that the terror of America as a post-industrial superpower may be never-ending.

Regardless, the unlikely return of horror comics in black-and-white magazines is not only a clever exploitation of a loophole but also an important advancement of comic book aesthetics that many argue were stunted by the Comics Code.[83] In this era, crime comics (less specifically targeted by the Comics Code) remained largely absent; however, horror comics (more specifically targeted by the Comics Code) returned against all odds in this significant but short-lived way. Benton tries to explain the fading popularity of horror in the late '70s and early 80s: "The end of the 1970s horror comics boom nearly coincided with the resignation of Richard Nixon from the presidency. Perhaps the time for ferreting out the evil within us had ended now that our nation's nightmare was over and our fascination with the gruesome underpinnings of our psyche and society were waning."[84] His "perhaps" identifies his argument as speculation but the ebb is related not only to these political factors but also to the broader socio-economic factors co-opting horror at the time.

Horror is an eruption of the unconscious in the excessively organized framework of post-industrial society represented well by America as a superpower. As stated previously, horror comics represent the widespread anxieties of common people in ways that are excessive, sometimes gratuitous, and often resistant to the authority of the powers-that-be. More particularly, resistance is catalyzed through the experience of fear and disgust, through contact with the monstrous that forces the individual to connect the self and the tale as well as the individual and cultural unconscious.

In this era, horror is presented in narrower and more radical ways with black-and-white magazines like *Creepy* and independent films such as *Night of the Living Dead*. But horror is also presented in broader and more tempered ways with comics like *Tomb of Dracula* and blockbusters like *Jaws*. And the fact that it seems to disappear for another short period merely sets the stage for another, perhaps more dramatic eruption.

With the advent of the direct market and the industry-wide move to target adults, comics creators Alan Moore, Neil Gaiman, Mike Mignola, and others would have opportunities to refine horror aesthetics in ways that will be explored in the upcoming chapters. In addition to the above definition, the resurgence in horror comics not only dialogues more openly with horror traditions but also develops approaches that critique the conventions of the genre and the medium. And with these contemporary horror comics creators, themes that become apparent in these first two eras form the foundation of the horror comic's resurgence beginning in the 1980s.

First, horror is always tied to anxieties of the culture, with the genre reaching new heights in the civilized world. Even when horror stories evoke a sense of the past in its contemporary setting (such as *Tomb of Dracula*), the space represents a distance from the familiar needed to expose the false surety of the industrial and post-industrial situation.

Second, horror is a natural outgrowth of the morally determined repression of American culture with a trajectory ranging from the Puritans of New England to the Communist fighters of Washington, D.C. When horror exposes the dark underbelly of the American dream (like EC's domestic dramas), the purveyors of good taste react violently and sometimes with grave consequences for horror creators.

Third, horror is tied to the language of psychoanalysis and Marxism because the ideas that led to contemporary horror are similar to the ideas that led to psychoanalysis and Marxism. While not a psychoanalytic or Marxist screed, this monograph will demonstrate how horror works in terms related to those theories to disrupt the fiction of the coherent self with things both fascinating and grotesque (such as *Creepy*'s psychopathic Santa).

And fourth, horror is a disruption of conventional boundaries between what is good and evil, safe and dangerous, appropriate and inappropriate, and desirable and disgusting (literally and figuratively exploring the darkness). As a consequence, well-established aesthetic rules are often disobeyed in horror to the seeming detriment of all we hold dear—and every horror host would readily admit that to you, quite directly, as the host breaks the fourth wall.

To different degrees (depending on the works discussed), these four themes will be referenced in the next four chapters examining the resurgence of horror comics. As I stated in *The Dark Night Returns*, I would consider Fredric Wertham's efforts to censor comics largely ineffective even without the resurgence of horror and crime comics. In addition to his general frustration with Congress turning the regulation of the industry back to the industry, his faulty critique is now not only largely rejected but also readily recognized as having missed the larger picture. Whatever one's opinion of crime or horror comics, it is clear that Wertham's frustration with comics existed on a superficial level (looking at acts of violence and not reading to the end of the story).

Moreover, while comics seem to have exorcised the ghost of Wertham as Bart Beatty claims,[85] they are still haunted by the specter of Bill Gaines, as he grows ever larger and more sinister (but in the best way). And with that in mind, parts of his congressional testimony will also be used as points of departure in each of the following chapters. Looking ahead to an outsider like Alan Moore, who brings us even more horrible stories that challenge the dominance of superheroes in the 1980s, I should acknowledge that the marginal and sometimes monstrous medium of comics makes us more malcontent and malevolent (but again in the best way). Please forgive the alliteration; I've obviously been spending too much time with horror hosts.

Chapter 2 Notes

1 Marv Wolfman, "Speaking with… Len Wein, part 1," Marv Wolfman.com, http://www.marvwolfman.com/marv/Speaking_With_Len_Wein_Part_One.html.

2 Most agree that his claims and support were faulty but some more than others; Carol L. Tilley, a library researcher, has argued that Wertham fabricated most of his support ("Seducing the Innocent: Fredric Wertham and the Falsifications That Helped Condemn Comics," *Information and Culture: A Journal of History* 47 [2012]: 383–413).

3 Trombetta comments on the triumph of authority: "By censoring the comics, the committee reasserted the hegemony of adults over children... it's pretty clear whose nervousness was assuaged by the Comics Code, and whose fear authored the deadliest injunction: there could be no stories that might 'create disrespect for established authority'" (Jim Trombetta, *The Horror! The Horror!: Comic Books the Government Didn't Want You to Read* [New York: Harry N. Abrams, 2010], 82). And Hajdu comments on Gaines's capitulation to authority: "Just five months after Gaines had faced down the U.S. Senate, defending not only his comics but the privilege of their creators and their readers to defy prevailing opinion, he capitulated on the very grounds upon which he had fought: taste. He surrendered to the parental authority he had defied ever since he had taken over his father's company, killing the comics he had always held dear as his own creation" (David Hajdu, *The Ten Cent Plague: The Great Comic-Book Scare and How It Changed America* [New York: Farrar, Straus, and Giroux, 2008], 289.)

4 These sentences play with the famous claim at the beginning of the *Communist Manifesto*; it refers to the powers of "old Europe" but fits this American situation in interesting ways.

5 Digby Diehl, *Tales from the Crypt: The Official Archives* (New York: St. Martin's Press, 1996), 96.

6 Ibid., 148–49

7 Text stories were formerly included in comics to justify a second-class mailing rate.

8 Richard J. Arndt, *Horror Comics in Black and White: A History and Catalogue, 1964–2004* (Jefferson, NC: McFarland, 2013), 5.

9 Bart Beatty, *Fredric Wertham and the Critique of Mass Culture* (Jackson: UP of Mississippi, 2005), 105.

10 Introduction, *Adventures into the Unknown* 60, American Comics Group (November–December 1954).

11 Ken Landau, "There's a New Star Tonight." *Adventures into the Unknown* 62, American Comics Group (March–April 1955).

12 Bart Beatty, *Fredric Wertham and the Critique of Mass Culture*, 163.

13 This gradual move to parody was abetted by morphine-addicted Bela Lugosi taking roles alluding to his role as Dracula in laughable Ed Wood productions (like *Glen or Glenda* and *Bride of the Monster*).

14 Wheeler Winston Dixon, *A History of Horror* (New Brunswick: Rutgers UP, 2010), 65.

15 David J. Skal, *The Monster Show: A Cultural History* (New York: Farrar, Straus, and Giroux, 1993), 259.

16 Ibid., 241. "A pioneer postmodernist, Vampira blurred categorical distinctions by wearing her costume offscreen as well" (David J. Skal, *The Monster Show: A Cultural History*, 242).

17 The myth of "Beauty and the Beast" was appropriated in an interesting way in *King Kong*. According to the character Carl Denham, the Beast was forced to fight the powers-that-be rather than be portrayed as a monster terrorizing humans. Later, Denham looks at Kong's corpse and says, "Oh, no, it wasn't the airplanes. It was Beauty that killed the beast!" After making the myth about a Machiavellian power struggle rather than a Christian ethic of love, the film places woman in position of power—but only by virtue of her traditional feminine attributes.

18 Robert Michael Cotter, *The Great Monster Magazines: A Critical Study of Black and White Publications of the 1950s, 1960s, and 1970s* (Jefferson, NC: McFarland, 2008), 35; David J. Skal, *The Monster Show: A Cultural History*, 269.

19 Although short-lived and financially unsuccessful, this magazine provides another link to the development of the Comix movement in the 1960s.

20 Although published much later (in the 1970s), Will Eisner's classic crime comic *The Spirit* was republished by Warren: first in *Eerie* and then as a separate magazine. While Warren's publications are alternately characterized as intentional in their focus and scattershot in their attempts to grab an audience, his commitment to the comics medium is apparent.

21 Robert Michael Cotter, *The Great Monster Magazines: A Critical Study of Black and White Publications of the 1950s, 1960s, and 1970s*, 33.

22 Other anthology programs also include *Boris Karloff's Thriller* and *Night Gallery* (Lorna Jowett and Stacey Abbott, *TV Horror: Investigating the Dark Side of the Small Screen* [London: I.B. Tauris, 2013], 87).

23 Ibid., 88.

24 Ibid., 90.

25 Ibid., 41.

26 Ibid., 42.

27 Quoted in Julia Round, *Gothic in Comics and Graphic Novels* (Jefferson, NC: McFarland, 2014), 36.

28 Richard J. Arndt, *Horror Comics in Black and White: A History and Catalogue, 1964–2004*, 6.

29 Mike Benton, *Horror Comics: The Illustrated History* (Dallas: Taylor Publishing, 1991), 63.

30 Russ Jones, Jack Davis, and Ben Oda, "Heh-Heh, Welcome–." *Creepy* 1, Warren (November 1964).

31 Archie Goodwin, Angelo Torres, and Ben Oda, "Monster Rally!" *Creepy* 4, Warren (June 1965), 8.

32 Terrence Fisher comments on how Dracula preys on the sexual weakness of his victims: "Fisher's Dracula inhabits an entirely moral universe, as do all the director's films, in which life is a struggle between temptation and redemption, perseverance and acquiescence" (Wheeler Winston Dixon, *A History of Horror*, 92).

33 Terrence Fisher, "Horror Is My Business," *Horror Film Reader*, ed., Alain Silver and James Ursini (New York: Limelight, 2006), 67.

34 Raymond Durgnat, "The Subconscious: From Pleasure Castle to Libido Hotel," *Horror Film Reader*, ed., Alain Silver and James Ursini (New York: Limelight, 2006), 45.

35 David A. Roach and John B. Cooke, *The Warren Companion: The Definitive Compendium to the Great Comics of Warren Publishing* (Raleigh, NC: TwoMorrows Publishing, 2001), 37. Jack Davis was embarrassed by the hearings and therefore by his work in horror (David A. Roach and John B. Cooke, *The Warren Companion: The Definitive Compendium to the Great Comics of Warren Publishing*, 39).

36 Richard J. Arndt, *Horror Comics in Black and White: A History and Catalogue, 1964–2004*, 6.

37 David A. Roach and John B. Cooke, *The Warren Companion: The Definitive Compendium to the Great Comics of Warren Publishing*, 11.

38 *Blazing Combat* presented war stories, a genre related to horror. The James Warren series had an anti-war tone and was short-lived (four issues).

39 Unlike France, the United States didn't make the film a full-fledged mainstream success, but the target audience for horror comics was smaller.

40 W. Scott Poole, *Monsters in America: Our Historical Obsession with the Hideous and the Haunting* (Waco: Baylor UP, 2011), 127.

41 David A. Roach and John B. Cooke, *The Warren Companion: The Definitive Compendium to the Great Comics of Warren Publishing*, 11.

42 One of the most obvious connections between comics and S&M culture can be found in the work produced by the down-on-his-luck Superman creator Joe Shuster, for 1950s magazines such as *Nights of Horror* (see Craig Yoe's *Secret Identity: The Fetish Art of Superman's Co-Creator Joe Shuster* [State College, PA: Harvey Abrams, 2009]).

43 "At her (and her stories') best, Vampi was fun and funny, sexy and scary, a combination of otherworldly innocence and smoldering beauty and sensuality that successfully utilized all the classic elements of the vampire story and gothic horror while remaining firmly rooted in the now... Designed by Trina Robbins, [her costume] was fetishistic yet cute... [In the 1990s] Vampirella was at the forefront of the 'bad girl art' trend of the 1990s–itself a cruelly ironic term. Sheena, the Phantom Lady, and Torchy–all these classic female characters were examples of 'good girl art.' That's merely pinups applied to comic panels, strips that are nothing but an excuse to showcase pretty girls. But since Vampi was a vampire, she was a 'bad girl.'" (Robert Michael Cotter, *The Great Monster Magazines: A Critical Study of Black and White Publications of the 1950s, 1960s, and 1970s*, 100–101). Cotter argues that earliest depictions of Vampirella's voluptuous body were not anatomically incorrect or beyond the realm of physical possibility.

44 Trina Robbins comments on Vampirella and her sense of herself as a feminist: "Nowadays, when some people hear I designed Vampi's costume, knowing what a feminist I am and how much I hate "bad girl" comics, they're confused, until I point out how much more she wore in those days, and how much today's Vampi is nothing like the original one. I recently had coffee with a woman who's teaching a class on super-heroines at UC Berkeley, and she told me how she grew up reading the original Vampi and how much she loved it because it was the only comic with a strong female lead" (David A. Roach and John B. Cooke, *The Warren Companion: The Definitive Compendium to the Great Comics of Warren Publishing*, 96).

45 "The definitive artist on Vampirella was Jose Gonzalez, whose dramatic close-ups set against wispy shadowy backgrounds defined the dream-like look for this black-and-white comic" (Mike Benton, *Horror Comics: The Illustrated History*, 66).

46 In a panel that does not contain his image, the local friar proclaims, "As these garments are plucked from you so may the evil be torn out of wicked and defiled flesh..." Centrally located in the panel is the witch whose naked body is obscured only by a well-placed leaf and she is surrounded by ogling villagers; the supposed "evil" in the flesh of the wicked witch is clearly desirable. And with no other female characters in the story, it extends the general sexism of *Vampirella*.

47 Mike Benton, *Horror Comics: The Illustrated History*, 68.

48 Richard J. Arndt, *Horror Comics in Black and White: A History and Catalogue, 1964–2004*, 7.

49 Robert Michael Cotter, *The Great Monster Magazines: A Critical Study of Black and White Publications of the 1950s, 1960s, and 1970s*, 93.

50 Mike Howlett, *The Weird World of Eerie Publications: Comic Gore that Warped Millions of Young Minds!* (Port Townsend, WA: Feral House, 2010), 54–55.

51 The depiction of the 1933 classic *King Kong* is notable because the remake was just released the year before (although weakly received by many horror fans).

52 *Creepy* and *Eerie* showcased a greater number of genres as the interest in other genres increased with few places to find such things at superhero-heavy DC and Marvel. (This trajectory reverses that of comic book anthologies in the 1950s that generally moved from genre diversity to horror exclusivity.) In film, drive-ins became the new hosts of other genres and B-grade entertainments: horror, science fiction, fantasy, and exploitation.

53 That is not to say everything in the magazines failed artistically at this time. "Thrill Kill" in *Creepy* No. 75 (1975) is an example of late-era excellence (David A. Roach and John B. Cooke, *The Warren Companion: The Definitive Compendium to the Great Comics of Warren Publishing*, 8, 12). Also Roach comments on some of the artists: "the Spanish artists from the Barcelona Agency…, within a year, had ransformed the company, bringing with them a new sophistication and exquisite draftsmanship. While fandom may have treated this revolution with a mixture of bemusement and apathy, the general public adored it and sales rose enormously" (12).

54 Jean Claude Romer, "Bloody New Wave in the United States," *Horror Film Reader*, ed., Alain Silver and James Ursini (New York: Limelight, 2006), 63–65.

55 Robin Wood, *Hollywood from Vietnam to Reagan… and Beyond* (New York: Columbia UP, 2003), 63.

56 However, this claim is complicated by the longer serial narratives associated with penny dreadfuls, pulp fiction, horror magazines, and horror movie sequels (especially with Universal and Hammer).

57 Lorna Jowett and Stacey Abbott, *TV Horror: Investigating the Dark Side of the Small Screen*, 47.

58 Ibid., 47–48.

59 Skywald would also be part of this change with continuing stories about Frankenstein and a different version of the Heap.

60 Julia Round, "Embedded Metafiction: Cain and Abel in DC Comics," paper presented at the PCA/ACA Conference, Seattle, WA, March 2016, 3.

61 *House of Secrets* was cancelled in 1956 with No. 80 and was revived in 1969 with No. 81, featuring Abel as a host.

62 In *Weird Mystery* No. 3 (part of DC's expanding roster of anthology horror titles in the early 1970s), Destiny, the host, clarifies that Cain and Abel are not connected to their Biblical namesakes. However, this seems an effort to forestall criticism, hard to accept in a comic that plays with the boundaries of storyworlds.

63 In a foreword in No. 189 illustrated in a cartoonish style by Sergio Aragones, Cain reveals the house to be a propped up façade concealing a pit that contains monsters.

64 This is clearly related to similar interactions in humor comics (with Dell characters) and superhero comics (with DC's Earth-1 and Earth-2) as well as the meet-and-greet with the authors in Grant Morrison's *Animal Man* (1990) and Dave Sim's *Cerebus* (1995).

65 Although outside the boundaries of the Code, this is a fairly conservative anti-drug message and far from the shocking cover content of *Shock SuspenStories* No. 12.

66 For more on these revisions, see Amy Nyberg, *Seal of Approval: The History of the Comics Code* (Jackson, UP of Mississippi, 1998), 140.

67 These changes to the Code are related to the cultural shift that caused the move to movie ratings (but the idea of comic books as kids' stuff still loomed large and a Code was still in place).

68 Randy Duncan and Matthew J. Smith, *The Power of Comics: History, Form, and Culture* (New York: Bloomsbury, 2009), 211.

69 Another favorite monster in superhero comics would be Man-Thing, but this swamp monster appeared in one of the earliest Marvel magazines: *Savage Tales* (debuting in 1971 and devoted mostly to pulp-fiction inspired fantasy stories with characters like Conan and Kull).

70 The regularly changing roster of creators with various Marvel (and DC) titles is important to mention because serial stories were often wobbly and destroyed the "open wound" potential of continuing horror stories. (This makes the comic series comparable to, though not as problematic as, the many horror movie sequels from Universal and Hammer Studios.) The comics industry factory model was still in place at this point and *Dracula* suffered less in narrative terms than other titles. For more on the complexities of serial storytelling with intertextual connections, see Shane Denson's "Marvel Comics' *Frankenstein:* A Case Study in the Media of Serial Figures."

71 Mike Benton, *Horror Comics: The Illustrated History*, 72.

72 Even with superheroes and fantasy heroes as part of the framework in place at Marvel, the zombie star of *Tales of the Zombie* became one of the strangest of their sympathetic monsters. The hero is not the lumbering flesh-eater of Romero's *Night of the Living Dead* as evidenced by his muscle-bound depiction (alongside a scantily clad damsel to save) on the second issue's cover painting by Boris Vallejo.

73 Other Marvel magazine publications should be mentioned such as *Savage Tales*: a showcase for sword and sorcery stories preceding the horror magazines by more than a year. Another was *Crazy*, linked to horror magazines as Marvel's attempt to imitate another controversial publication associated with EC: *Mad*.

74 Marvel also published horror anthology series in conventional comic book formats with titles that associated them with classic EC titles: *Crypt of Evil*, *Vault of Evil*, and *Dead of Night*. These served as testing grounds for horror and other genres such as science fiction but none made much of an impact, lasting less than two years.

75 Roy Thomas, "Ghosties and Ghoulies and Things That Go Bump in the Brain...," *Monsters Unleashed* 1, Marvel (March 1973), 16.

76 Randy Duncan and Matthew J. Smith, *The Power of Comics: History, Form, and Culture*, 47.

77 Bradford Wright, *Comic Book Nation: The Transformation of Youth Culture in America* (Baltimore: Johns Hopkins UP, 2001), 235–37.

78 Richard J. Arndt, *Horror Comics in Black and White: A History and Catalogue, 1964–2004*, 7. For the sake of brevity, Arndt romanticizes Warren's approach a bit as James Warren chased different profit trends with different publications. However, several factors in decision making prevented the growth of Warren publications.

79 Randy Duncan and Matthew J. Smith, *The Power of Comics: History, Form, and Culture*, 61–62.

80 The runs of these Marvel magazines lasted only two years, but the decisive shift in the market was made; in addition, Warren and Skywald magazines folded for a variety of reasons including weaker content and the move of horror back to traditional comics. Spinner racks in drug stores became the new source for comic books and the comic horror magazines didn't fit, moving out of sight of the comics consumer (Richard J. Arndt, *Horror Comics in Black and White: A History and Catalogue, 1964–2004*, 9).

81 Len Wein, Bernie Wrightson, Tatjana Wood, and Ben Oda, "Swamp Thing." *House of Secrets* No. 92, DC (June–July 1971), 8.

82 Charlton horror also published several horror titles in the 1970s such as *Ghostly Haunts*, *Midnight Tales*, and *The Occult Files of Dr. Spektor*. Yet while they represent the return of horror in the classic comic book format, their long-term impact is minor.

83 The advent of *Creepy* and *Eerie* coincided with the advent of the Comix movement and preceded other adult-oriented comics such as Will Eisner's *Contract with God* and European-influenced comics magazines like *Heavy Metal.*

84 Mike Benton, *Horror Comics: The Illustrated History*, 75.

85 "In determining who has exorcised the ghost of Fredric Wertham from the house of popular culture research…" (Bart Beatty, *Fredric Wertham and the Critique of Mass Culture*, 4). *Critical Study of Black and White Publications of the 1950s, 1960s, and 1970s, 93.*

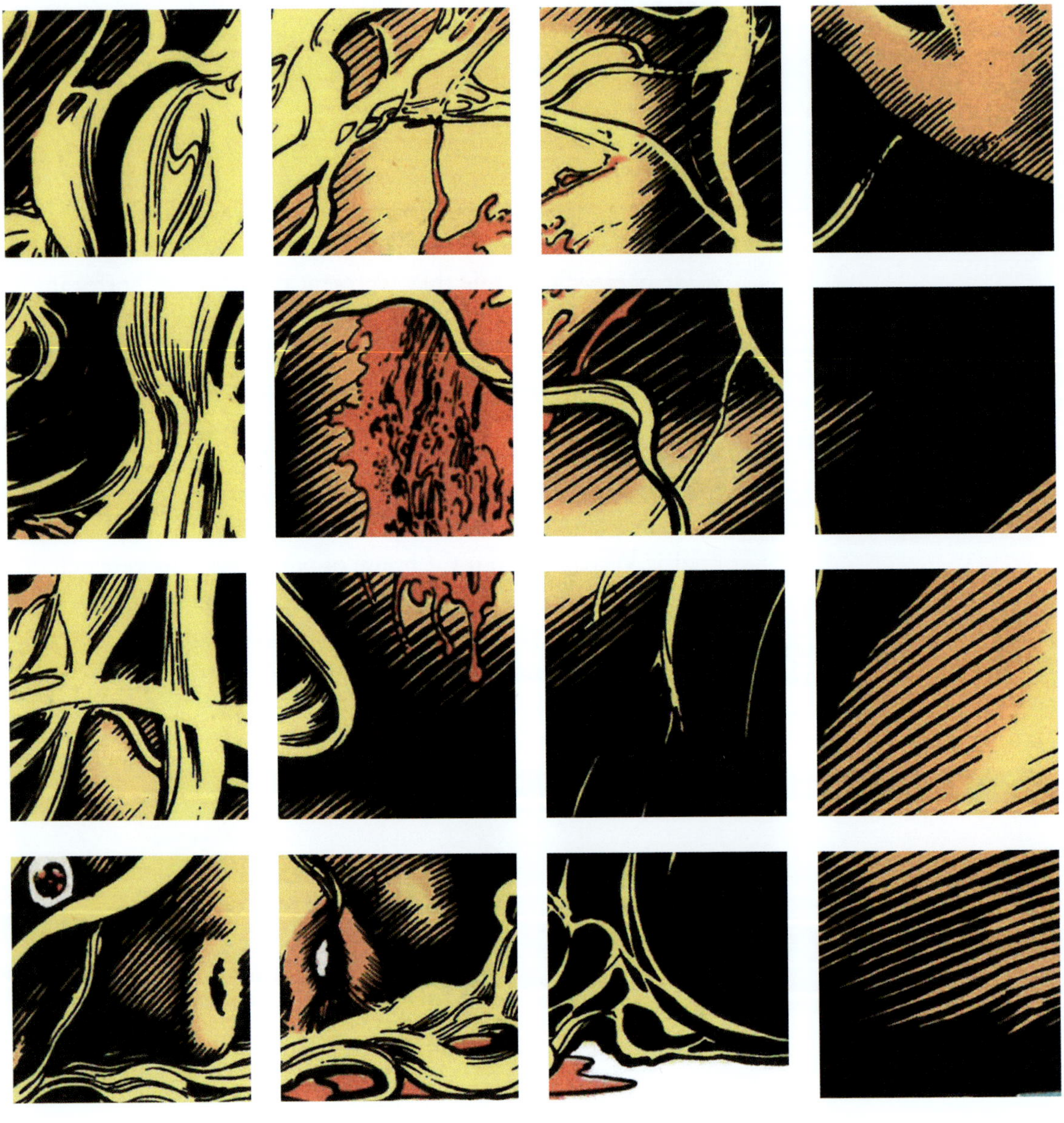

CHAPTER 3

A Monster More or Less Like Me: *Swamp Thing, From Hell,* and the Philosophy of Horror

Truth is a well-known pathological liar. It invariably turns out to be Fiction wearing a fancy frock. Self-proclaimed Fiction, on the other hand, is entirely honest. You can tell this, because it comes right out and says, "I'm a Liar," right there on the dust jacket.
Alan Moore[1]

The Big, Bad Comics Scare—So Big and Bad That It Jumps Over the Big (and Bad) Pond

Under the stress of mounting opposition and the effects of sleep-robbing diet pills, Bill Gaines composed a statement to be presented before the Congressional Committee on Juvenile Delinquency.[2] That statement ranged widely in content from the critical and political power of comic books as art to the harmless and meaningless pleasure of comic books as entertainment. While Gaines intended it as a defense of the industry, his statement (and subsequent responses to questions) worked better to capture comic books at a crossroads. Profiled in the remaining chapters, contemporary horror comics creators have found their motivation, approach, and justification at different points on those crossroads. Therefore, different quotations from Gaines's testimony will be used to represent each of these creators, their co-creators, and their works. In this chapter, that will be Alan Moore, Stephen Bissette, Rick Veitch, John Totleben, and Eddie Campbell, with particular reference to *Saga of the Swamp Thing* and *From Hell.*

In his testimony, Gaines stated, "[The comics industry] has stirred [readers'] imaginations, given them an outlet for their problems and frustrations, but most important, given them hours of entertainment.... We use the best writers, the finest artists, we spare nothing to make each magazine, each story, each page, a work of art."[3] This statement identifies the power of comic books to reach a vast number of readers in a meaningful and entertaining way as artworks. These basic ideas would be shared by Alan Moore, an English writer who became a giant in the American comic book industry and a fundamental part of the contemporary resurgence of horror comics. Moore argues, "[The comic book] is art, but it's not gallery art. It's cheaply available to a large number of people....

To me, mass production of the Mona Lisa is a bigger phenomenon than the original."[4] Moore sees comics not only as a mass medium but also as an art form that works by new rules, having the power to supersede high art in certain important ways.

This eventually powerful advocate for comic books came from England to America, and his status as a cultural outsider made him uniquely suited to revolutionize the comics industry. However, Moore (and England) was no stranger to American comic books and the controversies associated with them. In *A Haunt of Fears*, Martin Barker describes a situation in England parallel to the comics scare in the United States that even more directly targeted horror comics. In 1950s England, crusading pamphleteers argued against the influence of horror comics from America, only tangentially including crime comics and often referring to them just as American comics, as if America and horror were synonymous.

The anti-comics crusaders won unlikely allies in the British Communist party, who saw comics as part of the capitalist influence of the imperialist power of the United States. It is ironic that they seemed to miss that England also functioned as an imperialist power and that many horror comics, especially EC, railed against traditional American values. Regardless, American horror comics were removed from the stands in a much more direct way– not through industry self-regulation but through Parliament passing the Children and Young Persons (Harmful Publications) Act in 1955.[5]

In 1953, Alan Moore was born into a nation reacting to comics in this way, and as a comic book reader, he would read different imports–Marvel superhero comics. However, he would soon discover Eisner's artful *Spirit* and Kutzman's rebellious *Mad*,[6] embrace leftist politics, and produce his own Comix-like work. Eventually considered a political radical, Moore would offer a critique of both capitalism and communism in his work and words: "To me, politics does not divide into right-wing and left-wing, in that capitalism and communism are both just two different ways of ordering industrial societies, which have not been around for a vast amount of time and probably won't be around for a lot longer."[7] For a variety of reasons, Moore was brought over in the 1980s to work on mainstream American comic books in what was, ironically, a fairly conservative time in the comics industry and became "one of the most iconoclastic, rebellious, and freethinking figures in the medium."[8]

A Comics Creator So Creative That He Writes His Way Across the Big Pond

In the horror industry, things had been changing for some time with horror not only as a mass media production but also as an art form with the power to supersede high art in certain important ways. Although tentatively accepted by some American critics at the time of its release, Robert Wiene's *Cabinet of Dr. Caligari* was famously protested in America in 1921 and was only understood as expressionist art after a critics' poll from the Brussels World's Fair in 1958. Initially kept from release in 1932, Tod Browning's *Freaks* became an underground hit and part of a MOMA exhibit in the 1960s,[9] representing in part the counter-culture's appropriation of the term "freak." *Rosemary's Baby*, by the iconoclastic director Roman Polanski, and *The Exorcist*, by highly honored director William Friedkin, received widespread critical praise. And with the 1972 release of the English-made *Tales from the Crypt* starring Peter Cushing, the EC fan following suddenly became larger, creating a collector's market for EC horror comics.

While these examples indicate a new appreciation of horror and mass media, the popular appreciation of horror made it more of a commodity subject to conservative industry politics (effectively represented by simultaneously transgressive and conservative slasher films such as *Friday the 13th*). In this era when horror was art to some and commodity to others, Alan Moore would rise as a comics creator in England to a level that attracted the attention of DC Comics. Alan Moore continued to be politically engaged in the 1980s and was dismayed by neo-conservatism in the parallel movements of Margaret Thatcher in England and Ronald Reagan in the U.S.[10] In a time when the Cold War cooled, both leaders openly advocated the ideas of national power with a seemingly romantic attachment to 1950s Cold War conflict.

Working freelance in England, Moore wrote for *2000 AD*, *Warrior*, and *Marvel UK*: both one-offs and scripts for continuing series. In reference to Alan Moore's work with *2000 AD* publications (starting with *Future Shocks*), popular culture critic Lance Parkin argues that *Future Shocks* owed its mood and twist endings to the influence of EC and that "Alan mastered the form."[11] The most well-known of his continuing series would be *Marvelman* and *V for Vendetta*, in part because both were started with a failing British publisher and finished with American publishers. Both series took critical aim at the ideals of the power fantasy that undergirded the superhero comics as well as the politics of the Thatcher and Reagan administrations. His thoughtful, prolific, and well-received work attracted the notice of DC Comics, searching for ways to make more appealing comic series with mediocre sales.

Even though it connected with an older, potentially more reliable readership, the 1970s move to horror, as well as fantasy and science fiction, didn't radically increase sales. Bradford Wright states, "Engaging, thoughtful, and highly literate series like Marvel's *Tomb of Dracula* and DC's *Swamp Thing* found a devoted audience of older readers but failed to reach the kind of general market needed to make them profitable."[12] As a consequence, DC and Marvel fell back on the reliable if lackluster market cornered by their superhero stories but did keep many horror characters as part of the shared superhero universes. In a 1980s environment again dominated by superheroes, DC revived its formerly cancelled *Swamp Thing* as *Saga of the Swamp Thing* in 1982 and Moore was asked to write the series.

At that time, the series had been walking a line between the tropes of superhero and horror stories, and Moore seemed well suited for such an approach as Richard J. Arndt notes, "*Marvelman* and *V for Vendetta* had heavy horror overtones."[13] However, together with the campy Wes Craven *Swamp Thing* film in 1982 and the series' deep connections to the DC universe, *Saga of the Swamp Thing* was leaning toward superhero tropes and read more like an adventure series. With its weak sales in mind, Len Wein, the creator of *Swamp Thing*, was open to Moore's plan for a radical reinvention of the character that would take the series back to its horror roots.

Although still operating with the big business precedent of work-for-hire agreements ensuring that DC owned all creative work, DC attracted the anti-authoritarian Moore not only with a decent flat rate but also with the new precedent of royalties for creators. In addition, creators were allowed more creative control with B-list characters like Swamp Thing not tied to DC's major licensed characters. And so, beginning in 1984 in issue No. 20, Moore tied up the "Loose Ends" of the previous writer's run in several ways, most notably with Swamp Thing shot in the head—and dead—by the end of the issue. To avoid the convoluted wrap-up of No. 20, the usual starting point in collected editions of Moore's *Saga of the Swamp Thing* is the second issue of his run, "The Anatomy Lesson," illustrated by Stephen Bissette and John Totleben (soon joined in the run by Rick Veitch).[14] All three artists were graduates of the Joe Kubert School of Cartoon and Graphic Art[15] and were part of the growing professionalization associated with comic book creators in the 1970s and 1980s.

All (and Stephen Bissette in particular) were horror fans and anxious to fundamentally revisit to the horror of isolation central to Len Wein's vision of the "muck-encrusted monster"; this led to the effective pairing of Moore's narrative reconceptualization with Bissette and Totleben's visual reconceptualization of the Swamp Thing. In his initial presentation in *House of Secrets* No. 92 (1971), Swamp Thing's body creates for him a pathetic space between self-consciousness and unspeakable horror. However, when the lumpy half-man was re-envisioned for a regular series, the "muck-encrusted monster" would have a muscular physique similar to the body types of 1970s superheroes—something that fit a story arc less uncanny than its point of inspiration in *House of Secrets*. Alec Holland was victim of an accident that transformed him into the super-strong Swamp Thing. Even though he searched for a cure that he could never find, his new abilities allowed him to fight evil.

In "The Anatomy Lesson," rather than being Alec Holland trapped in a swampy body, Swamp Thing was revealed as a sentient piece of the swamp that mistakenly thought itself to be Holland. Bissette and Totleben not only made Swamp Thing's body humanoid but also incorporated within it characteristics drawn from the vegetative world of the swamp. The resultant story arc dealt with this "swamp god" exploring horror themes of abjection that not only undermined the typical superhero story but also made the uncanny a regular part of the series. Alan Moore describes his philosophy of horror as "sadistic": trying not to hit the same spot on the psyche because scar tissue will develop[16] (the converse too often the case with horror series and sequels). In the case of this story, Swamp Thing becomes less human and therefore more monstrous as a threat to his enemies but also as a being that defies the reader's well-accepted notions of humanity and consciousness.

No Longer a Black-and-White World But Rather a Green World Red with Blood

In "The Anatomy Lesson," Dr. Jason Woodrue reflects on an incident only to be revealed later in the course of the narrative. Three panels on the far left of the page reveal the setting (Washington, DC) seen from an apartment, and the panels are cut diagonally on their right side and set atop panels that reveal Woodrue's reflection in the window. In the three panels on the far right, Woodrue narrates the experience of a man pressing himself up against a rain-smeared glass that grows increasingly bloody in each panel: "He'll be pounding on the glass right about now...or maybe not now. Maybe in a while. But he'll be pounding, and...and will there be blood? I like to imagine so. Yes, I rather think there will be blood. Lots of blood.

Blood in extraordinary quantities."[17] In a grisly scene that recalls some of the demises in EC Comics, the most potent aspect is that the scene doesn't definitely exist in the real world of the narrative but somewhere between the real world and Woodrue's bloody imagination.

With this character, tone, and ambiguous space created for the story, "The Anatomy Lesson" then backtracks and describes Woodrue's research: an autopsy of Swamp Thing. Initiated by General Sutherland, the "old man" depicted at the beginning, the military man wants to know more about the creature. Woodrue, someone uniquely motivated as the Floronic Man, a plant-based DC supervillain, discovers that Alec Holland didn't survive the explosion of his sabotaged experiment; instead, the plants of the swamp absorbed not only his body but also his memories and consciousness. Working without a human conception of death, the swamp builds a sentient humanoid body that "thinks" it is Alec Holland.

Fig. 3.1
The Saga of the Swamp Thing No. 21, DC Comics, 1984, © DC Comics
A new era of horror comics is inaugurated with a complex and nuanced layout that presents the reader with the bloody speculations of Jason Woodrue.

When he hears Woodrue's initial findings, Sutherland unceremoniously fires him, something Woodrue takes very poorly. Locking the building with only Sutherland inside, Woodrue turns off the refrigeration unit that contained Swamp Thing. Subsequently, Woodrue continues his explanation of Swamp Thing from where the general cut him off. As green tendrils begin to grow from Swamp Thing's grey body, he narrates, "I'd have been able to explain that you can't kill a vegetable by shooting it through the head."[18] And Woodrue later speculates, "Perhaps he'll reach the basement in time to actually see it. Or perhaps not. And if the body is already gone...what will he do then, I wonder?"[19] Thereupon, Sutherland finds an empty refrigeration tank and runs from the scene, a depiction not described by Woodrue (suggesting this to be the "real" version of the story).

When Swamp Thing encounters Sutherland, the general asks him if he's intelligent and then asks if he's read the file describing his condition. In a form more wildly plantlike than before and with his words represented in an orange-brown and only roughly circular speech balloon, Swamp Thing confirms, "Yes... I... have read the file."[20] Although intelligent and capable of speech, Swamp Thing is clearly less human than before and his awareness of this fact makes him dangerous and quite frightening to Sutherland.

As the general flees Swamp Thing, the traditional grid layout of the panels on the page degenerates with more panels designed with unusual angles, laid sometimes atop and sometimes under other panels. This disruption in the typical linear progression of the visual reading experience makes the reader part of the terror that grips Sutherland with Swamp Thing as the unhurried monster that feeds that terror.

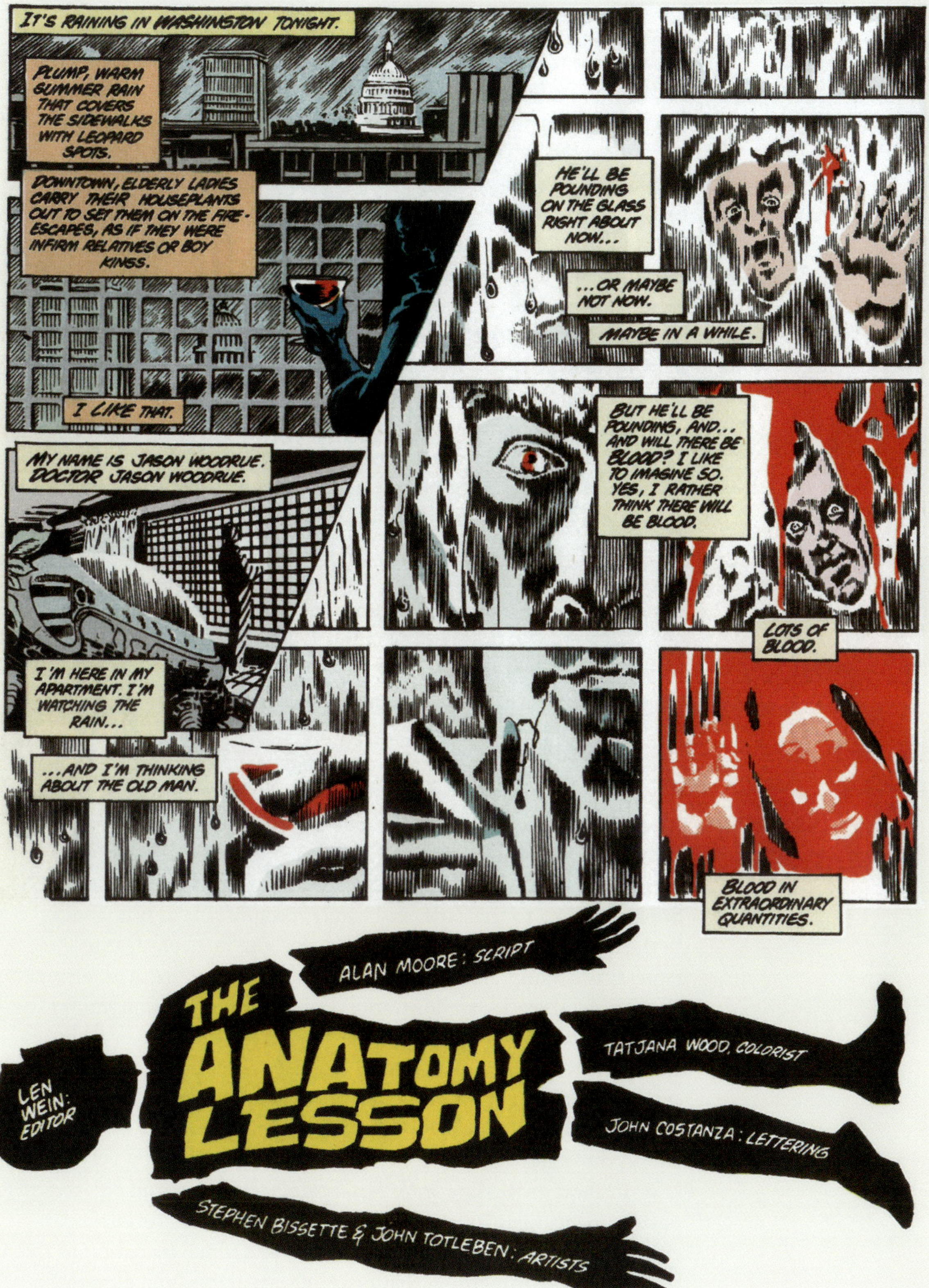

IT'S RAINING IN WASHINGTON TONIGHT.
PLUMP, WARM SUMMER RAIN THAT COVERS THE SIDEWALKS WITH LEOPARD SPOTS.
DOWNTOWN, ELDERLY LADIES CARRY THEIR HOUSEPLANTS OUT TO SET THEM ON THE FIRE-ESCAPES, AS IF THEY WERE INFIRM RELATIVES OR BOY KINGS.
I LIKE THAT.
MY NAME IS JASON WOODRUE. DOCTOR JASON WOODRUE.
I'M HERE IN MY APARTMENT. I'M WATCHING THE RAIN...
...AND I'M THINKING ABOUT THE OLD MAN.
HE'LL BE POUNDING ON THE GLASS RIGHT ABOUT NOW...
...OR MAYBE NOT NOW.
MAYBE IN A WHILE.
BUT HE'LL BE POUNDING, AND... AND WILL THERE BE BLOOD? I LIKE TO IMAGINE SO. YES, I RATHER THINK THERE WILL BE BLOOD.
LOTS OF BLOOD.
BLOOD IN EXTRAORDINARY QUANTITIES.
ALAN MOORE: SCRIPT
THE ANATOMY LESSON
LEN WEIN: EDITOR
TATJANA WOOD, COLORIST
JOHN COSTANZA: LETTERING
STEPHEN BISSETTE & JOHN TOTLEBEN: ARTISTS

When Sutherland reaches the window portrayed on the first page of the story, Swamp Thing smothers the general in the overgrown foliage of his chest (and it is clear the blood was in Woodrue's mind). Despite Swamp Thing's traditional role as hero in the series, this story is similar to one often seen in 1950s horror comics in which reanimated corpses take their revenge. While the extreme violence of vigilante heroes is almost always portrayed as acceptable, the reader not only experiences Sutherland's fear but also sees Swamp Thing operating without the humanity that had so long been part of his identity. In various ways (through narrative voice, panel structure, and previous story arcs), the reader is encouraged to identify respectively with Woodrue, Sutherland, and Swamp Thing: all main characters and all monsters in the story.

The radical twist Moore provides to the Swamp Thing story works in a way similar to EC's trademark twist by subverting expectations, but it takes place long before the last few panels and works with greater nuance. As Rick Veitch describes, "Alan Moore created one of the great, mainstream, comic scripting styles—and it's kind of simple. It's not that tricky. Mostly, it's based on irony. Almost every scene will end on an ironic note, although the irony is often seen from a different direction."[21] That irony relates not only what has come before but also what comes after in a serial narrative that encourages an identification with a plant that threatens basic ideas of the human self.

Swamp Thing subsequently begins to free himself of the personality of Alec Holland, and the shock of the friends who discover him results from their inability to discern his body from its surroundings. In "Swamped," the reader shares their difficulty as the form of Swamp Thing fills a splash page: a mass of vegetation firmly attached to the earth and barely recognizable as humanoid. In the next issue, "Another Green World," the first splash page represents Swamp Thing floating in a green space filled with elements of the natural world: an illustration lacking a separate foreground and background and not working in the Cartesian space of realistic art. Furthering this effect on both of these splash pages, the extradiegetic material of the story titles have typographic designs that resemble the swampy surroundings, and they nearly disappear within those surroundings.

In short order, *Saga of the Swamp Thing* articulates an eco-critical post-humanism via its narrative and illustration. This sets up an experience deeply threatening to identity as defined by reason in the Western world, something that discretely separates (and elevates) the figure from the ground. Meeker's *The Comedy of Survival* and Glotfelty's *The Ecocriticism Reader* reject the Cartesian claim that humankind has a superior place in the natural world.[22]

Refusing to recognize humanity's place within nature not only leads to practices that destroy the world essential to human survival. Refusing to recognize humanity's connection to the environment creates the illusion that human consciousness is a stable center separate from the currents of the natural world.

Moore's new direction for the series emphasizes Swamp Thing's body as something beyond the conventions of reasonable thought. Able to travel through the "green world" and reform his body at will, Swamp Thing shifts its priorities away from Alec Holland's quest for a cure and from a superhero's concern for civilization. Theorists as diverse as Jacques Lacan, Michel Foucault, and Judith Butler examine the post-human condition[23] and deconstruct identity with theoretical arguments similar to Alan Moore's aesthetic arguments. As Brian Johnson notes in "Libidinal Ecologies: Eroticism and Environmentalism in *Swamp Thing*," there is a "compatibility between deep ecology and deconstruction."[24] By asserting that traditionally defined human consciousness in the real world is a fiction, the post-human perspective causes profound anxiety for most[25]—an EC twist at a philosophical level.[26]

A Green Superhero Brings Darkness to the World of the Direct Market

Crossing impenetrable boundaries and violating sacred ideas is part of horror's methodology, something often physically represented by the mutilation and re-presentation of the body. In the horror films of the 1980s, this was done in some ways that served more conservative ends and in other ways that served radical ends conceptually similar to *Saga of the Swamp Thing*. In the former category were many of the slasher films of the Reagan era, like those in the *Friday the 13th* series, that used the slasher as a moral agent to punish those who acted as bullies or sluts. In many ways, this description of the slasher explains some of the fan devotion to horror movie serial killers like Jason Voorhees (*Friday the 13th*), Michael Myers (*Halloween*), and Freddy Krueger (*Nightmare on Elm Street*). However, other slasher films are in the latter category, like *Nightmare on Elm Street* with Freddy as an afterlife dream version of a child abuser murdering children of the parents who killed him. Seeming to be Wes Craven's commentary on his earlier exploitation revenge film *The Last House on the Left*, *Nightmare* demonstrates that fan identification with Jason is more complex and transgressive.

After John Carpenter solidified the slasher formula in *Halloween*, he made *The Thing*, a politically engaged horror film that would fail at the box office just weeks from the amazing success of Steven Spielberg's *ET* in 1982.[27]

While *ET* offered a mild criticism of a secretive government through a child's love for an ugly alien, *The Thing* radically revised its Red Scare source material and presented the horror of a culture living in fear. Based on *The Thing from Another World* (in which the monster is a highly evolved form of vegetable life), *The Thing* also uses motifs from *Invasion of the Body Snatchers*, in which pods replace humans.

After an isolated research station discovers an alien that can replicate humans, the team is systematically duplicated and eliminated; the two left at the end hold each other hostage in the freezing cold, not trusting one another because they might not be who they say they are. The means by which the film presents this bitter commentary on Cold War culture is an alien lifeform complete at the cellular level and capable of invading host bodies. Brilliant special effects present human bodies that become gaping jaws and dismembered heads that walk away like spiders. While offering no sympathy for the monster (or anyone else), this now well-regarded film is politically in line with Moore, depicting the fear of a consciousness in a shape unlike that of the human form: the essential starting point of Moore's *Swamp Thing*.

Due to the growing environmental awareness in the 1980s, the cultural impetus for a "green superhero" can be readily understood. In *Alan Moore: Comics as Performance, Fiction as Scalpel*, Annalisa Di Liddo describes Swamp Thing in this way, "After this transformation, the dreadful swamp-bred hybrid becomes a peculiar mystical creature that, thanks to its vegetable identity, can perceive the vital pulse of the earth and of the natural world. Swamp Thing is thus endowed with a proper 'pantheistic consciousness' that urges it to fight against the threats of growing industrialization and uncontrolled urban expansion."[28] And as comics scholar Maggie Gray states, this environmental focus places *Swamp Thing* directly in line with the Gothic tradition: "Swamp Thing serves to both elaborate the Gothic scale of the threat to environmental destruction and to conceptualize an ecological sensibility of alternative attitudes and values less founded in the technocratic domination of nature."[29]

With threats to the eco-system posed by various monstrous characters, this reorients the superheroic story but still positions Swamp Thing as a hero fighting against monsters outside the self. As Moore jokes, "I've probably done more comics about the horrors of nuclear power than I've done about the delights of windmills."[30] And so this semi-heroic vestige of the previous Swamp Thing persists; with "The Nukeface Papers," Moore enacts an EC-like political commentary with a destructive radioactive waste-swilling antagonist who is a by-product of factory culture.

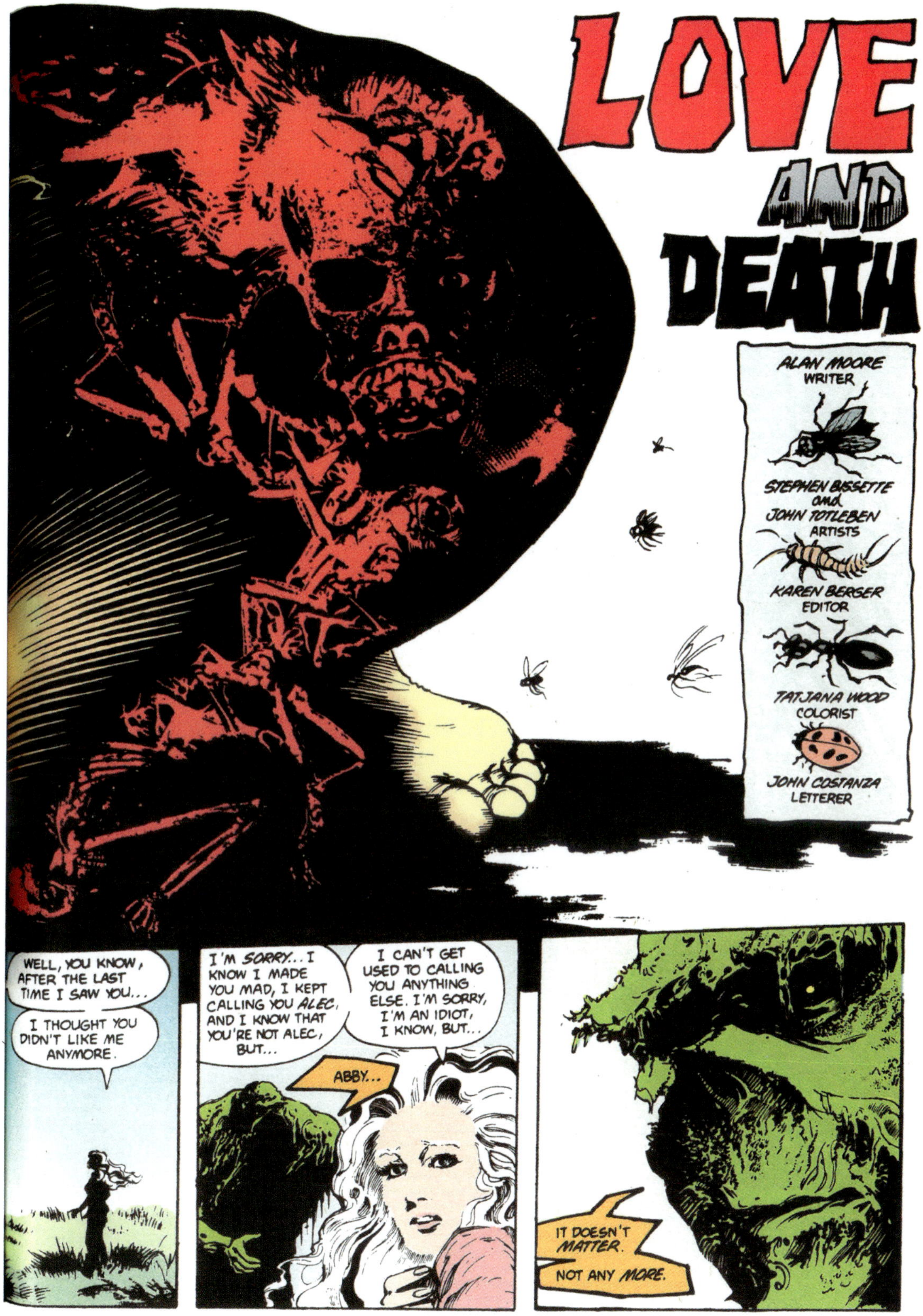
LOVE AND DEATH
ALAN MOORE
WRITER
STEPHEN BISSETTE
and
JOHN TOTLEBEN
ARTISTS
KAREN BERGER
EDITOR
TATJANA WOOD
COLORIST
JOHN COSTANZA
LETTERER
WELL, YOU KNOW, AFTER THE LAST TIME I SAW YOU...
I THOUGHT YOU DIDN'T LIKE ME ANYMORE.
I'M SORRY... I KNOW I MADE YOU MAD, I KEPT CALLING YOU ALEC, AND I KNOW THAT YOU'RE NOT ALEC, BUT...
I CAN'T GET USED TO CALLING YOU ANYTHING ELSE. I'M SORRY, I'M AN IDIOT, I KNOW, BUT...
ABBY...
IT DOESN'T MATTER.
NOT ANY MORE.

The following issue, "A Halo of Flies" (No. 30), depicts abject content less sexual but more violent with Arcane leading a group of horribly disfigured undead. When both issues were submitted to the Comics Code Authority for approval, No. 29 was not approved but No. 30 was approved despite the large number of walking dead in it. (After the Code's 1971 revision, they were the only monsters still thought to be prohibited without a history in "classic" literature.) Due to rising sales of *Saga of the Swamp Thing*, DC published No. 29 without Code approval, relying on older readers who frequented the direct market comics stories rather than newsstands or drug stores.

This decision needs to be emphasized in three major ways. First, while *Swamp Thing* was an intellectually challenging comic book, No. 29 had no clear moral justification like the anti-drug story in *The Amazing Spider-Man* No. 96 to 98. Second, with DC's corporate conservatism in mind, DC's choice demonstrated the insignificance of Code approval to their sales. Third, this decision led to running without Code approval from issue No. 31 forward, with DC marketing to the committed comic book store buyer rather than the casual newsstand or drug store buyer.[34] This dramatic marketplace shift would lead DC (as well as Marvel and many new independent publishers) to rethink comics as kids' stuff–something only challenged previously outside the mainstream by the Comix movement, Will Eisner's *Contract with God*, and Dave Sim's *Cerebus*.

With a horror title, DC caught up with trends that identified readers who would not grow up and out of their comic book reading habit. With issue No. 31, *Saga of the Swamp Thing* simply became *Swamp Thing* and ran the subtitle "Sophisticated Suspense" in place of the Comics Code approval. This transition emboldened Moore, Bissette, Veitch, and Totleben to increase the intellectual rigor and taboo-breaking of a title known for such things. Exploring the implications of "The Anatomy Lesson," the shift in Swamp Thing's character became an increasingly important locus of the uncanny.[35] Swamp Thing worked as a disembodied consciousness: traveling through the earth, controlling plant life separate from his body, and reforming his body at will (leaving husks of past bodies in his wake). While Cartesian thought identifies the mind as superior to the body, the Western world connects one mind with one body and Swamp Thing's existence independent of one body is a new kind of horror.

When the Swamp Thing is identified as a threat by overgrown civilization, Lex Luthor colludes with the government to permanently separate Swamp Thing from the earth. As a consequence, his disembodied consciousness floats through the universe and only occasionally reforms in the bizarre environments of alien planets.

Without the ability to control his presence in the so-called real world, Swamp Thing lives out the ultimate horror associated with a paradigm challenge mounted by eco-criticism; Swamp Thing has no true individuality in the real world but is subject in all ways to his physical environment.

Dreams and Visions: Intertextual Ex-Hosts and Sexual Vegetables

By revisiting DC horror history, No. 33 further explores Swamp Thing's nature (a loaded term) and questions the integrity of the individual by questioning the integrity of the story. The reader learns that the original "Swamp Thing" story in *House of Secrets* actually took place in the past, and the current Swamp Thing lives as part of a recurring phenomenon governed by the "Green" order. Easy to misread as a simple reconciliation of conflicting stories (often done to simplify overlong superhero histories), the story engages with horror comics history in a pointed, intertextual way.

The cover is a variation of *House of Secrets* No. 92, with a lumpy Swamp Thing again in the background but with the original story's Linda replaced by Abby in the foreground. The story begins with Abby in a dream where she encounters the horror hosts, Cain and Abel, from *House of Mystery* and *House of Secrets*. With layouts that defy conventions in which each panel is self-contained and separated by a gutter, each page is a full-page spread of different images in the narrative separated by a swirl of mists from the drawn landscape. In addition, other images in the narrative are placed atop or inset within the aforementioned images, frustrating a straightforward reading of her dream experience.

At a graphic level, it is unclear whether those panels are self-contained or part of a sequence, and so, they consequently exist as both. This ambiguity is tied to a conversation between Abby and Abel in which he states, "Some strange stories have intruded upon your life lately…." She understandably responds, "Stories? Everything that's happened to me has been real…." And host Abel (who is typically more timid than his brother, Cain) counters with "Oh please, it was just a figure of speech. Don't take offense…. You see, in a way, everything is made of stories."[36] Since the images on the page are also *figures* of speech, the visual and textual work together to reject certainty in terms of visual realism and comic book semiotics (creating a liminal space between the real and the imaginary like that described by Tzvetan Todorov).

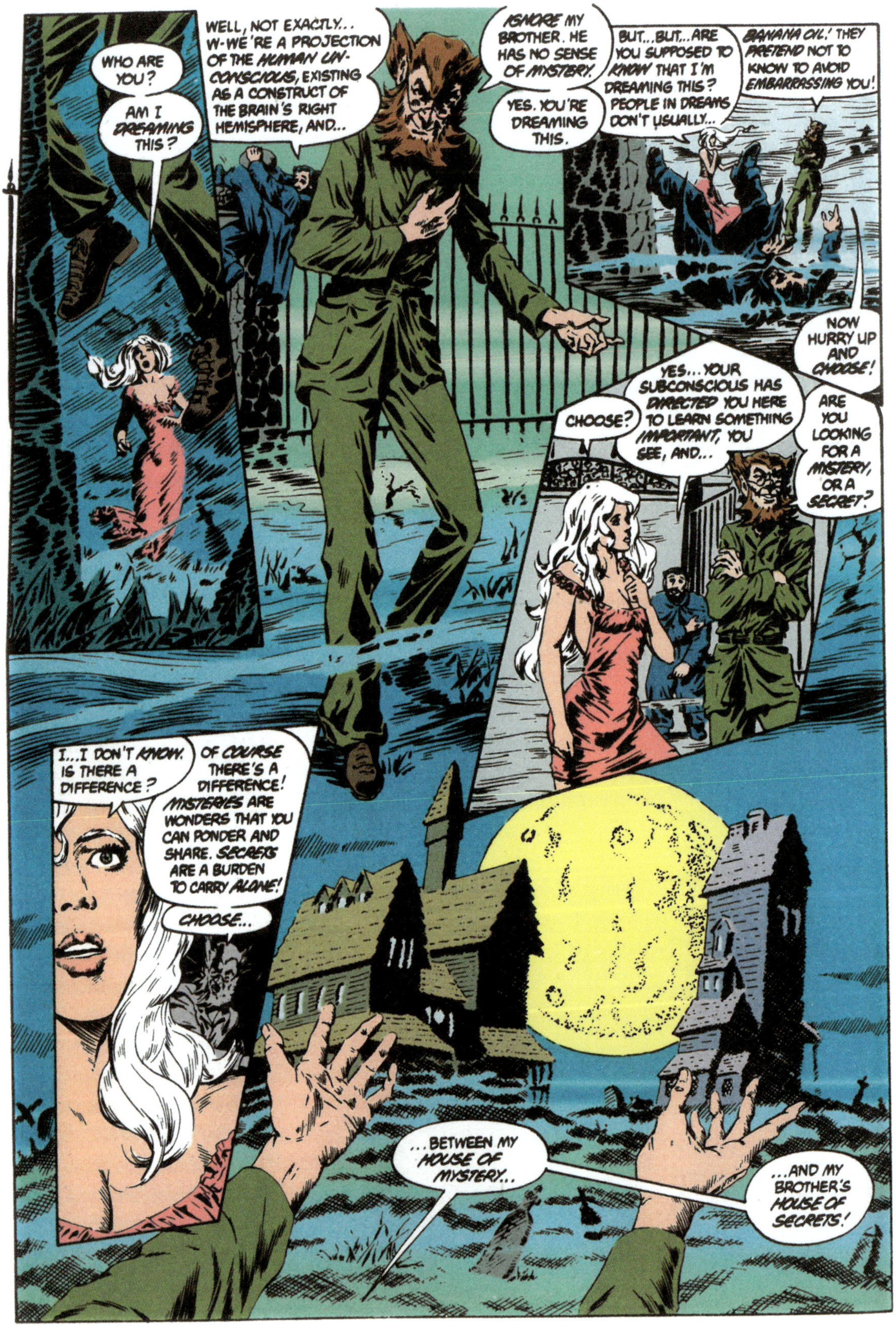
WHO ARE YOU?
AM I DREAMING THIS?
WELL, NOT EXACTLY... W-WE'RE A PROJECTION OF THE HUMAN UN-CONSCIOUS, EXISTING AS A CONSTRUCT OF THE BRAIN'S RIGHT HEMISPHERE, AND...
IGNORE MY BROTHER. HE HAS NO SENSE OF MYSTERY.
YES. YOU'RE DREAMING THIS.
BUT... BUT... ARE YOU SUPPOSED TO KNOW THAT I'M DREAMING THIS? PEOPLE IN DREAMS DON'T USUALLY...
BANANA OIL! THEY PRETEND NOT TO KNOW TO AVOID EMBARRASSING YOU!
NOW HURRY UP AND CHOOSE!
CHOOSE?
YES... YOUR SUBCONSCIOUS HAS DIRECTED YOU HERE TO LEARN SOMETHING IMPORTANT, YOU SEE, AND...
ARE YOU LOOKING FOR A MYSTERY, OR A SECRET?
I...I DON'T KNOW. IS THERE A DIFFERENCE?
OF COURSE THERE'S A DIFFERENCE! MYSTERIES ARE WONDERS THAT YOU CAN PONDER AND SHARE. SECRETS ARE A BURDEN TO CARRY ALONE!
CHOOSE...
...BETWEEN MY HOUSE OF MYSTERY...
...AND MY BROTHER'S HOUSE OF SECRETS!

Fig. 3.3 *The Saga of the Swamp Thing* No. 33, DC Comics, 1985, © DC Comics Reintroducing DC's horror hosts, "Abandoned Houses" re-presents Swamp Thing's history as a non-linear dream in which the reader participates.

Abel then presents the story from *House of Secrets* No. 92, reprinted exactly as the story originally appeared in 1971. Easy to mistake as a simple reprint (often done to help artists cope with the grind of a monthly schedule), the story-within-a-story serves an important function. The narrative style of Len Wein and artistic style of Bernie Wrightson clearly differ from the narrative style of Alan Moore and the artistic style of John Totleben. Ruining the reality effect of a consistent style, this side-by-side presentation again disrupts conventions and adds to the experience of unreality. Through the story, Abby supposedly learns a secret about Swamp Thing's nature, a point reinforced within the frame of her dream with Cain and Abel. Despite the horror host Destiny's claim in DC's *Weird Mystery* No. 3 that the Cain and Abel hosts are unrelated to their Biblical namesakes, Abby's dream ends with Cain's murder of Abel. Cain explains that his brother will be back and they'll do this again because, "It's all we have to do now that nobody wants to hear the stories anymore.... It's our punishment for doing it the first time." When Abby says it's not fair for Abel to be killed again and again for something Cain did, Cain replies, "Of course it's fair! I'm being punished for being the first predator... and he's being punished for being the first victim."[37]

This sequence clearly connects the horror hosts to Biblical counterparts and defies a claim made in the 1970s to avoid controversy. Horror continues to live beneath the surface despite attempts to contain it; in this case, the boundaries between stories disappear and controversy is invited. Furthermore, in this dream, the reassuring notion of Cain's guilt determined by his choice to commit violence is undermined because violence is an unavoidable (and unending) consequence of the brother's relationship. As Abby wakes and attempts to write down her "secret," she is interrupted and forgets ideas without corollaries in a world shaped by traditional notions of reality. As a result, the horror story secret remains only with the reader, whose subsequent reading of *Swamp Thing* will be affected by something not "real" in Swamp Thing's world.

"Rite of Spring" (the next issue) then challenges the reader to confront dominant order constructions of the real more directly via a threat to the real posed by Swamp Thing's abject body. In an earlier issue, the Floronic Man consumed a tuber growing on Swamp Thing's body, and his villainous history allowed the act to be understood as forbidden, disgusting, and perhaps even evil. However, Abby grew to love Swamp Thing and their sexual union would be consummated through her consumption of a tuber growing on Swamp Thing's body.[38]

Of course, the reader no longer has the luxury of regarding eating Swamp Thing's body in just one way. In addition to embracing the strangeness of a relationship between a human and a sentient plant, comics scholar Eric Berlatsky argues this story represents "Moore's abiding interest in gender, feminism, and 'queer' sexualities…."[39]

Spending less time separate from the earth, Swamp Thing's plant form is increasingly less human and more grotesque in the classical sense of the grotesque–simultaneously an object of fascination and repulsion. Swamp Thing's body becomes less readily available as a site of identification for readers and most characters with the exception of Abby and a few others. Abby's sexual union with Swamp Thing begins with a kiss and a claim that evokes a Romantic poet's portrayal of nature. Abby claims, "It's like lime… but not as sharp"[40] (and she likes lime).

But as a whole, the series had begun to rely less on typical plot movement and "The Rite of Spring" is an issue devoted solely to the psychological union of Swamp Thing and Abby during their first sexual encounter. The Swamp Thing slows her excitement in order to grow a tuber on his body and give it to Abby to consume. This leads to a psychedelic reaction and an out of body sexual communion: an encounter described by some post-humanist thinkers as the abandonment of "meat puppets."[41] In *Pornography and Silence*, Susan Griffin identifies Cartesian objectivity as the basis for pornography because it fetishizes the body,[42] but even if this story is the opposite of pornography, the strangeness of this boundary-erasing experience is accentuated.

In reference to this consumption of the tuber, Moore commented on it in specific reference to Code expectations: "I'm getting a whole motif of eating going on in *Swamp Thing*. I think it can be very disturbing. It's difficult to really frighten people [but this is not a Comics Code problem]…. They don't like a lot of sex and violence. But if you don't fixate on sex and violence, that leaves you with a lot of room to do things."[43] Along those lines, Abby's experience with Swamp Thing works in terms not directly connected to drugs (another area prohibited by the Code) but should be readily recognized as something like a drug experience.

Even if the reader moves past civilization's taboo against consuming another's body, Moore doesn't counterbalance the reader's potential unease by making nature beautiful in conventional terms. Abby finds wonder in unexpected places within the Swamp Thing's body as suggested by this interchange. Abby states, "And these little stars… these little jewels of light that drift about inside you… I don't have any of those." And Swamp Thing explains, "No. Those…are… insects."[44]

The visual component of Abby's post-human reverie is revealed to be bugs in the body, a standard horror trope usually used to create revulsion. Furthermore, Abby continues the reverie with, "There is no contradiction... only the pulse... the pulse within the world" in order to incorporate the visual presentation of a rat with bloody maws tearing apart another rat.[45]

Swamp Thing's body subsequently evolves as an object of fascination in part due to its disgusting and therefore horrific nature. Several issues later, when a sick bird dies in Swamp Thing's hands, he shoves its body into his own describing the process for Abby with a dispassionate analysis: "Death... shall nourish life... and nothing... shall be wasted. Is this... incomprehensible... to you?"[46] His question indicates a primal reaction that takes place at least at an unconscious level in the woman who has become his lover. And several issues later, Swamp Thing visits Abby at her home by traveling through the sewer and growing a new form as he emerges from her toilet. It is interesting to note that the initial expression on *his* face seems to be one of embarrassment, and not surprisingly, their subsequent encounter does not go well.

Abby's sexual experience with Swamp Thing has clearly not pushed her completely beyond the boundaries established by humanism (very notably, continuing to call Swamp Thing "Alec" and to think of Swamp Thing as male).[47] Swamp Thing's body evokes the "powers of horror" described by Julia Kristeva, but encounters with the abject do not readily lead to an embrace of that which is disgusting–the recognition of the essential breakdown between the subject and the object.

Monsters in a Factory Culture: The Dark Knight Goes Green

In narrative and visual terms, Moore, Bissette, Veitch, and Totleben continue to explore this uneasy tension between the green world of Swamp Thing and the ever-encroaching world of civilization at odds with him. In particular, civilization reacts to Abby's sex life in an arc that forcibly reinserts Swamp Thing into the DC superhero universe and makes Swamp Thing less of a superhero and a superhero more of a monster. Accused of "crimes against nature" (usually reserved for people who have sex with animals), Abby flees Louisiana but is rearrested in Gotham City in No. 51 "Home Free". When Swamp Thing emerges, he makes an angry move to the city and predictably, to confront the city's protector, Batman.

As forces marshal on all sides (mostly against the increasingly sympathetic Abby), she carries into a courtroom a rose given to her by the Gotham City Women's Action Group. When she drops it to the floor, Swamp Thing erupts from it in a splash page that multiplies the beauty of the flower with countless roses but also depicts the violent explosion of the wooden floor and showcases the notably deranged visage of Swamp Thing. At odds with the surroundings, he terrifies people in the courtroom and attacks those who threaten him with arms that grow from the floor, with a body that lacks all traditional integrity. Swamp Thing tells them to release Abby and threatens, "I have tolerated your species… for long enough…. If nature were to shrug…or raise an eyebrow…then you should all be gone."[48] With terms that anthropomorphize nature, Swamp Thing makes nature more threatening and assumes the role of villain or monster to Gotham City as he rescues Abby.

As the natural world overruns Gotham, Batman fights Swamp Thing with giant saws and defoliants, the tools of people who have devastated natural environments in the name of civilization.[49] Animating multiple humanoid versions of himself, Swamp Thing beats Batman into bloody submission and then appears in Commissioner Gordon's office as a giant Swamp-Thing head to declare, "Nowhere… is safe. No one… is safe."[50] As appearances of Swamp Thing become increasingly bizarre, his monstrous nature is juxtaposed with a portion of Gotham's citizens embracing Swamp Thing and this Gotham as a new Eden. With the Swamp Thing as the new monstrous entity that people both fear and desire, Batman acknowledges his defeat and argues with the mayor for Abby's release (referencing other monsters such as the Martian Manhunter, Hawkman, and Superman).

Through this profound and philosophical treatment of Swamp Thing, Alan Moore revolutionized horror in the comics industry in a time that was primed for this change. Horror would flourish in both the blockbuster and independent film markets in the 1980s (unlike other B-movie genres such as science fiction and fantasy, which became increasingly dependent on blockbuster budgets). Horror would similarly succeed with mainstream comics publishers like DC with its Vertigo imprint, and with Code-free independent publishers such as Pacific and Eclipse[51] with *Twisted Tales* and *Alien Encounters*.[52]

In addition, Alan Moore would revolutionize the comics industry in general. While artists attracted comic book collectors for more than a decade, Moore fully realized the fan followings for writers.[53] This worked well for DC, who published many of Moore's superhero and cultural commentaries such as *Watchmen*, *Batman: The Killing Joke*, and *V for Vendetta* (all stories with horror overtones).[54]

And DC changed policies for freelancers, establishing a royalty system in the mid-1980s, but comics creators were only beginning to realize a sense of artistic independence with Moore at the forefront of this realization.

When Dave Sim put out the "High Society" collection of *Cerebus*, he sold it through direct mail and not through Diamond distributors, which supplied comic book stores. In retaliation, Diamond refused to distribute *Puma Blues*, another Sim publication, thus demonstrating how a distributor for comic book stores, the new hope for adult comics, had the power to limit a creator's freedom. In response to this (and years of the comic book factory culture), Dave Sim, Scott McCloud, Stephen Bissette, Rick Veitch, and others would try to realize ideas pioneered by Neal Adams in the 1970s with a "creator's bill of rights" for comics professionals. In a way that anticipated this sentiment, Moore resented the control companies exerted over his work and ended his relationship with most British publishers in 1985 and with DC in 1987. Although DC ran *Swamp Thing* without Code approval in 1984, the company later wanted to impose a rating system on their comics, and this was Moore's breaking point.

Together with Frank Miller, Howard Chaykin, and Marv Wolfman, the writers officially protested: an incident that simultaneously demonstrated that some things stayed the same in the industry but others changed. For instance, Moore's voice as a creator was not only widely heard but also taken seriously. While the creators mounting the protest had notable fan followings, their serious company consideration is remarkable as Wolfman was the only one who was a full-time DC employee and should have had a formal say on corporate policies. These freelance creators associated with a new wave of horror and crime comics now had power that threatened the corporate conservatism,[55] and they moved their increasingly controversial work to the independent publishers.

An important tangential note is that Rick Veitch, sympathetic to the protest but not a formal participant, took over *Swamp Thing* not only as artist but also as writer when Moore left in 1987. In years to come, he would regret not leaving at the time "because Jenette's standards came back to haunt me a few years later"[56] (referring to Jenette Kahn, DC editor). Exploring many of the same themes in the *Swamp Thing* run he shared with Moore,[57] Veitch wrote a time travel story that pushed further Moore's space travel story (something initially proposed to Moore by Veitch). The most famous part of the arc was its climax "Morning of the Magician"– taking Swamp Thing back to the time of Jesus's crucifixion–because it was never published.

While initially approved by Jenette Kahn, DC was acquired by Warner Bros. and the protests of *The Last Temptation of Christ* were causing significant problems for another studio, Universal Pictures.[58] With artwork mostly completed by Michael Zulli, "Morning of the Magician" depicts Swamp Thing satiating Jesus's thirst with a plant that resembles Swamp Thing's face (his eyes portrayed as the bursting berries that produce the juice).[59] Subsequent to its acquisition by Warner Bros., DC made some conservative decisions influenced by a larger corporation tied to many media forms and cultural constituencies, and the story was rejected. Following in Moore's footsteps, Veitch not only produced a story with taboo material but also resigned when the story was rejected; he never finished it. In solidarity, his intended successors–Neil Gaiman and Jamie Delano–left with him.[60] This example shows that Moore had an indirect but profound influence on notions of comics as art with integrity, and comics professionals as creators who had rights and opportunities outside the big two superhero publishers.

Loving the Horror of It All: Taboo as a Publication and a Way of Life

Swamp Thing artist Stephen Bissette would identify horror as his first comics love and do his best to take advantage of opportunities created by Moore's success and direct market publishing. At the instigation of Dave Sim (later of little help due to his problems with Diamond), Bissette designed a black-and-white horror magazine anthology for the direct market to debut in 1988. With absolutely no consideration of the Code in regard to its content, *Taboo* was an expensive, perfect bound publication featuring well-known names in the new creator-driven comics field: Chester Brown, Neil Gaiman, Michael Zulli, Charles Burns, Charles Vess, and others.

As an anthology, *Taboo* harkened back to the horror comics of the 1950s and 1960s but also embraced the emerging "graphic novel" culture in form and content. Bissette states, "When we launched Taboo, we had a manifesto... it opened with a quote from David Cronenberg, which was, 'Horror is showing the unshowable and speaking the unspeakable.'... If it doesn't disturb you, please don't even send it. Don't waste my time." [61] Bissette rejected many prominent comics creators who pitched conventional horror stories with vampires, werewolves, and the like, wanting something more clearly suggested by the title. "Part of what defines the horror genre to me is exploring the deepest crevices of who and what we are... anything that goes to those extremes, once it crosses a certain parameter or boundary, becomes horrific by nature."[62]

While Bissette found talented creators who embraced this concept, much of comics culture was reluctant to support profoundly disturbing horror despite the popularity of related work in other mediums—such as work by Stephen King and Clive Barker and the films *Night of the Living Dead*, *The Texas Chainsaw Massacre*, and *Eraserhead.*[63] Printers often refused to print Taboo, comic book stores often refused to sell it, and Bissette lost money on the venture but it is the epitome of a cult phenomenon and a forerunner of things to come.

As Arndt describes it, "*Taboo* died not so much from low sales, although that may have been a factor, but from the combination of the shifting tumult of self-publishing, co-publishers' problems, [and] the distributors intrigues of the early 1990s... Not content to copy what had gone before, Taboo built on the foundations of dead, moldering magazines and raised its own horrible edifice."[64] At this crossroads in comics publishing, several of the serialized works in *Taboo* would go on to become works published on their own by the creators who owned them. Most notable was the work that Alan Moore and Eddie Campbell produced for *Taboo* (after Bissette rejected several of Moore's other scripts): *From Hell.*

While the demise of *Taboo* was frustrating for many, comics were nevertheless in a promising period of transition when content concerns were less relevant and power was shifting away from the industry and toward the creators. However, promising to some was threatening to others. In 1984, the article "Darkness in the Mall" in *Psychology Today* expressed concerns with adult content seen with work by creators including Howard Chaykin and Frank Miller (the specific titles mentioned being hybrids between science fiction and crime as well as superhero and crime). Failing to draw attention to its Fredric Wertham-type cause, little else was seen along these lines until 1989 when a higher profile piece was published in *The New York Times.*

In "Drawing on the Darkside," Joe Queenan, senior editor at *Forbes*, targeted many violent superhero comics but focused the majority of his criticism on Alan Moore's *Watchmen* and *V for Vendetta.* He offers a condescending overview of what he considers the falsely sophisticated veneer of Moore's work: "[A] boy who laughs when he finds out his mother committed suicide by drinking Drano [and] a child hacked to pieces and fed to German shepherds... is all in the service of a sophisticated literary technique called 'foreshadowing...'"[65] With tendencies like Wertham in *Seduction of the Innocent*, Queenan works from decontextualized pieces of evidence rather than holistic readings; focusing on a violent scene at the beginning of Neil Gaiman and Dave McKean's *Black Orchid*, he misses how the protagonist retreats from society to protect her daughter rather than exacting revenge on the villain.

Suggesting that comic books are "playing with the same fire that nearly destroyed it in the early 1950s," Queenan makes then-head of the Comics Code Authority and Archie president Michael Silberkleit, into the piece's hero, using his (slightly quizzical) words to close the piece, "If you fell to Earth from Mars and picked up a comic book, you would be very disillusioned."[66] Despite the growing recognition of Moore's name, it elicited no more reaction than *Psychology Today*'s article, indicating that culture was moving past the idea of comics as kids' stuff to be regulated. With comic books' move to the direct market for collectors who didn't pass along their purchases, they escaped widespread scorn. Instead, public protests and congressional initiatives put pressure on the music, television, and video game industries to develop rating systems.[67]

Moreover, classic horror comics would serve as inspiration not only for contemporary horror comics creators but also for other contemporary horror creators such as Stephen King and George Romero[68] with mass appeal and critical respectability. In the 1980s, Stephen King had ascended to popularity through early works like *Salem's Lot* and *Cujo* and moved to critical acclaim with works like *Thinner* and *Misery*; in addition, the books *Carrie*, *The Dead Zone*, and *The Shining* were box office hits as films artfully adapted by auteur directors Brian De Palma, David Cronenberg, and Stanley Kubrick respectively. George Romero was initially derided as master of the gross-out exploitation horror film with *Night of the Living Dead*, but it became one of the most profitable horror films of its time. In addition, a favorable critical shift of opinion took place within the first five years of its release; he was recognized as having created a monster movie for his time and with its sequel, *Dawn of the Dead*, was identified as an unconventional but important social critic.

Thanks to fanzines, comic book stores, and two British-made films in 1972 and 1973,[69] EC horror comics had moved from relative obscurity to fringe popularity. And in 1982, George Romero would direct *Creepshow*, based on Stephen King stories and specifically identified as an homage to EC horror comics. With a seal of approval from King and Romero, EC's *Tales from the Crypt* had the cachet that it needed to become a series on HBO, spearheaded by Hollywood producer Joel Silver. After moderate success with original programming, HBO wanted to take advantage of its position as a cable channel free of network restrictions with money to produce high-quality series. With *Tales from the Crypt*, HBO executive Bill Mesce argues HBO found what it wanted with a "morality play always ending with karmic justice dispensed in Grand Guignol bucket-o'-blood fashion... The hit-making pedigree of the men behind the series gave HBO something it hadn't had before: a free-flowing conduit to Hollywood's A-list. Crypt became Hollywood cool."[70]

In addition to the EC archive offering a seemingly endless source for quality horror stories, *Tales from the Crypt* also had the Crypt-Keeper (in the television series, a zombie-like figure controlled by four puppeteers). With the same personality as the comic book host, he again became a well-known icon, full of puns, black humor, and subversive potential as a breaker of the fourth wall. While the Hollywood association may imply a commodification and neutralization of EC horror, HBO was a new type of TV network and had a reason to remain R-rated controversial. As Mesce suggests, the forbidden and illicit pleasures of EC horror were mainstream cool (running from 1989 to 1996), no less disturbing but nevertheless embraced and acclaimed.[71]

The Monsters of Overgrown Civilization: From Whitechapel and From Hell

The governments of the United States and the United Kingdom took pride in their overgrown civilizations of the Western World as the Berlin Wall fell and the dissolution of the Soviet Union became imminent. George Bush and Margaret Thatcher evoked nostalgia for the Cold War pastimes of their respective histories, extolling the values of capitalism as a triumph over communism. At the same time, fascination grew not just for the fiction genre of horror but also true crime and stories of serial killers, setting the imminently respectable in the mainstream alongside the ultimate depravity at the fringes. True crime had lived long as a sub-genre but catapulted to prominence with Norman Mailer's *The Executioner's Song* in 1979 with many less literary and more sensational cases to follow.

Coverage of serial killers exponentially increased with profilers of murderers, past and present, like John Wayne Gacy, Charles Mason, and Jeffrey Dahmer. Crime reporter Thomas Harris produced best sellers with the fictional serial killer Hannibal Lecter, and FBI profiler John E. Douglas produced best sellers like *Mind Hunter* based on his cases. While various corners of English society harkened back to Victorian ideals, new books on Jack the Ripper would regularly appear, usually to great fanfare and public interest. After being critical of the contemporary United States in *Watchmen* and England in *V for Vendetta*, Moore would confront Victorian history and Jack the Ripper with fellow Englishman Eddie Campbell in *From Hell*. Even though something of a hybrid of true crime and horror, the first six parts running in *Taboo* and its horror elements fundamentally revised its true crime elements.

On a superficial level, it covers the same journalistic ground as true crime, based on extensive research and providing annotations. However, the factual basis associated with mystery and true crime is subverted to portray Victorian culture as the source of a post-industrial culture that, through its design, produces radical discontents.[72] Denying the satisfaction that accompanies revealing the murderer at the end, *From Hell* questions ways of knowing prescribed by Enlightenment culture.[73] Furthering themes established in *Swamp Thing*,[74] civilization, especially in the overgrown form inaugurated by the Industrial Revolution in England, produces monsters like Jack the Ripper.

After extensive research, Moore developed a plot based on a popular theory, not in order to identify the "truth" of a historical whodunit but in order to confront the fascination with the serial killer. Moore explains, "Ten years of wading through the material, the literature, not just Jack the Ripper but all of these fuckers. All these little apologies for human beings. They're not supermen. They're not supermen at all. They're not Hannibal Lechter."[75] At the beginning of Moore's project to demystify the cultish interest in the serial killer, the narrative works, in orthodox true crime terms, to provide a rationale for the Whitechapel murders. Prince Albert marries Annie Crook, a commoner, with whom he has a child, and Queen Victoria subsequently takes steps to separate them and cover up their relationship. With the help of the royal physician Sir William Gull, Annie is institutionalized and surgery is performed to make her of unsound mind.

Unfortunately for the sake of the cover-up, Annie's friends, a group of prostitutes, know about the royal connection and blackmail a friend of Prince Albert to pay criminals who threaten them. For this reason, Gull murders the women in a spectacularly violent fashion to throw off any investigator trying to find a rational explanation for the crimes. In this way, the crimes are robbed of the mystique generally associated the serial killer whose mind is nearly incomprehensible to society. Instead, the blame for the killings is placed squarely on those who protect the ideals of Victorian society. However, the series is more complex than this overview suggests in its portrayal of the seemingly irredeemable culture that produces a serial killer.

From Hell refuses to focus its sole attention on the detective and criminal, the profiler and the serial killer—a typical relation for true crime; the focus is diffuse and includes numerous characters from various walks of life, most notably well-rounded representations of prostitutes.[76]

In consequence, stereotypical judgments of "those" people based on class, gender, and sexuality are made problematic at best. And the moral ambiguity is accentuated by the move away from narrative and iconographic conventions of traditional comic books like the narrative box and thought balloon.[77] Without an omniscient narrative voice to pass moral judgment on the prostitutes, the reader is not distanced from the suffering of victims, and without inner monologues to explain the horrible acts, the reader is not privy to rationales that make sense of the monstrous.

Rather than deal with the Whitechapel murders after the fact, the prostitutes–typically objectified in life and in the reconstructions of the crimes–are portrayed not only as victims but also as sympathetic people with tragic lives. As Zoe Brigley-Thompson states in "Theorizing Sexual Domination in *From Hell* and *Lost Girls*," "Writing from the perspective of female survivors of violence, Moore is at his most appealing; though his writing about sex and brutality can verge upon the exploitative, he sometimes reveals an unexpected sympathy with dominated women."[78] In reference to the potentially exploitative, Brigley-Thompson explains how the elements of a scene depicting a john having sex with a prostitute in an alley prevents its gratuity; through Campbell's particularly small panels, the claustrophobic nature of the experience (and the social circumstances that give rise to it) is accentuated.[79]

Also, the way the women dialogue with one another develops their voices as individuals in a community and serves as a striking contrast to Gull's long-winded pontifications that isolate him from everything (except a corrupt idea of culture). At the same time, their ability to see what society hides makes them sympathetic, in opposition to the experience of "blindness" used to represent Gull's character (via black panels, negative space, and dislocations of text and image).[80]

Critics have suggested that the killings are gratuitous and dramatically silence the female voices,[81] but Mary escapes Gull and later casts his disembodied spirit "back to hell."[82] In this way, Moore uses Mary as an agent to redress the sexism of crime and horror narratives by putting her alongside the pot-bellied police inspector Frederick Abberline and the fraudulent psychic investigator Robert Lees. And since Mary and the other women elicit sympathy, their deaths cannot be accepted like those of sluts in slasher stories and are, therefore, truly abject.

Due in part to its length and excessive detail, the thirty-two pages that depict Gull gutting his final victim is not a transgressive pleasure but rather a disturbing horror that disrupts any notion of coherency. Refusing to connect sex and power in a pornographic way, the horror story makes the oppression of these prostitutes distasteful at the very best. And with no traditional hero who might restore social order, *From Hell* demonstrates how the media of contemporary civilization creates a monster with no opposing force.

As Gull extends his killing spree, reporters write sensationally about the "leather apron" killer and eventually send a forged letter to the police, "we're a whole new style of journalism, Mr. Gibbs, and we're inventin' it right 'ere."[83] In reaction to this letter, Gull changes his method of operation to better suit its contents and eventually produces the famous "From Hell" as an extension of this new character. Through a dynamic that falsifies canonical "evidence," Moore sets up a relationship between the killer and culture by suggesting that from the start Jack the Ripper was an invention: a device of intersecting plots. Ultimately, the killer is a "heightened media presence" that is mythologized by a variety of sources that are cobbled together.[84]

The notion that monstrosity is an unavoidable consequence of culture is an argument implicit within Gull's speculations about architecture. When he identifies phallic skyscraping architecture as a monument to London's achievement, Campbell places the reader in a low-angle perspective and the massiveness of the architecture diminishes the reader and creates anxiety. Di Liddo makes a broader connection between the city's architecture and the architecture of the page layout stating, "Moore and Campbell thus underline the oppressive presence of the city, which invades almost all the space the panel offers to the reader.... The rigorous geometrical structure of the page mirrors the precision of the morbid calculations Gull uses to foster and justify his insanity."[85]

As Gull moves beyond the motivation provided by Queen Victoria toward something more mystical, the comic book creates a pervading sense of dread by making maps and the panels that contain the abject. And as Gull moves in this direction, Moore seems less committed to demystification of the Whitechapel murders as the mystery of Gull's mind takes center stage. As Gull's language approximates Moore's own one-liners with phrases like "our lunatics were prophets once and had a prophet's power," he begins to have visions of the future.[86] Especially when he kills, he sees images of televisions, post-industrial skyscrapers, and cubicled offices with desktop computers.

Moreover, Gull seems to be able to interact with different people at the different points in history he sees in his visions. While this cements the idea of the Victorian era as the starting point for the post-industrial age of serial killers, it also gives the killer genuine power (something not exclusively created by the media of his time). Some of the foremost criticism has been over the way the work denaturalizes and then later naturalizes Gull's actions (deconstructing and then reconstructing Jack the Ripper through the textual practices of the comic itself).

In her comparison of *From Hell* and Iain Sinclair's *White Chapell, Scarlet Tracings*, English scholar Christine Ferguson states, "*From Hell*'s own rampant intertextuality provides a fitting stylistic counterpart to, and arguably aesthetic endorsement of, the murderous bibliomania that drives its antagonist.... Less sex than text murderer, Gull the monster is incanted into being by words that have been scripted elsewhere, that write on him just as he attempts to inscribe the symbols of male domination on his victims' bodies."[87] By making Gull the one who knows, Moore seemingly reinscribes the male power dismantled by other parts of the narrative.[88]

However, *From Hell*'s roots as a horror story (particularly as a horror story started in *Taboo*) explains this awkward tension in the work; the former critique doesn't collapse as a consequence of this tension, but this tension serves to demonstrate how a cultural critique is easily lost (the ultimate horror). The visions decisively take away *From Hell*'s identity as true crime and add to its identity as horror (taking away the reader's role as a detective capable of explaining an uncanny phenomenon). By taking away the reader's full critical position as an outsider capable of understanding Victorian England, *From Hell* reveals a different type of story.

From Phallic Skyscrapers to Horror in a Strip Club (and Other Moore Terrible Things)

Undoing the desire to solve the mystery and separate oneself from the horror, Moore and Campbell reveal how people are implicated in their culture. When Mary Kelly, one of the prostitutes, leaves London and presumably escapes Gull, she leaves a note for Inspector Abberline, who had been meeting her. Regularly giving Mary Kelly money and not taking sex and always treating her with respect, Abberline then exits the pub and has a constable arrest "a filthy fuckin' whore"[89] who approaches him. While this married man's overreaction to the prostitute may indicate a certain amount of guilt, it also shows how the culture that makes Gull also makes Abberline.

Good and evil, truth and untruth, strength and weakness are binaries that lose meaning in *From Hell*, and Gull's visions of the "truth" of future history should not be understood as a validation.

With everything that one thinks of as a fiction (like Gull's "From Hell" construction of Jack the Ripper), the Ripper's influence can't be ascribed to one man alone, and Gull's visions then become part of the unreliable fabric of *From Hell.* The connections between past and future serve as validation in linear terms of modernism but *From Hell* is a tale of postmodern horror in which all semiotic connections are subject to interpretation.

Campbell's use of variant styles works on multiple levels that prevent an easy identification of what is real or true within the context of the work. Mostly utilizing a somewhat naturalistic style filled with cross-hatching, Campbell's art often takes on the appearance of a rough sketch. When Lees describes the fraudulent nature of his visions at the beginning of the comic, the images that depict Lees and Abberline at the seashore exist somewhere between finished and unfinished, truth and fiction. Consequently, the certainty that should accompany an important revelation in a true crime story is made unstable, something that then characterizes the work as a whole.

In addition, Campbell varies his style in a way that ruins the realistic effect that a consistent style would convey, and thereby presents an open interpretation of the facts; he develops an ambiguous relationship between visuals that represent the omniscient narrative's perspective, the subjective character's perspective, and the compromised reader's perspective. When Gull visits Queen Victoria, the illustrations representing Gull's perspective (and the reader's perspective) use cross-hatching and charcoal-like blotting typically meant to distinguish a figure from the background. However, in these thirteen panels, Queen Victoria is blotted from easy recognition by the darkness that surrounds her. The inability to separate an individual from surroundings is quite notably associated with the individual in English society who should be subject to nothing and no one.

At other points, Campbell replicates art of the Victorian period, like the watercolor and lithograph,[90] but the quick transitions between these styles prevent them from evoking period authenticity. When works of art by William Hogarth and William Blake are included and are later imitated within scenes of the story, these links may seem like visionary connections between the Jack the Ripper murders and the phallic skyscrapers of the future—historical recurrences that are unassailably meaningful. However, as certain as these connections seem to be, they presuppose the author, and the reader can stand outside time and organize these moments together in meaningful patterns.

In "Madness and the City: The Collapse of Reason and Sanity in Alan Moore's *From Hell*," Monica Germana states, "That Moore's reworking of the Whitechapel murders ambiguously plays with visibility is also made clear by the other visions experienced by Gull, which implicate the novel's resistance to linear time."[91] When Blake and Gull share a vision of one another and Gull becomes the horrific figure in Blake's painting, the reader is left to contend with the notion that there is no separation between the maker and the made, the signifier and the signified. The horror of the story is that there is no detective, no meaningful clue, and no way in which culture produces a clear retreat from serial killers that Moore called "these fuckers… these little apologies for human beings."[92]

Despite the distance Moore tries to put between himself and the too convenient aspects of the well-known Stephen Knight theory that serves as the basis for *From Hell*, he admits that such conspiracy theories have an attraction: "Yeah, in that throughout the whole case there's all these kind of odd little connections, little coincidences, the same names, you know, it's a strange eerie little kind of era of information."[93] As much as Moore may want to present his version of Jack the Ripper as a straightforward critique on post-industrial society, his anxieties about culture's power are too pervasive to portray himself as the philosopher who makes it out of the cave.

Consequently, the annotations traditionally used to separate fact from fiction become something more subversive, as suggested by Di Liddo.[94] The way Moore departs from the objective language of the annotation becomes more pronounced throughout Appendix I, with Moore telling the reader to "work it out yourself" and offering information "just in case it helps." At the very end, Moore identifies his personal connection to the reader as "your friend," who "wish[es] you all a safe and happy night."[95] Serving as the chatty "dear reader" narrator of a Victorian novel, Moore not only demonstrates a tension within the impulses of Victorian culture but also rescinds his authority over his work.

Appendix I is all text, but Appendix II is a picture book that describes bits of information through narrative boxes accompanied by illustrations. The picture book presentation transitions to a comic book presentation in which the speech of characters compete with the narration. The "facts" included are not only history related to the Jack the Ripper case but also history related to the mythologizing of Jack the Ripper in works like Stephen Knight's *Jack the Ripper: The Final Solution*. Furthermore, referring to the quantum uncertainty principle that necessitates the researcher to map every conceivable position ("the super-position"), the narrator claims, "Jack's not Gull… Jack is a super-position."[96]

With this scientific metaphor used to describe Jack the Ripper, Moore simultaneously undermines his research-based authority and the visionary power of his version of Gull.

Most importantly, Moore uses the final page of Appendix II to depict his experience at Ten Bells, a public house associated with the Whitechapel murders, where he (and the reader) watches a stripper perform. While the last few panels move outside to Hawksmoor's Christ Church, and the flight of a bird from the steeple can be seen by the reader, Moore comments, "We were looking at the naked women dancing when it flew away."[97] The page juxtaposes the stripper and the bird in flight and creates tension through Moore's use of "we," a pronoun that includes himself and the others at Ten Bells (with the reader also as one of those others).

Moore and the reader live in a culture that commodifies Jack the Ripper (Ten Bells was formerly called The Jack the Ripper) and objectifies women as sexual victims (the stripper dances to "Jack, Jack, Jack your Body"). "We" participate in it all, and we are the monsters made by an oppressive post-industrial society. While *From Hell* is not a hosted horror comic book in the traditional sense, Gull and then Moore serve in indirect ways as hosts for the reader and transgress the boundaries that keep the reader safe from horror. In the end, this horror comic doesn't diminish the horror by explaining it or by separating the story from the life of the reader.

In Moore's life, he undermines a certain sense of self with free will when he claims to be a magician who worships a second century snake god but then admits he might be fooling himself (that the snake god might just be a variation on a sock puppet). When life is not recognized as performative, this leads to the problems experienced and enacted by Gull in *From Hell*. In this way, Moore goes further in his sociological critique than Freud in *Civilization and Its Discontents*; Germana states, "*From Hell* seems to suggest... civilisation cannot exist without madness. Simultaneously, in order to maintain power, and to counteract the subversive forces represented by the concurrent uprisings of the socialist and feminist movements at the end of the nineteenth century, reason must accommodate the irrational form of madness."[98]

Moore would examine these accommodations more in works that less directly address horror themes but more directly address horror literature in *The League of Extraordinary Gentlemen* (featuring Dr. Jekyll, Dorian Gray, and Mina from *Dracula*). And his taboo-breaking cultural reevaluation would continue with *Lost Girls*, his erotic interpretation of *Alice in Wonderland, Peter Pan*, and *The Wizard of Oz*.[99]

And much later, Moore would produce comics inspired by H.P. Lovecraft stories, but ultimately *Swamp Thing* and *From Hell* best represent his great contribution to the resurgence of horror comics.

Through intellectual and profoundly disturbing horror stories that attack culturally determined notions of identity, Moore paved the way for many other creators working in the comics industry. In particular, he laid the groundwork on which DC would build Vertigo, an adult, horror-focused imprint that became the home of Neil Gaiman's *Sandman*. However, it would be Gaiman himself who crafted the title able to survive the collapse of the comic book collector's market in the 1990s with its mythic exploration of the thin line that separates the real world from the nightmare.

Chapter 3 Notes

1 Dave Sim and Alan Moore, "Correspondence: *From Hell*, part 3: A Conversation Between Dave Sim and Alan Moore," *A Moment of Cerebus*, last modified Sept. 27, 2015, http://momentofcerebus.blogspot.co.uk/2015/09/correspondence-from-hell-part-3.html.

2 David Hajdu, *The Ten Cent Plague: The Great Comic-Book Scare and How It Changed America* (New York: Farrar, Straus, and Giroux, 2008), 262.

3 "Testimony of William M. Gaines, Publisher, Entertaining Comics Group, New York, NY," *TheComicbooks.Com*, last modified 2016, http://www.thecomicbooks.com/gaines.html.

4 Guy Lawley and Steve Whitaker, "Alan Moore," *Alan Moore: Conversations*, ed., Eric Berlatsky (Jackson: UP of Mississippi, 2012), 39.

5 This was repealed in 1969.

6 Tasha Robinson, "Interview: Alan Moore," *The Onion A.V. Club*, last modified June 25, 2003, http://www.avclub.com/article/alan-moore-13821.

7 Tasha Robinson, "Interview: Alan Moore," *The Onion A.V. Club*, last modified Oct. 24, 2001, http://www.avclub.com/article/alan-moore-13740.

8 Eric Berlatsky, "Introduction," *Alan Moore: Conversations*, ed., Eric Berlatsky (Jackson: UP of Mississippi, 2012), vii.

9 David J. Skal, *The Monster Show: A Cultural History* (New York: Farrar, Straus, and Giroux, 1993), 21.

10 Annalisa Di Liddo, *Alan Moore: Comics as Performance, Fiction as Scalpel* (Jackson: UP of Mississippi, 2009), 111.

11 Lance Parkin, *Magic Words: The Extraordinary Life of Alan Moore* (London: Aurum Press, 2013), 147.

12 Bradford Wright, *Comic Book Nation: The Transformation of Youth Culture in America* (Baltimore: Johns Hopkins UP, 2001), 247.

13 Richard J. Arndt, *Horror Comics in Black and White: A History and Catalogue, 1964–2004* (Jefferson, NC: McFarland, 2013), 10.

14 Rick Veitch initially served as ghost artist for Steve Bissette; Veitch indicated Bissette had difficulty with the workload (Jeremy Pinkham, "The Rick Veitch Interview," *The Comics Journal*, last modified May 24, 2013, http://www.tcj.com/the-rick-veitch-interview/).

15 The school was established in 1976.

16 Mike Benton, *Horror Comics: The Illustrated History* (Dallas: Taylor Publishing, 1991), 79.

17 Alan Moore, Stephen Bissette, Rick Veitch, John Totleben, and Tatjana Wood, *Saga of the Swamp Thing*, vol. 1 (New York: DC, 1987), 1.

18 Ibid., 15.

19 Ibid., 16–17.

20 Ibid., 18.

21 Jeremy Pinkham, "The Rick Veitch Interview."

22 Another important work in the field is Lawrence Buell's *The Future of Environmental Criticism: Environmental Crisis and Literary Imagination* (Malden, MA: Blackwell, 2005). While in part an overview, it charts the field's likely evolution (as the title promises). One of the areas explored is the relationship between eco-criticism and post-humanism.

23 One of the most significant texts in the field is Robert Pepperell's *The Posthuman Condition: Consciousness Beyond the Brain* (Portland: Intellect, 2003). The "posthuman condition" is a term that some scholars prefer to post-humanism, arguing that the posthuman is a state rather than a mode of thought.

24 Brian Johnson, "Libidinal Ecologies: Eroticism and Environmentalism in *Swamp Thing*," *Sexual Ideology in the Works of Alan Moore: Critical Essays on the Graphic Novels*, ed., Todd A. Comer (Jefferson, NC: McFarland, 2012), 19.

25 Rosi Braidotti's *The Posthuman* (Malden, MA: Polity, 2013) surveys the field and teases out its implications to conceptions of the environment. Braidotti rethinks the categorical distinctions between human beings and other forms of life, and this serves as an excellent connection to eco-criticism.

26 These ideas may not be new as sometimes suggested by the post-humanists, representing a persistent, alternate mode of thought (like the Gothic in the midst of the Enlightenment); see Colin Beineke's "'Her Guardiner': Alan Moore's Swamp Thing as the Green Man" (*ImageText: Interdisciplinary Comics Studies* 5, last updated 2010, http://www.english.ufl.edu/imagetext/archives/v5_4/beineke/) on the connection between Swamp Thing and traditional Green Man folklore.

27 Wheeler Winston Dixon, *A History of Horror* (New Brunswick: Rutgers UP, 2010), 134.

28 Annalisa Di Liddo, *Alan Moore: Comics as Performance, Fiction as Scalpel,* 51.

29 Maggie Gray, "A Gothic Politics: Alan Moore's Swamp Thing and Radical Ecology," *Alan Moore and the Gothic Tradition*, ed., Matthew J.A. Green (Manchester: Manchester UP, 2013), 60.

30 Gary Groth, "The Alan Moore Interview," *The Comics Journal*, last modified June 13, 2012, http://www.tcj.com/the-alan-moore-interview-118/.

31 Guy Lawley and Steve Whitaker, "Alan Moore," 29.

32 Qiana J. Whitted, "Of Slaves and Other Swamp Things: Black Southern History as Comic Book Horror," *Comics and the US South*, ed., Brannon Costello and Qiana J. Whitted (Jackson: UP of Mississippi, 2012), 192.

33 George Khoury, *The Extraordinary Works of Alan Moore* (Raleigh, NC: TwoMorrows, 2008), 93.

34 Randy Duncan and Matthew J. Smith, *The Power of Comics: History, Form, and Culture* (New York: Bloomsbury, 2009), 94–95.

35 Matthew J.A. Green connects Moore's ideas about the abject to his participation in the Gothic tradition: "[H]is work enhances our understanding of the uncanny and abject while further illustrating David Punter's sense that the Gothic 'serves to demonstrate… the perverse in the very ground of being'" (Matthew J.A. Green, "Alan Moore and the Gothic Tradition," *Alan Moore and the Gothic Tradition*, ed., Matthew J.A. Green (Manchester: Manchester UP, 2013), 4).

36 Alan Moore, Stephen Bissette, Rick Veitch, John Totleben, and Tatjana Wood, *Saga of the Swamp Thing,* vol. 2 (New York: DC, 2009), 181.

37 Ibid., 194.

38 This experience is unintentionally shared with others in No. 43 ("Windfall") when Abby's friend distributes another tuber from Swamp Thing (with positive and negative results determined by the psychology of the consumers).

39 Eric Berlatsky, "Introduction," xii.

40 Alan Moore, Stephen Bissette, Rick Veitch, John Totleben, and Tatjana Wood, *Saga of the Swamp Thing,* vol. 2, 26.

41 I use this terminology because it is part of the rhetoric used to describe sexual relationships in a post-human theory. For more on this, see Michael Hauskeller's *Sex and the Posthuman Condition* (New York: Palgrave Macmillan, 2014).

42 Brian Johnson, "Libidinal Ecologies: Eroticism and Environmentalism in *Swamp Thing,*" 20.

43 Guy Lawley and Steve Whitaker, "Alan Moore," 37.

44 Alan Moore, Stephen Bissette, Rick Veitch, John Totleben, and Tatjana Wood, *Saga of the Swamp Thing,* vol. 2, 213.

45 This story and the Swamp Thing's subsequent sexual relationship with Abby are discussed by Brian Johnson in "Libidinal Ecologies: Eroticism and Environmentalism in *Swamp Thing*" and by Matthew Candelaria in "Green Love, Red Sex" (*Sexual Ideology in the Works of Alan Moore: Critical Essays on the Graphic Novels*, ed., Todd A. Comer [Jefferson, NC: McFarland, 2012], 28–39). Johnson emphasizes the liberating effects of their union and Candelaria the troubling consequences.

46 Alan Moore, Stephen Bissette, Rick Veitch, John Totleben, and Tatjana Wood, *Saga of the Swamp Thing,* vol. 3 (New York: DC, 2010), 169.

47 Abby's reaction is prefigured in the bait-and-switch cover of No. 25 on which Swamp Thing erupts from the swamp and grabs a horrified Abby by the leg. (Since Abby is also scantily clad, this also recalls covers to horror comics from the 1950s.)

48 Alan Moore, Rick Veitch, Alfredo Alcala, Tatjana Wood, and John Costanza, *Swamp Thing* 52 DC (September 1986), 16.

49 Gray argues this portrayal of Batman robs him of his Gothic trappings, making him a representative of well-ordered civilization. "Although Batman is possibly the most Gothic of superheroes, it was his technocratic aspect that was emphasized in these issues, echoed by a depiction of Gotham, not as a city of dark alleyways or neo Gothic architecture, but a modernist bastion of steel and glass laid out in a strict grid plan" (Maggie Gray, "A Gothic Politics: Alan Moore's *Swamp Thing* and Radical Ecology," 51).

50 Alan Moore, John Totleben, Tatjana Wood, and John Costanza. *Swamp Thing* 52 DC (October 1986), 17.

51 Eclipse would publish *Marvelman* (retitled *Miracleman* to avoid copyright entanglements with both DC and Marvel), republishing work from *Warrior* and completing the series with new work from Moore.

52 Direct market sales of controversial comics were enabled in part with the establishment of the Comic Book Legal Defense Fund in 1986 (officially incorporated by Denis Kitchen in 1990). It was initially established to defend the manager of Friendly Franks who was arrested for distributing obscenity for selling *Omaha the Cat Dancer*, *Weirdo*, and others.

53 Eric Berlatsky, "Introduction," vii.

54 Also notable within *Watchmen* is the presence and metatextual commentary provided by *The Black Freighter* comic book. There are no superhero comics in this world of costumed heroes, and horror comics, like *The Black Freighter*, are prevalent.

55 "I'm not naïve enough to expect any big corporation to behave morally.... So, yeah, to some degree anyone who is working for a corporation is morally compromised to a point" (Gary Groth, "The Alan Moore Interview").

56 Jeremy Pinkham, "The Rick Veitch Interview."

57 Veitch portrays the post-human elements in various ways in Nos. 71–86. Sexual encounters between Swamp Thing and Abby are often depicted more literally and moments frozen to deemphasize eroticism and emphasize the strangeness. He continues to portray difficulties in the relationship between Swamp Thing and Abby, perhaps best represented by Abby's mistaken attempt to interact with an abandoned shell of Swamp Thing. And he presents other strange variations of Swamp Thing's body as determined by literal and figurative circumstance (such as his thinking mind as a tree that grows out of his head).

58 While the story encourages post-Cartesian ideas through its extra-biblical material, the central story is fairly orthodox in its presentation of Jesus. Jesus is not portrayed as a "hedge wizard" as Karen Berger suggests in the letters column of *Swamp Thing* No. 89 (meant to explain her rejection of Veitch's script).

59 Swamp Thing thinks, "If this man is who... I think he is... then he faces a grisly future indeed. I offer a drink... of purest fruit nectar... to soothe his contemplations" (Veitch, Rick and Michael Zulli, unpublished manuscript of *Swamp Thing* 88, *20th Century Danny Boy*, last Modified October 22, 2011, http://ohdannyboy.blogspot.com/2011/10/morning-of-magician-swamp-thing-meets.html).

60 The incident was thoroughly covered by *The Comics Journal* in "Newswatch: Rick Veitch Quits Swamp Thing: Scheduled Successors–Gaimen [*sic*] and Delano–Also Resign" (*The Comics Journal* 129 [May, 1989]: 7–11). In addition to cataloguing Veitch and Zulli's complaints, the article describes other crucifixion storylines published by DC: a *Batman* story in which a Batman imposter was crucified, a *Green Arrow* story in which a stripper is crucified, and a *Dr. Fate* story in which a vampire drinks Christ's blood at the foot of the cross.

61 Chris Dahlen, "Steve Bissette: Interview," *The Onion A.V. Club*, last modified Jul 23, 2009, http://www.avclub.com/article/steve-bissette-30751.

62 Ibid.

63 Stephen Bissette, "Taboo is Taboo," *Taboo* 9, Kitchen Sink (September 1995), 124.

64 Richard J. Arndt, *Horror Comics in Black and White: A History and Catalogue, 1964–2004*, 10.

65 Joe Queenan, "Drawing on the Dark Side," *The New York Times*, published April 30, 1989 (no posting date) http://www.nytimes.com/1989/04/30/magazine/drawing-on-the-dark-side.html?pagewanted=all.

66 Ibid. For all the article's failures, it does cite some justifiable examples of the DC and Marvel's gratuity and recommends alternative artists like Spiegelman, Peckar, and the Hernandez brothers.

67 Congressional hearings on music took place in 1985 in response to pressure from the Parents Music Resource Center to force the industry to develop a ratings system. Congressional hearings on television first took place in 1952 and later in the 1960s, 70s, 80s, and 90s, eventually leading to the Telecommunications Act of 1996 (overhauling the Communications Act of 1934 and requiring an industry-based rating system). Congressional hearings on video games took place in 1993, and the Video Game Rating Act 1994 was introduced to force the industry to develop a ratings system.

68 Mike Benton, *Horror Comics: The Illustrated History*, 5.

69 *Tales from the Crypt* was made as a film in 1972 starring Peter Cushing and was followed by *Vault of Horror* in 1973 (Digby Diehl, *Tales from the Crypt: The Official Archives* [New York: St. Martin's Press, 1996], 153).

70 Bill Mesce, *Inside the Rise of HBO: A Personal History of the Company that Transformed Television* (Jefferson, NC: McFarland, 2015), 191. *Tales from the Crypt* followed another revival, *Twilight Zone: The Movie* (a modest success in 1983) and a short-lived television revival. It would precede another movie return to anthology horror, *Tales from the Darkside: The Movie* (a weak success in 1990).

71 Robert Zemeckis (producer of *The Frighteneers* and the remakes of *House on Haunted Hill* and *Thirteen Ghosts*) comments, "They're like a guilty pleasure that appeals to the dark side, the murderous rage that every human has in them. They give you a healthy outlet to take pleasure in that fantasy, a pleasure that we all enjoy, even though we don't want to admit it" (Digby Diehl, *Tales from the Crypt: The Official Archives*, 161).

72 This works against nostalgic readings of Victorian culture and makes into a nightmare what Thatcher celebrates (Monika Pietrzak-Franger, "Envisioning the Ripper's Visions: Adapting in Alan Moore and Eddie Campbell's *From Hell*," *Neo-Victorian Studies* 2 (Winter 2009/2010): 166).

73 Brian Michael Bendis's roughly contemporaneous *Torso* retells and "solves" Eliot Ness's unsolved serial killer case; despite the bureaucratic impediments to justice, this work is more linear and provides some satisfaction for the true crime reader. And despite the bureaucratic impediments to justice, the film version of *From Hell* focuses on the handsome detective and provides far too much satisfaction.

74 Through its overrun urban setting, *From Hell* serves as the antithesis of ecological awareness set forth in *Swamp Thing*. This is emblematically represented by the tiny twig on city street at the killer's feet: an isolated and frustrated representation of nature.

75 Barry Kavanagh, "*From Hell*," *Blather.Net*, last modified Oct. 17, 2000, http://www.blather.net/projects/alan-moore-interview/from-hell/.8.

76 As mentioned, the film version of *From Hell* does the opposite, focusing on a handsome detective who solves the murders; even though he cannot expose the conspiracy, he uses his knowledge to save the prostitute whom he loves (reducing her as a prop in the plot's movement).

77 Moore mentions his early move away from thought balloons early in his career: "And you don't need thought balloons either" (David Roach, Andrew Jones, Simon Jowett, and Greg Hill, "Gary Leach and Alan Moore," *Alan Moore: Conversations*, ed., Eric Berlatsky [Jackson: UP of Mississippi, 2012], 12).

78 Zoe Brigley-Thompson, "Theorizing Sexual Domination in *From Hell* and *Lost Girls*: Jack the Ripper versus Wonderlands of Desire," *Sexual Ideology in the Works of Alan Moore: Critical Essays on the Graphic Novels*, ed., Todd A. Comer (Jefferson, NC: McFarland, 2012), 76.

79 Alan Moore and Eddie Campbell, *From Hell* (Marietta, GA: Top Shelf, 2006), chapter 3, page 4.

80 Monika Pietrzak-Franger, "Envisioning the Ripper's Visions: Adapting in Alan Moore and Eddie Campbell's *From Hell*," 159.

81 Ibid., 179.

82 Alan Moore and Eddie Campbell, *From Hell*, 14:23.

83 Ibid., 7:38.

84 Monika Pietrzak-Franger, "Envisioning the Ripper's Visions: Adapting in Alan Moore and Eddie Campbell's *From Hell*," 160.

85 Annalisa Di Liddo, *Alan Moore: Comics as Performance, Fiction as Scalpel*, 76–77.

86 Throughout his career, Moore became more committed to his belief and practice of magic and suggested that some of his works (particularly *Promethea*) were enactments of his magical practice: "One of the problems [with being creative and believing in magic] is, when you start to do that, in effect you're going to have to step off the edge of science and rationality" (Steve Rose, "Moore's Murderer" *The Guardian*, last modified Feb. 1, 2002, https://www.theguardian.com/film/2002/feb/02/sciencefictionfantasyandhorror.books).

87 Christine Ferguson, "Victoria-Arcana and the Misogynistic Poetics of Resistance in Iain Sinclair's *White Chapell, Scarlet Tracings* and Alan Moore's *From Hell*," *Literature Interpretation Theory* 20 (2009): 57. Ferguson initially commends Moore for broadening his version of the Jack the Ripper story but ultimately sees it as a failure: "Moore and Campbell's occulted historical pastiche resounds with the ethical gestures and concerns that seem dismayingly absent from Sinclair's novel [*White Chapell, Scarlet Tracings*].... The most significant impediment, however, to Moore and Campbell's attempts to distance themselves from the (b)latent misogyny of Ripper nostalgia lies less in their commitment to the same metaphysics of textual determinism that drive Sinclair's Victoria-arcana"(56).

88 "*From Hell*, through its dense weave of quotations, allusions, and historical detail, in itself seems to create a divine text that cannot be de-naturalized or de-mythicized... and in the process mythicizes masculine violence in a highly disturbing way"

88 *continued*
(Mervi Miettinen, "'Do You Understand How I Have Loved You?': Terrible Loves and Divine Visions in *From Hell*," *Sexual Ideology in the Works of Alan Moore: Critical Essays on the Graphic Novels*, ed., Todd A. Comer [Jefferson, NC: McFarland], 2012, 99).

89 Alan Moore and Eddie Campbell, *From Hell*, 11:15.

90 Annalisa Di Liddo, *Alan Moore: Comics as Performance, Fiction as Scalpel*, 82.

91 Monica Germana, "Madness and the City: The Collapse of Reason and Sanity in Alan Moore's *From Hell*," *Alan Moore and the Gothic Tradition*, ed., Matthew J.A. Green (Manchester: Manchester UP, 2013), 145. "What Is the Fourth Dimension" by Charles Howard Hinton is brought into the narrative by Howard's father and Gull's friend. Also, a conventional sense of time is resisted through the use of the gutter as well as the opening and closing pages of Chapter 2 (a collage of disconnected pieces of dialogue set in completely black panels):
"This 'stupendous whole' is precisely what Campbell's first page of black and dialogue represents: as we finish the chapter and encounter the dialogue that we were given in fracture form against the black background, and returning to the first page we can see it as a spatial representation of various periods of Gull's life that 'coexist' in one physical space. It is hard to imagine a medium better suited than comics to the staging of such a notion" (Seamus O'Malley, "Speculative History, Speculative Fiction: Alan Moore and Eddie Campbell's *From Hell*," *Graphic History: Essays on Graphic Novels and/as History*, ed., Richard Iadonisi [Newcastle: Cambridge Scholars Publishing, 2012], 171).

92 Barry Kavanagh, "*From Hell*," 8.

93 Ibid., 6.

94 Annalisa Di Liddo, *Alan Moore: Comics as Performance, Fiction as Scalpel*, 81.

95 Alan Moore and Eddie Campbell, *From Hell*, Appendix I: 42.

96 Ibid., Appendix II: 16

97 Ibid., Appendix II: 24

98 Monica Germana, "Madness and the City: The Collapse of Reason and Sanity in Alan Moore's *From Hell*," 152.

99 On Moore's argument against shame in his work *25,000 Years of Erotic Freedom*, "Moore has provided these erotic flights with a socially-redeeming and shame-diffusing alibi" (Brian Johnson, "Libidinal Ecologies: Eroticism and Environmentalism in *Swamp Thing*," 27).

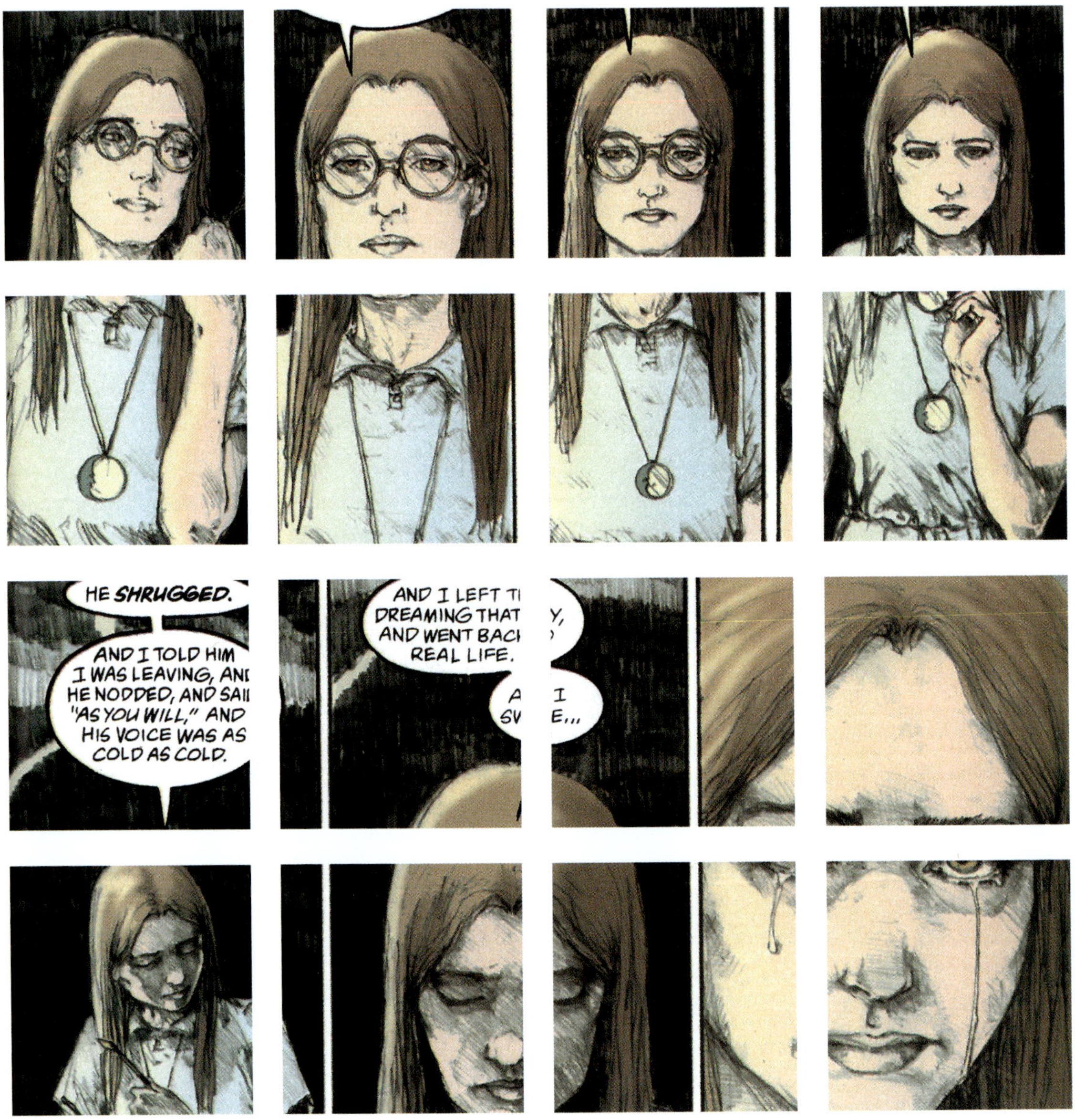
HE SHRUGGED.
AND I TOLD HIM I WAS LEAVING, AN HE NODDED, AND SAI "AS YOU WILL," AND HIS VOICE WAS AS COLD AS COLD.
AND I LEFT T DREAMING THAT Y, AND WENT BAC REAL LIFE.
A I SW E...

CHAPTER 4

Son of the Monster: Sandman and the Mythology of Vertigo

I'm trustworthy. Hold my hand. We will walk together, you and I, into the dark places and it's gonna be okay, because I'm holding your hand. And they look at you and they trust you and they listen to you. And you take them by the hand and you walk into the dark places with them; then you let go of their hand and you run away. That's storytelling.
Neil Gaiman[1]

Entering the Realms of the Fairy Folk: The Direct Market as a Burgeoning Marketplace

In his statement at the congressional hearings, Bill Gaines asked the rhetorical question, "What are we afraid of? Are we afraid of our own children?"[2] (a question that demonstrated how much Gaines was out of touch with the political climate). Shaped by Cold War paranoia, the general populace was afraid of its own children and was deeply disturbed by "The Orphan," in *Shock SuspenStories* No. 14, about a young girl's designs to make herself an orphan. Clearly feeling that the artistry of an O. Henry surprise ending didn't justify such a story, many committee members put forth questions asking Gaines to justify this story that subverted parental authority. Herbert Hannoch said, "Everybody reading that would think this girl would go to jail. So the O. Henry finish changes that, makes her a wonderful looking girl?... You think it does [children] a lot of good to read these things?" And Gaines replied, "I don't think it does them a bit of good but I don't think it does them a bit of harm, either."[3] Forsaking the justifications of social activism and an artistic precedent, Gaines quickly pivoted to the pleasure of horror, something unsatisfying to most politicians at the hearing who found horror comics distinctly unpleasant.

Regardless, this commentary would be echoed decades later by Neil Gaiman, who describes the pleasure of horror in his essay "Ghosts in the Machines." While the title makes reference to Gilbert Ryle's partial rejection of Cartesian rationalism, Gaiman focuses on the childlike fear of the supernatural: "Why take such pleasure in tales that have no purpose but, comfortably, to scare?... It's good to be a child again, for a little while, and to fear—not governments, not regulations, not infidelities or accountants of distant wars, but ghosts and such things that don't exist, and even if they do, can do nothing to hurt us."[4] Answering the question in part because he writes horror stories for young readers as well as adults, Gaiman suggests that horror stories provide a type of manageable fear. At the same time, while his statement about ghosts might seem reassuring, it is hard to keep categories distinct (Ryle's argument after a fashion) with "even if they do" allowing for the reality as well as the fantasy of ghosts. Gaiman identifies his work in horror comics as dark fantasies that please the reader but do so like EC stories at more than one level with a subversiveness that politicians feared and that Gaines couldn't hide.[5]

Like Alan Moore, this eventual comics superstar would come from England, part of a full-fledged British invasion of the United States during an interesting era for horror and comic books. Alongside a similar resurgence for the crime genre, classic and contemporary horror was no longer published just in mass market paperbacks. With classic authors like Edgar Allen Poe and contemporary authors like Stephen King, horror was now being regularly published in hardcover and trade paperback formats. While it didn't necessarily change the content of comic books in the direct market, certain publishers were becoming more interested in a format change specific to comics: book length and book format publications that collected series and presented wholly original long-form stories. Although the term did not originate with him, comics innovator Will Eisner brought the idea of the graphic novel to the mainstream and the evolutionary move in that direction became more apparent in the 1980s and 1990s.

However, the big two comics publishers, DC and Marvel, guided the market as they had for some time and slowed the transition to the graphic novel format. With new life in the superhero genre thanks to titles like *The Dark Knight Returns* and *Watchmen*, sales of traditional pamphlet-style comics were again booming. And with back issue costs skyrocketing, investor speculation drove many buyers motivated less by content and more by future monetary value.

Soon the direct market stores that represented the high hopes of art comics advocates such as *The Comics Journal* became superhero novelty shops. The high priced comics were not full-fledged graphic novels but expensive foil-covered variants of regular superhero comic book issues from DC and Marvel. And many black-and-white publishers that initially provided a place for alternative voices and genres became publishers trying to imitate the success of Eastman and Laird's *Teenage Mutant Ninja Turtles*.

As stated by comics critic Michael Dean, "Direct market can be said to have rescued comic books," but various problems "isolated comics and their readers from the rest of the world as if they'd been sealed in a tomb."[6] This quotation points out a fundamental shift and emerging problem for comic books that formerly had been widely read; the new audience was more devoted but isolated and often made purchases regardless of content (based on what *Wizard* magazine identified as the next hot title). In other words, while comic book buyers were now more devoted, they were a smaller group who ironically were becoming less likely to critically read the comic that they bought. And once again in comics history, artistry was becoming less relevant and superheroes were thriving.

However, this collector's market for superhero comics would be short-lived, and the reader's market for comic books and graphic novels would be most clearly sustained by horror comics, particularly by Neil Gaiman's *The Sandman* and DC's adult imprint Vertigo. When the superhero collector's bubble burst and comic book sales dropped in 1993, much of the credit for the success of Vertigo horror titles would be given to DC editor Karen Berger. Identified by Gaiman as "the single most terrific editor anybody could ever want,"[7] Berger had served as the editor of *House of Mystery* in the 1980s (making several notable appearances with Cain in the final issues). After helping to promote the early run on Alan Moore's *Swamp Thing*, she is often associated with "the British invasion" of mainstream comics in the 1980s.

This influx of talent from England was not as uniform as many assume with Brian Bolland and Dave Gibbons preceding Alan Moore and Neil Gaiman, and with Jamie Delano and Grant Morrison following sometime after Moore's success with *Swamp Thing*. Regardless, Berger would be closely associated with Gaiman's initial DC work and with the growth of horror as a genre within the DC superhero universe. Vertigo was created to house ongoing DC series that appealed to older readers, like *Swamp Thing*, *Hellblazer*, and *The Sandman*,[8] and the imprint grew increasingly independent unlike Marvel's much later established MAX line (solely featuring superhero stories with R-rated content).[9]

Featuring characters that worked outside the tropes that governed superhero stories, these series were essentially separated from that universe, and "DC gave horror comics a venue when it launched its Vertigo imprint."[10] Vertigo was established shortly before the collector's market fell apart and DC utilized it to explore markets not primarily driven by the interests of male teenagers and collectors. Comics scholar Matthew Pustz argues, "DC also began marketing these products more aggressively to an audience not accustomed to buying comic books....The new Vertigo audience included college-age young adults, women, readers of Anne Rice novels, and those interested in the occult [including] Goths."[11] This new sort of brand identity was based largely on groundwork established by *The Sandman*, whose sales nearly doubled those associated with *Swamp Thing*.[12]

But when *The Sandman* began its run in 1989, its following was the result of a natural phenomenon more than a marketing strategy, which enabled Vertigo to survive the collector's market bust relatively unscathed. Neil Gaiman would follow in Alan Moore's distinctive footsteps in conceptual and sometimes literal ways, writing for Eclipse's *Marvelman/Miracleman* series after Moore left, and nearly writing Swamp Thing with Jamie Delano after Rick Veitch left.[13] With excessive humility, Gaiman joked about his part in the British invasion, "Alan Moore got to be the Beatles and, along with Grant Morrison, I was Gerry and the Pacemakers."[14] While his early influences include straightforward fantasy works by G.K. Chesterton, C.S. Lewis, and J.R.R. Tolkien, his later influences include darker material by Ray Bradbury, Michael Moorcock,[15] and H.P. Lovecraft. In fact, Gaiman identifies Lovecraft as his primary guide in horror reading, "The odd thing is that the finest gift from Lovecraft was less the Cthulhupoid stuff and more some amazing pointers at things he was influenced by...'Supernatural Horror in Literature'...was like being handed a road map for where I should be reading and what I should be looking for."[16]

Gaiman began his career at DC with his long-time illustrative partner Dave McKean on *Black Orchid*, a revisionist superhero story cited as offensive by Joe Queenan in the article "Drawing on the Darkside." While depicting violence in explicit ways (Queenan's complaint), the series ultimately rejects the violence of the superhero power fantasy. Thus, Gaiman's interest in subverting conventional narratives would be apparent from his start at DC, especially when paired with McKean's somewhat abstract and challenging artwork. In fact, the original script for *Black Orchid* included DC dream characters including Cain, Abel, and the superhero known as the Sandman.[17]

While none of them appeared in the final script, it indirectly led to Gaiman's proposal for a series featuring the Golden Age superhero. Like Moore's proposal for *Watchmen* with the Charlton characters, it was rejected, but Gaiman was encouraged to write another, which led to a wholly original Sandman character: the basis for his landmark series.

Far from being a superhero, Gaiman's Sandman, named Morpheus, was part of a pantheon of gods who influenced various aspects of human experience (in his case, dreams). With a mythic scope, the series readily moved into the fantasy realms of dreams and nightmares with no clear sense of what was real. While employing traditional horror figures ranging from occultists to serial killers, *The Sandman* became widely known as a dark fantasy about the nature of storytelling itself. Dark fantasy is a sub-genre that combines elements of fantasy and horror, portraying history as complex and depicting magic, human society, and divine power as corrupt. In recent years readily associated with contemporary Goth culture, dark fantasy accurately describes specifics of *The Sandman*, such as the physical appearance and fashions of Morpheus himself. In further reference to this link, the bands Siouxsie and the Banshees and Bauhaus, distinct starting points for Goth culture, were part of the music culture Gaiman covered as a reporter and critic in the 1980s.[18]

Goth Culture: The Obvious Child of Alt Rockers and Vampires, Sadomasochism and Nihilism

These 1980s music groups intended to lyrically and musically represent Romantic ideas of the Gothic period but also synthesized them with other ideas, and the points of synthesis range from horror to nihilism, from the Marquis de Sade to David Bowie. With pale skin and black clothes in styles borrowed from S&M culture, Goth fashions broadly signify their preference for death and nothingness over life and meaning.[19] The narrative precedents for this culture include the Byronic variations on the vampire (starting with Polidori's *The Vampyre*), stories in which sympathetic monsters who have an undeniable relationship with death are set apart from society. Since subcultures are smaller parts of culture at large and defined in opposition to the mainstream, it would seem that dark fantasy would have a limited appeal. And yet regardless of how much a subculture identifies itself in oppositional terms (hippies, punks, goths), they are tied to history and essential parts of culture at large.[20]

And while goths may be parodied within mainstream culture, the narratives that embed their values often permeate contemporary vampire stories like Anne Rice's *Vampire Chronicles* (beginning with *Interview with the Vampire*).

Introducing Louis, a world-weary vampire, the story portrays the pathos-heavy experience of seeing with "dead" eyes, both beautiful and tragic. As horror scholar Nina Auerbach describes the vampires of the *Vampire Chronicles*, "Its vampirism is a select club, a fraternity of beauty and death."[21] By embracing the pan-sexuality often associated with Goth culture, Rice portrays homosexual attraction between vampires, something Auerbach notes as new ground broken within the world of horror. "Rice's infraction of this final Stoker-instigated taboo brings a special electricity."[22] While some variations of the wholly evil vampire persist in works like Stephen King's *Salem's Lot*, the angst-filled vampire would become the standard in other works like Whitley Strieber's *The Hunger* (treating vampirism as addiction and adapted as a film starring Goth icon David Bowie).

As a category that brings genres together, dark fantasy has a history that, of course, predates Goth culture and also extends beyond vampire fiction. With twentieth-century origins in the pulp fiction publications of Gertrude Barrows Bennett, the genre borrows from fantasy, adventure, and science fiction to present a world with an overwhelming feeling of dread. The category is broad enough to include Charles Grant's *Nightmare Seasons* (horror mysteries) and Michael Moorcock's Elric series (sword and sorcery based on *The Threepenny Opera*). And film representations include *Legend, The Dark Crystal*, and *Labyrinth* (again with Bowie), with Gaiman citing *The Dark Crystal* and *Labyrinth* as inspirations for his own work.[23] In 1987, horror author Clive Barker made his debut as a film director with *Hellraiser*, an exceedingly gruesome tale of a man resurrected by his lover as a skinless corpse through the blood of murder victims. With a puzzle box reputed to open a portal to a realm of pleasure, he releases leather-clad monsters who destroy him; these are neither angels nor demons but vile creatures who don't distinguish between pain and pleasure.[24]

While the *Hellraiser* films depict a more horrific, distinctly S&M side of Goth and dark fantasy, the increasingly popular films of Tim Burton demonstrate that the subculture was beginning to redefine the mainstream. With films that included the neo-Expressionist *Batman* with Michael Keaton, Burton produced the ultimate dark fantasy parable in *Edward Scissorhands*. Featuring teenage heartthrob Johnny Depp as the titular character, the film brings together Goth subculture with classic horror films, also starring Vincent Price as the kindly (if slightly mad) scientist who created Edward. Designed as a Goth figure in skin tone, hair style, and clothing, Edward lives his life with scissors for hands because the scientist died before providing him with real hands. Ultimately, persecuted in a Technicolor suburbia, the misunderstood representative of fringe culture must deal with the monstrosity of an exaggerated 1950s American culture.

As opposed to the outsider perspective on Goth in *Hellraiser*, the insider perspective of *Edward Scissorhands* presents an emo Gothic Frankenstein creature as a sympathetic ambassador to the masses for the subculture's macabre death obsession. Moreover, with a self-conscious humor seen in the even more broadly appealing *The Nightmare Before Christmas*, Tim Burton acknowledges the performative in Goth culture. As Paul Hodkinson suggests in *Goth: Identity, Style, and Subculture*, all subcultural groups include a wide range of people and ideas within a set of loosely connected and self-consciously appropriated signifiers. When looking for a home in America, Neil Gaiman jokingly refers to his desire for an Addams family house,[25] an icon of anti-American Americaness. As seriously as he and critics might take the dark fantasy of *The Sandman*, Gaiman still recognizes his Goth leanings are indebted as much to the look of Morticia Addams[26] as a philosophy of nihilism.

But while *Edward Scissorhands* would serve as a quaint horror parable for Goth culture, *The Sandman* would serve as a dynamic horror mythology for Goth culture (and mainstream culture as well). Looking back on the series, Gaiman states, "If somebody had told me, 'hey, your job is to create a new mythology for the millennium,' I would have told them to shove it."[27] Nevertheless, the series has been understood in these terms, with Stephen Rauch writing a book-length analysis of *The Sandman* based on work of the well-known scholar of mythology Joseph Campbell. Even Fantagraphics, a press that rarely devotes books to genre comics published in the mainstream, published a collection of what it refers to as the "mythology" of The Sandman.[28] Regardless, the mythic story of The Sandman begins as it should as part of a line of comics nurtured by editor Karen Berger—heavily inflected by horror tropes reworked for Gaiman's own purposes.

With Lovecraftian overtones and picture frame panel designs reminiscent of *The House of Mystery*, *The Sandman* begins in 1916 with Roderick Burgess, an Aleister Crowley character, using sorcery to bind the physical embodiment of Death. However, he accidentally summons the embodiment of Dream, Morpheus, whom he keeps imprisoned for fear of retribution from the eternal forces related to him. Continuing his quest for immortality, Burgess tries to negotiate with Morpheus, a pale-skinned, black-haired man who is largely unresponsive. His viewpoint is represented by a fish-eye distortion within circular panels, which visually makes his perspective seem stranger than that of the occultist. Burgess keeps Morpheus captive until Burgess dies, and then Morpheus becomes the responsibility of Burgess's son, someone less capable but equally vile.

The stretch of his imprisonment lasts until his jailers make a mistake in 1988, and a large part of the story is spent with the dreaming and sleeping gone often horribly awry during Morpheus's imprisonment. After he dons suitably Gothic clothes and escapes, Morpheus punishes Burgess's son with the unending experience of nightmares, some of which the reader sees. Because Morpheus explains the punishment to him in a way that seemingly addresses the reader and breaks the fourth wall, this excessive punishment for things done wrong has the feeling of EC horror.

Fig. 4.1
The Sandman No. 1, DC Comics, 1989
© DC Comics
The interaction between Morpheus and his captor features the Dream King also speaking to the reader like a classic horror host: sinister and contrary but more abstract.

Once free, Morpheus goes about retrieving the lost artifacts of his power, leading him to other occult and dream figures in the DC universe such as the Alan Moore creation John Constantine, and the dream-altering villain Doctor Destiny. Especially with the Doctor Destiny portion, the series establishes the precedent of manipulating page layout to create a nightmarish experience that questions what is known and what is "real" for a character who walks in the realm of dream. The end of the initial eight-issue story arc is a long conversation between Dream and his older sister Death (the embodiment sought by Burgess at the start). While pale-skinned, wearing an ankh, and appropriately decked out in Goth fashions, Death is unexpectedly playful and challenges the grim Morpheus to think differently about himself after the humiliation of imprisonment: "You are utterly the stupidest, most self-centered appallingest excuse for an anthropomorphic personification on this or any other plane! An infantile, adolescent, pathetic specimen! Feeling sorry for yourself because your little game is over, and you haven't got the balls to go and find a new one!"[29]

In addition to introducing a larger framework with his siblings, known as the Endless, who govern humanity (Destiny, Desire, Despair, Delirium, and Destruction), this issue reveals that immortals like Death work beyond stereotypical associations. Moreover, the story arc reveals Gaiman's interests in mythic figures that set Sandman apart from the superhero trends of the 1980s: "It's interesting because at the time, John Byrne had just taken over *Superman* and had announced that he was making Superman less powerful because he had become too powerful and you couldn't write interesting stories about people that were too powerful. That started me thinking, 'Well, no, actually you *can*, because what makes a person interesting or not interesting isn't how powerful they are, but *who* they are.'"[30] In many ways, Morpheus understands himself in traditional terms as a god-figure: a powerful, unchanging arbiter of human affairs. However, the series is a quest of sorts to determine how he copes with the realization that he might not be what he thinks while he negotiates the contentious relationships he has with his siblings.

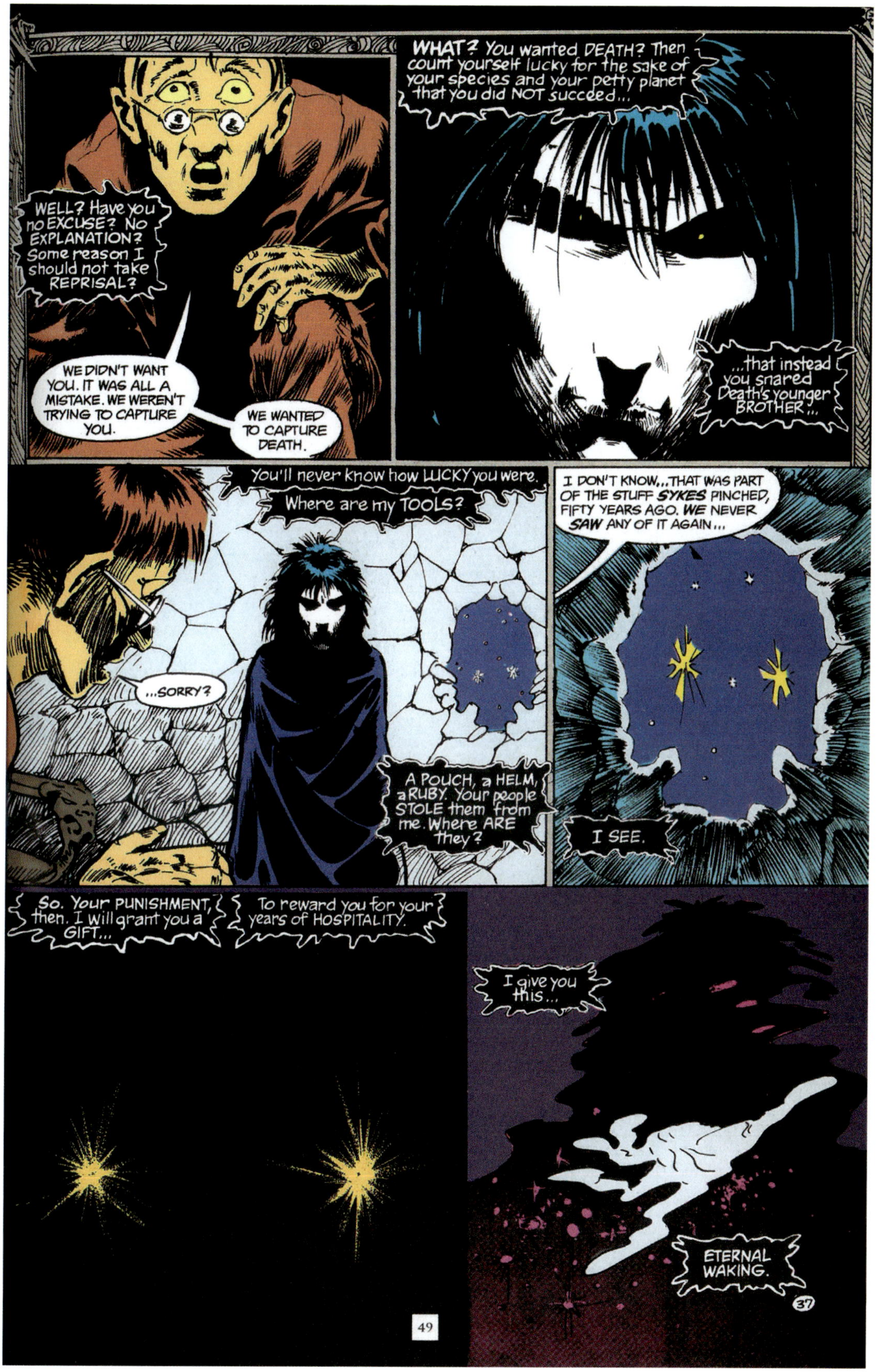
WELL? Have you no EXCUSE? No EXPLANATION? Some reason I should not take REPRISAL?
WE DIDN'T WANT YOU. IT WAS ALL A MISTAKE. WE WEREN'T TRYING TO CAPTURE YOU.
WE WANTED TO CAPTURE DEATH.
WHAT? You wanted DEATH? Then count yourself lucky for the sake of your species and your petty planet that you did NOT succeed...
...that instead you snared Death's younger BROTHER...
You'll never know how LUCKY you were.
Where are my TOOLS?
...SORRY?
A POUCH, a HELM, a RUBY. Your people STOLE them from me. Where ARE they?
I DON'T KNOW... THAT WAS PART OF THE STUFF SYKES PINCHED, FIFTY YEARS AGO. WE NEVER SAW ANY OF IT AGAIN...
I SEE.
So. Your PUNISHMENT, then. I will grant you a GIFT...
To reward you for your years of HOSPITALITY.
I give you this...
ETERNAL WAKING.
37
49

Dark Fantasy Goes to Dark Places with Pale Skin: Myth, Anti-Myth, and Something Else

The second arc explores machinations against Dream by Desire and Despair who discover Rose Walker, a "dream vortex" capable of uniting imaginations and destroying the world. After rescuing Rose from a monstrous serial killer and dream creation known as the Corinthian, Morpheus informs Rose that he must kill her in order to protect the world from destruction. However, Rose's grandmother (and the victim of a sleeping sickness that occurred during Morpheus's imprisonment) takes Rose's place as the vortex and seemingly dies a natural death. In the end, Desire reveals that she impregnated Unity during her sleeping sickness, hoping that Morpheus would kill the dream-inspired Rose and thereby destroy himself. Although far from heroic in typical terms defined for human beings, Morpheus maintains order, reprimands Desire, and achieves something at least vaguely moral in human terms.

In fact, when Morpheus captures the Corinthian, the nightmare had been attending a convention for serial killers (identified as a "cereal convention"); with a significant dose of EC black humor in the narrative, the story confronts the post-industrial nightmare of the serial killer, and Morpheus defeats the killers by revealing the ridiculousness of their grandiose ideas: "You disappoint me, Corinthian. You, and these humans you inspired… A nightmare created to be the darkness and the fear of darkness in every human heart…What have you wrought, Corinthian? Nothing.
Just something else for people to be scared of, that's all. You've told them that there are bad people out there. And they've known that all along."[31] His words deconstruct the serial killer in a way different from Alan Moore and as David Bratman states in "A Game of You–Yes, You," "[T]he sheer ludicrousness of the notion [of the serial killer convention] is what makes pursuing it seriously black humor rather than sick: watching these sociopaths network, or failing to network, and failing to control their murderous urges despite the practical necessity of doing so. We see how pathetic they really are: fanboys worshipping a nightmare."[32] As a Goth-like character informed by the eternal, Morpheus provides a vitally important perspective on this nightmare and dismisses it in a self-conscious and unconventional way.

Morpheus's development has been read in mythic and rather heroic terms especially by Rauch in his aforementioned study of *The Sandman*, using Joseph Campbell to connect mythology and the sacred,[33] dreams[34] and Jung's collective unconscious.[35]

In the series, Morpheus later descends into the underworld to save the lover he damned, searches the earth for Destruction, his long-lost brother, and gives up his life as part of an inescapable order of events (replaced by another in the eternal role of Dream). The epic nature of these incidents almost necessarily suggests intentionality and development.[36] As literary scholar Annalisa Castaldo argues, "Throughout the series, characters comment on Dream's changes, which he at first denies and never completely accepts. Gradually, he realizes that the isolation of imprisonment imposed by another has made his self-imposed isolation, based in his sense of duty, intolerable."[37]

With a narrative that in its bare bones seems to have a monomythic structure, readers might be tempted to understand Morpheus's story as a linear progression, but that is inaccurate and far from its underpinnings as Gothic dark fantasy. Gaiman himself speaks to the problem with seeing *The Sandman* as a story of character development: "[T]he joy of Sandman and Morpheus himself, the central character, is that he really doesn't change. In many ways, that is the tragedy of "The Sandman," a character who, if only he could change, he would have a story with a much happier ending. And "The Sandman" is a tragedy. An incredibly upbeat tragedy..."[38] Gaiman's playful description of the series as "an incredibly upbeat tragedy" evokes the more eternal and otherworldly perspective of Morpheus; this perspective is suggested by an overall narrative design that doesn't consistently focus on Morpheus (making him a minor character in the dreams of other characters and presenting his story in a non-sequential way often interrupted by the dream-related short stories). In fact, Gaiman moves the story away from intentionality and order with his statement, "If any thing [sic], it's a bumbling little tragedy in which the real tragedy is just that people act like people and sometimes lousy things happen."[39]

Literary scholar Nick Katsiadas develops a connection between Campbell, Jung, and Romanticism as a means of rejecting *The Sandman* as a linear myth, focusing on "how Morpheus's identity connects with Romantic revisions of the power of myths and the artist's organic, cyclical imagination."[40] And in "Freedom, Damnation, and Milton's *Paradise Lost* in Neil Gaiman's *The Sandman*," Joakim Jahlmar argues the story moves far beyond the typical morality of the epic: "In Sandman, there is... a suggestion that teleology, the belief that evil serves a greater good, presents the divine plan as evil, and therefore, in Nietzsche's view of existence and the world, is justifiable only aesthetically."[41]

As a result, the horror experience of *The Sandman* results from a move outside conventional mythology into the surreal in which things are not ordered in ways typical of the conscious world. The series utilizes dreams to present a Goth perspective that disrupts traditional meaning-making.

The idea of the dream and nightmare has been an explicit part of the horror genre in narrative terms since Coleridge's "Rime of the Ancient Mariner" and in visual terms since Fuseli's "The Nightmare." However, its disruptive power became more apparent in the twentieth century through the surrealist paintings of Salvador Dali ("The Persistence of Memory") and the surrealist films of Louis Buñuel (*An Andalusian Dog*).[42] Through radically different composition and editing, their works became threatening to conventional sensibilities regardless of their content–but even more so when their content was questionable (with the association made between Jesus and the Marquis de Sade in Buñuel's *The Golden Age*). Typical horror comic book stories with nightmare themes include "Orgy of Blood" in Skywald's *Nightmare* No. 1 in which a man relates to his psychologists his bizarre, repeated nightmares of vampire attacks; ultimately, he would realize that the visits to the psychologist were the dream and the attacks the reality.

Closer in time if not medium to *The Sandman* would be Wes Craven's *Nightmare on Elm Street* in which the supernatural serial killer Freddy Krueger has the power to kill teenagers in their dreams. This slippage between the real and dream world creates not only a fear of falling asleep for characters but allows the narrative to function in unreal ways that intensify the horror experience for viewers. Seemingly aware of his role as a performer, Freddy acted like the wisecracking hosts of 1950s horror comics before returning to the narrative as a real threat to the teenagers (as described by communications scholar Ian Conrich): "Freddy is the confident performer, the host, the showman, and the comic.... Like a comedian, Freddy... functions disruptively in relation to the fictional world, by manipulating, destroying, or even completely altering its structure."[43]

Perhaps more relevant to the dark fantasy of *The Sandman* would be David Lynch's television show *Twin Peaks*, a horror soap opera about a serial killer in a small town. The FBI investigator is able to track this killer, possessed by a strange spiritual presence, through the investigator's dreams rather than his logic. The show resists the detective genre with what Lorna Jowett and Stacey Abbott call "the anti-narrative of cinematic surrealism... the dream code is not solved through logic...but through further clues, riddles, and visions....

[In so doing,] *Twin Peaks* unsettles the audience… [by] the uncanny and liminal world between the conscious and the subconscious, in which reality is infused with the qualities of dreams and nightmares."[44] In his "Definition of the Fantastic," Tzvetan Todorov suggests that this breakdown of the distinct boundaries of reality and fantasy make the reader less distinctly separate from the experience of horror.

Many other horror pieces at that time explore the porous boundaries between reality and fantasy and concomitantly between fact and fiction. *Misery*, a book by Stephen King, portrays a woman who kidnaps an author because he plans to kill his fan-favorite heroine and deviate from his well-known style.[45] *Candyman*, a film produced by Clive Barker, depicts a folklorist who investigates the urban legend of the Candyman monster and becomes part of the story either in reality or in her mind. *New Nightmare*, a film produced by Wes Craven, follows the making of a sequel in the *Nightmare on Elm Street* series and makes the monster part of the script's reality but also part of the making of the *New Nightmare* film itself.[46] Eventually, Stephen King would reinvent his dark fantasy *Gunslinger* series by inserting characters from his self-contained horror novels (and himself as the author), thereby creating a complex intertextual relationship between the story and the reader.[47] The idea of stories as variations on the real is part of the oral culture folktale tellers approach to life, but the shift toward literacy causes categorical distinctions between what is real and what is not to be much more important. In the wake of the disappearance of the superhero collector market, the comic book industry moves to the bookstore-friendly graphic novel (something partially solidified with the success of collections of *The Sandman*); and yet while *The Sandman* becomes a critically approved part of literate culture in terms of format, its content works in opposition to literate culture.

The Dream and the Reality (and the Horror) of the Graphic Novel

As cultural critic Hayley Campbell notes in *The Art of Neil Gaiman*, "Gaiman was about to become part of the linchpin in a major shift in comics publishing, and in comics finding their way into regular bookshops."[48] With the move into the bookstore, comic book readers would pursue more specialized interests, wait for the collections by favorite creators, and pay big money not readily available to the broad comic book audience of the past. Pustz notes, "Most of these paperbacks sold for around twenty dollars, adding to the idea that the comic's audience was primarily adult."[49] The fourth collection of *The Sandman* series, *Season of Mists*, would be one of the first contemporary collections published in hardcover.[50]

And Gaiman was keenly aware that *The Sandman* kickstarted this strange phenomenon of comic book collections. "I was a 16-year-old comic reader in 1977 and the idea that I would have been reading a comic that would have been first published in 1957 and ended by 1965 and that it would have been relevant at all, that would have been a really strange idea back then."[51]

Most comic book work continued to be published monthly and was only later collected, but more and more graphic novels at this time were being conceived as self-contained long works. Opting to retain the strangeness he associates with such collections and self-contained works, Gaiman rejects "graphic novel" as a term and thinks of the comic book primarily as something published monthly in a pamphlet format. In his passionate defense of the First Amendment and rationale for the Comic Book Legal Defense Fund, he describes comic books almost exclusively as something sold in monthly installments at direct market comic book stores.[52] In terms of his own process, he regularly mentions his fear of *The Sandman*'s cancellation in the first year (not plotting far beyond that year) and his inability to carefully revise the early parts of *The Sandman* like he did his prose novels (not developing a classically defined narrative integrity).[53] Thinking of comic books in these terms is a significant choice for Gaiman because it situates him in line with the folktale teller and at the margins of literate culture. And it is a self-conscious choice for someone like Gaiman, who became a superstar author and eventually had the freedom to do otherwise (like Stephen King who in 1996 engaged in the pulp fiction practice of publishing *The Green Mile* in serial form).

What Walter Ong refers to as secondary orality is a digital-age means of intentionally employing folktale practices to activate folk culture ideas in a playful, self-conscious way.[54] Through a mix of intuition and self-consciousness, Gaiman developed a storytelling practice in *The Sandman* that employs and deconstructs myth at the same time, what English scholar Joakim Jahlmar refers to as "metamyth."[55] Gaiman has been called one of "the top ten living post-modern authors" by the *Dictionary of Literary Biography*,[56] an honorific that is somewhat unclear given the endless ways in which postmodernism can be defined. However, Gaiman recognized that *The Sandman* was not just a myth but a myth about myths and a story about stories: intertextual and metatextual.[57] Through *The Sandman*, he questions conventional meaning: undermining clear divisions between reality and dream, fact and fiction, right and wrong, true and false: "Everything is welcome. Nothing is untrue. All is true.

In theory, you think the whole structure would collapse under a neatly eroded suspension of disbelief. But in actual fact, it worked fairly well."[58] Elsewhere, Gaiman connects this idea with the experience of a scary holiday for a child yet to be taught that some things are false: "On Halloween, I believed in everything."[59]

In his introduction to the second collected volume of *The Sandman*, Clive Barker describes how Gaiman's approach threatens familiar places with terms generated by the genre of horror:

> [In Gaiman's] kind of fantastique... the whole world is haunted and mysterious. There is no solid status quo, only a series of relative realities, personal to each of the characters, any and all of which are frail and subject to eruptions from other states and conditions. One of the finest writers in this... mode is Edgar Allan Poe, in whose fevered stories landscape, character–even architecture–become a function of the tormented, sexual, anxious psyche of the author; in which anything is possible because the tales occur within the teller's skull.[60]

In addition to describing a world where everything true is eerie, Barker connects characters to writers (and later to readers). The boundaries between what is real and what is not have been removed, and Barker wonders, "Is it perhaps the freedom from critical and academic scrutiny that has made the medium of the comic book so rich an earth in which to nurture this second kind of fiction?"[61]

Barker's point is interesting but shouldn't be read as a silver lining of the Comics Code, the consequence of a capitalist industry wanting to survive in a hostile market and willing to define its product as entertainment that can be regulated as obscenity (rather than as art that is subject to academic scrutiny). Of course, folktales are never consciously identified as tales of the folk by their tellers and much less as art that works in cooperation with other "texts" through literary devices like allusion. With this in mind, Gaiman clearly inhabits contradictory positions: understanding comics as a mass market product that should be protected like art by the First Amendment. This conflict, which is not seen as a conflict by Gaiman, is addressed by two other commentators on *The Sandman* collections, Stephen King and Harlan Ellison.

In an introduction to one of the last *The Sandman* collections, King states,

> The stories…[are] works with the clarity of fairy tales and the subversive undertone of top-drawer modern fiction…. There's so much referral–self and otherwise–and cross-referencing going on here that it's damned near Joycean. Or Proustian. Or ovarian. Or one of those damned things they're always nattering on about in English 202…. Gaiman doesn't do it pretentiously, thank God; that would be boring (and a little mean). It's for fun, like the scribbles of marginalia in *Mad Magazine*."[62]

Posing as an intellectual everyman (something to be discussed more in Chapter 5), King identifies the connection between fairy tales, modern fiction, and intertextuality associated with modern literary masters[63] (or something more bodily). He makes porous the boundaries between low culture and high culture, terms used in the campaign against comics in the 1950s; Gaiman's sophisticated allusions become "the scribbles of marginalia in *Mad* magazine," something that satisfies the worthy end-goal of fun.[64] In contrast, Harlan Ellison represents a push-back characteristic of a 1950s high culture perspective in his introduction to the fourth collection of *The Sandman* (the first to be published in hardcover). In what can be characterized as a long, condescending, back-handed compliment, Ellison's introduction dismisses Gaiman's practices in subtle ways.

After a diatribe on excellence versus mediocrity, Ellison describes how Gaiman's talent "reminds us of how much mediocrity we put up with," making Gaiman significant in contrast to the dearth represented by most comic books. Unlike King who appreciates Gaiman's intertextuality, Ellison criticizes Gaiman's allusions as superficial, calling attention to themselves:

> [J]ust in case the reader hasn't seen the 1941 Warner Bros. adaptation of Jack London's *The Sea Wolf*, in which Edward G. Robinson as the tyrannical freighter skipper Wolf Larsen quotes the quotation repeatedly, Neil bangs us over the head with the information that the aphorism comes from Milton's *Paradise Lost* (1667). Leaf ahead to that page and look at it. See what I mean? A *really* intellectual guy, secure in his own voluminous erudition, wouldn't have bothered making sure we know how goddam sharp he is. Now, I'm not saying Neil isn't as sharp as he wants us to believe he is, I'm merely suggesting that he is so intent on building all the buttressing into his fictional structure that he makes certain we perceive of what excellent granite is made the basement slab.[65]

His immediate concern is with the tendency to garner information from a lesser, more recent point of origin (*The Sea Wolf* film, not even *The Sea Wolf* novel or *Paradise Lost* itself): a typical concern of literate age high culture. Although he identifies himself as sometimes doing the same and reading comics in his youth, Ellison is clearly uncomfortable with Gaiman's project–perhaps due to his misreading *The Sandman* as "a compelling internally-consistent universe."[66]

A fictive universe where "nothing is untrue" cannot be consistent, at least in a post-Enlightenment world informed by Cartesian precepts, but that inconsistency is essential to *The Sandman*, where dreams are not a departure from the real. The series takes place as much in the world of dreams as in the so-called real world, and this is established from the start with Morpheus's move back into his dream realm. Through his conversation with horror hosts Cain and Abel (real parts of his dream realm that can travel to other realms), it becomes apparent that dreaming is a space where fiction comfortably exists alongside the so-called fact. Cain and Abel are clearly the DC horror hosts, and Abel names his new pet gargoyle after his imaginary friend Goldie. And despite the horror host Destiny's attempt to dissociate them from their Biblical namesakes in *Weird Mystery* No. 3, Gaiman picks up where Moore left off with them in *Swamp Thing* No. 33: as brothers forever reenacting the primal act of fratricide. (Incidentally, Destiny himself shows up later in in the series as one of Morpheus's brothers, another member of the D-named divine order of siblings called the Endless.)

In addition to the humor of Morpheus's conversation with Cain and Abel followed by the horror of Abel's murder, the pathos of their relationship is compounded by the alternate story crafted by Abel. Alive again and speaking to his new pet gargoyle, he ignores his bruised and bleeding eye: "I'll, um, tell you a story, Goldie.... It's a secret story. It's a story of two brothers. And they, uh... they loved each other very much and they were always nice to each other. Nice and brotherly. And the elder brother would never hurt the younger brother. Never. And they lived in the same house.... I'm really not crying. It's only blood."[67] The six panels in which the story is told depict Abel on his doorstep: two panels in each of the three columns with the large vertical gutters separating the columns and depicting drops of blood falling to the ground. Artists Sam Keith and Mike Drengenberg use the gutters, typically negative or dead spaces, to portray, as Clive Barker suggests, the "frail [boundaries of stories] subject to eruptions from other states." This use of Cain and Abel represents what will be a long line of intertextual references linking high and low culture as equally viable in the world of dreams (and Dream).[68]

In fact, Lyta Hall, the daughter of the Golden Age Wonder Woman, plays a major role in the life of Morpheus, a role intertwined with mythic figures like the god Loki, the fairy Robin Goodfellow, and the monstrous Furies. She conceived a child with Hector Hall, the *Sandman* superhero who is the son of the Golden Age Hawkman and Hawkgirl, but Hector was killed before she gave birth. Visiting Hector in dreams during Morpheus's imprisonment, Lyta married him and temporarily halted her child's development. After Morpheus informed her that her child belonged to the Dreaming, she lived in constant fear that Morpheus would take her child, Daniel. When Loki stole Daniel, she suffered a nervous breakdown, enabled the Furies to destroy the Dreaming, and inadvertently forced Morpheus to sacrifice himself to protect his realm. However, as a consequence, Daniel would assume Morpheus's former role as Dream, the governor of the Dreaming.

While this story seems to work in orderly terms established by Greek tragedy (in which an attempt to escape fate ensures its realization), it clearly reveals the intertextual web on which *The Sandman* relies. Moreover, the series works in other ways to subvert the narrative structures that represent the values of modern Western culture. After being goaded by his sister, Desire, Morpheus decides to save Nada, an African woman he cast into hell for refusing his offer of marriage. Although her story is initially presented as an orally transmitted African myth earlier in the series, the hell Nada inhabits looks much like a hell shaped by Christian mythology, Milton's *Paradise Lost*, and Doré's illustrations of *Paradise Lost*. And Cain, protected by the mark placed on him by God, is initially sent to Lucifer as an emissary safe from the possible aggressions of the fallen angel. However, just as important as the cross-pollination provided in cross-cultural and cross-medial terms is the way *The Season of Mists* sets up and frustrates readers' expectations. There is a poignancy to this frustration of expectations established in part by the "true" story told by *Paradise Lost,* a work that inserts a Biblical story into classical epic tradition that potentially rewrites the meaning of the source material.

Frustrating Even More Expectations: Even (and Especially) in the Gutter, Morpheus Is Not a Hero

Already the series had revised the resolution of conflict typical of quests in minor ways with the revenge of Morpheus that follows his imprisonment. When he confronts Doctor Destiny as an adversary who possesses an object of Morpheus's power, Doctor Destiny is not attacked but moved into a dream realm where he is tiny and Morpheus is enormous.

When he saves Rose from the Corinthian and a convention filled with serial killers, the means by which he dispatches the killers are words that dismiss their ideas (as already mentioned). Regardless, *The Season of Mists* is even more particularly designed with the typical hallmarks that precede a quester's violent confrontation with his enemy through Morpheus's farewells to old friends, safeguards for his realm's future, and armaments with which to do battle.

And hell is appropriately horrific, at odds with the "civilized" quest of Morpheus, with demons of infinite and disgusting variety who torture the damned (most often by rending their flesh). Yet, when Morpheus arrives in hell, Lucifer informs him that he has no plans to fight in order to keep Nada. "I give you my word that while we are within the bounds of hell, I will do nothing to harm you.... I'll tell you what's happened to your lady-love...Now do you still want to know what's going on?... I've quit."[69] The next three panels, in which Morpheus faces the reader with various expressions of astonishment, approximate the reaction of the reader set up by this narrative and the general narrative of modern Western culture to expect something quite different.

Although it is in reference to a later story, Bratman makes a statement that applies to much of *The Sandman*: "It's hard to count the number of ways Gaiman violates the rules of good writing."[70] Of course, those violations are intentional, and the freedom to move from cultural scripts is important at many different levels to *The Sandman*. In *Season of Mists*, Lucifer moves away from his culturally determined script and gives Morpheus the keys to hell, creating new problems but also opening up new possibilities. For the damned in hell, it means moving away from a notion that they maintain because it is a source of pride: they are so dramatically evil that they have made a mark in opposition to the creator.

When Lucifer tells the horribly tortured and disfigured Breschau that he may leave, he responds, "I... will... not... leave.... My name was whispered by mothers to terrify their babes into obedience. I am Breschau who bathed in the blood of children." When Lucifer claims that he has tortured himself enough, Breschau responds, "It's not me that is torturing me....Did you not hear? I–am Breschau. Yes, I know. But no one today remembers your name."[71] The idea of himself as essentially monstrous helps Breschau sustain the illusion of his power, but Lucifer argues that he can only be monstrous when defined relatively in relationship to culture–and no one now remembers his name.

Lucifer literally embraces the abject, with all its power to destabilize, at the very end of this issue in a panel where he tongue-kisses Mazikeen, a demon whose half-rotten profile faces the reader. (However, he makes no acknowledgement that this act or Mazikeen, whose half-preserved face is beautiful, is disgusting in any way.) Shortly thereafter, he says to Morpheus, "And what will they do on earth... I wonder... when the dead start coming back?"[72] With the image of Mazikeen and these words, the reader likely has expectations for a walking dead story so long prohibited by the Code, but as the reader should realize, *Season of Mists* does not provide an expected horror experience.

Instead, the story of Charles Rowland is situated between the two halves of this story in which Morpheus receives the keys of hell and decides what to do with them. Mostly a flashback to the recent events in the life of the now dying Charles, this issue is the only representation of how Lucifer's actions affect people "on earth." Stranded at his boarding school over the holidays, the dead return as blank-eyed but otherwise rather normal figures going about boarding school routines in a sinister way. Three bullies return from the dead and kill Charles, but a young boy named Edwin Paine returns from the dead and attends him in his final moments (and after he dies). When Death comes to collect Charles, he realizes that his new friend Edwin is staying and Charles chooses to stay with him (revealing that Death has no divine power to force him to go).

As Charles and Edwin depart, Charles comments on the mundane cruelties that he sees enacted by the risen dead: "They're doing the same things they always did. They're doing it to themselves. That's hell." In this way, he reinforces the notion introduced with Breschau, that the horror show of hell is not separate from one's self but within one's self and willfully experienced. Edwin responds with a line that is somewhat more traditional but nevertheless emphasizes the idea of choice and resists the idea of a stable and unchanging identity: "I don't think I agree. But you don't have to stay anywhere forever." As they leave the boarding school hand-in-hand, Charles says, "We might as well make the most of it. Just take it as it comes." "Death, you mean? Or life?" Edwin queries. "Either. Both. Anyway, I think we've learned all we're going to at school. Now: let's see what life's got to offer us..."[73] Revising conventions of stories about the walking dead (and boarding schools), Gaiman works to also break down a fundamental dividing line for human experience—life and death—and make it a playful matter of choice as the dead boys go to see "what life's got to offer."[74]

At the artistic level, Matt Wagner illustrates this story at the center of the *Season of Mists* while Kelly Jones illustrates the rest of the arc. In addition to marking a difference between the story of Morpheus and that of Charles in visual terms, Wagner designs panels in notably different ways, and this is nowhere more apparent than on the second page, where Charles relates his dreams to Edwin.

Within panels drawn with jagged lines, the reader is made privy to bizarre images from Charles's dreams, with only the first and last panels representing the "real" world of the dying boy. However, those two panels are presented in surreal ways that make the real world disorienting (like the first with Charles viewed from above and at an angle, seemingly a panel set within a panel and set at a strange angle). More importantly, the panels are small and allow space to depict something in the gutter and behind the panels: the only image of Morpheus in the story, a figure surrounded by a web that partially spills over to the gutter space on the next page. Gaiman had already taken away Morpheus's status as a questing hero and even as a conventional protagonist by making him into a minor or nonexistent character in the series with individual issues devoted to self-contained stories like one about a cat's dreams. However, this is something much more.

In addition to complicating the Cartesian space within the panels (consisting of a foreground and background) by adding another background, this move complicates the gutter. Clearly not a marker of the simple transition in time, Morpheus inhabits the crypt space and between the panels Morpheus becomes something more or at least other than a character. Occupying the space between, he becomes a disruption of time (a conventional story unit), simultaneously working as character, setting, and plot elements; he is the fabric of the story that problematizes its conventional workings. And with this presentation, readers have a sense of Morpheus–staring straight toward the reader–as the host who reveals a self-conscious approach to the deconstructive power of Dream. When stymied by rules (like those of a boarding school), the idea of freedom from rules is enabling, and breakdown between boundaries is potentially exciting.

However, freedom might not be enabling or exciting and might be frustrating and fearful because such a reorientation necessitates the end of a fundamental way of understanding. In a way that prefigures Lyta's fruitless attempt to defy fate, the angel Remiel presents a case to Morpheus for God to have the keys to hell (alongside other figures from many cross-cultural mythological traditions who make their own cases). When Morpheus agrees to give the keys to him, God informs Remiel that he will be the new ruler of hell. He responds with "Hell is for the Evil.... I will rebel. Like Lucifer. I will protest. This is wrong.... But–how can I rebel?

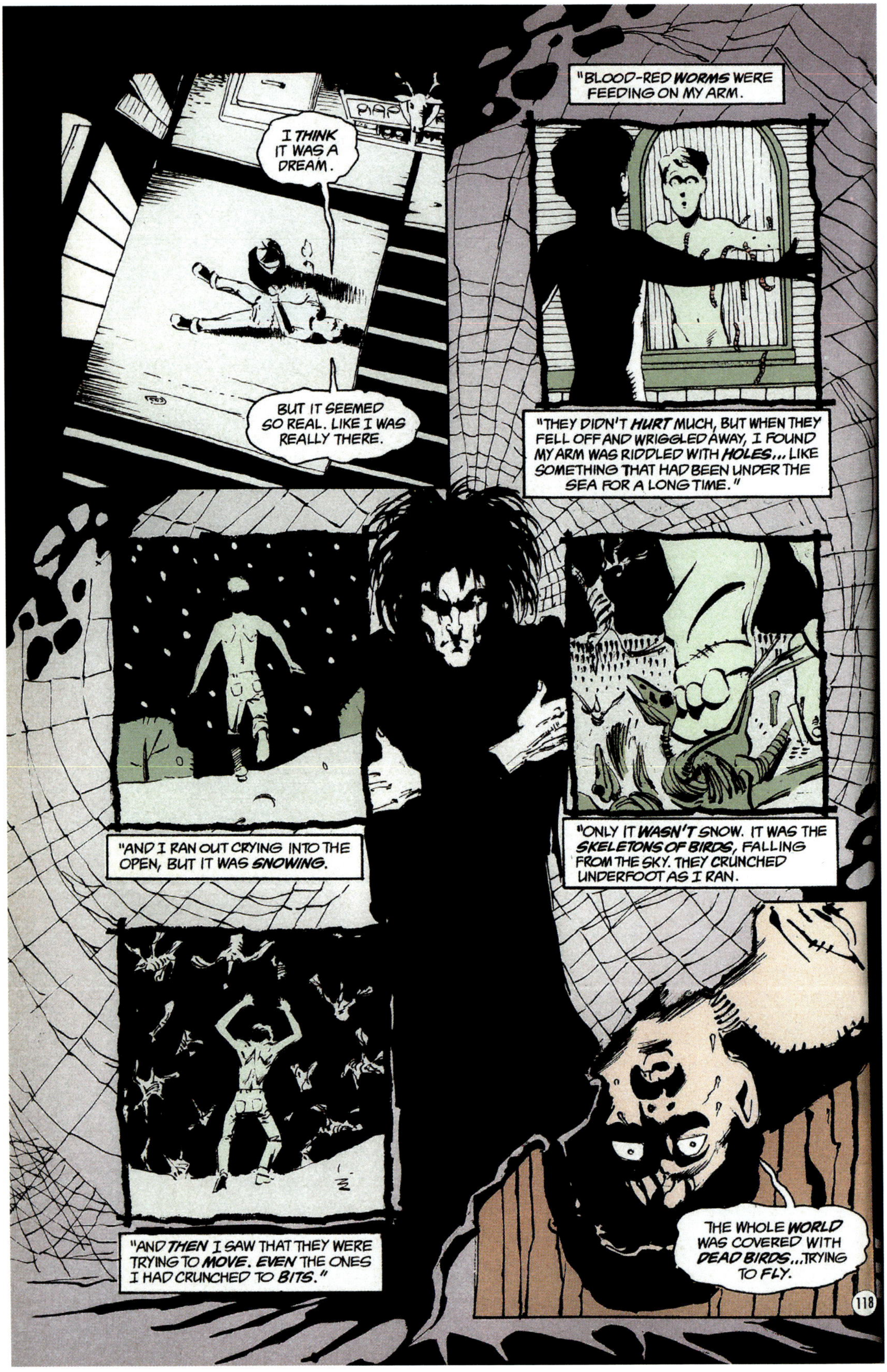
I THINK IT WAS A DREAM.
BUT IT SEEMED SO REAL. LIKE I WAS REALLY THERE.
"BLOOD-RED WORMS WERE FEEDING ON MY ARM.
"THEY DIDN'T HURT MUCH, BUT WHEN THEY FELL OFF AND WRIGGLED AWAY, I FOUND MY ARM WAS RIDDLED WITH HOLES... LIKE SOMETHING THAT HAD BEEN UNDER THE SEA FOR A LONG TIME."
"AND I RAN OUT CRYING INTO THE OPEN, BUT IT WAS SNOWING.
"ONLY IT WASN'T SNOW. IT WAS THE SKELETONS OF BIRDS, FALLING FROM THE SKY. THEY CRUNCHED UNDERFOOT AS I RAN.
"AND THEN I SAW THAT THEY WERE TRYING TO MOVE. EVEN THE ONES I HAD CRUNCHED TO BITS."
THE WHOLE WORLD WAS COVERED WITH DEAD BIRDS... TRYING TO FLY.
118

Where could I go if I did?"[75] Almost immediately recognizing the problem with his idea of rebellion, he later decides what must change is his idea of hell. While the torture of evil-doers continues in hell, he explains, "We do not do it to punish you. We do it to redeem you. Because afterward, you'll be a better person... And because we love you." To this, one of the tortured (likely committed to the same line of thought as Breschau) states, "But...you don't understand... That makes it worse. That makes it so much worse."[76] The chance for redemption and the realization of love is painful to this tortured soul because it exists in a place where one thing is not separate from another.[77]

Fig. 4.2
The Sandman No. 25, DC Comics, 1991
© DC Comics
By occupying the "crypt" space of the gutter, Morpheus not only complicates Cartesian space but also disrupts the conventional passage of time between panels.

Dark Fantasy Goes from the Weird to the Queer: "Other" Stuff in *The Sandman*

In his interviews, Gaiman is less political than Alan Moore, and in his work, Gaiman doesn't engage political issues in ways that are overtly political and characteristic of Moore. However, *The Sandman* does address contentious contemporaneous political issues important to Goth identity and often represented problematically within horror fiction: gender and sexuality. While women were arguably in a better position in both social and political terms in England and the United States in the 1980s, the Thatcher and Reagan administrations represented a conservative and perhaps reactionary stance in regard to women's rights (ironically with Margaret Thatcher as the first female prime minister in England). And as homosexuality was decriminalized in the 1980s, a backlash against women, homosexuals, and others outside the heterosexist norm took shape and gained support through the rhetoric of family values.

Prominent actions include Thatcher's Clause 28 preventing local authorities from supporting alternatives to heterosexual family life, Pope John Paul removing support from gay Catholic organizations, and Jesse Helms referring to homosexuals as degenerates in the name of family values (in *Newsweek* in 1994). Sexism, along with heterosexism, has long been part of horror fiction, as women in horror literature and film regularly occupy the object position, to be saved and to be ogled. Prominent examples of this sort of objectification can be seen in sources as diverse as Bram Stoker's *Dracula*, many Universal monster movies, and most post-Goodwin *Creepy* titles and Skywald magazines (mentioned in Chapter 2). And in *Monsters in the Closet*, Harry Benshoff argues that monsters in horror movies from the 1930s through the 1970s are regularly coded as homosexuals to be destroyed, reinforcing prejudices against the sexual other.

However, the genre is not uniformly dismissive of people othered by gender and sexuality as women often represent the means to defeat the monster (as in the classic *Nosferatu* and the contemporary *Alien*). Despite the male-centered conservatism that could be read into slasher films of the 1970s and 1980s, this simple reading is made problematic by Carol Clover in *Men, Women, and Chain Saws*. Clover suggests the male gaze of the killer is subverted as the viewer submits to the power of the mothering body with the nurturing woman left alone to oppose the killer (in *Halloween*, *Nightmare on Elm Street*, and others). And in addition to Universal's *Frankenstein*, with a sympathetic monster coded as homosexual by James Whale, alternative sexualities have long been part of vampire stories outside the somewhat dominant Stoker tradition with not entirely monstrous Byronic figures. Although not vampire fiction per se, Oscar Wilde's *The Picture of Dorian Grey* is recognized for portraying homosexual characters in both coded and overt ways in which an alternative lifestyle is monstrous largely by society's standards.

Goth culture presents gender and sexuality as fluid constructs in its general ideas and outward expressions in fashion. While Tim Burton's Goth primer, *Edward Scissorhands*, does not deal overtly with gender or sexuality, the film depicts the tragic consequences of alterity in the wake of a conservative culture's backlash. With this history as part of Gaiman's world, *The Sandman* presents gender and sexuality in ways more subversive than Alan Moore, making more indistinct the separations between man and woman, heterosexual and homosexual and others. As mentioned earlier, the publisher sought a different audience for *The Sandman*[78] and this enabled Gaiman's self-conscious decision to openly deal with issues of gender and sexuality. In terms of his approach, Gaiman states quite simply, "I tended to alternate between what I thought of as male story lines... and more female stories."[79] While this suggests a Virginia Woolf-inspired first wave feminist approach to gender, he pushes further in another interview: "Language is sexist. You can fight this or you can get it to work with you."[80] Gaiman begins to cover ground central to Julia Kristeva and Luce Irigaray's critique of psychoanalysis with the idea that culture can be written in a more gynocentric way. Recalling narrative innovations already covered, the narrative itself works with a structural (or post-structural) approach that undermines systematic limitations of straight male storytelling.

Throughout *The Sandman*, communities of characters are extremely diverse, and cultural outsiders often become central while cultural insiders are revealed as monstrous. In *The Doll's House* arc, Rose lives in a boarding house that includes Hal, a nightclub drag performer, Chantal and Zelda, a lesbian couple, and Ken and Barbie, a heterosexual couple. As might be expected from their names, Ken and Barbie are a caricatured, yuppie-like couple whose strict gender identities seem informed by the Mattel dolls for girls. At a critical point with Rose as the vortex for the Dreaming, Barbie cries in bed (due to her patriarchally determined helplessness), and the horny Ken reacts badly to her (due to his patriarchally determined self-centeredness).

But Barbie's story is not a simplistic critique of heterosexist culture as she returns, divorced, as the central protagonist in *A Game of You*. When she revisits a stereotypical dream of being a princess, the fantasy land is revealed to be not of her own making and leads to the horrific death of her toy-inspired companion Wilkinson. The aid offered by her friends outside the Dreaming inadvertently results in the death of another companion (but this one from the "real world"): the preoperative transsexual Wanda. When "she" is buried as Alvin Mann, Barbie replaces the name on the tombstone and dreams of Wanda as a woman (demonstrating how her ideas have moved beyond cultural constraints with gender and sexuality less clearly fixed).[81]

In "Empowering Voice and Refiguring Retribution: Neil Gaiman's Anti-Feminism Feminist Parable," Aaron Drucker demonstrates that Gaiman resists the straightforward, empowered female hero characteristic of second-wave feminism: "Lyta [Hall] serves as a figure for feminist tropes in Gaiman's fantasy, constructed to ironically critique the second-wave feminist archetypes of empowerment in a male-constructed narrative of the feminine in the world of dreams."[82] When Lyta releases the furies to attack Morpheus and the Dreaming, her act of vengeance undermines her power and ensures an outcome she does not want.[83] Instead, as Ally Brisbin and Paul Booth argue in "The Sand/wo/man: The Unstable Worlds of Gender in Neil Gaiman's *Sandman* series," Gaiman makes gender (and sexuality) a performance, an infinite cycle of revelation and rediscovery characteristic of third-wave feminism.

The emphasis of the cyclical (as opposed to the linear) in identity formation necessarily leads to a consideration of the Endless specific to gender and sexuality. These siblings visually appear to be a divine Goth community, difficult to clearly identify from external signifiers as masculine or feminine, male or female, or heterosexual or homosexual.

While some have relatively stable gender and sexual identities, others do not, and the most notably fluid is Desire (shaping herself by virtue of the human experience s/he governs). While depicted as a woman more often than a man, s/he appears as a man in notable ways such as impregnating Unity Kinkaid. In the Dreaming (not necessarily dissimilar to the real world), performance is actuality, something Desire does reactively as well as proactively. And while s/he serves as an antagonist to Morpheus, they are often visually and interpersonally indistinct (arguably more so than any other members of the Endless).

The Style of Art and the Art of Style: Endless Surrealism on the Cover and on the Mind

While the art and visual design of *The Sandman* has been mentioned, this chapter has primarily referred to Gaiman as the auteur behind the series. Whether or not that characterization is fair, it is a consequence of the fact that no one artist worked with Gaiman to give *The Sandman* a consistent look. This turnover is not unusual in the traditional comic book industry where artists were considered interchangeable, but the series clearly became a point of transition to a new shape for the comic book industry. However, the differences in style that once may have been considered to be a deficiency were often considered by critics as a generally positive feature (with styles complementing the specifics of story arcs). Gaiman suggests there was clear intentionality along these lines and states, "Alan Moore told me that when you write for specific artists you should... play to their strengths... 'It makes you look good,' he explained."[84] And he not only wrote for artists brought to him but eventually for artists he specifically sought for certain arcs or stand-alone issues.

Critical approval of the series' variation in style indicates a move away from a desire for classical principles of consistency and realism. Regardless of how naturalistic any one artist's style might be, it would look less realistic when placed before or after another artist with even a slightly different style; the difference prevents the reality effect that results when a reader becomes accustomed to an artist's style. Thematically, this worked to the benefit of a series that sought to problematize the conventional experience of the real. Moreover, many of the artistic styles intentionally departed from rules that govern visual realism such as that of Marc Hempel for *The Kindly Ones* arc, whose style looks like "stained-glass windows."[85]

Marc Hempel is followed by Michael Zulli, whose more naturalistic style is ironically used to represent Morpheus's wake in the Dreaming (and in quick succession, the final two issues are illustrated by two other artists: Jon J. Muth and Charles Vess). In any case, the dream-like positioning of two styles that are different and seem to not belong in the same "space" is a precedent established by the one artist most consistently associated with the series: Dave McKean.

Inspired by surrealist painters and filmmakers,[86] McKean's cover art for *The Sandman* regularly mixes styles and works like collages to bring together various art objects. Although the initial covers create a panel-like border for the central image, there is no conventional way to "read" the cover as one might a comic book page. The painted images are not clearly ordered or associated with one another, and even individual images borrow from dream logic; in the same space figures overlap in impossible ways and/or allow smaller views not suggested by the larger image such as the mosaic pattern inside (or is it atop?) the head and chest of the figure on the cover of issue No. 5. Moreover, even the deceptive familiarity of the panel strips as borders is disrupted with issue No. 7 where an image "cut" from the central panel is placed atop the left-side border. In addition, the partial image of a door in one of the right side panels extends into the central panel with a doorknob, and the collage structure allows the viewer to imagine (or not) that the cutout of the hand in the central panel is reaching for the doorknob.

Throughout the series, McKean's covers become more experimental and seemingly less tied to the interior story. Unlike the classic comic book tease cover that showed something that never happened in an interior story and was subsequently dismissed by an angry reader, McKean's abstract designs encourage the reader to make creative connections. And while those connections are potentially less frustrating than a misleading tease, they are also potentially more disturbing as the reader is robbed of a sure narrative (and even spatial) context for what is seen. For instance on No. 44, details of skeletal remains can develop ominous overtones when placed inside (or is it atop?) a segmented surface painted sloppily in red and set alongside difficult to identify details of internal organs or roots in the ground? The difficulty for a reader trained to read for certain information is the disorientation caused by McKean's artwork that suggests something other, something unknown, and therefore haunting.

And as Gaiman envisions the Endless, their divine Gothic order reverses the expectations for the divine, and the nature of their existence summarizes the disorientation so important to *The Sandman*.

After Desire attempts to destroy him, Morpheus cautions her to temper grandiose notions of herself as a mover of events: "We of the Endless are the servants of the living—we are not their masters. We exist because they know, deep in their hearts, that we exist.... And we do not manipulate them. If anything, they manipulate us. We are their toys. Their dolls, if you will."[87] In addition to reversing the typical power relationship between gods and humans, Morpheus removes the notion of primacy: that the existence of gods preceded that of humans. And perhaps even more significantly, the idea of knowing is conflated with belief, and the power of knowing/believing is all that sustains the Endless. Rather than wholly independent, they are wholly dependent beings that exist only in the story-space of the human mind.[88]

Fig. 4.3
The Sandman No. 71, DC Comics, 1995
© DC Comics
With a history that dates back to ancient Greece and The Sandman's "Game of You," the witch Thessaly returns to offer her thoughts on Morpheus to the reader.

Thereby, the inner and outer are collapsed. This is revealed to be more than just Morpheus's opinion in *Brief Lives*, in which Morpheus seeks Destruction, the sibling who abandoned his role as an embodiment of Destruction. Surrounded poignantly by the vastness of the starry sky, Destruction, who has seen destruction (and creation) continue without his governance, extends Morpheus's thoughts:

> I can pretend that things last. I can pretend that lives last longer than moments. Gods come, and gods go. Mortals flicker and flash and fade... But I can pretend.... The endless? The endless are merely patterns. The endless are ideas. The endless are wave functions. The endless are repeating motifs. The endless are echoes of darkness, and nothing more. We have no right to play with their lives, to order their dreams and desires. And even our existences are brief and bounded.[89]

With the idea that the Endless are in fact finite, Destruction indulges in the refrain that he can nevertheless pretend. If anything remains, it is the pretend, the belief, the dream that allows opposing things to be true simultaneously, and this gives fantasy the value given to reality, and fiction the power given to fact in an Enlightenment world. If these playful ideas are taken seriously, *The Sandman* exists because of the readers. After the death of Morpheus (but not the death of Dream), "In Which a Wake Is Held" (No. 71) features characters of all sorts who have played roles in the series. When they eulogize Morpheus, they are most often situated within the panels so that they directly address the reader, reinforcing the reader's power to accept or reject their stories. The title of the next issue, "In Which We Wake," is word play with the idea of the wake as funereal celebration and also of waking from sleep—but not the Dreaming (the setting for the issue). And quite significantly, waking is something that "we" do.

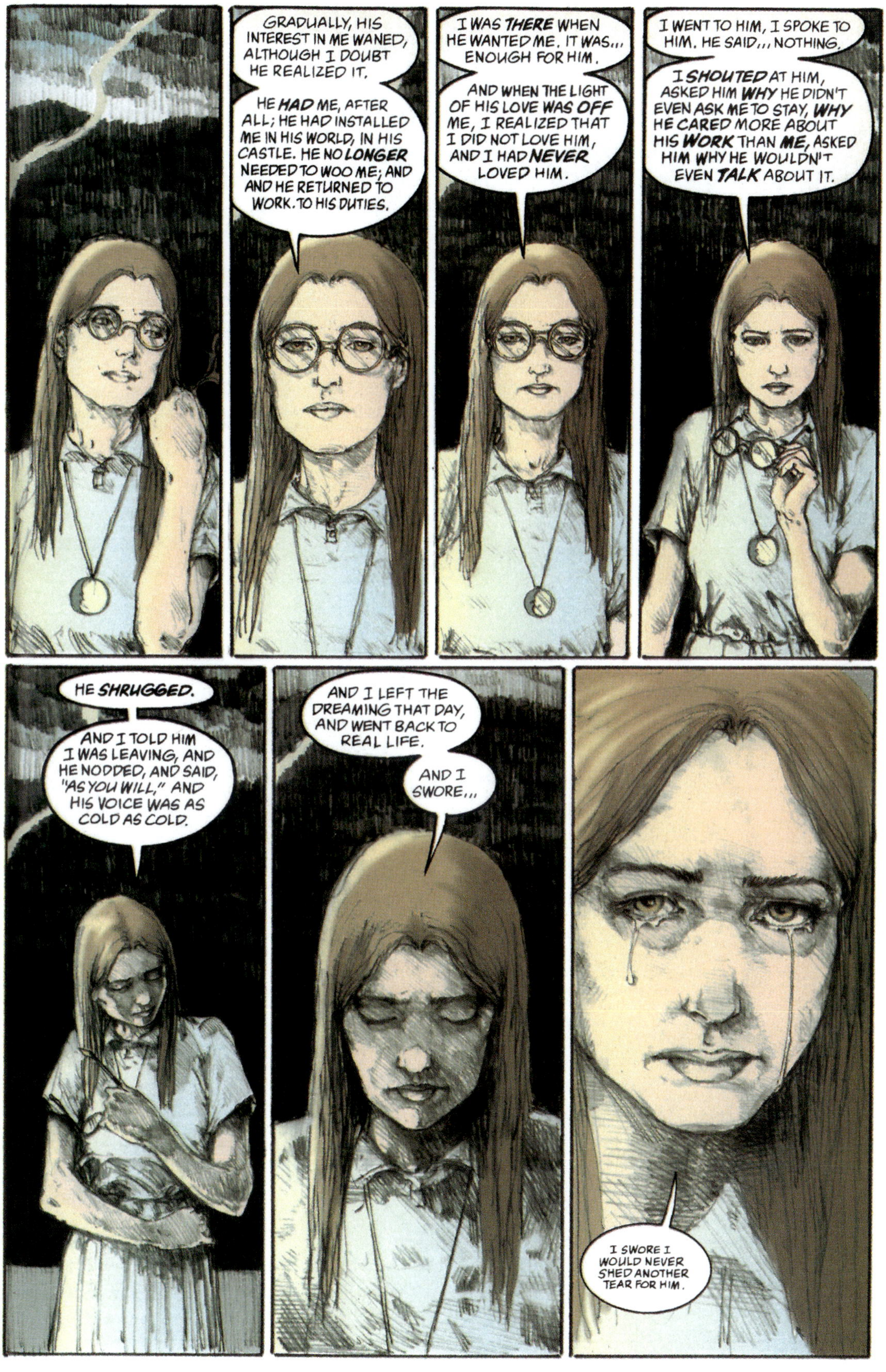
GRADUALLY, HIS INTEREST IN ME WANED, ALTHOUGH I DOUBT HE REALIZED IT.
HE HAD ME, AFTER ALL; HE HAD INSTALLED ME IN HIS WORLD, IN HIS CASTLE. HE NO LONGER NEEDED TO WOO ME; AND AND HE RETURNED TO WORK. TO HIS DUTIES.
I WAS THERE WHEN HE WANTED ME. IT WAS... ENOUGH FOR HIM.
AND WHEN THE LIGHT OF HIS LOVE WAS OFF ME, I REALIZED THAT I DID NOT LOVE HIM, AND I HAD NEVER LOVED HIM.
I WENT TO HIM, I SPOKE TO HIM. HE SAID... NOTHING.
I SHOUTED AT HIM, ASKED HIM WHY HE DIDN'T EVEN ASK ME TO STAY, WHY HE CARED MORE ABOUT HIS WORK THAN ME, ASKED HIM WHY HE WOULDN'T EVEN TALK ABOUT IT.
HE SHRUGGED.
AND I TOLD HIM I WAS LEAVING, AND HE NODDED, AND SAID, "AS YOU WILL," AND HIS VOICE WAS AS COLD AS COLD.
AND I LEFT THE DREAMING THAT DAY, AND WENT BACK TO REAL LIFE.
AND I SWORE...
I SWORE I WOULD NEVER SHED ANOTHER TEAR FOR HIM.

In "A Midsummer Night's Dream" (No. 19), the most highly awarded and often studied story in *The Sandman* series,[90] William Shakespeare laments his second-class status alongside Christopher Marlowe to Morpheus in the Dreaming. Shakespeare then breaks down the barrier between his life and Marlowe's most famous story by making a Faustian bargain with Morpheus and enabling him to give the fantastic a home in his stories. Sitting alongside the fairy folk Titania and Auberon, Morpheus states, "Things need not have happened to be true. Tales and dreams are the shadow-truths that will endure when mere facts are dust and ashes, and forgot."[91] Clearly connected to other ideas presented by Dream and Destruction, Castaldo describes it further: "[Shakespeare's] versions [of stories] have, in fact, become the 'great stories' not because they are mythical connections to a greater reality, but because they have helped to shape our culture's knowledge about itself."[92] The tale builds to the famous ending of Shakespeare's *Midsummer Night's Dream* in which Puck, like a horror host in this comic book context, breaks the fourth wall with an invitation to participate in the dream.

The final issue of the series (No. 75) does not end at a traditional point like Morpheus's death, funeral, or wake but with Morpheus's other visit to Shakespeare, in this case concerning *The Tempest*. Perhaps the very first dark fantasy, the play features a magician who destroys his books (the source of his power) and who acknowledges his dependence on the audience in a soliloquy. As a whole, *The Sandman* works to destroy the static power of the written word's authority and move into the dynamic post-author territory suggested by Michel Foucault and encouraged by the "new" media of the twentieth and twenty-first century.[93] The fear associated with this move is that there is no clear source, center, or position that might allow a person to justify the self as right in opposition to the other as wrong. While *The Sandman* builds toward a wake, it is in its entirety a funerary celebration of the death of the conventional ways of knowing based in the binaries of the Cartesian world. Represented so well by the unexpected giddiness of Morpheus's sibling, Death, this is the dark fantasy of the series.

More on the Experience of Vertigo: A Sandman, Hellblazer, and Preacher Walk into a Comic Book Store...

Three years after *The Sandman* became part of the fledgling Vertigo experiment, Neil Gaiman's initial run on the series came to an end. Early in the run, Gaiman expressed a desire for *The Sandman* to end with his last issue, and according to Gaiman, even the thoroughly supportive Karen Berger indicated that's just not how things are done in the comics industry.

Subsequently, Gaiman regularly mentioned his planned conclusion and that he would continue working with DC only if the series ended at that point.[94] Whether or not DC's hand was forced by the fear of losing a writer whose star was rising, *The Sandman* did end at No. 75 and set a meaningful precedent in the mid-'90s; outside the long-established superhero industry, the vision of creators became more important than the continued use of company-owned characters. In addition to the profitability of a continued relationship with Gaiman, DC was likely also influenced by the fact that buyers now followed creators as much as characters (and with careful marketing, trade collections of Neil Gaiman's *The Sandman* would have a long life of sales in the bookstore).

While DC's motivation here may not have been any more purely idealistic than Bill Gaines's motivation to showcase EC creators, this choice moved DC closer to the possibilities suggested by the way Gaines ran his company. Of course, Gaiman treated *The Sandman* like something he could own: a bit more like a text of the literate age than a tale of the folk era. But he did so largely to protect the series from a corporate system inclined to cheapen and merchandise ideas (something also done by Mike Mignola and Eric Powell and discussed more extensively in the next chapter). *The Sandman* would sporadically continue with Gaiman in several subsequent volumes: the picture book *The Dream Hunters* (1999), the short story collection *Endless Nights* (2003), and the prequel *Overture* (2013). Moreover, other writers were allowed to play with Sandman characters in *Death: At Death's Door, The Dreaming, Lucifer*, and *Dead Boy Detectives* (featuring Charles Rowland and Edwin Paine). And ultimately, *The Sandman* is a testament to the ideals of folktale-based horror: something encouraged by the comic book form itself with profound implications in a post-industrial culture.

Founded with *Swamp Thing, Sandman*, and the *Swamp Thing* spin-off *Hellblazer*,[95] Vertigo continued to work outside the conventions associated with superheroes, seeking adult audiences (especially those interested in horror). Producing series not related to one another in their own self-contained worlds, the creators owned their work. The two horror series most significant to the imprint in the 1990s would be *Hellblazer* (a DC property) and later, *Preacher* (a creator-owned property). Both written and drawn by creators from the UK, the series had transgressed social and moral boundaries in ways similar to other horror comics thus far profiled. Based on Alan Moore's John Constantine character (an occultist in a hardboiled detective's rumpled trenchcoat), Jamie Delano's run on *Hellblazer*[96] was more overtly political than *The Sandman* and even Moore's *Swamp Thing*.

With Constantine, readers encountered a haunted man willing to use dark magic and sacrifice his own morality for what might or might not be the greater good. However, this post-punk character is set against the monstrous excesses of the Thatcherite England, and the personal horror of his sinister compromises seems trivial in comparison to the political abuses portrayed on Constantine's telly.

The Irish writer Garth Ennis eventually took over *Hellblazer* and segued into his own original series in 1995 with *Preacher*—a pastiche of various genres including horror, crime, and the Western. Following the quest of Jesse Custer, a preacher empowered by the spiritual offspring of an angel and demon, Jesse's ragtag group fights against a divine bureaucracy that protects itself through ultraviolent means. His quest is to find God, who has apparently abandoned his heavenly post, in order to hold God accountable for his radically fallen world. Exploring the most extreme depravities in ways that are explicitly depicted, the series emphasizes a Quentin Tarantino-like male bonding between Jess and an amoral vampire who helps him; alternately horrifying and comic, radical and conservative, *Preacher* is easily one of the most sacrilegious comics of the 1990s. The series editor, Stuart Moore, felt the need to justify its depictions of sex and violence to DC executives but not its disturbing religious themes;[97] this may suggest not much had changed within the industry in terms of the superficial content-based readings that led to the prohibitions of the Comics Code.[98] However, the simple fact that the series was published by the once conservative bulwark of DC (and that it found a devoted audience) suggests otherwise. An evisceration of big government's faith in itself, *Preacher* argues that no such faith is justified in this world or the next.

Horror comics returned to the mainstream in the United States with titles initially set in the DC superhero universe like *Swamp Thing* and *The Sandman*, due in large part to an influx of talent from the UK. In regard to this phenomenon, comics critic B. Keith Murphy states,

> Had British comic writers been exposed to the heavily formulaic American superhero comics as the status quo rather than as a rare import, it seems unlikely that Moore, Gaiman, and such contemporaries as Garth Ennis and Grant Morrison would have provided such a fresh and insightful approach to a rather old and tired genre. Therefore, in one of those odd coincidences, the Harmful Publications Act, which was created in the wake of the success of EC's line of American horror comics in Britain, actually has served to protect young British minds—but not so much from the exposure to the 'harmful and dangerous' ideas and images of the genre. Instead, by protecting British minds from stereotyped American comic books, the Act allowed the modern version of the genre to blossom.[99]

Perhaps that unblemished outsider perspective is what American horror comics needed to move beyond the limitations of the Comics Code and the superhero genre within the industrial framework of comic book publishing. Regardless, DC's Vertigo imprint represents an industry showcasing a dangerous genre (and allowing it to again be dangerous) through the visions of Alan Moore, Neil Gaiman, and others. While Gaiman followed in Moore's footsteps, *The Sandman* would be the series that changed the ideas of the industry, the medium, and its audience in a way that enabled Mike Mignola and Eric Powell to make a frontal assault on the critical institutions that determine what is acceptable. Those changes not only enable an assault via the offbeat horrors of Mignola's *Hellboy* and Powell's *The Goon*, but they also promise that these creators have a freedom that will not be stolen by the industry or culture at large.

Chapter 4 Notes

1 "Interview-Neil Gaiman, Likely Stories," The Dreamcage, http://www.thedreamcage.com/2016/04/interview-neil-gaiman-likely-stories.html.

2 "Testimony of William M. Gaines, Publisher, Entertaining Comics Group, New York, N.Y.," *TheComicbooks.Com*, last modified 2016, http://www.thecomicbooks.com/gaines.html.

3 Ibid.

4 Neil Gaiman, "Ghosts in the Machines," *The New York Times*, last modified Oct. 31, 2006, http://www.nytimes.com/2006/10/31/opinion/31gaiman.html.

5 Likewise, Gaiman identifies the appeal of "weird fiction": "a holiday in unearthly beauty and oddness, from which you might not always safely return" ("Exclusive Interview: Neil Gaiman on the Weird," *Weird Fiction Review*, last modified Nov. 1, 2011, http://weirdfictionreview.com/2011/11/exclusive-interview-neil-gaiman-on-the-weird/).

6 Michael Dean, "The Young Cannibals: How Phil Seuling and a Generation of Teenage Entrepreneurs Created the Direct Market and Changed the Face of Comics," *The Comics Journal* 277 (July 2006): 49.

7 Claire E. White, "A Conversation with Neil Gaiman," *The Internet Writing Journal*, last modified March 1999, http://www.writerswrite.com/journal/mar99/a-conversation-with-neil-gaiman-3991.

8 These DC series became Vertigo series with the following issues: *Swamp Thing* 129, *Hellblazer* 63, *Sandman* 47, and *Doom Patrol* 64.

9 In the 1970s, DC seemed less committed to horror than Marvel with Marvel's B&W magazines, but Marvel has since fully committed to the multimedia production of superhero stories. Marvel built a stronger superhero film presence, and their adult lines became MAX (superhero stories with adult content) and Icon (creator owned titles with no promotion).

10 Randy Duncan and Matthew J. Smith, *The Power of Comics: History, Form, and Culture* (New York: Bloomsbury, 2009), 91. Vertigo also published other alternative genre work with general success: *100 Bullets* (crime), *Fables* (fantasy), and *Y: The Last Man* and *Transmetropolitan* (science fiction).

11 Matthew J. Pustz, *Comic Book Culture: Fanboys and True Believers* (Jackson: UP of Mississippi, 1999), 84.

12 Hayley Campbell, *The Art of Neil Gaiman* (New York: Harper Design, 2014), 105.

13 Neither wrote *Swamp Thing* as planned, resigning when DC refused to publish Veitch's *Swamp Thing* issue featuring Jesus.

14 Geoff Boucher, "Neil Gaiman: 'Alan Moore got to be The Beatles.... I was Gerry and the Pacemakers,'" *Hero Complex*, last modified Dec. 2, 2008, http://herocomplex.latimes.com/uncategorized/neil-gaiman-ala/. Vertigo should be seen as the house that Alan Moore built; in addition to *Swamp Thing*, one of the other major titles first absorbed in the line (discussed later in this chapter) is *Hellblazer*, a spin-off of *Swamp Thing*.

15 Hank Wagner, Christopher Golden, and Stephen R. Bissette, *Prince of Stories: The Many Worlds of Neil Gaiman* (New York: St. Martin's, 2008), 3.

16 "Exclusive Interview: Neil Gaiman on the Weird," *Weird Fiction Review*.

17 Hayley Campbell, *The Art of Neil Gaiman*, 96.

18 In 2010, Gaiman married Amanda Palmer of the Dresden Dolls described as "Brechtian punk cabaret" (part of the dark cabaret sub-genre of contemporary Gothic music).

19 Lauren M.E. Goodlad and Michael Bibby, "Introduction," *Goth: Undead Subculture*, ed., Lauren M.E. Goodlad and Michael Bibby (Durham: Duke UP, 2007), 1–3.

20 Julia Round draws connections between Goth and fanboy as subcultures in *Gothic in Comics and Graphic Novels* (Jefferson, NC: McFarland, 2014), 36.

21 Nina Auerbach, *Our Vampires, Ourselves* (Chicago: U of Chicago P, 1995), 154.

22 Ibid., 154.

23 Tasha Robinson, "Interview: Neil Gaiman," *The Onion A.V. Club*, last modified Sept. 28, 2005, http://www.avclub.com/article/neil-gaiman-13953.

24 In reference to the S&M pain aesthetic in *Hellraiser*, Wheeler Winston Dixon states: "Central to the conceit of the film is the puzzle box–the "torture box"–that contains all the pain and the suffering imaginable in this, or any, world" (Wheeler Winston Dixon, *A History of Horror* [New Brunswick: Rutgers UP, 2010], 157).

25 John Krewson, "Interview: Neil Gaiman," *The Onion A.V. Club*, last modified Feb. 3, 1999, http://www.avclub.com/article/neil-gaiman-13579.

26 Dark fantasy is not without comic book precedents: *Creepy* and *Eerie* with fantasy and science fiction and Marvel with Conan and Kull (a pulp fiction connection). However, they usually lack the self-conscious aspects that are an increasing part of this genre. As a synthetic genre (fantasy/science fiction/horror), it questions the conventions of each genre.

27 "An Interview with Neil Gaiman," *Gothic Beauty*, last modified Dec. 1, 2004, https://www.gothicbeauty.com/2004/12/an-interview-with-neil-gaiman/.

28 Joe Sanders, *The Sandman Papers: An Exploration of the Sandman Mythology* (Seattle: Fantagraphics, 2006).

29 Neil Gaiman, Sam Keith, Mike Dringenberg, Malcolm Jones III, Robbie Busch, and Todd Klein. *The Sandman: Preludes and Nocturnes* (New York: DC, 1995), 219

30 Geoff Boucher, "Neil Gaiman: 'Alan Moore got to be The Beatles.... I was Gerry and the Pacemakers,'" *Hero Complex*, last modified Dec. 2, 2008. http://herocomplex.latimes.com/uncategorized/neil-gaiman-ala/.

31 Neil Gaiman, Mike Dringenberg, Malcolm Jones III, Chris Bachalo, Michael Zulli, Steve Parkhouse, Robbie Busch, and Todd Klein, *The Sandman: The Doll's House* (New York: DC, 1995), 172.

32 David Bratman, "A Game of You–Yes, You," *The Sandman Papers: An Exploration of the Sandman Mythology*, ed., Joe Sanders (Seattle: Fantagraphics, 2006), 44.

33 Stephen Rauch, *Neil Gaiman's* The Sandman *and Joseph Campbell: In Search of the Modern Myth* (Holicong, PA: Wildside, 2003), 17.

34 Ibid., 22.

35 Ibid., 23.

36 "[T]he seed of his death was planted more than three thousand years earlier by his son Orpheus's refusal to accept death as the natural course of things" (Kathryn Hume, "Neil Gaiman's Sandman as Mythic Romance," *Genre* 46 [Fall 2013]: 358).

37 Annalisa Castaldo, "'No More Yielding than a Dream': The Construction of Shakespeare in *The Sandman*," *College Literature* 31 (Fall 2004): 100.

38 Geoff Boucher, "Dream a Little Dream: Neil Gaiman on the 20th Anniversary of '*The Sandman*,'" *Hero Complex*, last modified Dec. 1, 2008, http://herocomplex.latimes.com/uncategorized/dream-a-little/.

39 Robert K. Elder, "Gods and Other Monsters: A Sandman Exit interview and Philosophical Omnibus," *The Neil Gaiman Reader*, ed., Darrell Schweitzer (Holicong, PA: Wildside, 2007), 56. In reference to structuring stories in line with Joseph Campbell's monomyth, Gaiman states, "I think I got about half way through *The Hero with a Thousand Faces* and found myself thinking if this is true– I don't want to know. I really would rather do it because it's true and because I accidentally wind up creating something that falls into this pattern than be told what the pattern is" (Tim E. Ogline, "Myth, Magic, and the Mind of Neil Gaiman: A Conversation with the Dream King," *Wild River Review*, last modified August 1, 2007, http://www.wildriverreview.com/4/worldvoices-neilgaiman.php.).

40 Nick Katsiadas, "Mytho-auto-bio: Neil Gaiman's Sandman, the Romantics, and Shakespeare's The Tempest," *Studies in Comics* 6 (2015): 66.

41 Joakim Jahlmar, "'Give the Devil His Due': Freedom, Damnation, and Milton's *Paradise Lost* in Neil Gaiman's *The Sandman: Season of Mists*," *Partial Answers: Journal of Literature and the History of Ideas* 13 (June 2015): 268.

42 Surrealism has occasionally but notably appeared in the work of Windsor McCay, Robert Crumb, and Rick Veitch.

43 Ian Conrich, "Seducing the Subject: Freddy Krueger," *Horror Film Reader*, ed., Alain Silver and James Ursini (New York: Limelight, 2006), 226–27.

44 Lorna Jowett and Stacey Abbott, *TV Horror: Investigating the Dark Side of the Small Screen* (London: I.B. Tauris, 2013), 160–61, 163.

45 This has been read as King's reaction to his fans' rejection of his fantasy novel *Eyes of the Dragon*.

46 Although *New Nightmare* was not an enormous success, Craven's next film, *Scream,* would be, and it made similar comments on storytelling and horror: "Scream... contained numerous references to other horror films, and the killers themselves are two horror aficionados whose fascination with the genre structures their mayhem.... addressing... the increasingly blurred lines of media representations and reality" (W. Scott Poole, *Monsters in America: Our Historical Obsession with the Hideous and the Haunting* [Waco: Baylor UP, 2011], 220).

47 In an interview with Stephen King, Gaiman gushes, "[W]hen people in the far future want to get an idea of how things felt between 1973 and today, they'll look to King" (Neil Gaiman, "Popular Writers: A Stephen King Interview." Neil Gaiman's Journal. Last modified April 28, 2012. http://journal.neilgaiman.com/2012/04/popular-writers-stephen-king-interview.html).

48 Hayley Campbell, *The Art of Neil Gaiman*, 114. Aside from collections of strips and origin stories, this contemporary process really begins with Frank Miller's *The Dark Knight Returns* and Alan Moore's *Watchmen,* but the bookstore market was most fully realized with *The Sandman*.

49 Matthew J. Pustz, *Comic Book Culture: Fanboys and True Believers*, 86.

50 Hayley Campbell, *The Art of Neil Gaiman*, 117.

51 Geoff Boucher, "Dream a Little Dream: Neil Gaiman on the 20th Anniversary of '*The Sandman*,'" *Hero Complex*, last modified Dec. 1, 2008, http://herocomplex.latimes.com/uncategorized/dream-a-little/.

52 Claire E. White, "A Conversation with Neil Gaiman."

53 Hayley Campbell, *The Art of Neil Gaiman*, 114.

54 With reference to *Twin Peaks*, David Lynch bridges this strange space between the intentional art film and the improvisational thrill of unplanned developments in serial storytelling. Killer Bob is the evil spirit central to the story but only after the camera accidentally caught in a shot Frank Silva, a set dresser–a shot Lynch was determined to keep.

55 Joakim Jahlmar, "'Give the Devil His Due': Freedom, Damnation, and Milton's *Paradise Lost* in Neil Gaiman's *The Sandman: Season of Mists*," 260.

56 Hank Wagner, Christopher Golden, and Stephen R. Bissette, *Prince of Stories: The Many Worlds of Neil Gaiman*, 1.

57 Kathryn Hume, "Neil Gaiman's Sandman as Mythic Romance," 345.

58 Robert K. Elder, "Gods and Other Monsters: A Sandman Exit interview and Philosophical Omnibus," 78.

59 Neil Gaiman, "Ghosts in the Machines."

60 Barker, Clive, "Introduction," Neil Gaiman, Mike Dringenberg, Malcolm Jones III, Chris Bachalo, Michael Zulli, Steve Parkhouse, Robbie Busch, and Todd Klein, *The Sandman: The Doll's House* (New York: DC, 1995) 6.

61 Ibid., 6.

62 Stephen King, "An Introduction," Neil Gaiman, Bryan Talbot, John Watkiss, Michael Allred, Michael Zulli, Shea Anton Pensa, Alec Stevens, Gary Amaro, and Todd Klein, *The Sandman: World's End* (New York: DC, 1994), 12.

63 King chooses James Joyce as one of his examples, coincidentally the one modern author to which Gaines referred in his congressional testimony due to the obscenity case against *Ulysses*.

64 Marginalia in manuscripts from the early literacy of the European medieval period have become essentially important to future readers' interpretation of those manuscripts.

65 Harlan Ellison, "Introduction," Neil Gaiman, Kelly Jones, Mike Dringenberg, Malcolm Jones III, Matt Wagner, Dick Giordano, George Pratt, P. Craig Russell, Steve Oliff, Daniel Vozzo, and Todd Klein, *The Sandman: Season of Mists* (New York: DC, 1992), 11.

66 Ibid., 9.

67 Neil Gaiman, Sam Keith, Mike Dringenberg, Malcolm Jones III, Robbie Busch, and Todd Klein. *The Sandman: Preludes and Nocturnes*, 78.

68 In regard to the big two superhero publishers, the DC universe is more open to a narrative in which many realities have equal validity. While the imaginary stories of Superman (like "The Amazing Story of Superman-Red and Superman-Blue!") were carefully separated from the canonical story, Gardner Fox reintroduced Golden Age superheroes in a Silver Age universe with Earth-2. Subsequently, many stories were developed that featured other universes, including Earth-prime (our world), and comics creators often crossed over into superhero universes.

69 Neil Gaiman, Kelly Jones, Mike Dringenberg, Malcolm Jones III, Matt Wagner, Dick Giordano, George Pratt, P. Craig Russell, Steve Oliff, Daniel Vozzo, and Todd Klein, *The Sandman: Season of Mists* (New York: DC, 1992), 72.

70 David Bratman, "A Game of You–Yes, You," 42.

71 Neil Gaiman, Kelly Jones, Mike Dringenberg, Malcolm Jones III, Matt Wagner, Dick Giordano, George Pratt, P. Craig Russell, Steve Oliff, Daniel Vozzo, and Todd Klein, *The Sandman: Season of Mists*, 76.

72 Ibid., 87.

73 Ibid., 140.

74 These characters would later have their own series: *Sandman Presents: Dead Boy Detectives* (Ed Brubaker, Bryan Talbot, Steve Leialoha [New York: DC, 2008]).

75 Neil Gaiman, Kelly Jones, Mike Dringenberg, Malcolm Jones III, Matt Wagner, Dick Giordano, George Pratt, P. Craig Russell, Steve Oliff, Daniel Vozzo, and Todd Klein, *The Sandman: Season of Mists*, 177–78.

76 Ibid., 216–17.

77 In the "end," Nada–still unwilling to marry Morpheus–is reincarnated with no memory of him, and Lucifer tentatively acknowledges God after a conversation about personal tragedy and the beauty of the sunset. Najwa Al-Tabaa notes, "Perhaps this is what redemption entails–a second chance at happily ever after" ("Hell Can Be Good for You," *Neil Gaiman and Philosophy: Gods Gone Wild!* ed., Tracy L. Bealer, Rachel Luria, Wayne Yuen (Chicago: Open Court, 2012), 78. However, that claim requires an unconventional definition of "happily ever after": no princess with the prince and no reparations made for past actions.

78 Pustz states, "*Sandman* was the only series read by many people, especially spouses and significant others of broader comic fans" (Matthew J. Pustz, *Comic Book Culture: Fanboys and True Believers*, 86). And Gaiman states, "If I did anything, I think the biggest thing I did was just help break down this peculiar gender divide....Guys would be getting Sandman and most of them would have said to their significant females 'please read comics'... and the female person would read it and go 'where are the rest of them?' And then what would normally happen is when they broke up the female person would now go out and normally have the Sandmans with her, and then get a new male person and say 'read these'" ("An Interview with Neil Gaiman," *Gothic Beauty*, https://www.gothicbeauty.com/2004/12/an-interview-with-neil-gaiman/, accessed August 17, 2017).

79 Quoted in Hank Wagner, Christopher Golden, and Stephen R. Bissette, *Prince of Stories: The Many Worlds of Neil Gaiman*, 31–32.

80 Robert K. Elder, "Gods and Other Monsters: A Sandman Exit interview and Philosophical Omnibus," 64.

81 Gaiman distances himself from positions taken within the text (such as that of the moon, which doesn't accept Wanda as a woman) (Ally Brisbin and Paul Booth, "The Sand/wo/man: The Unstable Worlds of Gender in Neil Gaiman's Sandman Series," *The Journal Of Popular Culture* 46 [2013]: 25).

82 Aaron Drucker, "Empowering Voice and Refiguring Retribution: Neil Gaiman's Anti-Feminism Feminist Parable in *The Sandman*," *Feminism in the Worlds of Neil Gaiman: Essays on the Comics, Poetry, and Prose*, ed., Tara Prescott and Aaron Drucker (Jefferson, NC: McFarland, 2012), 81.

83 Ibid., 97.

84 Joseph McCabe, *Conversations with Neil Gaiman and His Collaborators: Hanging Out with the Dream King* (Seattle: Fantagraphics, 2004), 3.

85 Ibid., 6. Late in the series, Gaiman influenced these decisions (originally seeking *Hellboy*'s Mike Mignola for the arc, another artist whose iconographic style departs in notable ways from the real).

86 Dave McKean provided artwork for the DVD rerelease of Dalí and Buñuel's *An Andalusian Dog*.

87 Neil Gaiman, Mike Dringenberg, Malcolm Jones III, Chris Bachalo, Michael Zulli, Steve Parkhouse, Robbie Busch, and Todd Klein, *The Sandman: The Doll's House*, 226.

88 The idea of story space as a "real" dimensional plane is argued by Grant Morrison (the third major leg of the British invasion authors) as well as Stephen Bissette.

89 Neil Gaiman, Jill Thompson, Vince Locke, Dick Giordano, Danny Vozzo, and Todd Klein, *The Sandman: Brief Lives* (New York: DC, 1994), 13, 16.

90 The story won the World Fantasy Award and has been often discussed in scholarship: Annalisa Castaldo's "'No More Yielding than a Dream': The Construction of Shakespeare in *The Sandman*" in 2004; Julia Round's "Transforming Shakespeare: Neil Gaiman and *The Sandman*" in 2010 (*Beyond Adaptation: Essays on Radical Transformations of Original Works*, ed., Phyllis Frus and Christy Williams [Jefferson, NC: McFarland, 2010], 95–110); and Nick Katsiadas's "Mytho-auto-bio: Neil Gaiman's *Sandman*, the Romantics, and Shakespeare's *The Tempest*" in 2015 (among others).

91 Neil Gaiman, Kelly Jones, Charles Vess, Colleen Doran, Malcolm Jones III, Robbie Busch, Todd Klein, *The Sandman: Dream Country* (New York: DC, 1990), 83.

92 Annalisa Castaldo, "'No More Yielding than a Dream': The Construction of Shakespeare in *The Sandman*," 105. The story also plays with the idea of identifying the "original" source for great plays (a concern for literate cultures but not folk cultures).

93 Foucault's death of the author is something I discuss in relation to comic books in *The Meaning of Superhero Comics* (Jefferson, NC: McFarland, 2012).

94 Hayley Campbell, *The Art of Neil Gaiman*, 120.

95 Introduced in *Swamp Thing* in 1985, *Hellblazer* became a regular series in 1988 and a Vertigo title in 1993.

96 The series was originally meant to be titled *Hellraiser* but was retitled after the release of the Clive Barker film.

97 Stuart Moore, "Introduction," in Garth Ennis, Steve Dillon, Matt Hollingsworth, and Clem Robbins, *Preacher, Book 2* (New York: DC, 2013), 2.

98 It does suggest things changed a bit from the 1930s when Universal cut a line from *Frankenstein* in which Victor claims now he knows what it feels like to be God.

99 B. Keith Murphy, "The Origin of *The Sandman*," *The Sandman Papers: An Exploration of the Sandman Mythology*, ed., Joe Sanders (Seattle: Fantagraphics, 2006), 21.

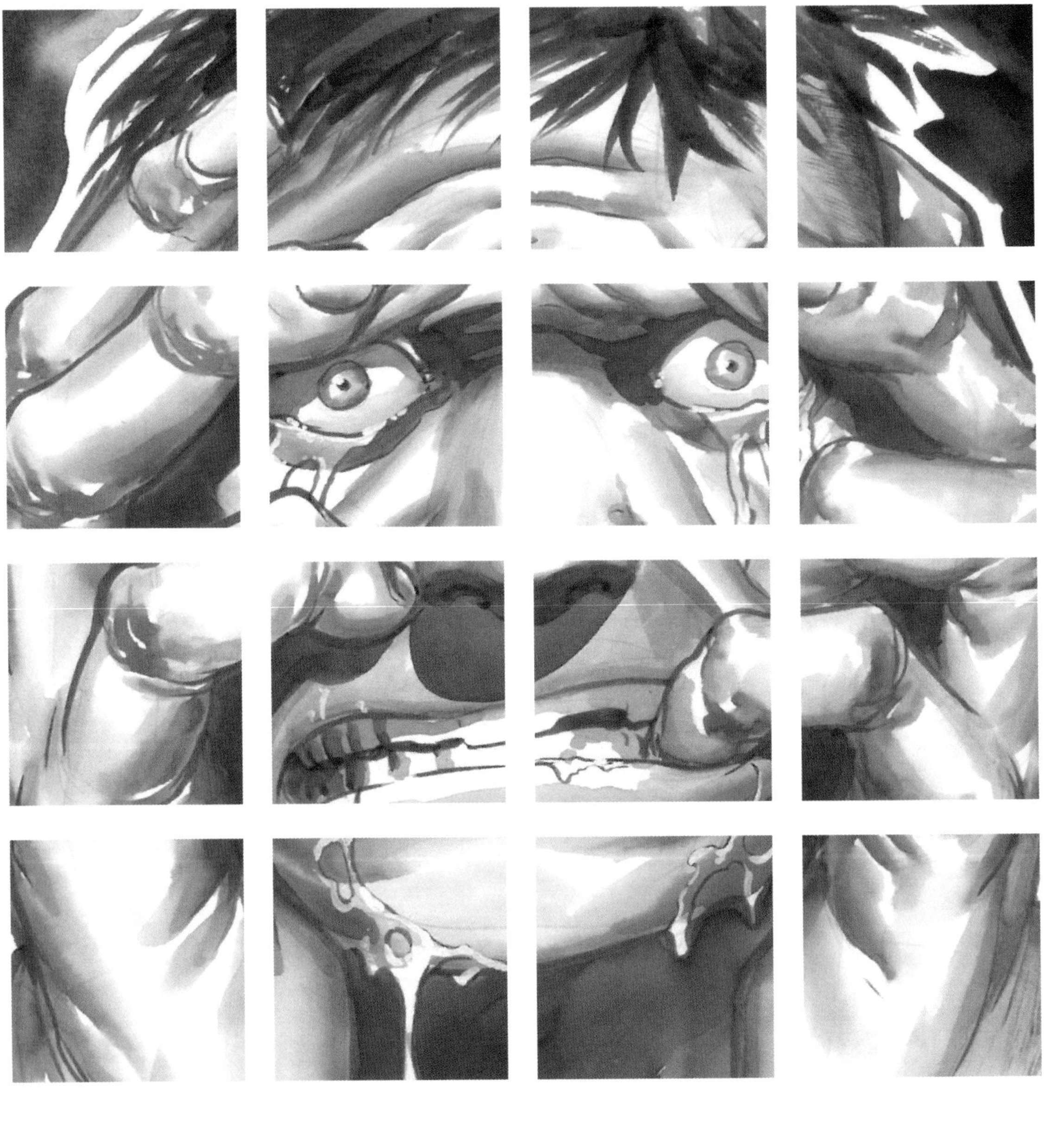

CHAPTER 5

The Monster Kills: *Hellboy*, *The Goon*, and Accolades for Contemporary Folktales and Pulp Horror

It's one of the problems you run into in a mainstream comic—lots of them have the illusion of change, but because all these are huge properties owned by giant companies, they're never really gonna let you keep a Superman dead, never gonna let you cut a Batman in half and keep half of him alive.
Mike Mignola[1]

The Bad Taste of Horror Goes Down So Easy (and Threatens the Powers-That-Be)

In regard to Bill Gaines's testimony before Congress, most scholars of American history, media, and comics would agree that his situation was impossible to "win" (and the blame for the Comics Code assigned to him from contemporaneous comic creators was unfair). Influenced by Wertham and the turning tide of public sentiment, most politicians already made up their minds and rallied to find ways to discredit whatever he said; questions were constructed to indict rather than inquire. The most successful line of questions were those designed to question the good taste of crime and horror comics, an issue that Gaines opened in his testimony: "Some may not like [horror comics]....That's a matter of personal taste."[2] Later came the now-famous questions about the infamous decapitated head on the cover of *Crime SuspenStories* No. 22.

Estes Kefauver said, "Here is your May 22 issue. This seems to be a man with a bloody ax holding a woman's head up, which has been severed from her body. Do you think this is in good taste?" Gaines replied, "Yes, sir, I do, for the cover of a horror comic. A cover in bad taste might be holding the head a little higher so that the neck could be seen dripping blood from it and moving the body over a little further so that the neck of the body could be seen to be bloody." Kefauver further observed, "You have blood coming out of the corner of her mouth," and Gaines curtly clarified, "A little."[3] Once Gaines acknowledged that gore was part of the comic's scare formula, the degree to which gory things were depicted was beside the point.

In addition to being indefensible as art thanks to these comments, horror was little other than bad taste (something rectified years later by the critical approval of creators such as Alan Moore and Neil Gaiman). However, rather than distance themselves from the idea of bad taste, certain creators such as Mike Mignola (creator of *Hellboy*) and Eric Powell (creator of *The Goon*) would proudly own bad taste.

The Goon one-shot, *Satan's Sodomy Baby*, featured an all-text cover with the title *Satan's $@#%* Baby* bound over the illustrated cover of the issue. Its text reads, "This comic contains material unsuitable for children. It's filled with vile, morally reprehensible subject matter. Subject matter that is quite possibly illegal in some states, and if it's not, it should be.... Do not open this comic if you have strong religious convictions or even the smallest bit of human decency. Do not open this comic if you love Satan.... In fact, unless you have no strong feelings about anything, this probably isn't the comic for you."[4] Using typical comics iconography to replace the offensive word in the title, Powell uses humor that is both broad and wry to identify his work as inappropriate for people who care about anything other than empty entertainment. Unlike Gaines's rather measured response above, Powell has been quoted as saying, "I'm going to do whatever I want to do, and if people like it, that's awesome."[5] While bad taste was a dangerous indulgence for Bill Gaines, it becomes an important right with Mike Mignola and Eric Powell.

Unabashedly inspired by "lesser" horror stories ranging from obscure folklore to pulp horror magazines and B-grade Universal film monster mash-ups, these creators take up the cause articulated within Bill Gaines's seemingly misguided statements (that most in the industry wanted the general public to forget). Mignola and Powell are devoted to producing the type of horror deemed unacceptable within the formerly dominant discourse of high culture. In fact, Mignola's *Hellboy* and Powell's *The Goon* make overt moves in textual and extra-textual ways to resist the respectability endowed on these series by critical accolades and industry awards. In this way, these creators enter a long-standing debate about whether comics should be accepted due to their good merits or rejected due to their lack thereof with a third position: that comics should be embraced due to their lack thereof.

In the 1950s as the comics scare gained momentum, Milton Caniff, the creator of *Terry and the Pirates* and *Steve Canyon*, made an impassioned argument for comics: "Children are natural critics. No lobby can reach them....

The portrayal of the blackness of evil which makes virtue white by contrast, and, as in all folktales, the desire to emulate the St. George of the moment slaying the current dragon, is a healthy and stable instinct to arouse."[6] While not shying away from questionable content in comics, Caniff's argument is based on two caveats: comics are for the tough-to-educate demographic of children and comics present evil to evoke a positive moral response from the readers. Likewise, in the oft-cited *The Uses of Enchantment: The Meaning and Importance of Fairy Tales* (1975), Bruno Bettelheim argues for the idea that evil should be presented in fairy tales and against the idea that children should be protected from such things.

For Bettelheim, children must be allowed to make their own decisions (in line with the assertion that they are "natural critics"), not goaded by a moral tacked on by someone like Charles Perrault. While a moral should not be overtly stated in fairy tales, Bettelheim suggests this form of children's literature leads children to certain conclusions due to its narrative design: "The figures and events of fairy tales… suggest ever so subtly how these conflicts may be solved, and what the next steps in the development toward a higher humanity might be… the fairy tale reassures, gives hope for the future, and holds out the promise of a happy ending."[7]

Like Caniff with comics, Bettelheim ignores the fact that folk and fairy tales were not designed with children as their exclusive audience (even when Perrault collected them in the 1600s). While his argument against protecting children works in opposition to Wertham's approach, he nevertheless understands only certain material as appropriate for children: "Most important of all, since the fairy tale guarantees a happy outcome, the child need not fear permitting his unconscious to come to the fore in line with the story's content, because he knows that, whatever he may find out, he'll live 'happily ever after.'"[8] With a limited notion of how the unconscious works, Bettelheim's definition of the fairy tale is extremely restrictive and artificial, as tales from oral culture that have tragic and disturbing endings are defined as myth.[9]

These arguments from Caniff and Bettelheim are implicitly echoed by Gerard Jones, an author of comics and other comic book studies, in his nuanced, multimedia study, *Killing Monsters: Why Children Need Fantasy, Superheroes*, and *Make-Believe Violence* (2002). Based on valid scientific studies of children (and therefore at odds with Wertham), Jones looks at the impact of disturbing content such as violence in film, television, comic books, and video games. Although more broad-based and liberal in approach (suggesting that certain types of fantasy don't help but don't hurt either), Jones's conclusion is still somewhat conservative, looking at the end result of citizenship versus juvenile delinquency.

Bettelheim's basic argument has often been used not only to justify fairy tales but also other forms of literature and media with objectionable content (because horror stories often end with the monsters being killed). However, not all fairy tales and horror stories end this way, and a more inclusive perspective would be that of Bettelheim's contemporary, Angela Carter. Well known for fiction that reworks fairy tales in subversive ways, Carter is also responsible for major collections of fairy tales and essays on fairy tales not as systematic but just as important as *The Uses of Enchantment*. Rather than focus on how fantasy narratives can serve to improve morality in the real world, Carter's early work "employed fairy-tale motifs in unusual ways to test the limits of realism."[10]

In 1977, Carter assembled her first compendium of fairy tales, a Charles Perrault collection in which she streamlines the translations and adds another moral in addition to the one supplied by Perrault. For instance, while Perrault's moral for "Bluebeard" is somewhat abstract, focusing on how the satisfaction of curiosity leads to "a thousand regrets," Carter's moral is more literal, ironic, and critical: "It is easy to see that the events described in the story took place many years ago. No modern husband would dare to be half so terrible, not to demand such an impossible thing as to stifle her curiosity. Be he never so quarrelsome or jealous, he'll toe the line as soon as she tells him to."[11] By questioning the stable meaning of fairy tales, Carter reveals how Perrault's moral may only be reinforcing a specific cultural perspective through a stereotype of women: outdated and yet still reinforced by an oft-read "classic" text.

In 1979, Carter produced related works with *The Bloody Chamber* and *The Sadeian Woman*—one a collection of her retellings of fairy tales and the other a study of how the taboo writing of the Marquis de Sade enables women to move beyond sexual objectification. *The Bloody Chamber* showcases the strong women, sexuality, violence, and horror Carter sees as central to fairy tales through Red Riding Hood werewolf stories like "The Company of Wolves." She describes her method as follows: "My intention was not to do 'versions'... but extract the latent content from the traditional stories and use it as the beginnings of new stories... and the latent content is violent and sexual."[12] Refusing to describe her stories as adaptations, she engages in the tradition of tale tellers who orally transmitted fairy tales—entertaining with stories made startling and relevant because they drew on concerns of the surrounding world.

In the 1990 introduction to the Virago collection of fairy tales, Carter emphasizes that the ideas in fairy tales are drawn from their historical contexts. She acknowledges that so-called fairy tales feature fewer fairies and more talking beasts and identifies them as "remade again and again by every person who tells them, the perennially refreshed entertainment of the poor."[13] In addition to the way their interpretations have changed, their content has changed, making the moral meaning of the tales even less certain. And with the emphasis on entertainment, the didactic ends of these "violent and sexual" stories are lost. Instead, she argues, "Mother Goose... is going to entertain you, to help you pass the time pleasurably, one of the most ancient and honorable functions of art.... Fairy tales are devoted to the pleasure principle... pleasure itself threatens authority. Which of course,... it still does."[14] The reference to the pleasure principle suggests these tales connect with the unconscious (something more dynamic than Bettelheim implies) and work against the conscious control of moral authority on which civilization depends.

Blue-Collar, Low-Brow, and Damn Right: Horror Is King, Winning Awards for Better or Worse

When stories simultaneously entertain and question morality, they are derided as things in bad taste, making the pleasurable experience of those stories something that induces guilt. As John Fiske argues in *Understanding Popular Culture* (1989), the regulation of taste in the mass culture of contemporary capitalism reinforces the identity and position of those in power through sexism, racism, and classism. However, Fiske also suggests this strategy of control is successful only up to a point because popular culture that exists on the fringes of culture (like comic books) has the means to subvert. With this in mind, the late 1990s and 2000s are an interesting time in the United States for the medium of comic books and the genre of horror, both of which were gaining a degree of critical respectability and institutional approval.

Gradually appropriated as things of good taste, the older ideas of the institutions of high culture pushed back in a variety of ways against comic books and against horror. In the midst of critical approval of the comic book work of Alan Moore and Neil Gaiman (including the Hugo for Moore and the World Fantasy Award for Gaiman), the major breakthrough for comic books was the special Pulitzer given to Art Spiegelman for *Maus* in 1992.

Inspired by Comix, the underground comics movement associated with 1960s counterculture, Spiegelman operated outside the mainstream comics industry and the industry's Comics Code. More of an outsider than Moore or Gaiman, Spiegelman, through this position, enabled critics to explain why *Maus* works as art and deserves the "special" variation of the prestigious Pulitzer.

In the *Village Voice*, Elizabeth Hess would claim, "Spiegelman is an original, a hybrid artist who has genuinely created a new form.... *Maus* is not exactly a comic book... comics are for kids."[15] What Spiegelman does as an auteur of graphic literature supposedly has little to do with the mass culture history of comics because comics are not art but entertainment only fit for children. In this way, the traditional standards of high culture can be maintained alongside the low opinion of comics because Spiegelman's work is fundamentally new (or at least a hybrid of more respectable forms). In essence, this argument allows a graphic novel like *Maus* to enter the mainstream unfettered and justifies Spiegelman's subsequent position as a special contributing artist for the *New Yorker* without question. As a result, comic books that continue to operate with other things deemed unacceptable in the past, like horror, can still be rejected–and yet in Angela Carter's terms, this causes them to be dangerous to the purveyors of high culture.

Less particular to the medium and more particular to the genre, Stephen King won the Medal of Distinguished Contribution to American Letters from the National Book Foundation in 2003. Unlike Spiegelman, who was long dissociated from the mainstream comics industry, King was long associated with the mainstream horror industry and therefore, the reactions from arbiters of culture would include outright rejection. One of the most well-known representatives of literary high culture, Harold Bloom, set forth his vehement reaction in the *Los Angeles Times*:

> The decision to give the National Book Foundation's annual award for "distinguished contribution" to Stephen King is extraordinary, another low in the shocking process of dumbing down our cultural life. I've described King in the past as a writer of penny dreadfuls, but perhaps even that is too kind.... By awarding it to King, they recognize nothing but the commercial value of his books, which sell in the millions but do little more for humanity than keep the publishing world afloat.[16]

Drawing a line back to the penny dreadfuls (which may be "too kind"), Bloom claims King is part of a popular tradition that debases humanity and cannot be welcomed into the high culture that serves humanity.

In King's acceptance speech, he addressed his blue collar origins as a struggling author, far from class privilege, and in turn identifies the artificial divide between popular and high culture:

> For far too long the so-called popular writers of this country and the so-called literary writers have stared at each other with animosity and a willful lack of understanding. This is the way it has always been. Witness my childish resentment of anyone who ever got a Guggenheim. But giving an award like this to a guy like me suggests that in the future things don't have to be the way they've always been. Bridges can be built between the so-called popular fiction and the so-called literary fiction. The first gainers in such a widening of interest would be the readers, of course, which is us because writers are almost always readers and listeners first.[17]

In "Challenging the Divide? Stephen King and the Problem of 'Popular Culture,'" Dorothee Birke shows how these identity politics persist, despite his multi-millionaire status, in King's *On Writing* (and how they determine how his popular fiction serves humanity): "A culture 'from the people for the people,' as he well understands, hinges on the biography of the individual writer rather than on his work: his work can only be classified as 'popular' if he comes across as authentic."[18] King's commitment to his role as a regular guy allows him to reach a wide audience, and the resulting authentic entertainment serves as a protest against the few trying to enforce good taste. The good taste that prohibits horror protects the questionable authority of an overgrown and self-serving civilization.

While Moore and Gaiman seem to be rhetorically closer to the aesthetic mandates of high culture, the previous chapters indicate how far their work is outside those mandates. And in reference to the goal of fairy tales and popular culture to entertain, Gaiman succinctly moves past the academic expectations of high culture to horror as entertainment in his introduction to *The Art of Horror*:

> I know that... I should talk about primal fears, about shapes and shadows moving in the darkness, beyond our primitive fires, about the way things that frighten us can inspire us; I should tell you about monsters and miracles, and how closely they are linked.... And it's not that they aren't important.... But the thing I kept seeing, kept thinking, kept wanting to say, as I looked through this remarkable book, was something else. Something far more important.... It's really fun.[19]

Even though associated with a multimedia conglomerate that wanted to maintain profitability, Vertigo comics was shaped by Moore and Gaiman who pushed boundaries. And, Vertigo was not the only comic book publisher that encouraged the resurgence in horror, and with other, more independent publishers, the new comics scare would be in very bad taste.

The Very Image of Bad Taste and the Dark Horse on the Cultural Fringe

Eventually becoming the third largest publisher, alongside DC and Marvel, Image comics would be the result of the convergence of changes to superhero comics, the comics marketplace, creators' rights, and the star system associated with comics creators. Due in large part to the success of DC's *The Dark Knight Returns* and *Watchmen*, superhero comics became "grim and gritty": crime-influenced hyper-violent stories that stressed the authoritarian power of superheroes. Even *Superman*, seemingly not conducive to such narratives, did so with the violent "Death of Superman" storyline, resulting in an overblown event generally identified as the end of the collector's market.

A central figure in this grim and gritty era would be the fan favorite artist Todd McFarlane, who worked on the follow-up to Frank Miler's *Batman: Year One* and a popular run of *The Amazing Spider-Man* that he wrote as well as illustrated. McFarlane would eventually leave *The Amazing Spider-Man* over "creative differences" that centered on McFarlane wanting to put a spear through a supervillain's eye and editor Danny Fingeroth refusing to let him do so. McFarlane became the leader of a large number of comics creators who left Marvel (including other "star" creators like Jim Lee, Rob Liefeld, and Marc Silvestri) and McFarlane soon after founded Image comics.[20] The catalyst for McFarlane's departure is interesting because it involved violence to the eye (the form of violence most hated by Fredric Wertham) and because it centered his freedom to do what he wanted (not a sophisticated creators' rights position rejecting the industry). With Image established with the release of McFarlane's *Spawn* and a few other titles right before the collector's bubble burst (1992), Frank Miller would interpret this move as a coordinated attack against corporate practices: "They never should have been given an inch, those old publishers.... The old machinery tried to retool... [but, Todd McFarlane] rallied his fellow comics superstars to abandon the sad old Marvel comics.... While Marvel staggers on, still an industry giant, its roar has gone hollow, and its feet of clay are visible to all."[21] With tough, overly dramatic talk, Miller captures the spirit of the times and of the overly aggressive superheroes that populated the Image titles.

Aside from making provisions for creators to own their work, the most interesting aspect of Image comics was McFarlane's *Spawn*. In addition to carrying on the violent power fantasies of superheroes at the time, Spawn was a superhero character who borrowed less from crime comics and more from horror comics. When black ops assassin Al Simmons is betrayed and killed, he sells his soul in hell to have the power to see his wife again and avenge his death. However, as with most Faustian bargains, the details are not clear, and Al's benefits do not live up to his expectations; he returns to Earth five years later, disfigured and amnesiac, in a garish superhero costume and with demonic powers that make him more evil with each use.

At the cost of his own relative goodness, Spawn exercises violent retribution against various criminals such as Billy Kincaid–an ice cream vender who happens to be a transvestite child molester and killer that Spawn hangs by chains and impales with ice cream treats. With a poem hung on Kincaid's body, "Boys screamed and girls screamed so I made him scream and scream and scream…,"[22] it is clear that McFarlane was not peddling the sophisticated prose of Edgar Allan Poe. However, his horror-based superhero appealed to the target demographic of teen males (colorfully described by Frank Miller): "Todd McFarlane has that visceral connection to the reader…. there's a moment when you're fourteen years old and you take your penknife out and your carve a swastika on your desk at school–Todd McFarlane *owns* that mind!"[23]

Marketed as a radical departure from DC and Marvel, *Spawn* borrowed from 1970s superhero horror with a superhero costume and deformed face that didn't move far beyond Marvel's Morbius. Nevertheless, he brought this character to a new era unfettered by Comics Code prohibitions against violence, profanity, and sexuality. Moreover, McFarlane took advantage of direct market superhero fan expectations with the quick move by Image to create an interrelated superhero universe. And with variant covers encouraging collectors rather than readers[24], McFarlane doubled down on the comics book store as a novelty shop when the collector bubble burst. With the establishment of McFarlane Toys in 1994, action figures and sculptures were produced of Spawn characters as well as other horror movie and video game characters–very profitable by comic book store standards for an increasingly specialized audience.[25]

Furthermore, the toy line production of Angela, Neil Gaiman's *Spawn* character, demonstrated how Image's practice didn't live up to its policy, violating a creators' rights agreement and making Image look more like DC and Marvel. As a consequence, Image's promising start seemed to be amounting to less than what Vertigo and other independent publishers promised, and many fans reacted negatively.

Matthew Pustz states, "fans [were] critical of what they perceive as destroying the industry: the lack of children's comics, the overreliance on crossover stories that are so complex that they automatically limit the series' audiences, the high price of comic books, and the abandonment of accessible non-comic shop retail outlets."[26] Thankfully this is not the end of the Image story, but it would take shifts from McFarlane's youthful business practices to make it into the company that publishes *The Walking Dead* (the subject of Chapter 6).

More significant to horror comics in the 1990s is Dark Horse, a company founded in 1986 during the direct market boom alongside other promising (but eventually defunct) publishers like Eclipse,[27] Comico,[28] and First.[29] Unlike Vertigo, none of the these publishers were tied to an established publishing company, and their ventures were consequently riskier. However, Dark Horse's growth was slow and steady, and the publisher weathered the end of the collector's market through its broad base of readers. The company had focused on adult readers, not with R-rated superhero content but with the sophisticated reinvention of genre material like Paul Chadwick's *Concrete*—a contemplative work about a man transformed into a rock-like "thing."

With a hardline devotion to creators' rights, Dark Horse eventually attracted star writers such as Frank Miller, who produced *Sin City* (1991) and *300* (1998). And their more innovative titles were balanced (but not troubled) by the tried comic book practice of producing titles based on trademarked characters, including the *Star Wars* and *Indiana Jones* franchises.[30] Balancing its identity as an outsider and insider, Dark Horse succeeded with its comics where others had not in ideological and commercial terms, and this success allowed Dark Horse to publish the most significant horror titles of the late 1990s and early 2000s. In addition to the wide selection of horror franchise titles (*Aliens, Predator, Planet of the Apes, The Thing, Army of Darkness*, and *Buffy the Vampire Slayer*), Dark Horse produced a variety of original horror titles, most notably Mike Mignola's *Hellboy* and Eric Powell's *The Goon*.

The Devil in the Details: Rediscovered in the Fullness of an Empty Past

In the 1980s, Mike Mignola began his career as a work-for-hire artist at Marvel and DC with well-known characters including Daredevil, The Incredible Hulk, The Phantom Stranger, and Batman. Preferring to illustrate the fantastic, such as large mythical beasts, he toyed with concepts that he could develop as his own property (over the years working with independently minded creators like Jim Starlin and Howard Chaykin).

He eventually settled on a devil creature dubbed Hellboy on a team of superhero-like paranormal investigators embroiled in the supernatural stories (necessitating that Mignola draw monsters from the folklore that he loved). Initially conceived as a means to the end, *Hellboy* would become a complex synthesis of horror, adventure, and superhero stories with a bit of crime (with Hellboy being beat up at least as often as the average hardboiled detective).

With his favorite comic book series being *Tomb of Dracula*[31] and favorite artist Frank Frazetta,[32] Mignola has points of inspiration in comic book horror, but *Hellboy* "relies heavily on fusion."[33] Mignola also pulls from other sources such as the stories of Robert E. Howard and H. P. Lovecraft as well as folktales from around the world. Mignola reflects, "I wanted to do a big monster/ action kind of thing, but I also wanted to use all these folktales, fairy tales, and mythology things that I've always liked [and] wanted to do things with. It was really like taking everything I like and putting it in a bowl. Sometimes it works, sometimes it doesn't, but it's a lot of fun."[34] In addition to avoiding terms like "inspiration" typically associated with artistry, Mignola describes his end-goal as pleasing himself and doesn't suggest that his mash-ups necessarily succeed; nevertheless, it is always entertaining, but whether he thinks it's fun for him and others too is unclear.

Literally rendered red devil figures with horns are plentiful in 1950s horror comics. They are typically portrayed as emissaries of hell summoned by black magic and tricking the hopeless summoner out of power and into damnation (such as "Hangman's House" in *Suspense* No. 5). Hellboy moves beyond this framework and even beyond a Faustian superhero like Spawn with the devil figure as the protagonist known as the "world's greatest paranormal investigator" (a moniker reminiscent of pulp fiction adventure heroes). In that capacity, Hellboy would be paired up with other paranormal characters (such as the fish-man Abe Sapien) as part of the government-sponsored Bureau of Paranormal Research and Defense (BPRD). Such monster teams had precedents in comic books like *The Legion of Monsters* (collecting Marvel's horror heroes in the 1970s) and the Creature Commandoes (collecting classic monsters together in DC's *Weird War* in the 1980s).

Regardless, the paranormal investigation portion, more than the team, would be more important because it served as the vehicle to bring together various folktale, pulp fiction, and comic book stories. While this also has comic book precedents with the Werewolf Hunter in *Rangers* comics in the 1940s and *The Occult Files of Dr. Spektor* in the 1970s, the most important connection here would be to the television show *The X-Files* in the 1990s.

Inspired in part by an earlier show, *Kolchak: The Night Stalker*, Chris Carter's series began its run in the same year as *Hellboy*. Following the paranormal investigations of two FBI agents, the series reveals the nefarious workings of a government run for the benefit of a select few, which covers up all knowledge of an impending alien invasion. Setting aside the series' often terrifying overall science fiction arc, *The X-Files* also features stand-alone horror episodes that draw on diverse sources for inspiration. Perhaps most importantly, the series' maxim "trust no one" applies to the series itself with semi-regular parody episodes undermining the integrity of its various genres and the series' own mythology. Sharing the government distrust, doomsday paranoia, and self-effacing humor of *The X-Files*, *Hellboy* is designed so that the stories depict their horrific content in ways that alternately terrify and poke fun; this strange alternation leads away from anything that resembles a jump scare and toward something that is more self-conscious and curiously dreadful.

Drawn to the Earth during WWII by Nazi occultists, Hellboy is adopted by the paranormal investigator Professor Bruttenholm and raised in the United States. *Hellboy*, which is mostly set in a vague contemporary time, has an on-going connection to the past or more accurately, the series[35] develops a sense of pastness. Aside from the fact that Hellboy has a history that begins in WWII, the *Seed of Destruction* mini-series establishes the existence of a folktale past as an important part of a story comprised of actual history as well as folktales alongside comic books, horror fiction, and other pulp fiction sources. Alan Moore describes Mignola as "crafting a work as good as everyone remembers the original being... [blending the past] with how we see things now and with our visions for the future."[36] Like steampunk science fiction that portrays the future as it was imagined in the futurist stories of early twentieth-century pulp fiction, *Hellboy* portrays the past as it was imagined in the contemporarily set stories of the early twentieth-century pulp fiction, thereby creating a familiar but uncanny space for Hellboy to inhabit.

Based on a story written by Mignola, the script for *Seed of Destruction* is written by John Byrne (well-known for his retcons of *The Fantastic Four* and *Superman*).[37] While his approach is more text-heavy than Mignola's thereafter, the long-winded expositions suit the atmosphere with a Lovecraftian sense of an uncanny setting and mood. Based on the historical figure of the mad monk, Grigori Rasputin is employed by the Nazis but uses their resources to realize his own ends: raising the supposed key to Earth's destruction (later known as Hellboy).

In the ceremony, he chants with appropriately anachronistic language and poetic syntax, "Chained in heaven are they. Seven is their number. Bred in the depths of the ocean, neither male nor female are they. They are as the howling wind, which knoweth not mercy, which knoweth not pity."[38] Like an occultist who worships Cthulhu, Rasputin develops a Lovecraftian worldview that is revealed to be the world of *Hellboy*. This revelation is told through a story about Bruttenholm, Hellboy's "father," who led an expedition to ancient ruins like those in Lovecraft's *At the Mountains of Madness*.

For Mignola, horror is based largely on mood created by bringing together elements both familiar and horrifying: "I had the luxury of cobbling together a series of images… And as you read across it, it does create some kind of mood."[39] In addition to the historical context of WWII, the historical referent of Rasputin, and the classic fiction of H.P. Lovecraft, the pulp fiction and superhero strands of the narrative also become apparent with the American team sent to stop the Nazis. In addition to a classic pulp fiction team with supernatural expertise ("[a] professor,… paranormal Whiz Kid, and… England's top medium"), their effort is led by the rough and tumble outsider: "And in charge of this Looney Toon party is me [Sergeant George Whitman], a guy who never heard the word 'paranormal' before a week ago."[40] The team also features a Captain America stand-in, the Torch of Liberty, who Whitman declares, is "Funny to see… standing there, having a cup of Joe with the rest of the guys."[41] While this comment works within the narrative because the character is accustomed to seeing the Torch of Liberty on newsreels, it also approximates the reader's experience as disparate elements are quickly assembled.

However, this combination is not simplistic and makes *Hellboy* more than derivative, as evil Nazis serve an end in the larger story in which a demon questions his own evil. Without cheapening the past with parody, Mignola maintains the good-humored earnestness of the source materials and simultaneously provides something more sophisticated in his evocation of pastness. The admiration of past narratives that refuses to be nostalgic is represented by one of the supposed artifacts presented in the opening sequence: a photograph featuring the American team of G.I.s, paranormal researchers, and a costumed superhero together with a scrawny giant-handed demon boy.

From the start of the series, Mignola's style negotiates between a flatter and more iconic comic book style and a more realistic and naturalistic illustrative style. With the transition from the bold colors of the "real" world to the black and white of the photograph (a panel dramatically isolated on the page), a reality effect is created that cements these disparate styles together as a meaningful whole.

The photograph works as a sort of prosthetic memory, which simultaneously provides nearness to and distance from these figures not only to be admired but also to be understood as a cultural artifact. However, this does not mean that Mignola's love and careful scrutiny of the past completely prevent him from finding the whole thing a bit funny and injecting humor into the series.

Fig. 5.1
Hellboy: Seed of Destruction No. 1, Dark Horse, 1994, © Mike Mignola
Hellboy negotiates between an iconic comic book style and an illustrative magazine style with the photograph as a "real" memory of a past that never existed.

It Is the Best of Times: The Ultimate Agent of Our Destruction Is So Funny

The obvious starting point for a discussion of humor in the series is Hellboy himself, who, despite his point of origin and demonic nature, is quite different from the brooding and overwrought superhero of Todd McFarlane's *Spawn*. Unlike most horror in the Western tradition, *Hellboy* doesn't waste time with skeptics or hysterics who cower from Hellboy (or other monstrous team members of the BPRD): "Generally, a large crimson-skinned demon (complete with cloven hooves, a tail, and horns (which he does file off) might shock everyday people in Mignola's world, but it is rarely even commented upon as unusual."[42]Despite the striking red of his skin that works in contrast to the muted colors of Hellboy's world, Hellboy keeps his horns filed to stubs, giving him a more human appearance and forcing him to negotiate between his identity as a demon and other roles. As a grown "man," Hellboy shares some things in common with the superhero (his extremely muscular physique and super-strength), the hardboiled detective (his rumpled trenchcoat and thick skin), and the adventure hero (his big guns and military supply belt).

Although *Hellboy* tales are often quite sophisticated with folktale monsters as metaphors, Hellboy charges into situations less as an archeologist or paranormal investigator and more as a strong man ready to fist fight with monsters. In addition to regularly receiving beatings worthy of a gumshoe in a crime story, Hellboy works much like a Doc Savage type adventure hero with a stress more on Doc Savage's open shirt and less on Doc Savage's mind as an inventor and researcher.[43] He not only has a giant fist and uses violence as a first resort, he also maintains a certain amount of detachment from danger—ever ready with adventure hero quips to comment on the absurdity of his situation. In *Seed of Destruction*, Rasputin explains the intricacies of Ragna Rok and Hellboy's instrumental part in the end times with typical Lovecraftian gravity: "If you kill me you will never know who you are!

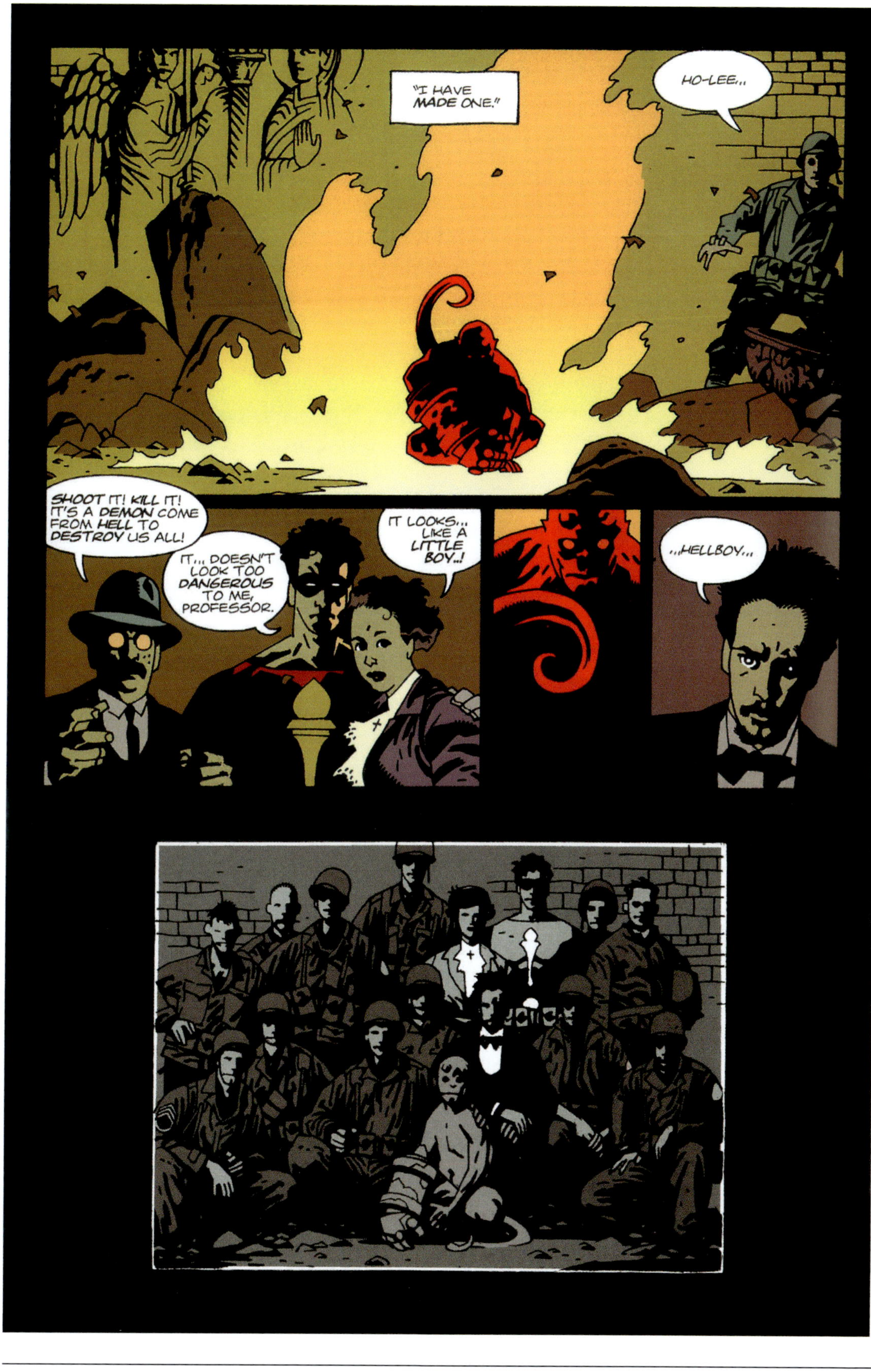
"I HAVE MADE ONE."
HO-LEE...
SHOOT IT! KILL IT! IT'S A DEMON COME FROM HELL TO DESTROY US ALL!
IT... DOESN'T LOOK TOO DANGEROUS TO ME, PROFESSOR.
IT LOOKS... LIKE A LITTLE BOY..!
...HELLBOY...

You will never understand the power inside you." However, Hellboy remains pragmatic, punches him and plainly replies, "Yeah, you're right. But I can live with it!" The sorcerer volleys back, "I will see you crawl before me! This is not the end!!" And as Hellboy picks up his skull to crush it, Hellboy dryly comments, "Well… it is for you."[44]

This dynamic would be part of *Hellboy* from the start seen in "Hellboy: World's Greatest Paranormal Investigator," a four-page preview story from *The Comic Buyer's Guide*. Therein, many pulp fiction hallmarks are centralized, including the rescue of the scantily clad woman from the evil Nazi scientist, a head suspended in a jar of fluid, and his henchman, a mechanically augmented ape who was developed by the scientist's experimentation. Mignola intended these silly characters in this promotional piece to be at least somewhat ridiculous and funny. But he later takes them seriously, and they become part of the growing mythology of the *Hellboy* series. In folktale fashion, a seemingly incidental or disposable detail is folded into a future retelling or extension of the story. Likewise, and perhaps more importantly, while Hellboy's grumpy yet plucky demeanor initially appears as just a mechanism through which fun can be poked, his personality becomes part of the series' heavy pathos in relation to the inevitable doom-bringing evil of his destiny.

Along these lines, Mignola states, "…what I'm *reading* now is probably a lot of the same stuff that Neil Gaiman's got on his bookshelf. I've got the same books, I can make the same references. So I'm taking the same subject matter but treating it in a more [Jack] Kirby-ish kind of way. There are things that Neil did in Sandman where I said, 'This needs a sledge-hammer fight!'"[45] Making light of his own process as slap-dash, Mignola crafts an everyman role for himself as a writer, something that parallels Hellboy's approximation of an ordinary man's reaction to his extraordinary situations. In reference to plotting *Hellboy* without Byrne as scriptwriter, he states, "First, it changed a little bit, then it changed a little more, and when I got to the mid-point of issue four it changed entirely. The last issue-and-a-half were re-done on the fly, and it had a totally different ending than I originally intended. It's a very weird ending–and I kind of like it."[46]

In regard to this description of his supposedly on-the-fly and artless composition, Mignola basically describes the arrangement of folktales that are developed without self-conscious scrutiny in oral cultures. This does not mean the end-result is in fact artless but rather something that works in opposition to the convention of the literate culture that Gaiman self-consciously questions in *The Sandman*.

This approach can be seen as a natural outgrowth of Mignola's love and implementation of folktales; he is an armchair anthropologist and postmodern folklorist who recognizes no discrete separation between types of stories and eras of time. Mignola states, "I like so many different aspects of the narrow confines of this supernatural horror literature, that in the same story I'm trying to cram in this old folklore a subtle kind of account of some kind of atrocity like that, but also put in some old movie kind of thing."[47] With no intention of cheapening atrocities, Mignola describes the broadening of a folktale narrative to include contemporary movie narratives as something quite natural.

In addition to the juxtaposition of material drawn from often studied folklore and often derided B-movies, Mignola speaks more about the synthesis of folktales in *Hellboy*: "I feel okay taking it further away from the source material. I will always try to direct people back to the original myths, though. But that's the nature of folklore: it changes with time."[48] While originality and endurance are tests for stories important to modern culture, Mignola asserts that folklore changes with time (and in essence, new renditions like those in *Hellboy* supply the important experience of pastness). This backward-looking disinterest in points of origin that can never be found in folk culture works in opposition to the idea of progress in industrial cultures influenced by the Enlightenment.

One of the earliest direct appropriations of a folktale ("Teig O'Kane and the Corpse") in a *Hellboy* short story would garner accolades from P. Craig Russell who describes it as "absolutely unique, with a deft wit, a sometimes gruesome sense of humor, and at all times a formal elegance."[49] The combination of gruesomeness and humor is natural (when considering the classic tone of comics horror hosts) but the descriptor of unique is not so natural (when considering the story as a folktale retelling). And the idea of elegance is at odds with Mignola's already-mentioned assessments of *Hellboy* in general and of this story in particular.

The contrast between those who want to validate *Hellboy* as a myth (an academic term used to describe folktales) and Mignola who wants to ground *Hellboy* as entertainment is regularly seen in the introductions to the collected editions of *Hellboy*. Trade paperback collections of monthly series are integral to the transition from comic book to graphic novel and are a format that's part of the growing respectability for the comic book on the American scene. While it creates space for introductions from luminaries such as Alan Moore, Jane Yolen, and P. Craig Russell to write about *Hellboy*'s grand scope, it also gives Mignola the opportunity to comment on his own work. He does this most extensively in the *Hellboy* short story collections comprised of tales deeply indebted to cross-cultural folklore.

His commentaries remove his appropriations from the idea of the grand scope in history and a formal elegance in art. In reference to "The Corpse," Mignola explains the comic was the result of fulfilling certain practical considerations; the story was originally published in *Advance Comics* in two-page installments and that meant "[coming] up with a story where some new, strange thing would happen every two pages." Of course, considerations of time and space are not foreign to folktale tellers, but in a typical self-effacing style, Mignola states, "Several people I respect consider this to be the best *Hellboy* story I've done... I was convinced that it was the all-time worst story I had ever done. I don't remember why. Oh well..."[50] In addition to questioning others' favorable estimation of the story, Mignola questions his own ability to write something valid about the story with "I don't remember why" and lapses into colloquial speech with "Oh well." Mignola himself plays horror host in these collections with his wry wit becoming a regular part of the story through this playful paratext. And his low opinion here is definitely playful as Mignola has suggested in other places that the story was "a turning point" where he "was firing on all cylinders."[51]

It Is the Worst of Times: It Is Hell to Be a Demon (and a Working Class Guy)

Despite the supposed limitations of his abilities suggested in Mignola's trade paperback introduction, "The Corpse" lives up to much of its praise in regard to both its narrative and visual components. The first page is designed less with a Jack Kirby sense of kinetic action and more as a series of images that work together like a tableau with connected but self-contained story-based pictures. Using large blocks of darkness to represent shadow, the uppermost of the three panels is long and horizontal, depicting three figures carrying a body across a barely moonlit field. The second is also long and horizontal but a stark contrast from the other two in that it is largely white and showcases the title of the story, "The Corpse." At the same time, the panel features a detailed view of the corpse's face that could be a non-narrative depiction of one of the main characters but also could be a cinematic move into the scene depicted in the first panel. The third panel is the largest, a square splash page image of an ominous, spike-headed mostly hidden figure in front of the shadows of barren trees (someone who will be revealed in a parallel plot thread featuring a supernatural kidnapper). With a centrally positioned square text-box within the lower half of that panel, simple but formal script represents a frightening text description of fairies from William Allingham's "The Fairies."

The design of the first page not only sets up the narrative, but also evokes older traditions in illustration through a creative composition of comic book elements. In a comic that might deserve the description "elegant," Mignola moves into a "gruesome" and yet "witty" tale in which a baby has been replaced by a fairy imposter and Hellboy agrees to bury a talking corpse in Christian grounds in order to retrieve the abductee. In terms of the two-page intervals with "new, strange" twists, the story follows the original folktale with the corpse rejected from a series of gravesites. While the story ends with a fist-fight with a giant monster, there are poignancies in narrative and visual terms that make careful use of pulpy material: Hellboy's gruff demeanor is contrasted with his care for the baby, slapstick interaction between Hellboy and the corpse is contrasted with the fairy culprit's description of his dying race, and big action scenes are contrasted with elegant visual puns (like the self-reflexive corpse's finger pointing to a detail of the corpse's finger pointing in the next panel).[52]

In "The Corpse on Hellboy's Back: Translating a Graphic Image," English scholar Laura O'Connor describes how the source material for "The Corpse" was described by Douglas Hyde during the Irish revival as a means of weaning Irish people off their dependence on English "penny dreadfuls and shilling shockers."[53] Hyde is in part motivated by his desire for an indigenous Irish culture, but nevertheless does something quite common to elevate common folk stories to a higher level within literary culture; he makes them superior to whatever is readily accepted as the low entertainment. In a curious way, while others describe folklore as myth and try to elevate *Hellboy* as something that lives up to those standards, Mignola does something contrary; he lowers *Hellboy* not in opposition to folklore but in connection to folklore.

In his introduction to the *Hellboy* story "The Baba Yaga," Mignola clarifies that the folktale source works in ways not dissimilar to his own stories: "I made up that business about counting dead men's fingers, but (believe it or not) the thing about Baba Yaga counting spoons is an actual Russian folktale."[54] Folklore has an absurdity similar to comic books, pulp fiction, and B-movies from the 1950s, and this narrative experience of the abject is central to *Hellboy*'s alternative view of culture.

In *Hellboy's World: Comics and Monsters on the Margins*, Scott Bukatman indicates Mignola is likely quoting Gregory Peck's Ahab in *Hellboy* rather than Melville's, and comic book artist Gary Gianni says, "[Mignola's] high regard for classic foundations is mingled in a refreshing manner with pulp material from the 30s and 40s, as well as horror films and other comics."[55] His "high regard" for classics should not be associated with high culture's regard but rather an appreciation for something that earns a space alongside low humor's ability to entertain.[56]

Hellboy is a celebration of all that is low because low culture is really the only cultural option in the series. While *Hellboy* is often well-structured, poignant, and full of social commentary, such things are done only in contexts that are highly entertaining and resistant to high culture meaning-making. For instance, "Hellboy in Mexico, or A Drunken Blur" is based largely on a funny sketch and depicts Hellboy, at one drunken point in his Mexican travels, teaming up with Mexican wrestlers to fight paranormal fiends (leading to a story-within-a-story where Hellboy is tragically forced to kill a former friend). The frame story ends with children in a broken down theater watching films of Hellboy as a Mexican wrestler.

Endings that refuse to explain the supernatural menace or unpack the feelings of the characters are common in a seeming effort to realize what Angela Carter identified as the heart of fairy tales: entertainment. While that doesn't mean they lack meaning, they are not overburdened with certain meaning and by lacking a specific moral, they become more significant to culture at large: dynamic, pregnant with potential meanings, and consequently full of pass-along value. In "The Crooked Man," based on a folktale retold by pulp writer Manly Wade Wellman, Hellboy travels to the Appalachian mountains and finds a man who wants to atone for his early life seduction by and initiation as a witch. Although thinking himself damned by his actions, he wants to save Cora, another person initiated, but in her case, motivated by tragic circumstances. With the Melungeons of Appalachia identified as the source of witchery, the story may seem to reinforce a stereotype of the Melungeons, but English scholar Joseph Michael Sommers offers a nuanced reading of this story situated in a comic book series that examines "the interstitial narratives formed in an interplay of history, religion, mythology, and other discourses through the lens of popular narratives."[57]

> While the Melungeons are still antagonists in "The Crooked Man," the goal is not the disestablishment of the prior dominant discourse of tyrannical viewpoints. Instead, the tyranny is held up to the voices of the impoverished and focused into a public, dialogical conversation so that the audience can make a more nuanced and complex assessment of those once viewed only by the terms of a monological tyranny. Mignola provides the reader of *The Crooked Man* with such an opportunity, using the special circumstances surrounding *Hellboy*'s somewhat novelistic/somewhat folkloric narrative, to liberate the Melungeons from their historical prison and to laugh at centuries of oppression.[58]

This openness in a retelling of a story seemingly designed to oppress represents the broad attempt to identify what is central to the series and the story of Hellboy himself. As a synthetic folktale, *Hellboy* addresses the concerns and anxieties of the common folk, especially through the character of Hellboy, the wise-cracking horror destined to bring about the apocalypse.

The long story arc of *Hellboy* is complicated, beginning long before his summoning by Rasputin during WWII and involving power struggles between Rasputin, Hecate, the Baba Yaga, Nimue, and other figures drawn from world folklore. Hellboy is the product of a union between a seventeenth-century witch and the demon Azzael, who outfitted the offspring with the "right hand of doom," instrumental in bringing about the apocalypse. Once summoned to Earth, Hellboy fights against his destiny (choosing to destroy monsters that threaten humans), but he is often subject to the many forces hoping to use him for their evil ends. Despite his choice to be an agent for good with the BPRD and on his own, as media scholar Scott Bukatman describes, "he is an event to be investigated."[59]

Through much of the series, Hellboy avoids consciously dealing with his destiny, and he mentions this strategy during an uncharacteristic reflection at the end of "Right Hand of Doom"–something added only for the collected edition. In a conversation with Kate Corrigan of the BPRD, Hellboy says, "You know how I live? I never deal with what I am. I don't think about it, I just do my job, which usually involves me beating the crap out of things a lot like me. But I don't like to think about that."[60] While his encounters with werewolves, vampires, and witches are horrible in their own terms, the larger horror is the dread that Hellboy's end is evil regardless of his choices.

Mignola connects Hellboy's dilemma with the concerns of an ordinary "working class guy": "How do I keep this character being this kind of blunt, matter of fact guy and have him deal with this huge stuff? On one hand, I think it's kind of a funny image that Hellboy is just some working-class kind of guy who just so happens to also be the beast of the apocalypse."[61]

Although exaggerated, this dread lurks on the edge of the conscious experience of the ordinary guy in post-industrial culture, and there is a bitter humor to this awareness in a world supposedly able to perfect itself.[62] Nevertheless, the biggest pitfall for Hellboy, as Mignola articulates it, is not this situation but "[keeping] his head buried in the sand."[63] Along these lines, The Island (written in the wake of Guillermo del Toro's *Hellboy* film) metaphorically depicts the consequences of refusing to acknowledge one's circumstance and thereafter reveals many of the particulars concerning Hellboy's destiny as a destroyer. At the beginning, Hellboy is "not thinking about it," drinking with a lively group of guys who are revealed as long-dead sailors gathered in a ship's hold. When an ancient spirit then appears to share the specifics of Hellboy's future, the horror of his surroundings is balanced out by Hellboy's angry but humorous threat, "Don't mess with me lady. I've been drinking with skeletons."[64]

In del Toro's introduction to *Conqueror Worm*, he laments his inability in the *Hellboy* film to replicate "the cold, velvet backdrop of blackness from which [Mignola's] characters emerge... his hyper-expressionist lighting."[65] While the film was commendable in its own right, del Toro struggles with Mignola's compositions on film, dealing with a material world where lighting produces shadow, a darkness from which characters emerge. And yet while Mignola's style is somewhat realistic, it also works in another way that, as Scott Bukatman claims, not only "establishes generic expectations for the knowing reader" but also is an "enveloping mass."[66]

The first issue of *Conqueror Worm* presents masses of blackness (not necessarily shadow) that act as negative space and invite the reader to understand them not as absence but presence.[67] About "spirits of the void" returning in a Nazi space capsule, the issue begins with the blackness of space, followed by the darkness of the sky alongside the black shadow of the mountain, and then followed by the shadow of the mountain in front of another more clearly illuminated. This move toward more detailed images of the Earth continues until a castle is revealed and BPRD agent Lobster Johnson is clearly depicted in an attack on Nazi agents.

But the reader's ultimate arrival at the action of an unfolding story is less important than the cosmic blackness within the panels on the first three pages, which are connected only through portions from Edgar Allan Poe's "Ligeia." Resisting the kind of panel-to-panel momentum associated with an artist like Jack Kirby and described by a theorist like Scott McCloud, "*Hellboy* creates something of a ruminative and intertextual space for the reader to occupy."[68] This space is descriptive of the type of interaction thus far described between texts and other texts and between texts and readers, something that moves back and forth rather than just progressing in a linear fashion to the end.

And the story of Hellboy is one of voids to be filled: Hellboy leaving the BPRD when he questions their methods; Liz Sherman's life-sustaining power taken to restore the life of Roger the Homunculus; or Hecate's evil reign ending only to enable the fairy Gruagach to replace her with the dangerously unstable Nimue.[69] Much more about stasis, *Hellboy* does not move to a conventional, heroic end, and consequently Hellboy does not respond to his call when he discovers he is a descendent of King Arthur. If he fought in a cause identified by Morgan le Fay and Queen Mab, his ascension to power would forsake his desire to be an ordinary guy with an ordinary girl[70] and push him toward his destiny as king of hell.

Nevertheless, Hellboy has a fantastic fist fight with Nimue (now a giant dragon) because the readers shouldn't expect less from a superhero/gumshoe/adventure hero/demon like Hellboy. And despite his attempts to avoid his destiny, Hellboy is dragged to hell by the vindictive Nimue demonstrating that some decisions may be better than others, but they are all some variety of wrong. While the collision of things that don't belong together remain together (the Hellboy of Mignola's *Hellboy in Hell* is just as mouthy in the underworld), the humor is something that catalyzes great fear within the series. Mignola states, "Horror is a weird thing. To me, the most horrible thing in *Hellboy* is the idea that you are pre-destined to do something evil."[71] Referring to Lovecraft's sublime affect, Bukatman describes Hellboy in part as a "conceptual engagement with overwhelming powers… [that] threatens all that we understand; it threatens human existence itself–hence the experience of horror as opposed to more straightforward terror."[72] While being a monster is broadly funny up to a point, the series ends with a much narrower sense of humor that recognizes the absurdity of his position (and of our own) dealing with forces beyond our control.

From Comic Relief to Outright Spoof: A Bad Taste (in Your Mouth) with The Goon

With folktales, there is no value placed on an original, privileged starting point; instead, value is placed in the common, the shared, and the current—and the horror story comes out of that tradition. Celebrating what is forbidden by high culture is just as thrilling as disseminating what is entertaining to the common people. Working along lines similar to *Hellboy* but more tastelessly humorous would be Eric Powell's *The Goon*: a pastiche of bad horror movies, crime story clichés, and arm-chair existentialism. Tuned more directly into what Mark Voger would call "the monster craze" (a kitschy collector's market for horror starting in the 1950s), *The Goon* celebrates the love of the aberrant and scatologically moves from one joke to another dealing with abject subject matter.

In the critical surveys of twentieth-century horror literature and film, special derision has been reserved for the sensational attempts to secure an unsophisticated audience and make money. For instance, *Frankenstein Meets the Wolfman* is often identified as such an offering, "originally conceived as a joke by Curt Siodmak in the Universal cafeteria during a long lunch break as he and fellow writers struggled to come up with a new angle for the Frankenstein story."[73] However, the improbable thrill of seeing these monsters together is enhanced for many by a tacitly understood absurd humor that propels it in the first place. Ed Wood films like *Bride of the Monster* were designed to feature Bela Lugosi in a way that seriously referenced his role as Dracula; but poor acting, screenwriting, and directing made the films funny and generated a cult following that appreciated its unintended camp.

In the 1980s and 1990s, the space between the gravity of horror and the levity of camp was explored in various ways and places. Narrated by Vincent Price and directed by John Landis (after his semi-humorous *American Werewolf in London*), Michael Jackson's "Thriller," a horror-themed music video, was not released as expected on MTV but at movie theaters in 1983. Opening with a familiar horror premise (Michael Jackson transforms into a Wolf-Man and pursues his girlfriend), the sequence is revealed as a movie watched by Jackson and his girlfriend. After they leave the theater, the "real" Jackson and his girlfriend are pursued by zombies until Jackson becomes one and dances with the zombie horde to the song "Thriller." Demonstrating the facility of horror to revise the real, the video serves as an indicator of the entertainment value of horror, especially when it becomes less serious and somewhat campy.[74]

After the failure of the now classic *The Thing*, John Carpenter made another box-office loser but cult favorite, *Big Trouble in Little China* (1986). A strange amalgamation of horror, kung fu, and action, the film featured an excessive performance by Carpenter favorite Kurt Russell, starring as a hero impossible to take to seriously (much like the rest of the film).[75] While the film is excessive (and therefore humorous) in its use of B-movie genre clichés, the cult status of the film results from the unclear extent of Carpenter's humorous intentions. Sam Raimi's successful but low-budget cabin-in-the-woods horror film *Evil Dead* (1981) was continued (or remade) with *Evil Dead 2* (1987) in which Raimi embraced the unintentional humor of the first with broad slapstick–and the sequel was more successful than the original.

As the 1990s embraced horror comedies with books such as Christopher Moore's *Practical Demonkeeping* (1992) and television series such as Joss Whedon's *Buffy the Vampire Slayer* (1992–1997), the 2000s also thrilled to new monster mash-ups with *Freddy vs. Jason* (2003) and *Alien vs. Predator* (2004) (continued in comic book form by Dark Horse). While *Hellboy* was humorous, it avoided both camp and outside references for the sake of spoof, differentiating it from *The Goon*, the major horror comedy comic following it in 1998. Borrowing from crime in a more obvious way (like Howard Chaykin's mostly serious but equally offensive horror crime comic *Black Kiss*), *The Goon* would undercut horror in general and its own narrative in particular even while it developed a tragic trajectory for its protagonist.

Eric Powell would begin his work on *The Goon* in 1998 with the independent publisher Avatar, but frustrated with the company, he began self-publishing the series in earnest in 2002.[76] Following the story of the Goon, an enforcer for the gang leader known as Labrazio, the horror influences are apparent at the start with zombies, werewolves, and talking skeletons appearing in the first three pages. Pitted against a rival gang of the undead led by the "Zombie Priest," the improbably tough Goon is an ugly, muscle-bound visual amalgamation of Popeye and Dick Tracy. Feverishly working to always set up the next sick joke involving the Goon, his buddy Frankie, and more horrible monster-related violence, the series focuses less on a fully coherent plot and more on the glee of bringing together an evil scientist, a giant squid, and a vampire seductress.

For instance, when the Zombie Priest transforms a chimpanzee into a fifteen-foot "great zombie chimp", the Goon reacts in a way that downplays any drama in an already absurd conflict by accentuating the ridiculousness of his life in general: "I draw the line at giant dead monkeys. I've put up with the redneck werewolf, the little guy with the bowling ball on his hand, I'll even put up with the big man-eating rats. But this is all I can take tonight! I'm going home!" Unfortunately, the monster attacks, and the Goon hits the chimp in the stomach, causing him and Franky to be covered in intestinal fluid; the Goon simply says, "I... got... it... in... my... mouth.[77] Expanding on the idea of the Goon with a literal bad taste in his mouth, the series consistently makes the argument that there is no such thing as good taste in horror.

Like Mignola, Powell doesn't justify his aesthetic choices but does describe what he does in terms of personal preferences: "*The Goon* is a blender of everything I like. I like horror and noir stuff.... While I don't give the book a specific time period, it's heavily influenced by that feel. It's an amalgam of stuff that I either care for as a subject, or like to draw."[78] This juxtaposition led to an entertaining comic that sold well and generated interest at Dark Horse, ultimately publishing *The Goon* after its self-published three-issue run.[79] And even though it would never forsake the essentials (set-ups for the next gross-out joke or fist fights with another giant monster), the series became more than those things so notably established in the initial run. Even in these first few issues, the Goon is revealed not only as a goofy strongman but a tragic hero who lost a loved one and fell into a life of crime.[80] In addition, the crime/horror synthesis is a much more direct address of everything that troubled Fredric Wertham and led to the establishment of the Comics Code. Evoking a general mood cut free of a specific time and place, the setting enables an even wider amalgamation of various pulp fiction, comic book, and B-movie horror material than *Hellboy*.

Comparing Mike Mignola's approach to his own, Powell argues, "I hate drawing hip pretty people and modern things.... I do like drawing monsters, dilapidated buildings, ugly people, and old cars. Mike created a world where he incorporates the folklore and Lovecraftian horror he loves. I created one where I could do the Pythonesque B-movie monster stuff that I love."[81] With Wally Wood, Jack Davis, and Will Eisner (in addition to Mike Mignola) as influences, his style becomes increasingly tied to traditional illustration techniques and grounds the absurdity (suggested by Monty Python humor) of the authority-flouting frenetic series.

The Point of Humor in Bad Taste Is the Bad Taste (Or The Point of a "Knife to the Eye!")

With the Goon and Frankie working as mob enforcers, *The Goon*'s narrative positions them as criminals, and that makes the potty humor and super-violence with monsters more pointed as violations of the Comics Code. Aside from one police officer in the first issue (who happens to be corrupt), most of the series never depicts a threat of penal consequences and rarely suggests that an outside political authority exists. And so with an undead gang threatening everyone's way of life, the reader comes to appreciate the relatively amoral Goon and libidinous and ultra-violent Frankie. Community is represented at Norton's Pub with the Goon, Frankie, a werewolf, a talking spider, a friendly zombie, and other dregs of society, and the future is represented by a football-playing, malicious, child street gang (visually resembling Hal Roach's Little Rascals) who refer to themselves as the "Little, Unholy Bastards."

The subversion of the conservative values of American culture is clear in *The Goon* Christmas specials, the first of which sports a cover in the style of Norman Rockwell's *Saturday Evening Post* paintings. Although Powell tends toward a cartoonish style that employs caricature and extreme exaggeration for humor, he also uses more detailed line drawings in sepia tones to evoke the color of early 20th century illustration and a painterly style somewhat like that of Rockwell. In the case of this cover, the design is specific to that of *Saturday Evening Post* covers, unavoidably evoking associations with the quaint family-oriented content of Rockwell. Depicting the Goon sleeping in a chair as a stand-in for Santa Claus, small monstrous gnomes surround him, tear apart the toys, and prepare to shoot him in the head. The story itself begins with children around a hearth in anticipation of Santa's visit only to be eaten by the small creatures depicted on the cover. After the bereaved mother begs the Goon and Frankie to find her children, they discover the ugly gnomes are Santa's elves, and Santa is a cruel task-master who tortures them. And after Father Christmas shakes the gnomes until they vomit out the children (alive but horribly traumatized), Frankie angrily asks, "Hey, if you exist, how come you never brought me nuthin'?!" The giant and imposing Santa replies, "Because you're a rotten little [expletives scratched out], that's why!"[82] In addition to delivering this bit of anti-nostalgia that removes wholesome values associated with Santa, this tirade accurately describes Frankie, the reluctant and not very heroic child-rescuer.

Doll-eyed like little Orphan Annie, the little (but disproportionately large-headed) Frankie takes the most direct "stab" at the concerns of Fredric Wertham. With a visual appearance similar to innocent humor comics characters from the 1950s, Frankie engages in the most reprehensible violence with glee. In a dream-like crossover with *Hellboy*, Frankie attacks the giant squid they all fight with a "knife to the eye!" (the text rendered in bold isolation within its own panel). Since only the antecedent and aftermath and not the knife to the eye are visually represented, the reader becomes (as Scott McCloud might suggest) an accomplice to the crime. And since the victim is a monstrous creature in league with the Zombie Priest, the reader can participate in Frankie's glee over the type of violent act most reprehensible to Wertham.

Fig. 5.2
The Goon: Rough Stuff, Dark Horse, 2010, © Eric Powell
A new breed of horror hosts, the Goon and Franky introduce not only the story but also the series's artistic changes, current publishing situation, and monetary end goals.

The Goon purposefully situates itself as the lowest of low-brow entertainment, even further than *Hellboy* from the sort of respectability garnered by Moore's *Swamp Thing* and Gaiman's *Sandman*. For instance, the first collection of *The Goon* is titled "Rough Stuff," not only in reference to the Goon's method of operations but also to Powell's estimation of its low quality. In the text introduction to the third edition that Dark Horse deems worthy of a trade paperback collection, Powell uses crass terms to describe the volume's supposed lack of artistry and greedy goals: "The only reason that I'm allowing this book to be printed again is because I also like to see when artists I like sucked. I weather the embarrassment because I love you readers so much. That, and I got bills to pay."[83]

In the two-page comic book introduction to the same volume (subtitled the "Milking-It-for-All-It's-Worth Edition"), the Goon and Franky break the fourth wall like horror hosts to comment on the content. The Goon says that in addition to him no longer looking "like a shaved mule,... the biggest change has been our financial situation [with Dark Horse as their publisher]."[84] In short order, a butler tries to serve them sushi and Franky kills him with a broken bottle: gratuitous violence meant for laughs, which shows the reader little has changed in this socially unacceptable comic book. Curiously, this is in slight contrast to other introductions in subsequent trade paperbacks by other creators who sometimes emulate Powell's irreverent style but also situate the series within respectable comic book traditions (like that of Will Eisner).[85]

In No. 8 of the Dark Horse series, Powell further highlights the emerging tension between his low opinion of the series and others' high opinion by hijacking the beginning of a Goon story to comment on *The Goon*'s first Eisner Award nominations.

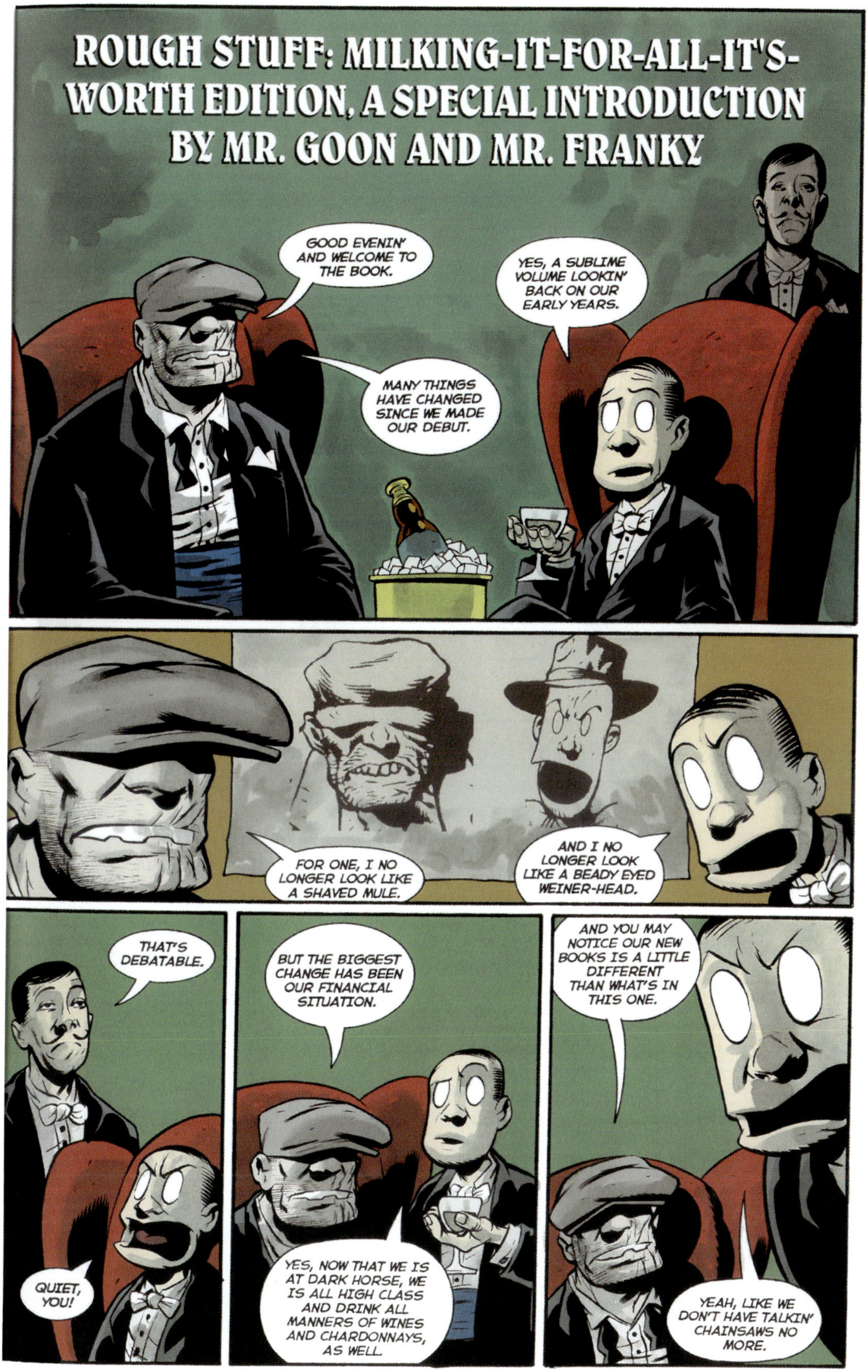
ROUGH STUFF: MILKING-IT-FOR-ALL-IT'S-WORTH EDITION, A SPECIAL INTRODUCTION BY MR. GOON AND MR. FRANKY
GOOD EVENIN' AND WELCOME TO THE BOOK.
YES, A SUBLIME VOLUME LOOKIN' BACK ON OUR EARLY YEARS.
MANY THINGS HAVE CHANGED SINCE WE MADE OUR DEBUT.
FOR ONE, I NO LONGER LOOK LIKE A SHAVED MULE.
AND I NO LONGER LOOK LIKE A BEADY EYED WEINER-HEAD.
THAT'S DEBATABLE.
QUIET, YOU!
BUT THE BIGGEST CHANGE HAS BEEN OUR FINANCIAL SITUATION.
YES, NOW THAT WE IS AT DARK HORSE, WE IS ALL HIGH CLASS AND DRINK ALL MANNERS OF WINES AND CHARDONNAYS, AS WELL.
AND YOU MAY NOTICE OUR NEW BOOKS IS A LITTLE DIFFERENT THAN WHAT'S IN THIS ONE.
YEAH, LIKE WE DON'T HAVE TALKIN' CHAINSAWS NO MORE.

Franky directly addresses the reader to introduce Peaches Valentine, "a simpleton," drooling and clad only in a t-shirt, underwear, and slippers; Peaches spends a page and half (fourteen panels) defecating, smearing his feces on his face, and finally lifting a sign reading "2004 Nominee for Four Eisner Awards." At that point, two beatnik intellectuals debate the deeper meaning of Peaches' actions, leading Franky to shoot Peaches in the head and complain, "Sometimes a simpleton-playin'-in-his-own-filth-and-getting-shot-in-the-face joke is just a simpleton-playin'-in-his-own-filth-and-getting-shot-in-the-face joke!" However, that doesn't stop the intellectuals who yell, "He's pointing his phallic representation of man's mortality at us! Run!"[86] With Will Eisner often identified as the father of the "graphic novel" (a term more respectable than comic book), an Eisner Award is a near equivalent of a National Book Award for comic book creators. But such approval for the series seems to run contrary to Powell's goals of celebrating and finding humor in his own bad taste and the bad taste of his readers. In order to remain in a position where he defies authority, he must remain in even worse taste as critical establishments change definitions to accommodate his type of work.

Along those lines, he fiercely asserts his right to bad taste in a conflict with a fictional crusader named Margaret Snodgrass (described by Powell as "a right-wing Bible thumper from Alabama").[87] Powell supposedly didn't run his intended content for No. 18 of *The Goon*, a story titled "Satan's Sodomy Baby." According to the introduction to No. 18, the story is one of "demonic sexual assault on the unsuspecting buttocks of a backwoods rube and the progeny of said union."[88] Within the published content of that issue, Franky finds a copy of *Satan's Sodomy Baby* and is so distracted that he's useless to the Goon in his fight against a "swamp devil" monster. Among other things, he complains, "This book was written by an idiot! There's no way I would do that without rubber gloves and a few beers in me!"[89] This commentary continues throughout and serves as an issue-long intertextual reference to the story published as a one-shot. Powell's invented controversy led to big sales for the highly offensive cross between *Deliverance* and *Rosemary's Baby* (an issue never republished in trade paperback versions).

Comments on Amazon, GoodReads, and the letters page to *Satan's Sodomy Baby* indicate readers consider the introduction to No. 18 a ploy to generate those big sales. Nevertheless, most reviewers don't seem to hold this low-brow salesmanship against Powell but appreciate the blurring of fact and fiction and love of the comic despite its bad taste or due to their bad taste.

In reference to the humor that propels this fairly tasteless comic, Powell argues, "The safe predictable joke is never funny. If it makes me laugh and it's not overtly harmful to anyone, I'll usually throw it in the book. *Satan's Sodomy Baby* is a different story. The book was so over the top out of spite.... When the distributor started flipping out over the word sodomy and said the only way it was going to get released was through the porn catalogue, it pissed me off. I said fine. If you're going to make me release it with porn, I guess the gloves are off. So I made it really obscene."[90]

One of the notable aspects of this commentary is that distributors still participate in a system that encourages them to be the arbiters of good taste. And even more important is that prohibitive mandates are often counterproductive, not only making the forbidden more appealing but also creating a motivation for further rebellion. *Satan's Sodomy Baby* was a fairly tasteless exercise with the Goon trying to pound the rather cute Harvey-style devil baby back into the buttocks of the back woodsman from where he came. Powell's awareness of the abject nature of this forbidden humor can be seen in the departure from the narrative at "the end,"with Franky pulling back the text of "the end" isolated in its own panel. Subsequently, a series of panels looks increasingly closer at a woman's breast with the last panel portraying Powell as the unwashed and perverted creator behind it all.

The Tragic End of a Working Class Guy (Adding to the Tragic Beginning and Middle)

Powell's self-conscious humor appears elsewhere, including No. 32 in which Eric Powell interrupts the main story to argue that rape can be funny—with a robot and Frank Darabont, director of *The Shawshank Redemption*.[91] And yet while *The Goon* resists authority through the shocking implications of its jokes and aesthetic violations, the series works with much more than the juvenile delinquent in mind. Not just a parody like the *Scary Movie* series, "the stories go anywhere from completely absurd to, with *Chinatown*, overly dramatic and serious," Powell notes.[92] Although the emphasis is most often on *The Goon*'s absurd world, the failure of all authority to make things better is *The Goon*'s drama and its horror. In addition to the general absence of benevolent authority figures, the people with power invariably abuse that power, and that abuse has had tragic consequences for the Goon and other characters.

The "overly dramatic" stories are usually put in close quarters with the most absurdly comic material such as No. 1 in the second Albatross Exploding Funnybooks series.

Beginning with an EC-like story of a thief who is trapped by ghosts in the mansion where he hides his loot, the issue quickly transitions to the Goon driving down the street with a squid on his car. And while the first two issues of the first series focus on humor, the third issue depicts the past story of Labrazio killing the Goon's mother-figure and the adolescent Goon killing his cruel boss (revealing his longtime role as Labrazio's enforcer to be a sham). Since *The Goon* is a horror comic that features undead characters, Labrazio is not gone for good, and the Goon later faces many issues that he has repressed. In another comic/tragic contrast, the introduction that features Peaches Valentine defecating is followed by an eloquent story that connects the loss of a tragic "vampire dame" to the Goon's own past experience in Chinatown. After the vibrant four-color presentation of the Peaches Valentine sequence, the central story is muted in color that highlights Powell's more realistic style (ending with a slightly distorted detail of the Goon's contemplative face).

Fig. 5.3 *The Goon: Chinatown and the Mystery of Mr. Wicker*, Dark Horse, 2007, © Eric Powell The Goon looks in the mirror and at the reader in a series of five splash pages designed to reveal the horror (rather than the humor) of his dreadful life.

And most notably, after No. 18 and *Satan's Sodomy Baby*, Powell takes a break from the regular series to produce *Chinatown and the Mystery of Mr. Wicker* in a graphic novel format. It opens with a full page of text indicating "This ain't funny," visually accompanied by the shadowy face of a gargoyle creature frozen in an expression somewhere between anger and humor. Thereafter, Powell blends his characteristic style with a more painterly, illustrative style in sepia tones and selective color reminiscent of *Creepy* magazine. In the story, the Goon is subject to the capricious, out-of-control Chinatown crime lord who just happens to have mystical powers. Most horrifying for fans is not the Goon's near death conflict with the crime lord/dragon god but the emotional breakdown of this consistently cartoonish and humorous character. When his true love leaves, his breakdown is depicted over the course of five splash pages focused exclusively on his pained facial expressions (an experience after which he indiscriminately murders not a monster but an ordinary human being).

The best example of a sympathetic character implicated within the system and with no justifiable claim to authority is the Buzzard, a former sheriff who chooses not to protect his town from the Zombie Priest. When all his people become zombies, he kills them, and the Zombie Priest casts a spell on the sheriff. Becoming a different sort of zombie (a living man with an insatiable hunger for carrion), the monstrous Buzzard nevertheless seeks revenge, something that will not serve the people or the soul he lost.

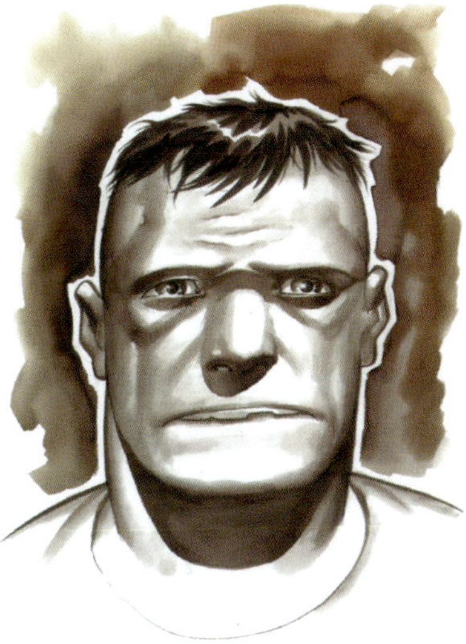
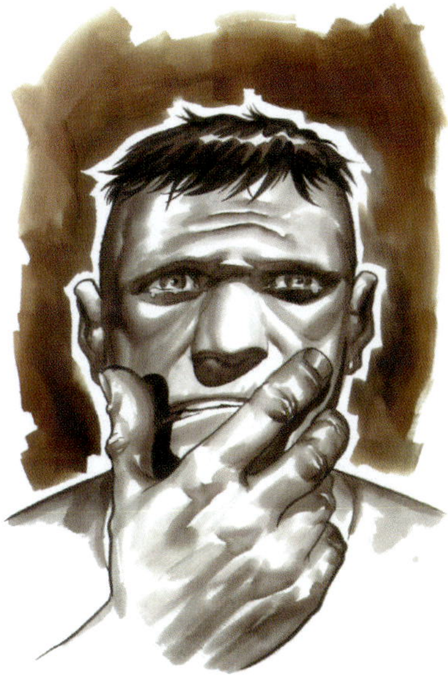
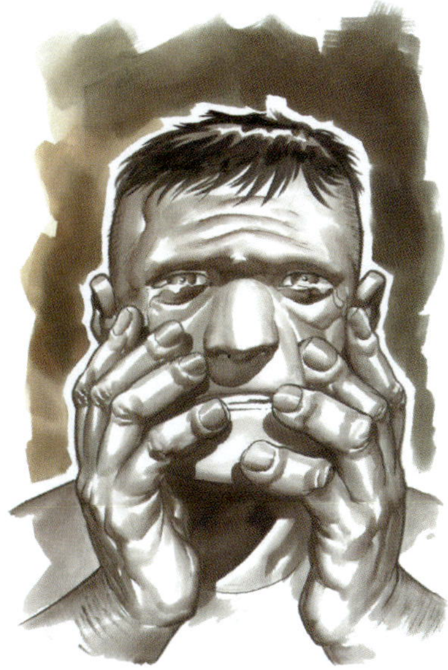
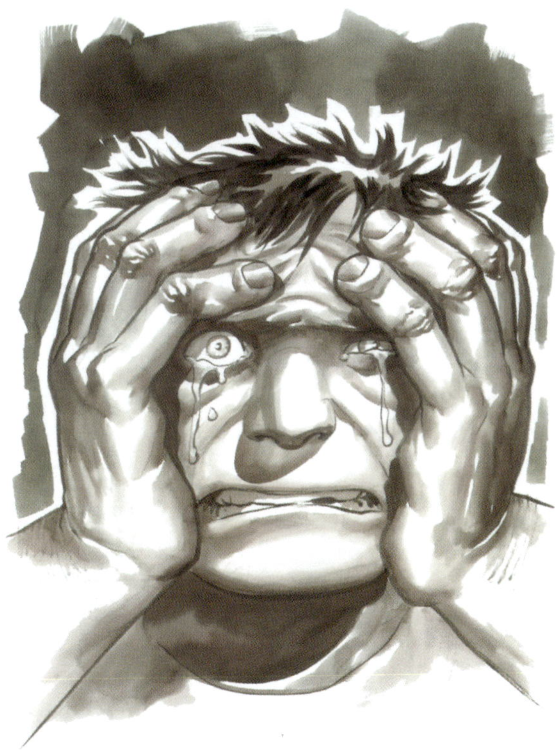
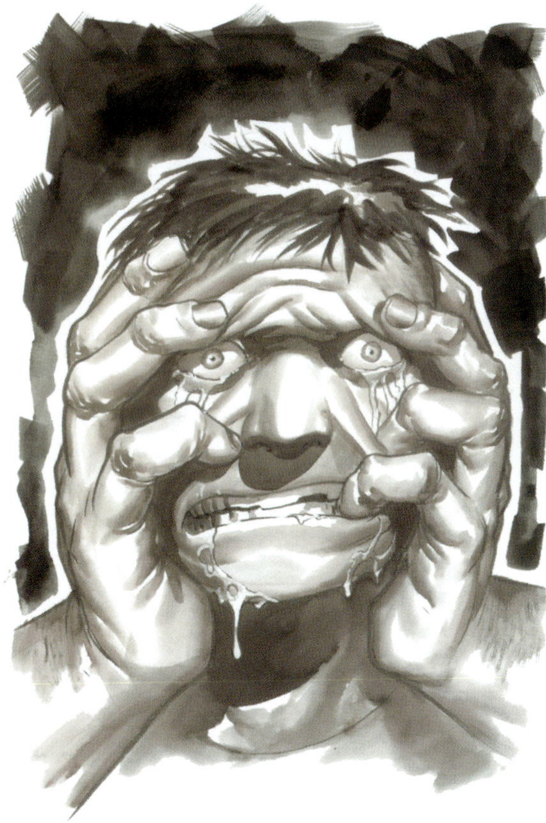

In a fairly poetic and very serious spin-off series devoted to the character, the Buzzard states, "The tarnished luster of the world can break you down. And it's hard to be alive and so broken"[93]; he subsequently fails to save a young boy placed in his charge. As the ultimate representation of a broken system and the authority figures it produces, the Buzzard eats the bloody remains of humankind to continue traveling a meaningless path.

At the end of the meeting of Hellboy and the Goon in *The Goon* No. 7, Hellboy crosses back into his own world and says, "We'll just pretend that didn't happen."[94] While it might be well and good for Hellboy to put up this pretense, the crossover is not as gimmicky as other crossovers between titles often are, and in many ways, it is very natural. This has everything to do with the porous boundaries established in these series that implicitly and explicitly synthesize and spoof material from folktales, literature, and film considered to be both high art and low entertainment.

Regardless of their frequent borrowings from other sources, both creators have been fiercely protective of their creations, maintaining control over the so-called Mignolaverse and the world of *The Goon*. In limited degrees, other creators have been invited to play in these worlds, but both creators maintain a level of control associated with *Concrete*, a pioneering Dark Horse title identified by Powell as a precedent: "When *Concrete* comes out, it's always Paul Chadwick. That's the way *The Goon* is going to be.... If *The Goon* book is coming out, I'll be doing 90-percent of the work involved."[96] Likewise, Mignola also writes, co-writes, and/or oversees all spin-off titles in the Mignolaverse including titles devoted to the BPRD, Abe Sapien, and Lobster Johnson. Their refusal to rescind control and share their creations may seem in conflict with their tendency to borrow, but their position has everything to do with their historical situation within a specific industry.

Since comic book publishers have a history of ignoring creators' rights and treating creators like factory workers, Mignola and Powell are not seeking authority so much as they are preventing the abuse of their work from the powers-that-be.[97] While asserting creative control may be a double-bind for creators who passionately produce folklore, it is important that working class guys prevent their stories from being reshaped to serve the interests of media conglomerates.[98] With this in mind, their business decisions, like their horror comics, serve as a protest against industrial society, identifying their frustrations with power as it is typically exercised against the ordinary people. As opposed to *Spawn*, which treats power as the means to win, *Hellboy* and *The Goon* treat power in itself as a problem.

Power can be expressed in a variety of ways, such as through the cultural approval of the Eisner Awards (which both series have often won). In reference to Stephen King's National Book Award speech, Mignola and Powell would heartily align themselves with King's working class identity but would be largely unwilling to build a bridge between the old boys' club and the working class (too long identified by the old boys as lower). *Hellboy* and *The Goon* treat encounters with monsters not as horrifying but entertaining, and what becomes horrifying is the way their working class heroes run out of options as indiscriminate authority marshals against them. As *Hellboy* and *The Goon* veer toward stories of poignant loss, Mignola and Powell offer no apologies for their work and revel in their supposed lack of expertise as writer/artists.

Drawing on a history of the fantastic, including things outside the realm of social respectability, these creators celebrate comic book content that shocked those who burned comic books in the 1950s and laugh at their fear of the void. This laughter serves to undermine the mission of critics in the 1950s who claimed that comic books were wholly separate from the esteemed arts within high culture and that this lower status meant that they should not be read. Rather than validate a high culture precept by arguing that comics are art, Mignola and Powell base their work on "bad" taste and keep their work on the margin, outside respectability.[99] The intentionality of their position beyond the confines of the increasingly irrelevant Comics Code is certainly debatable, but the impact is nevertheless consequential.

While not making an overt political statement, both series give comic books power that only comes from being in bad taste, horrifying the cultural elite, and staying outside the system. Outside society is where popular horror now thrives in literal terms with the zombie and the apocalypse that comes in its wake: something so effectively realized in Robert Kirkman's *The Walking Dead*. With the success not only of the comic book but also its television variant, Kirkman brings to an enormous audience the experience of uncertainty, disgust, and horror, revealing it to be an experience that most people desire.

Chapter 5 Notes

1 Craig Grannell, "An Interview with Mike Mignola, Part 6," *RevertToSaved*, last modified August 17, 2008, http://reverttosaved.com/2008/08/17/an-interview-with-mike-mignola-part-six/.

2 "Testimony of William M. Gaines, Publisher, Entertaining Comics Group, New York, NY," *TheComicbooks.Com*, last modified 2016, http://www.thecomicbooks.com/gaines.html.

3 Ibid.

4 Eric Powell, *Satan's Sodomy Baby* 1, Dark Horse (April 2007), cover.

5 Brian Heater, "Interview: Eric Powell Pt. 1 [of 2]." *The Daily Cross Hatch*, last modified Feb. 24, 2009, http://thedailycrosshatch.com/2009/02/24/interview-eric-powell-pt-1-of-2/.

6 Quoted in David Hajdu, *The Ten Cent Plague: The Great Comic-Book Scare and How It Changed America* (New York: Farrar, Straus, and Giroux, 2008), 173–74

7 Bruno Bettelheim, *The Uses of Enchantment: The Meaning and Importance of Fairy Tales* (New York: Vintage, 2010), 25.

8 Ibid., 32.

9 Ibid., 26–27.

10 Jack Zipes, "Introduction: The Remaking of Charles Perrault and His Fairy Tales," *Little Red Riding Hood, Cinderella, and Other Classic Fairy Tales of Charles Perrault*, ed., Angela Carter (New York: Penguin, 2008), viii.

11 Angela Carter, *Little Red Riding Hood, Cinderella, and Other Classic Fairy Tales of Charles Perrault*, ed., Angela Carter (New York: Penguin, 2008), 10.

12 Quoted in Helen Simpson, "Introduction," Angela Carter, *The Bloody Chamber* (London: Vintage, 2006), vii–viii, ix.

13 Angela Carter, *Angela Carter's Book of Fairy Tales* (London: Virago, 2007), xi.

14 Ibid., xiv–xvi.

15 Elizabeth Hess, "Meet the Spiegelmans," *Village Voice*, Jan. 14, 1992, 87.

16 Harold Bloom, "For the World of Letters, It's a Horror," *Los Angeles Times*, last modified Sept. 19, 2003, http://articles.latimes.com/2003/sep/19/opinion/oe-bloom19.

17 Stephen King, "National Book Award Acceptance Speech," *National Book Foundation*, last modified 2003, http://www.nationalbook.org/nbaacceptspeech_sking.html No. .WSSHRTOZMk8.

18 Dorothee Birke, "Challenging the Divide? Stephen King and the Problem of 'Popular Culture,'" *The Journal of Popular Culture* 47 (2014), 532. She also mentions *Misery* as another way that King comments on the culture industry (a novel mentioned in Chapter 4). I would add to this *Desperation,* in which a critically acclaimed but unfulfilled author has a horrifying experience and decides to write horror.

19 Stephen Jones, *The Art of Horror: An Illustrated History* (Milwaukee, WI: Applause Books, 2015), 8.

20 Randy Duncan and Matthew J. Smith, *The Power of Comics: History, Form, and Culture* (New York: Bloomsbury, 2009), 121.

21 Frank Miller, "Introduction," in Todd McFarlane, Steve Oliff, Reuben Rude, and Tom Orzechowski, *Spawn, Book 1* (Fullerton, CA: Image, 1998), 3.

22 Todd McFarlane, Steve Oliff, Reuben Rude, and Tom Orzechowski, *Spawn, Book 1* (Fullerton, CA: Image, 1998), 120.

23 Charles Brownstein, *Eisner/Miller* (Milwaukie, OR: Dark Horse, 2005), 132.

24 Dirk Deppy refers to the "Image frenzy" created in part by *Wizard* magazine, a speculator's magazine identifying the next hot comic to buy. "Suicide Club: How Greed and Stupidity Disemboweled the American Comic-Book Industry in the 1990s," *The Comics Journal* 277 (July 2006): 70. Randy Duncan and Matthew J. Smith describe the same phenomenon in *The Power of Comics: History, Form, and Culture,* 74–75.

25 The figures and sculptures are based on the *Spawn* universe, *The Walking Dead*, unlicensed horror characters (classic monsters, historical killers, twisted fairy tales, and twisted Land of Oz) and licensed characters (Leatherface, Jason, Freddy Krueger, Edward Scissorhands); they also include video game characters and sports figures.

26 Matthew J. Pustz, *Comic Book Culture: Fanboys and True Believers* (Jackson: UP of Mississippi, 1999), 179.

27 Established in 1977, it published *Detectives. Inc.*, *Ms. Tree*, and *Miracleman.*

28 Established in 1982, it published *Mage*, *Grendel*, *Robotech*, and *Johnny Quest.*

29 Established in 1983, it published *American Flagg!*, *Nexus*, and *Dreadstar.*

30 It also published previously established but less-famous comic book characters like *Usagi Yojimbo* and handsome reprint collections representing controversial chapters of comic book history (like *Crime Does Not Pay* and the *Creepy*, *Eerie*, and *Vampirella* magazines).

31 "For *Hellboy* Creator Mike Mignola, the Real Horror Is Hollywood," *Wired*, last modified Oct. 12, 2012, https://www.wired.com/2012/10/geeks-guide-mike-mignola/.

32 Stephen Weiner, Jason Hall, and Victoria Blake, *Hellboy: The Companion* (Milwaukie, OR: Dark Horse, 2008), 216.

33 Ibid., 12.

34 Christopher Irving, "Raising Hellboy: Mike Mignola on the Development of Hellboy and His Work Past, Present, and Future," *The Hellboy Archive*, last modified 2007, http://completehellboy.com/interviews/1996-2007/1998/.

35 Throughout this chapter, I will refer to *Hellboy* as a series for the sake of convenience. However, it would be more accurate to refer to *Hellboy* as a series of limited series. In addition, the trade paperbacks collect not only the various series but also short stories scattered in different places such as anthologies and promotional magazines.

36 Alan Moore, "Introduction," Mike Mignola, James Sinclair, and Pat Brosseau, *Hellboy: Wake the Devil* (Milwaukie, OR: Dark Horse, 1997), 1.

37 *Hellboy* debuted as a limited series, a format better designed to protect the creators; with no clear end, an on-going series promotes the character at the expense of the creators and the creative team can be readily replaced.

38 Mike Mignola, John Byrne, Mark Chiarello, and Matthew Hollingsworth, *Hellboy: Seed of Destruction* (Milwaukie, OR: Dark Horse, 2003), 7.

39 Christopher Brayshaw, "Between Two Worlds: The Mike Mignola Interview," *The Comics Journal* 189 (August 1996): 71.

40 Mike Mignola, John Byrne, Mark Chiarello, and Matthew Hollingsworth, *Hellboy: Seed of Destruction*, 6.

41 Ibid.

42 Joseph Michael Sommers, "Crooked Appalachia: The Laughter of the Melungeon Witches in Mike Mignola's *Hellboy: The Crooked Man*," *Comics and the U.S. South*, ed., Brannon Costello and Qiana J. Whitted (Jackson: UP of Mississippi, 2012), 224.

43 For a more direct representation of the Golden Age superhero and pulp fiction adventure hero, Mignola made Lobster Johnston part of the past history of the Hellboy Mignolaverse.

44 Mike Mignola, John Byrne, Mark Chiarello, and Matthew Hollingsworth, *Hellboy: Seed of Destruction*, 100.

45 Christopher Brayshaw, "Between Two Worlds: The Mike Mignola Interview," 86.

46 Tom Fassbender, "Mike Mignola Interview," *Ralf Hildebrandt*, last modified Jan. 17, 2007, https://www.arschkrebs.de/interviews/Mignola9704.shtml.

47 Christopher Brayshaw, "Between Two Worlds: The Mike Mignola Interview," 86–87.

48 Jason Heller, "Interview: Mike Mignola," *The Onion A.V. Club*, last modified July 24, 2008, http://www.avclub.com/article/mike-mignola-14279.

49 P. Craig Russell, "Introduction," Mike Mignola, James Sinclair, Matthew Hollingsworth, Dave Stewart, and Pat Brosseau, *Hellboy: "The Chained Coffin" and Others* (Milwaukie, OR: Dark Horse, 2003), 1.

50 Mike Mignola, James Sinclair, Matthew Hollingsworth, Dave Stewart, and Pat Brosseau, *Hellboy: "The Chained Coffin" and Others* (Milwaukie, OR: Dark Horse, 2003), 2.

51 Laura O'Connor, "The Corpse on Hellboy's Back: Translating a Graphic Image," *The Journal of Popular Culture* 43 (2010): 540.

52 Ibid., 548.

53 Ibid.

54 Mike Mignola, James Sinclair, Matthew Hollingsworth, Dave Stewart, and Pat Brosseau, *Hellboy: "The Chained Coffin" and Others*, 34. This is another one-shot that becomes important to the overall arc of *Hellboy*; in compositional terms, Mignola seems to work like a folktale teller.

55 Gary Gianni quoted in Scott Bukatman, *Hellboy's World: Comics and Monsters on the Margins* (Oakland: U of California P, 2016), 9.

56 This works in contrast to Harlan Ellison's appraisal of *The Sandman* (see Chapter 4).

57 Joseph Michael Sommers, "Crooked Appalachia: The Laughter of the Melungeon Witches in Mike Mignola's *Hellboy: The Crooked Man*," 218.

58 Ibid., 227.

59 Scott Bukatman, *Hellboy's World: Comics and Monsters on the Margins*, 78.

60 Mike Mignola, Dave Stewart, and Pat Brosseau, *Hellboy: The Right Hand of Doom* (Milwaukie, OR: Dark Horse, 2003), 117.

61 Shawna Ervin-Gore, "Mike Mignola Interview," Dark Horse Comics Last modified June 2002, http://www.darkhorse.com/Interviews/763/Mike-Mignola.

62 O'Conner makes this anxiety much more historically specific: "Hellboy's lack of malice and self-interestedness identifies him with ethos of G2s fighting a just war against Fascism as opposed to US involvement in a morally and politically questionable war in Iraq.... The moral ambiguity represented by Hellboy's Right Hand of Doom resonates with cultural anxieties about terrorist assaults and fear that the United States itself may wreak destruction upon the world. Visions of the apocalypse are a form of catastrophizing, a mode of imagining the eclipse of human agency" (Laura O'Connor, "The Corpse on Hellboy's Back: Translating a Graphic Image," 561).

63 Christopher Brayshaw, "Between Two Worlds: The Mike Mignola Interview," 89.

64 Mike Mignola, Dave Stewart, and Clem Robbins, *Hellboy: Strange Places* (Milwaukie, OR: Dark Horse, 2006), 70.

65 Guillermo del Toro, "Mike Mignola Is a Genius: An Unapologetically Subjective Introduction," Mike Mignola, Dave Stewart, and Pat Brosseau, *Hellboy: Conqueror Worm* (Milwaukie, OR: Dark Horse, 2003), 1.

66 Scott Bukatman, *Hellboy's World: Comics and Monsters on the Margins*, 37.

67 Mignola's economical use of words sets him apart from the tradition established by EC and continued with Moore and Gaiman. In many ways, Mignola constructs horror in visual terms, more like a designer. Lovecraft found language inadequate to represent horror and Mignola's large blacknesses represent that inclination.

68 Scott Bukatman, *Hellboy's World: Comics and Monsters on the Margins*, 151. Mignola's intricately designed covers combine elements in static collages that defy real movement in space, evoking both B-movie posters and the high art of Goya and Dürer (Christopher Brayshaw, "Between Two Worlds: The Mike Mignola Interview," 83).

69 Bukatman comments on another sort of void in *The Right Hand of Doom*: "There is a formal complexity here marked by fragmentation, enigma, and incompleteness–something approaching an illegibility... Mignola has yet to reveal the complete 'history of causes' that underlies the Hellboy mythos, opting instead for immanence and immersion" (Scott Bukatman, *Hellboy's World: Comics and Monsters on the Margins*, 181).

70 That ordinary girl is the one he rescued from the fairies in "The Corpse."

71 Gary Butler, "Mike Mignola on *Hellboy*," *The Hellboy Archive*, last modified April 7, 2004, http//completehellboy.com/interviews/1996-2007/apr-7-2004/.

72 Scott Bukatman, *Hellboy's World: Comics and Monsters on the Margins*, 50.

73 Wheeler Winston Dixon, *A History of Horror* (New Brunswick: Rutgers UP, 2010), 36.

74 "With its literal flashy display of boogying bogeys, 'Thriller' was an almost literal danse macabre for the go-go eighties, a leveraged buyout of Hans Holbein the Younger by modern entertainment conglomerates" (David J. Skal, *The Monster Show: A Cultural History* [New York: Farrar, Straus, and Giroux, 1993], 316).

75 Eric Powell is a fan of the film and wrote the *Big Trouble in Little China* comic book series from BOOM!

76 Powell would develop an early version of the character (Monster Boy) in *Best Cellars* No. 1.

77 Eric Powell and Dave Stewart, *The Goon: Rough Stuff* (Milwaukie, OR: Dark Horse, 2010), 26–27.

78 Hannah Means-Shannon, "It's a Battle for The Goon's Soul in 2015–Eric Powell in The Bleeding Cool Interview," *Bleeding Cool*, last modified Dec. 11, 2014, https://www.bleedingcool.com/2014/12/11/battle-goons-soul-2015-eric-powell-bleeding-cool-interview/.

79 Before Powell self-published *The Goon* under the moniker of Albatross Exploding Funnybooks, Dark Horse passed on the series.

80 Powell describes the series as character-driven, focused on the Goon and Frankie as buddies–not concept-or plot-driven like *30 Days of Night* (Hannah Means Shannon, "It's a Battle for The Goon's Soul in 2015–Eric Powell in The Bleeding Cool Interview").

81 Alex Dueben, "The Goon Show: An Interview with Eric Powell," *Ninth Art*, last modified Oct. 18, 2004, https://www.ninthart.org/display.php?article=936.

82 Eric Powell and Robin Powell, *The Goon: Nothin' But Misery* (Milwaukie, OR: Dark Horse, 2010), 109.

83 Eric Powell and Dave Stewart, *The Goon: Rough Stuff*, 6. "I've gotten much better as an artist and storyteller. I still suck. Just not as much" (Charles Webb, "Return of 'The Goon': An Interview with Eric Powell," *MTV.com*, last modified March 11, 2011, http://www.mtv.com/news/2621595/return-of-the-goon-an-interview-with-eric-powell/.).

84 Eric Powell and Dave Stewart, *The Goon: Rough Stuff*, 7. This type of metatextual and intertextual commentary is part of *The Goon* from the start with invented advertisements for the "Hey Mom! It's Educational! Billy Lobotomy Kit" and "The Atomic Rage," a hyper-violent Golden Age superhero with testicular cancer.

85 This is represented by Frank Darabont's introduction to *Heaps of Ruination* that compares Powell to Eisner.

86 Eric Powell, Robin Powell, Shaynne Corbett, Barry Gregory, and Ben Cocke, *The Goon: Heaps of Ruination* (Milwaukie, OR: Dark Horse, 2011), 97–98.

87 Eric Powell, *The Goon: Wicked Inclinations* (Milwaukie, OR: Dark Horse, 2006), 85.

88 Ibid.

89 Ibid., 99.

90 David Harper, "Artist August: Eric Powell (Interview)," *Multiversity Comics*, last modified Aug. 15, 2011, http://www.multiversitycomics.com/news-columns/artist-august-eric-powell-art-feature/.

91 Based on a story by Stephen King, *The Shawshank Redemption* contains a dramatic depiction of a prison rape. Incidentally, Darabont was the prime mover behind the development of *The Walking Dead* as a television series.

92 Brian Heater, "Interview: Eric Powell Pt. 1 [of 2]."

93 Eric Powell, Dave Stewart, and Nate Piekos, *The Goon: Death's Greedy Comeuppance* (Milwaukie, OR: Dark Horse, 2011), 105.

94 Eric Powell, Robin Powell, Shaynne Corbett, Barry Gregory, and Ben Cocke, *The Goon: Heaps of Ruination*, 94.

95 Brian Heater, "Interview: Eric Powell Pt. 2 [of 2]," *The Daily Cross Hatch*, last modified March 2, 2009, http://thedailycrosshatch.com/2009/03/02/interview-eric-powell-pt-2-of-2/.

96 Mignola comments on the ownership of creative work: "I think what surprises me more often is really how few people actually do it. I think it's such a practical business model… I shouldn't say that because it certainly isn't a proven commercial business model, but I do think it has so much potential for success" (Rich Barrett, "Our Interview with *Hellboy* Creator Mike Mignola," *Mental Floss*, last modified March 22, 2014, http://mentalfloss.com/article/55606/our-interview-hellboy-creator-mike-mignola).

97 With a movie adaptation that reveals then unknown secrets, Mignola asserted his ownership of *Hellboy* by producing Hellboy's back-story for *The Island* (Laura O'Connor, "The Corpse on Hellboy's Back: Translating a Graphic Image," 553).

98 Powell argues that the industry does not have the facility to grow over time: "The industry is lazy. We keep selling a rehash of a rehash because it has a built in audience to exploit. But that audience keeps shrinking because they are getting tired of it" (Dan Casey, "Comic Book Day: Eric Powell's a Total 'Goon,'" *Nerdist*, Last modified April 25, 2012, http://nerdist.com/comic-book-day-eric-powells-a-total-goon/).

99 Powell acknowledges that his marginal position is partly lost due to the success of *The Goon*: "I think the Goon is… underground, but it's not… .I don't feel like I fit in with the superhero comics and stuff like that, but at the same time I'm not a really small press or an independent, so I'm in this weird thing" (Quint, "Quint Talks with *The Goon* Creator Eric Powell about the Upcoming Animated Feature, "David Fincher, Paul Giamatti, and Much More!!!" *AintItCool.com*, last modified August 23, 2010, http://www.aintitcool.com/node/46242). Mignola experienced this due to widespread awareness of *Hellboy* through the feature films. See "For Hellboy Creator Mike Mignola, the Real Horror Is Hollywood," *Wired*, https://www.wired.com/2012/10/geeks-guide-mike-mignola/.

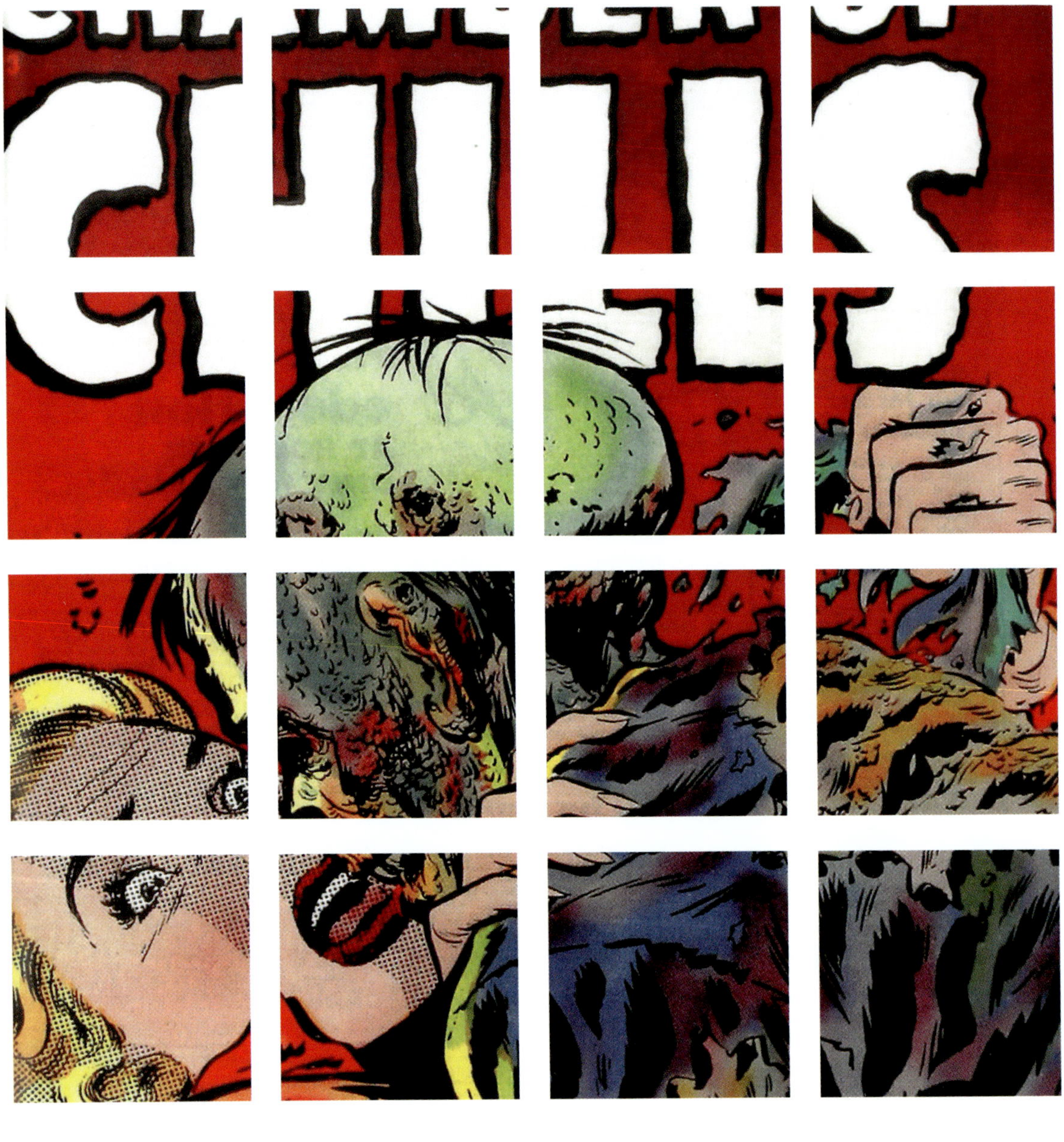

CHAPTER 6

The Monster Brought Back to Life Again: *The Walking Dead* and Horror Comics Even More Undead

I definitely have character arcs in mind for each character unless I kill them.
Robert Kirkman[1]

Gothic Traditions and the Really Weird Cowboy: Horror and Heroism in the United States

If Bill Gaines had a "gotcha" moment with Fredric Wertham during his statements to the congressional subcommittee, it was his criticism of Wertham's reading of the EC story "The Whipping." In a direct address, Gaines stated,

> "Dr. Wertham, I am happy to say, I have just been caught in a half truth.... He said there is a magazine now on the stands preaching racial intolerance.... There do appear in this magazine such materials as 'Spik' [sic], 'Dirty Mexican,' but Dr. Wertham did not tell you what the plot of the story was. This is one of the series of stories designed to show the evils of race prejudice and mob violence.... I am very proud of it, and to find it being used in such a nefarious way made me quite angry.[2]

Gaines revealed that Wertham had not read or accounted for the O. Henry twist ending and that his superficial interpretation missed the story's obvious message about the evils of racism. In addition to justifying questionable content in the service of a moral cause, this description charted the socially conscious territory often covered by EC horror. Although sometimes employing traditional monsters and the supernatural, the stories borrowed more heavily from the traditions of realism and naturalism than most others during the classic age of the comics scare. Even with its emphasis on the surprise ending, EC comics did not reject traditional story structure and aspired to something like the cultural criticism implicit in social realist texts like Upton Sinclair's *The Jungle*.

This territory would later be occupied by one of the most clearly influential comic books of the contemporary comics scare: Robert Kirkman's zombie epic *The Walking Dead*. Although it is a story of an apocalyptic future caused by monsters, Kirkman develops a strikingly realistic setting and employs a continuing narrative to go far beyond the ending of a 300-page novel or two-hour film (rejecting the artificiality of a discrete climax and resolution). Like EC stories that use monsters largely as a device to delve into psychological phenomena, *The Walking Dead* is a story that makes the physical presence of monsters less relevant to its narrative and themes. Along these lines, Kirkman himself identifies this monster tradition and his comic series as engaging in discrete social criticism: "The best zombie movies aren't the splatter fests of gore and violence with goofy characters and tongue in cheek antics. Good zombie movies show us how messed up we are, they make us question our station in society... and our society's station in the world... there's always an undercurrent of social commentary and thoughtfulness."[3]

The zombie tradition should be carefully charted because this tradition is the newest and most American of any thus far discussed (and Kirkman's series contributes significantly to the zombie's development as a cultural obsession). While there are certainly precedents for zombies in ancient folklore, their representation as the harbingers of a secular end of times is anchored in the twentieth and twenty-first centuries in the United States. As media scholar Kyle Bishop states, "the zombie is a fundamentally *American* creation."[4] In order to characterize the zombie, two of Jeffrey Cohen's theses in *Monster Theory* pinpoint the most prominent aspects of the contemporary zombie narrative: the monster's body is the cultural body,[5] and the monster is the harbinger of category crisis.[6]

Ancient folklore was less concerned than contemporary horror with labels that separate the walking dead into ghosts, vampires, and zombies. But the contemporary reference to zombies means something very specific: a horde of shambling, flesh-eating corpses who outnumber the living in a world no longer driven by the technology and morality of civilization. As W. Scott Poole argues, "Perhaps more than any other monster, they are 'made in America' as commodities for sale and distribution. This makes them important representations of what Americans fear, or desire, from the monster at the beginning of a new millennium."[7] Examining how these monsters represent the "cultural body" and our "category crises," many have read zombies metaphorically as a foreign invasion, infectious disease, terrorism, sin, and more. However, all monsters function as metaphors with meaning dependent on cultural context, and so American narratives should be examined as contributing to the zombie story.

In particular connection to *The Walking Dead*, Kirkman implements and deconstructs certain horror traditions in conjunction with the zombie: the Southern Gothic and Weird Western traditions.

In a broader literary context, the American Gothic represents the way the European Gothic has become part of the American literary tradition and is primarily associated with Edgar Allan Poe's critique of the national failure to confront history. The move from the European Gothic to American Gothic is often flippantly identified as the move from the haunted castle to the haunted house, identifying the supposedly shorter history of the United States. Regardless, in "The Fall of the House of Usher," the protagonist tries to soothe Roderick Usher, plagued by an illness connected to his aged house that also afflicts and seemingly kills Roderick's sister.[8] Overwhelmed by guilt and a sense of doom, Roderick cannot be diverted by the protagonist's story of a knight breaking into a dwelling, discovering a dragon, and slaying the beast. However, the triumphant end of the knight's story leads to the revelation that Roderick's sister was buried alive and hence the ultimate destruction of both siblings in their collapsing house.

The destruction of the family is connected to the Old World story, a reminder of an origin much older than their New World home and the ancient source of their strange ailment. This story represents the American Gothic argument that the United States has a longer history than most acknowledge, and haunting results from the sins of the often unacknowledged father. English scholar Teresa A. Goddu argues, "American gothic literature criticizes America's national myth of new-world innocence by voicing the cultural contradictions that undermine the nation's claim to purity and equality. Showing how these contradictions contest and constitute national identity even as they are denied, the gothic tells of the historical horrors that make national identity possible yet must be repressed in order to sustain it."[9] The contradictions include not only the false newness of the country but also the rights-of-man ideals that would be forsaken in the earliest part of nation-building through the institution of slavery and the abuse of native peoples.

The first of two regionally specific traditions tied to the American Gothic is the Southern Gothic, dealing with the tension between civilized exteriors and inhuman actions via the convention of the literary grotesque. In twentieth-century literature, the Southern Gothic includes the works of William Faulkner and Flannery O'Connor, neither of whom are horror writers per se. However, both developed characters invested in the superstructures of civilized culture and unwilling to acknowledge civilization's past sins–the quintessential stuff of grotesque characters.

Flannery O'Connor described this design of characters in the Southern Gothic best when she called Southern literature "Christ-haunted."[10] This model is very similar to that of less geographically specific, monster-free EC horror stories that use the American dream to define and distort their grotesque characters.

Regardless, the Southern Gothic leads to stories more clearly defined as horror, such as Anne Rice's *Vampire Chronicles*, Shaun Cassidy's *American Gothic*, and Charlaine Harris's *Southern Vampire Mysteries*. In reference to the television show *American Gothic* featuring a sheriff as a sinister, supernatural tempter, Lorna Jowett and Stacey Abbott state, "The show emphasizes the dichotomy between the polite and formal exterior of the South versus the interior truth of corruption and social decay in which deals are made… for personal or community gain."[11] And in reference to *True Blood*, the HBO show based on *The Southern Vampire Mysteries*, Jowett and Abbott argue that "beneath the veneer of Southern charm lies a world of drugs and drug-dealing, BDSM, intolerance, religious hypocrisy, and murder.… As the series progresses,… the abjectness of the vampire body is depicted in increasingly graphic, often grotesque detail."[12] In connection with its obsession with depravity underneath the propriety of small towns and suburban spaces,[13] the Southern Gothic horror narrative uses the grotesque and the monster to represent the cultural body. And through the Southern Gothic writer Cormac McCarthy, *The Road* critiques the cultural abject via the travel narrative (connected with the Western) in the post-apocalyptic future (connected with the zombie story).

The second of two regionally specific traditions tied to the American Gothic is the Weird Western, exploring the connection between civilization and savagery in characters that conquered the frontier. Similar to the way early Southern literature sought to justify slavery through works such as Thomas Dixon's *The Leopard's Spots* and Margaret Mitchell's *Gone with the Wind*, early Westerns sought to justify native oppression through works like the pulp stories of Buffalo Bill and John Ford's *Stagecoach*. However, in the mid-twentieth century, Westerns often dismantled the dichotomy that made cowboys civilized and good and Indians savage and evil with progressive films like André deToth's *The Indian Fighter* and more significantly, with John Ford's *The Searchers*. Featuring John Wayne as Ethan Edwards, a cowboy, ex-Confederate soldier, and Indian fighter, the movie portrays Edwards as a mirror of his Indian adversary. Made savage, ugly, and abject by his perception of his enemy, Ethan's grotesque behavior is generally seen as inappropriate in the supposedly civilized (though still quite savage) world.

Within the frame established by the Western as an American myth, the image of Ethan lifting his niece, who has been kidnapped and enculturated by Indian tribe, is haunting because it is unclear whether he intends to save her or kill her.

However, the Western only becomes truly weird in pulps and comics with the supernatural as an artificial plot device (the frightening costume of the Ghost Rider) or as an actual presence that threatens the civilized veneer of towns on the frontier. As media scholars Cynthia Miller and Bowdoin Van Riper argue, "The vampires, zombies, mummies, and ghosts of undead lay siege to a frontier tied to myths of freedom, independence, strength, and ingenuity, which serve as building blocks of our identities, both individual and collective."[14] More recently, this can be seen in Kathryn Bigelow's vampire Western film *Near Dark*, Stephen King's science fiction horror novel *The Gunslinger*, and in Garth Ennis's comic book *Preacher*, featuring John Wayne as a spirit-guide to the rebel Texas preacher navigating supernatural horrors. In short, the heroes and the monsters of Southern Gothic and Weird Western narratives are not distinct and expose the artificiality of the separation between civilization and the horrific animal impulses that undergird human behavior. And with haunting themes that spoil America's new nation future-orientation and promise of progress, their vision becomes one of an inescapable past that leads to an even more monstrous future.

Dawn of the Barely Read: The Mostly Cinematic History of Zombies

The deconstruction of American heroism and the establishment of the apocalyptic future is central to the zombie narrative, something that connects the Gothic past to America's future. "The zombie can... be seen as... a new monster for a New World that has facilitated the Gothic's ability to remain relevant in a post-industrial, cyberspace era. Unnatural death is now more horrific, pervasive, and far-reaching than [Horace] Walpole ever could have imagined, and the zombie works as a dramatic manifestation of this ever-present anxiety."[15] Bishop argues that zombie fiction becomes unique in horror history by skipping its literary stage and moving directly from folklore to film.[16] *White Zombie* (1932) and *I Walked with a Zombie* (1943) appropriate Caribbean myths of the Voodoo master who enslaves unwilling victims (making the zombie state into a metaphor for slavery). However, this would not be the only variation on the living dead motif in the United States, as corpses sometimes returned after unnatural deaths in the horror comics of the 1950s (usually to plague murderous or grief-stricken spouses).[17]

However, despite these precedents, the most influential source of the American myth of the zombie story would be Richard Matheson's post-apocalyptic novel *I Am Legend* (1954). With vampires created through communicable disease (the favorite explanation for zombies in years to come), Robert Neville fights back against the vampire horde as the last living human, and his fight for survival changes him in fundamental ways: "Neville's hatred of the vampires makes him into more of a monster than they are.... The zombie genre, especially in Romero's iteration, relied heavily on Matheson's novel, especially in its explicit satire of human attitudes toward the monster."[18] And yet unlike *I Am Legend*'s hard science fiction explanation of vampires as the living dead, George Romero's *Night of the Living Dead* (1968), the essential starting point for the contemporary zombie story, avoids any clear explanation for corpses coming back to life.

While the monsters' hunger for flesh and bites turns others into the living dead, *Night of the Living Dead* is more concerned with the way people cope with the onslaught (and suggests the monsters are not the problem to be solved). Focusing on a group of mostly unrelated people seeking shelter in a small house, Romero turns an ordinary space into something uncanny,[19] haunted by literal monsters and social dynamics that keep survivors from working together. This involves resistance to the clear leader of the group because he is black, demonstrating the film's direct engagement with social issues. As Romero produced the *Living Dead* series, this engagement is directly related to setting—with the home and a critique of the American family (*Night of the Living Dead*), the mall and a critique of American capitalism (*Dawn of the Dead*), and the military base and a critique of the military-industrial complex (*Day of the Dead*).[20]

Rejecting the timeless Gothic of Universal's monster movies and grounding the films in contemporary times and places, the Romero zombie movies are more than a blend of horror and disaster, and they craft monsters specifically as outgrowths of culture. Different from the immaterial nature of hauntings by ghosts or the Byronic sophistication of blood-consuming vampires, the primal and disgusting hunger of decaying zombies provides a new perspective on humanity. As an independent production, *Night of the Living Dead* wasn't seeking a broad audience and presented previously unseen levels of gore with its cannibal monsters that surprisingly resonated with a larger audience. "Romero toyed with the idea of cutting out the most explicit sequences (close-up after close-up of zombies eating entrails), but then decided that these scenes gave *Night of the Living Dead* the extra punch.... Thus, a new level of cinematic violence was born, and the horror film was changed forever."[21]

In addition, humans act in self-defense by violently killing the zombies in a variety of stomach-turning ways that destroy the brain but make the line between the humans and the monsters less distinct: "Romero-style zombies flagrantly defy the established boundaries of living and dead, confronting audiences with dangerous bodies that challenge the natural order of things."[22] At the same time, *Day of the Dead* makes zombies more sympathetic as experiments conducted on them (by increasingly inhuman human beings) reveal that the zombies have memories of their former lives. This identification with the enemy relates to the anxieties of the Vietnam War (its horrific images inspiring Tom Savini, makeup effects master for *Living Dead* films): "Horror films of the seventies and eighties began exhibiting symptoms remarkably similar to some of those suffered by victims of posttraumatic stress syndrome: startle reactions, paranoia,... and traumatic flashbacks."[23] These zombie narratives represented and processed individual and collective trauma in the United States, and Romero's first two films radically exceeded box office expectations.

Despite its lack of a literary tradition (something that justified other Code-skirting Marvel monsters of the 1970s), the zombie became part of the black-and-white Marvel horror magazine roster with *Tales of the Zombie*. With the bigger budget of *Dawn of the Dead* (1978), zombies became part of the popular culture but slipped into camp with Michael Jackson's *Thriller* and the Romero-less *Return of the Living Dead* (1985) in which zombies first cried out for brains.[24] With camp not far from parody, the zombie became fodder for black comedy with characters like Billy Butcherson in the horror comedy *Hocus Pocus*. However, Danny Boyle, an English director, would resurrect the American myth of the zombie in a realistic setting with *28 Days Later* (2002), a film focused on Jim, a character who wakes from a coma to find a devastated London overrun by fast-moving zombies.

Less about the living dead than the infected living, the zombie metaphor shifted in an era of quickly spreading viral pandemics and unanticipated attacks by faceless terrorists: "[T]he primary metaphor of the post-9/11 zombie world is of course terrorism itself."[25] Whether or not a direct point of inspiration, *28 Days Later* blames the zombie pandemic on animals subjected to experiments that "infected" them with violent experiences. Moreover, the film revisits themes in the underappreciated *Day of the Dead* as a military conclave rescues a group of survivors to collect women as sex slaves and breeders; and in the end, Jim uses zombies to attack the soldiers, the true monsters.

The zombie myth has evolved through a short but robust lifespan, first as a slave, then as an invader, and most recently as a catalyst as Julia Round argues, "Early themes... have now been replaced by a 'post-zombieism' that, although it claims to sustain the presence of these creatures, actually diminishes their role within their own narratives in order to better illustrate the existential plight of humanity: the real walking dead."[26]

Horror portrays and critiques the civilized individual estranged from the violent, sexual, and generally hungry self, and the zombie narrative portrays and critiques the monstrous human by stripping away the trappings of the post-industrial society. As Poole states, "America's apocalyptic tendencies grew throughout the 1980s, and by the 1990s had become intertwined with technological fears regarding the new millennium.... The very complexity of modern society, the intricate support systems that keep the lights on... has given a special twist to the theme of apocalypse in modern America."[27] In a post-human environment, post-Enlightenment thinkers in this zombie-filled world lose the notion that the future stretches long into the distance and offers endless opportunities to refine and perfect society. And in a post-Christian environment, Americans in this secular apocalypse have little reason to restrain savagery barely contained in the past. Debuting a year after *28 Days Later*, *The Walking Dead* significantly contributes to these ideas and pushes the zombie narrative into the radical post-zombie era of human monsters in America.

The Walking Dead and Runaway Success: Black and White and Dead All Over

Beginning with the independently published *Battle Pope*, a parody of superhero violence, Robert Kirkman later developed *Invincible*, a series for Image's superhero line in 2003. In the same year, he developed *The Walking Dead* with Tony Moore, the artist from *Battle Pope*, and worked to sell the idea to Image, whose reputation for company/creator relationships had improved in notable ways. With increasingly diverse offerings in genre and style, Image was understood by Kirkman as a company that shared profits and granted clear-cut deals to creators: "That's also the appeal of Image comics in general. Within your series, you're controlling everything. You're the owner."[28] With *The Walking Dead* a clearer move away from the mainstream of superhero comics, Kirkman found a home for the series whose title was the specific descriptor used in the Comics Code to prohibit the monsters now commonly known as zombies.

The Walking Dead adds most significantly to zombie horror through its on-going story, something tied to the serial nature of comics publishing and something often derided by high culture's advocates of classical narrative structure with a discrete beginning, middle, and end. Rather than understand a continuing (and seemingly never-ending) series as part of an entertainment industry that continues to manufacture what sells, Kirkman sees it as a radical opportunity: "With *Walking Dead*, the concept is a zombie movie that never ends.... If they don't die [in a movie], they ride off into the sunset, mostly in a helicopter and you never hear from them again.... I just wanted to explore a natural progression of events in that type of society."[29] Referencing zombie movies (especially with the helicopter escape at the end of *Dawn of the Dead*), Kirkman resists the closure that often makes horror bearable: the teleological promise of an ending. Working along similar lines, Kirkman states, "I always want to know what happens next. Even when all the characters die at the end... I just want to keep going."[30] The incredibly important point is that, for Kirkman, a story should continue without end regardless of the logic that guides a conventional narrative such as the resolution of the conflict for the central protagonist. Consequently, *The Walking Dead* promises the long whimper of people struggling under the monstrous weight of their own survival, charting the way this experience changes what was formerly known as society.

Aspiring to a realism often associated with zombie films, *The Walking Dead* is the contemporary horror comic book story least obviously constructed by an exterior force like text from an omniscient narrator and features nothing like the self-conscious frame commentary of a horror host. In addition, textual representations of a person's thoughts are not provided in thought balloons, but Kirkman and Moore (later Charlie Adlard) do manipulate the narrative in other ways afforded by the comic book form such as repeated images, panel size, and textually rendered sound effects. Nevertheless, the timeline is primarily linear and rarely ever departs from the "real" and consistent environment of a band of survivors in a decimated world overrun with zombies. The aesthetics of realism and naturalism are established in the first issue with an opening that borrows from the premise of *28 Days Later*. When sheriff's deputy Rick Grimes is shot on the last panel of the first page, he wakes in a hospital bed with a gasp in the very next panel (a splash page). With renderings of Rick and his surroundings that are intricate and shaded in a careful illustrative design, the perspective alternates between Rick's first- and third-person views but doesn't move beyond the scope of his own experience. His limited viewpoint and understanding that emphasize his isolation consequently become the reader's limited viewpoint and understanding.

While not quite painterly, the illustrative style (particularly of Adlard, who begins with No. 7) recalls the style inaugurated in horror comics with *Creepy*, and the black-and-white aesthetic adds to the bleak experience of the zombie apocalypse Rick is soon to discover. On the third page (divided as a nine-panel grid), the slow progress of a weakened Rick is depicted as he slowly moves from his bed in the first three, falls in the fourth, calls for a nurse in the fifth, and sits on the floor in the seventh and eighth in their wordless depiction of time passing. After moving into the hallway and discovering a corpse, Rick opens a locked cafeteria door to discover bloody and rotting corpses on their feet and moving towards him to attack. Despite a title and a general familiarity with the zombie genre that sets up the expectation of this discovery, his horror at the scene is transferred to the reader. Moore's panels have a cinematic shot/reverse shot rhythm, implicating the reader through both Rick's literal viewpoint and a depiction of Rick's emotional reaction. In addition, panel design creates a claustrophobic feel with each successive panel that depicts the zombie attack increasingly close and detailed, making his escape seem unlikely.

Kirkman's general philosophy is to avoid flashbacks and utilize techniques that engage the reader and add to the reality effect:[31] "Maybe that's because it seems more real to me, being able to put your own spin on things and being able to picture it yourself almost makes it feel like a novel. I'm putting the hard work on the reader instead of having the artist draw all the stuff."[32] "Maybe it makes things seem more real? Less like a work of fiction."[33] This verisimilitude makes the drama of fiction more exciting, but *The Walking Dead* doesn't function like an adventure, and sharing a character's traumatic experience reveals the potential cruelty of this sort of truth-telling in horror comics. In regard to the "truth" of *The Walking Dead*, the physical traumas are connecting to a conceptual trauma: the dismantling of the self-made hero of the American frontier who establishes and preserves democratic civilization. As "a continuing story of survival horror" (the tag-line associated with the series), the narrative reveals the pragmatic nature of the hero who becomes a survivor in a harsh environment. Rather than fight for the rights of man, the characters tap into their baser natures to reveal the fascism beneath the surface of the American heroic consciousness (as argued by John Shelton Lawrence and Robert Jewett in *The Myth of the American Superhero*).[34]

As a sheriff's deputy in Georgia, Rick Grimes immediately has associations with the Southern gentleman through his geography and the cowboy through his profession—complete with the sheriff's wide-brimmed "cowboy" hat.[35]

After again encountering the horror of his circumstances through a "living" skeletal corpse on the side of the road, he sheds a tear but then becomes a man of action. In his attempt to return home, Rick encounters Morgan (and his son Duane), someone able to explain the devastation: "All media shut down after a few weeks.... Before they stopped broadcasting they told us to relocate to the bigger cities. They said they could protect us all there. I figured I'd be better off taking my chances here."[36] In addition to reestablishing tenets of zombie mythology ("A good blow to the head will take 'em out"), Morgan sets up a typical heroic journey for Rick to rejoin and save his family in the bigger city: one likely to fail in a typical zombie narrative wherein populated areas are most dangerous. Regardless, the monsters threaten civilization, and the warrior hero fights to restore it (an intention marked by a typical sequence featuring Rick arming himself at the police station). When Rick and Morgan encounter a zombie behind a fence, Morgan, who plans to stay, tells the gun-toting Rick to "leave it be.... You may need that bullet later."[37] Despite this advice, Rick shoots the still-living but immobilized skeletal corpse on the way out of town as an act of mercy: a clear marker of civilization.

In this way, the first issue sets up a paradigm that will ultimately fail: one that finds meaning in the suffering of the hero who reasserts morality and rebuilds civilization. On the last page of the first issue, Rick's act of mercy is already called into question by emphasizing his isolation. Rather than demonstrate the moral triumph, the final three panels focus on ordinary moments that lack drama and special meaning; from a distance that prevents a clear view of his face, Rick is shown 1) walking to his car, 2) entering his car, and 3) driving away into the night (not a cowboy's sunset) with the emphasis placed on the desolate road. In the next issue, Rick runs out of gas and rides a horse to Atlanta—reestablishing his cowboy status—only to discover it overrun by zombies (barely escaping with the help of Glenn, another survivor). Led by Glenn to a survivor's camp outside the city, he is improbably reunited with his wife Lori, son Carl, and best friend (and fellow sheriff) Shane: building blocks for civilization that are, in short order, taken from him. In his absence, Lori slept with Shane, and Shane redefines his life in response to this new relationship and the zombie apocalypse, soon after breaking down and threatening Rick. Carl, trained to use a gun in self-defense against the zombies, shoots Shane in a moment ambiguous in regard to the hero's mission. When Carl states, "It's not the same as killing the dead ones, Daddy," Rick replies, "It never should be, son. It never should be."[38]

On one hand, this can be read as the cowboy passing on necessary skills and frontier wisdom to the next generation; on the other stronger hand, this can be read as the cowboy, savage for the sake of civilization, having no easy answers for a traumatized son. After all, he is a boy who has killed a father figure (the only other "official" authority figure), because that man had been fundamentally changed by the zombie apocalypse. The final page is a splash page that provides a high-angle perspective of the three characters, again with an emphasis on Rick's isolation as he comforts Carl and also with the nearby body of Shane in a pool of blood. In this case, the end result of violence is neither stylized nor sanitized to make it more appealing within a story supposedly about the redemptive powers of the American warrior hero.

Another Day, Another Apocalypse: The End of the American Hero and the Beginning of Survival Horror

In short order, Rick's priorities shift in a way typical within the zombie narrative, toward security, and other humans are recognized as threats equal to those posed by zombies. With this in mind, Carl's break from stereotypical heroic values is seen more fully in his execution of Ben, a troubled boy who kills his twin to see him come back as a zombie. In a world where decisions are based on ensuring the security of the survivor group, good must be understood in relative terms and not as a universal ideal. When the survivor group ascends a hill in an archetypal civilization-building moment, Rick looks down in a splash page close-up of his face and states, "It's perfect. We're home."[39] However, this reaction is ironic considering the preceding double splash page that depicts the prison that they see (anything but a perfect home by formerly established cultural standards).

Despite being suited to provide for their newly established needs, the prison is not perfect as the group itself is not secure, and a new member named Thomas murders two young girls within the prison. An enraged Rick attacks Thomas and asserts a new tribal order so that the group can deal with the threat from within. When Carl asks whether Thomas is dead from Rick's beating, Rick responds, "No. Not yet.... I'm making the best choice for all of us.... I'm in charge.... We do not kill. We do not tolerate it. That is our rule–our pledge. You kill. You die. No exceptions. Now–help me get Thomas up. We're going to hang him."[40] When Lori questions his trial-free mandate for capital punishment, a still angry Rick tells her to "shut the fuck up."[41]

In addition to establishing that human violence necessitates an equal level of retributive violence (the same way that a zombie attack does), Rick asserts his authority and undermines the group as a democracy in principle and action. While his leadership is questioned and democratic rule temporarily reasserted, other survivor groups later attack them for their resources. As the fear of humans outpaces that of the zombies as the others who threaten, Rick returns to his role as leader.

In fact, when the group joins a secure, suburban enclave of survivors, Rick rejects their idea of rebuilding a community based on democratic principles and plans to commandeer what they have in the name of security. In a panel that emphasizes the angry expression on his face and shrouds his face in shadow, Rick says to Glenn (and to the reader), "I don't care what these people say. This place is too important.... I want our guns back–and you're going to get them for us."[42] While Rick's position is that of a villain in a story of epic heroism, his position is that of a survivor in a story of the zombie apocalypse. And since the reader has participated in Rick's long and often tragic struggles, the need to marshal the strength to maintain order is readily understood. Kirkman states, "Is Rick sympathetic?.... Maybe he isn't. I don't know. I'm not sitting around worrying whether he's sympathetic or relatable. I think that would be a mistake. Rick is a good person at his core, so at his core, he is relatable and likeable... but he's going to make mistake after mistake because that's what people do.... Seeing people live through the events of the book, and watching how that changes them, for good or bad, hopefully makes them at least a little sympathetic, no matter what."[43] Quite notable in Kirkman's discussion of sympathy for Rick is that it does not lead to a sense that Rick will or can be an idealistic hero.[44]

The Walking Dead also undermines several other characters made popular with fans through the ways they initially exceeded conventional expectations for the warrior hero. Tyrese, who supports Rick and also leads the group, is depicted as a brave and effective zombie killer most notably during an incident within the prison. When attempting to "clean out" the prison gym of zombies, the small group of cleaners is overrun, and their quick escape leaves Tyrese, whom they presume to be dead, inside. When Rick returns with others to finish the horde off (undoubtedly now including a zombie version of Tyrese), they find sitting amidst the zombie corpses a still-human Tyrese, who says, "Rick. You're back. What kept you?"[45] Although the marriage of this image and quip represents a power fantasy (the thrill of a stylized resolution of the hero's violent action), Tyrese is hardly the selfless warrior hero, and the moment is tempered by his very recent past actions.

When his daughter and her lover make a suicide pact to shoot one another, he follows through, but she does not; upon making this discovery, Tyrese chokes the teenager to death. When he tells Rick, "Leave me. He'll be coming back soon, and I'm going to kill him again. Slower this time," the next panel features Rick's horrified reaction.[46] When he later sees Tyrese smiling as he burns their bodies, Rick (and the reader) can recognize that the emotional source of Tyrese's power is not the ideals typically associated with an American hero.

Likewise, Michonne wields a katana and efficiently beheads zombies but is quite clearly shaped by her abject circumstances. While on her own, she survives mostly undisturbed thanks to her chained and jawless zombie companions, whose scent prevents other zombies from recognizing she is alive. Scarred by her experience, she is cruel not only to her enemies but also other members of the group and frequently demonstrates signs of a dissociative disorder. Literary scholar Jeffrey Sartain suggests two possible ends in this era of the zombie:

> The values of ruggedness and self-determination classically associated with the Western genre in literature and film are an important part of the contemporary interest in the zombie story. Zombie stories' emphasis on the values of self-reliance and toughness often make the genre a testament to a version of masculinity that privileges narrow-minded individualism, but more progressive versions of the zombie tale, which emphasize community and consubstantial formations of identity, also exist.[47]

With its critique of ruggedness and self-determination, *The Walking Dead* fits into the latter category, but identity formation based on community (and also on the ethics of survival) is not necessarily healthier.

When one of Rick's friends is captured and partially eaten by a cannibalistic survivor group, Rick's group tortures and kills them all. When they first encounter the leader of the cannibals, a large panel presents Rick's group from the low angle of the leader, emphasizing their power and showcasing expressions indicative of their cruel intentions. Kirkman states, "I try not to be the glass-half-empty kind of guy. But I do feel like if society were to crumble, we would all be killing each other for resources. It's terrifying what a human will do to survive, you know? Monsters are real and they are us."[48] While violent retribution may be justified by certain narrative contexts (such as Rick biting the throat of a man who threatens to rape Carl), the habitual use of violence makes the survivor group less heroic and more monstrous.

The ultimate antagonism between survivor strategy and heroism can be seen with Eugene, who falsely claims to have the cure for the zombie disease so that Abraham and Rosita will protect him. When this sham is exposed, the revelation robs Abraham, Rosita, and the reader of a heroic quest that gives meaning to the repeated experience of violence.

Civilization and Its Pleasure Principle and Zombies and Their Discontents

As Kirkman's sympathy for Rick encourages the reader's sympathy for Rick (and other survivors), the reader's continued exposure to trauma makes abnormal and monstrous actions acceptable as coping strategies. After his son is attacked by zombies, Morgan finds a house where a father has killed his family and himself–a formerly unacceptable means of protection from zombies within a narrative that emphasizes survival at all costs. However, while this father's strategy is contrasted with Morgan's own, Morgan failed to protect his son from zombies, and this discovery then adds to Morgan's own trauma, demonstrating the cumulative nature of trauma in the comic series. And in general, the experience of trauma is seemingly unending, with yet another zombie attack in a supposedly safe place, preventing characters from establishing social routines and encouraging the "category crisis" suggested by Cohen's monster theory.

Moreover, it is not just zombie attacks that keep civilized patterns from reasserting themselves but the abject experience of all violence that prevents the typical organization of the self. Even the most understandable violence (killing zombies) is seen in graphic detail by the characters and the reader, and the graphic detail pushes the reader to disgust; such violence includes not only a series of zombie heads exploding from gunshots but also splash pages devoted to images like the smashed skull of a fan-favorite character like Glenn. Although typical of zombie narratives, the most disturbing killing and abject experience of violence results from the supposed necessity of killing family and friends who return as zombies.

For instance, when the borderline to Rick's settlement is marked by attackers with heads of settlement members on pikes, those heads return as zombies to be destroyed. Sartain states, "The role of the Other in Kirkman's epic… is filled by the living dead who are explicitly familiar yet truly alien versions of the people they face–the very definition of the uncanny. The familiarity of the zombies–the revelation that they are former neighbors, friends, and lovers–signals the series' identification and empathy with the Other, a critical trope… where a strict binary between self and Other gets deconstructed."[49]

Before Morgan encounters the family suicide, Rick discovers that Morgan had been living with his son as a zombie, keeping the boy chained but fed. After Rick gives a typical "that's not your son" speech, he leaves Morgan "to say goodbye," but after a shot rings out and Morgan leaves, a series of panels reveals he left his son alive and free to roam.[50] Often this sort of category confusion is reserved for the excessively cruel villain (the Governor and his zombie daughter) or the uncontrollably dangerous abnormality (Carol and her conversation with a zombie she allows to bite her): "I think I'll just talk to you from now on. You listen, you don't judge me.... I really hope you like me. [She allows the zombie to bite her.] Oh good... you do like me."[51] However, as already argued, the lines between heroic and villainous, normal and abnormal are blurred and lead to a blurring of the line between human and the monstrous.

Fig. 6.1

© *Chamber of Chills*, no. 23, *Harvey*, 1954 The desirable and disgusting are brought together in Rick's dream, a repeated horror motif depicted in a mirror image on the cover of *Chamber of Chills* in 1954.

In the first year of the series, Kirkman presents a debate in which Hershel, a well-grounded farmer who shelters Rick's group, questions Rick's claim that "Those things aren't human. They're undead monsters."[52] While Hershel's argument is clinical (that the "walkers" suffer from a disease), this connection to the living and the walking dead is established from the start. Moreover, the idea of trauma in Freud's *Beyond the Pleasure Principle* suits this study in general and this series in particular because the psychological repetition of trauma represents the unconscious death-drive: a desire for non-existence dismantling Cartesian notions of reality. Motivated by instincts associated with a soul-less animal, the zombies embody non-existence and push forward the continuing story of survival horror. With a resolution constantly deferred and survival needs blurring lines between human and the monstrous, the definition of reality breaks down.

In one of the few moves into the psychological space of characters, Rick dreams of Lori after she is killed. In his dream of the pre-zombie world, Rick saves Carl from a speeding car (a danger made obsolete by the zombie apocalypse) and Lori consoles the overwrought Rick with a kiss. The next panel presents them in a reverse perspective that represents the radical change wherein Lori is quite clearly a zombie giving a tongue kiss to her husband (a remarkably similar variation of the classic cover to *Chamber of Chills* No. 23). She berates Rick for his inability to protect her and he allows her to consume his body. While such category confusion is typical in a dream, this precipitates Rick's return to a means of coping with the trauma of his wife's death, a strategy that requires a willful ignorance of "reality." Earlier, but still after the failure of the phone system, Rick picked up a ringing phone and was astonished to find a woman speaking.

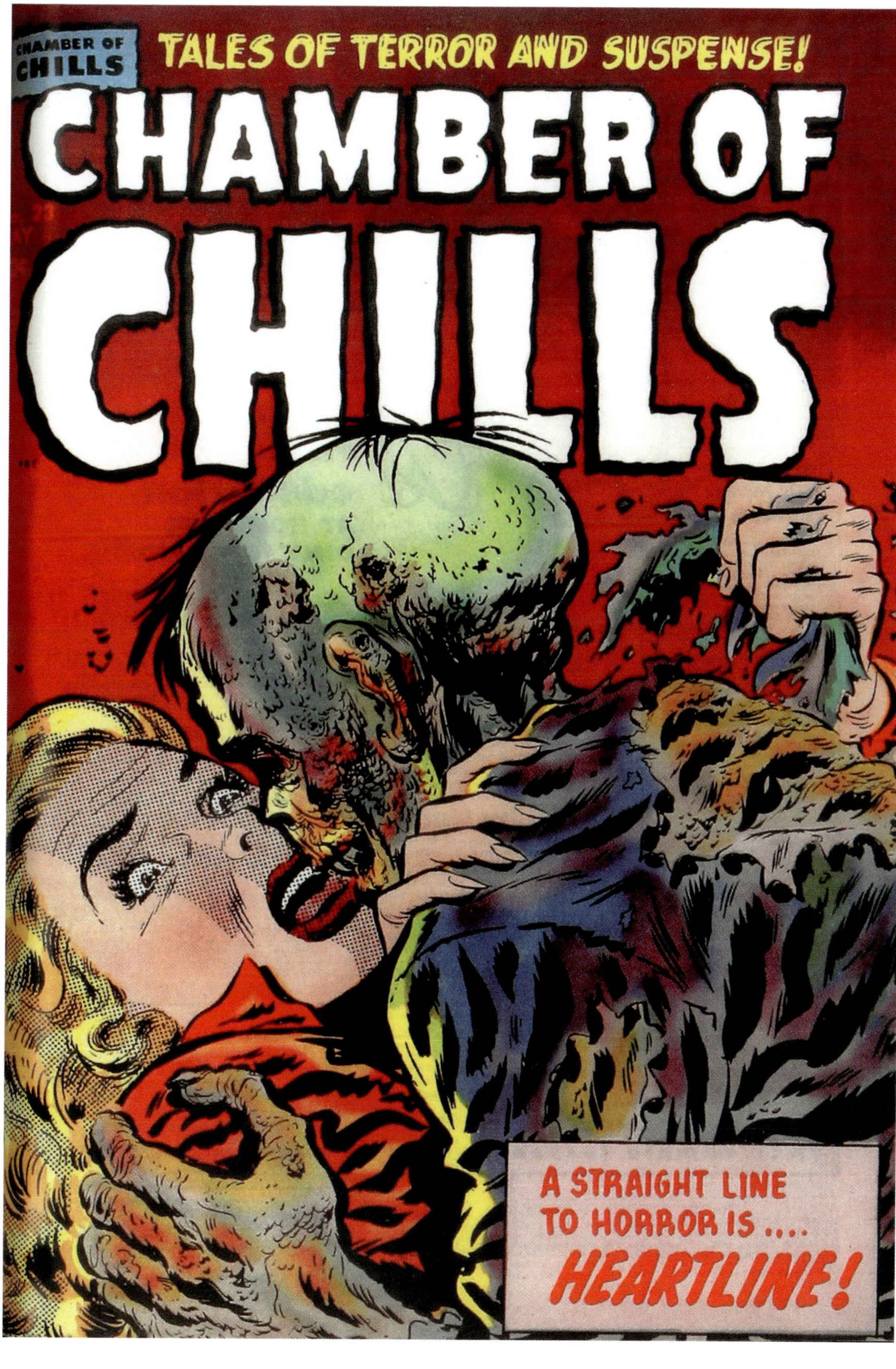
CHAMBER OF CHILLS
TALES OF TERROR AND SUSPENSE!
CHAMBER OF CHILLS
A STRAIGHT LINE TO HORROR IS.... HEARTLINE!

Eventually it became apparent that Rick invented the conversation with the woman (his wife Lori), but two aspects of this departure from the real are important to note. The reader "hears" the other end of the conversation through text on the page, something consequently believable until the speaker is revealed to be Lori. And after his dream, Rick takes the phone on the road to continue his conversations with Lori, something he does in front of Carl and even after he tells "Lori," "I think I need to stop doing this."[53]

While this category confusion can be interpreted as a dark night before the dawn, this confusion is a central theme of the series, seen more clearly as Rick and his group establish a settlement, suppress the zombie hordes, and create a feudal economy in relationship with other settlements. The disintegration of individual identity works prominently on a social level with Kirkman's obvious interest in the fictions that extend the American monomyth for heroes. In "Going to Ground: The Undead in Contemporary Southern Popular Culture Media and Writing," Taylor Hagood suggests that the series uses zombies as a means to critique the myth of the American South: "[I]t seems reasonable to discern a latent pro-Agrarian or at least pro-small town ethic in *The Walking Dead* that sees not the so-called Old South as the undead... but rather the real South, post-South, Atlanta South as the undead that has lost the value of 'helping folks out.'"[54]

However, few models of society, ranging from the small town to the suburb, actually work in *The Walking Dead*, and again, zombies must be seen as a catalyst that allows Kirkman to portray human beings as social monsters. A general interpretation from the introduction to *Undead Souths* encompasses the series more effectively with zombieism as a "highly communicable dis-ease with the instabilities of contemporary US and southern political economies."[55] As Bishop claims, "The Walking Dead isn't about zombies at all,"[56] and "For Kirkman, the zombies aren't metaphors for human failings; they are the catalyst that reveals the monstrous potential that has been exposed within us all."[57] Within the series, people do not need to be bitten to rise from the dead, because everyone literally carries the contagion that causes people to do so.[58] Early on, the survivors stay in a subdivision with the written warning, "All dead; do not enter," and in the prison, Rick makes a speech about who they are: "We already are savages... The second we put a bullet into the head of one of these undead monsters... We became what they are!... We are the walking dead!"[59] And subsequently, whenever someone states their community is not monstrous, that statement is undermined in very short order.

As Rick's group confronts other groups that want their resources (most notably those led by the Governor and then Neegan), their feudal mentality allows them to readily shift their hatred of the zombies as Other to the competing groups as Other. And sometimes, their hatred of competing groups seems appropriate as the leaders behave in heinous ways that outpace the moral violations of Rick's group. Neegan claims to Holly, one of Rick's group, "I really want you to understand… we're not monsters,"[60] but the panel depicts him kneeling over the gruesome corpse of a man he just killed by sticking a knife in his throat. Based on Neegan's sincere and not ironic expression, he believes he committed this act for the greater good (of saving Holly)–a consistent refrain of people who do terrible things in *The Walking Dead.* And yet the choices he makes for the "greater good" allow this leader to physically and emotionally abuse his people and enjoy the greatest part of their resources with impunity. Mindful that his rhetoric lines up with that of most nations in times of violent conflict, Kirkman never depicts the opposition groups simply as an Other that allows Rick's group to define itself as good.

Even after the zombie-head collector known as the Governor brutalizes Rick and rapes Michonne, the reader spends time with the Governor and his community in a way that humanizes the group before their attack on Rick's group. Although vulgar, violent, and manipulative, the Governor is also inspirational (with clever rhetorical strategies that believably persuade "normal" people) and affectionate (toward his people and his zombie child–something seen later with the more likable Morgan). The problem then becomes how Rick's group justifies its violent actions against competing groups like them but seen only as Other–clearly not internalizing the idea that they are the walking dead. And this problem is emphasized by Rick's one-on-one confrontation with Neegan on the field of their final battle.

Zombies and the Zombie Terror(ists): Postmodern, Post-Zombie Culture

According to Bishop, *The Walking Dead* works in historically specific terms in a post-9/11 era and "demonstrate[s] a new symbolic manifestation, one that reflects not cultural fears about what terrorists might do, but rather what the 'good guys' can do against potential or suspected terrorists."[61] Before the 9/11 attacks, most Americans perceived terrorism as something that took place somewhere else, and if an attack did take place in the homeland, the terrorists didn't inflict enough damage to threaten the body and soul of the United States.

Afterwards, that was no longer the case, but George W. Bush's "axis of evil" speech gave Americans a focus for their newly developed free-floating anxiety and led to a Cold War strategy for the "war on terror" (a strategy loosely connecting this time to the era that inspired Romero's zombie stories). However, as occupations of Iraq and Afghanistan lengthened and news of abuses at Abu Ghraib prison broke, it seemed conventional methods of warfare couldn't eliminate America's terrorist enemies and the idea of blame was complicated. The question of "why they hate us" didn't have a simple answer that restored values of American exceptionalism, and the potential for the abuse of power in a security-minded administration was more apparent.

In reference to the first year of the series, English scholar Michael Blouin argues that "during the year that saw the launch of the Iraq war–specifically 2003–Kirkman and Moore appear to cast zombies as a *threat against* which society can restore its 'lost traditions.'"[62] This idea is worth mentioning, because the first year works like the ruse that sets up the series' genuine claim about society–something later embodied by the rhetoric used by Rick to deceive Neegan. In a long conversation held during a suspension of hostilities, Rick pleads for the peaceful relations and a more open cultural exchange: "[We] can do amazing things… if we work together. We can establish a system of trade. Then we can build safer places to live. We can fix roads.… We could rebuild civilization… maybe even do a better job this time." At this point, an entire splash page is devoted to Neegan in wide-eyed surprise and after uttering a characteristic "Fuck," Neegan says among other things, "I've had it all wrong.… I think you're right."[63] At this point, Rick cuts Neegan's throat and he announces to Neegan's people that they need to surrender and that he will have a doctor save Neegan's life. With Rick employing the dream of civilization to make Neegan drop his guard, that dream becomes not only a fiction but also an untruth.

Rick is a huckster salesman at this point, and the dream is a figment to sell; while Neegan's default had regularly been sarcasm, his depiction implies genuine engagement that is betrayed by Rick as the warlord looking for an advantage. Since the reader is not privy to Rick's plan, the reader may also be convinced by the description of a society like the reader's own (but better) and therefore not just surprised but also confused by Rick's violence. More than a regression from intercultural cooperation to tribal hostilities, this moment suggests that the idea that society can improve is an illusion.

Rick's cynicism becomes more significant after Neegan's defeat because the narrative jumps forward in time to reveal that Rick has built the kind of civilization he described: a civilization in which it seemed he had little or no faith. Although the likely end of a heroic epic (such as Aeneas founding Rome after the fall of Troy), this relatively zombie-free society threatens to be the greatest horror.[64]

Previous attempts at civilization had failed, and all notable markers of civilization fell away during the zombie apocalypse, like religion, art, and the stockpiling of foodstuff. However, Father Gabriel establishes a church in the settlement of Alexandria, Carl begins his apprenticeship as a metalworker in a neighboring settlement, and Michonne sails a fishing barge in deep waters. Media scholar Sherryl Vint argues that, against all reason, "Rick [has] a desire for a sense of humanity that can persist beyond the zombie apocalypse—an investment in ideals of community, a condemnation of the autoimmune disorder that will sacrifice all for the sake of the self."[65] That desire seemed to be realized until long-term readers encountered Rick's final public interaction with Neegan. And subsequently, his ideals as leader contain a large performative element with Neegan's imprisonment (and not execution) described as what this civilization would expect.

The performative nature of leadership is outlined by King Ezekiel, the leader of a neighboring settlement who keeps a tiger for show: "I'm playing king. People want someone to follow. Makes them feel safe. People who feel safe are more useful, less dangerous… more productive. They see a guy with a tiger, start spreading larger than life stories about him… She protected me, helped me get here… Brought me the respect… and fear needed to set up shop here. I used to act in community theatre. The King Ezekiel bit comes as second nature to me."[66] While his community is real (relatively speaking), the basis for his community is not, and therein lies the same problems revealed with individual characters, except that in a group these problems will be amplified.

Beginning at home, Carl secretly visits Neegan, who seeks to undermine Rick's authority with his son; continuing on a grander scale, zombies at the edges of the settled territories are heard whispering and seen carrying weapons. Actually a nomadic tribe, they wear the skins of corpses, relinquish human names, and organize themselves like an animal pack, with ideas regularly suggested but not fully developed by Rick's group of survivors throughout the series. Their leader, Alpha, describes this to Rick, "You don't have a single thing to offer us…. You think you have accomplished much, but I look around at what you've done… and I see children playing a game of make believe. You've built a shrine to a long dead world. We are animals who always pretended we are not….

We don't allow the intelligence evolution has given us to make us weak. . . . This is a world for. . . the strong."[67] Encouraged by the unrelenting exposure to the abject, Enlightenment notions of both individuality and civilization disintegrate and "the whisperers" embrace the walking dead literally with their skin-wearing and conceptually with community organization beyond conventional morality.

This move toward the obvious presence and power of the abject was suggested by the changing depiction of an eye wound that Carl received from a gunshot. Initially depicted in a dramatic two-page spread with Carl's eye and part of his head missing from a life-threatening wound, Carl not only survived but also came to understand the wound as something that defined him. When Neegan takes Carl, he is thrilled by Carl's wound as well as his strength and links the two; in that sequence, the look of horror associated with the initial shooting is replaced by the look of determination from a young man with an empty eye socket like that of a zombie. And when a settlement first captures some of the whisperers, Carl meets Lydia, Alpha's daughter, who finds the uncovered wound not only interesting but also sexually exciting. Their first sexual encounter begins with her licking his open wound in real world foreplay reminiscent of his father's dream-kiss with his zombie wife (something in stark contrast to a horrified Rick waking from a nightmare).

While Carl initially claims Lydia for traditional civilization by putting his father's sheriff's hat on her head, he finds himself occupying a much more ambiguous liminal position in his later statement to Rick: "This world is my father and I've got it's [sic] looks."[68] After Carl crosses into the whisperers' territory to reclaim Lydia (given in exchange for captured settlers), Alpha marks their borderline with the impaled heads and disrupts the supposed triumph of Alexandria's civilized ways. Although the whisperers' strangeness and horrific violence make them a convenient Other, Lydia later reveals that her mother (and the whisperers) had never done anything like this and likely did so out of fear. Initially accepting this at face value, Rick encourages all the people of Alexandria and the related communities to not abandon their civilized ways in the wake of their anger and fear. But unable to control the fracturing groups and the subsequent mob violence, Rick visits Neegan, who finds a system like democracy unacceptable because it guarantees a leader's loss of control.

> Neegan lectures Rick,
> You're worried these people are turning against you…
> and you're worried about this while you have the best fucking boogie man ever falling into your lap? Leaders make up shit like this to stay in power. You couldn't imagine a better us versus them situation. People rallied behind you because dead people were fucking eating people… and you kept them safe from them…. They're calling for security. Make them feel secure. Make them feel safe… Watch them shut the fuck up….
> You're a good guy… You don't want to lie to these people….
> What I was pointing out to you is the truth of the situation. At worst, I'm suggesting you use that truth to manipulate people. And at the end of the day… if that keeps people alive… what's the harm?[69]

Rick quickly and readily creates the Other through a rudimentary propaganda campaign using the slogan "Silence the whisperers." When he is asked what happened to him to allow such tactics, raise a militia, and thereby undermine the principles central to Alexandria, he replies "I became a better leader."[70] Rick's earlier revelation about humans as the walking dead has been lost, and horror is now widespread, existing at an even larger social level. As this new ruse works with his own people, they chant his name, Neegan says "attaboy," and Rick truly believes the whisperers are the Other. And the fact that this is not the end of the series is irrelevant as the series clearly shows any "good" end is merely a prelude to human failure and the experience of abjection.

"The Story of Survival Horror Continues Here": The Zombie Apocalypse Will (Continue to) Be Televised

It is important to briefly consider the television adaptation of *The Walking Dead*, more so than any other film or television adaptation of the contemporary horror comics mentioned in this book. After Wes Craven's 1982 decent approximation of Len Wein and Bernie Wrightson's *Swamp Thing*, the film that followed Alan Moore's run on the series, *Return of the Swamp Thing* (1989), was campier than its predecessor; but even as camp, it was relatively weak and received poorly by critics as was the USA network television series (1990–1993). With the Hughes brothers as directors and Johnny Depp as an actor, *From Hell* (2001) looked promising, but the loosely adapted film became a conventional mystery/thriller and was coolly received by critics. Though Mike Mignola was involved in story creation and *Hellboy* (2004) was lavishly produced, the very strong film represented director Guillermo del Toro's vision more than that of Mignola (especially its equally strong sequel).[71]

Adapted as a television series in 2010, several things paved the way for the wide appeal of *The Walking Dead*, and the first would be growth of interest in and critical acceptance of zombie horror. In addition to zombie films, zombie horror found its central text with Max Brooks's *World War Z* (2006), a follow-up to his modestly successful but tongue-in-cheek *The Zombie Survival Guide*. Identified as "an oral history of the zombie war," the novel sets up an anthropologist's collection of first-person accounts that chronicle the devastation resulting from zombie attacks and the subsequent reclamation of civilization. Although civilization itself is of value, the idea of a collection with no central character moves the reader beyond the typical heroic narrative in which the center must hold. In addition, found-footage films like *The Blair Witch Project* (1999) and *Paranormal Activity* (2007) brought to the mainstream low-budget techniques associated with horror films like *Night of the Living Dead*.[72]

Exploitation horror and splatter films reached a wider audience thanks to *Saw* (2004) and *Hostel* (2005), often described as torture porn, with significantly more depictions of the explicit and the gross. But most important would be what Dean DeFino calls the "HBO effect," a trend resulting from the success of the subscription network's well-funded series that appealed to niche audiences, challenged viewers, and required long-term commitment. Along these lines, *The Sopranos* (1999) and *The Wire* (2002) are most often mentioned, but HBO's successful start with original programming was *Tales from the Crypt* (1989), and an adaptation of The Southern Vampire Mysteries' *True Blood* (2008) anchored the HBO lineup shortly before the development of *The Walking Dead*. Through the promise of an audience for this horror subgenre, its development could be sold, but many other factors ensured the quality of *The Walking Dead* in a format well-suited to the never-ending feel of Kirkman's vision.

Frank Darabont, whose horror resume includes writing *Tales from the Crypt*, *Nightmare on Elm Street 3*, and *Mary Shelley's Frankenstein*, worked closely with Robert Kirkman to develop the television series. More importantly, Darabont would adapt and direct several Stephen King works, including *The Shawshank Redemption* and *The Green Mile*, whose popularity and acclaim gave him the means to attract serious attention from AMC. With tight scripts, excellent performances, and superlative horror effects, the series debuted to impressive audience numbers that grew steadily throughout the six-episode season. The television series followed the general story arc of the comic book and was uncompromising in its depiction of zombie gore and human depravity driven by desperate circumstances (both increasing in intensity throughout the run of the series).

While the road had been paved for television anti-heroes by *The Sopranos* and *The Wire*, the combination of visual and conceptual horror pushed television boundaries. The gruesome content of *The Walking Dead* is unrelenting and therefore less acceptable in comic books and television shows with no clear end than in novels and films with a clear end. The graphic nature of *The Walking Dead* is comparable to that of Eric Powell's *The Goon*, but *The Goon* was always intended for a more specific and limited audience. This content (alongside its bleak themes) makes the extreme popular success of the series on a broad-based cable network surprising at the very least to the network executives who needed time to adjust to the idea. Although AMC doubled the number of episodes in the second season, the budget remained about the same, and the network focused promotion on its prestige period-piece series *Mad Men*. Clearly underestimating interest in *The Walking Dead*, the audience for the meagerly budgeted season nearly doubled, making it roughly three times that for *Mad Men*.

The passion for Kirkman's zombie world didn't belong exclusively to horror comic book readers (and the audience, which grew with the television series, often became readers of the comic series). With Kirkman's name now well known, he was interviewed by major new outlets like CNBC where he joked about the show's popularity: "People now are, you know, worrying about how to pay their mortgage and worrying about how they're going to afford groceries, and it's nice to sit on the couch and watch a simpler time, when people are just worried about being chased by zombies. It's really funny."[73] Although partly a quip, his statement identifies a desire for stories depicting something beyond overgrown civilization–something monstrous. Obscured by contemporary social dynamics, the fear of the zombie apocalypse reveals terrible truths, and the popularity of *The Walking Dead* is a consequence of its ability to go beyond superficial concerns to address and exercise fundamental anxieties.[74]

Although the television series has generally followed the comic book plot, there have been deviations: some minor, some major, and some becoming major over the course of time (as characters who die in the second year of the comic book series live into the seventh year of the television series).

For instance, the series introduced some new stories such as the first season's "Vatos" in which Rick comes into conflict with Latino survivors in Atlanta; such additions are not unexpected in adaptations and could be argued as necessitated by the constraints of episodic television. However, other new stories take more time and have a more profound effect on the direction of the series; these include the two-episode trip to CDC (where Rick learns everyone has the zombie contagion) and the half-season long trip to Terminus (where the survivors are not saved as promised but victimized). Character arcs were changed and include killing Andrea in the third year (who in the comic book series lives much longer and becomes Rick's lover, Carl's new mother, and Alexandria's community leader). And new characters were created for the television series, such as Darl, the popular backwoods biker, whose presence significantly affects the group dynamic (necessarily different from the group dynamic in the comic book series).

Reacting to comic fans' opposition to such changes, artist Charles Allard points out that the audience for the comic is 40,000 and the audience for the show is 5,000,000[75]; the implication is that the show runner is concerned with the largest number of viewers, and the number of upset comic book fans is inconsequential. However, this doesn't really address why changes are made, why fans are upset with the changes, and why Kirkman (deeply involved with the show) approves changes to his plot and characters. While comics fans may view the comic book version of *The Walking Dead* as a sacred text not to be altered, Kirkman does not, but he also does not view the television version as the improved and final draft. When asked whether he sees the television show as a "director's cut" of the comic book, Kirkman responds, "There are certainly some cool scenes where I think, 'Yeah, that's way better.' But it's not like I view the show as the final version, the version I got right. I like them both equally.... It's being able to sometimes do this and sometimes do that that's fun."[76] Like other creators of horror comics, Kirkman sees a folktale-like dynamism with his stories, and he welcomes the opportunity provided by the television series to explore the possibilities.[77]

Marvel Zombies Here, Archie Zombies There: Wertham's Shambling Corpse and Lots of Zombies Everywhere

In regard to alternate worlds, Kirkman explored this idea earlier with another comic book that uses zombies to overwhelm comics at the narrative and commercial levels as well. Spinning off a story in *Ultimate Fantastic Four*, Kirkman wrote *Marvel Zombies* (2005), a story about the Marvel superheroes in a universe overrun by a zombie virus.

Marvel's Ultimate titles (*Ultimate Spiderman, Ultimate X-Men*, etc.) started as a reboot of the Marvel universe where new readers can read Marvel superhero stories without the baggage of fifty years of continuity. However, Ultimate creators presented roughly the same Marvel superhero stories from the past with small variations (something that *Ultimate Fantastic Four* writers do regularly for about twenty issues).

However, in the twenty-first issue, Mark Millar develops a story in which Mr. Fantastic communicates with another Mr. Fantastic from a parallel universe that looks exactly like the original Marvel universe.[78] When the team crosses over, they discover the other Mr. Fantastic brought them to an Earth overrun by a zombie virus. Almost everyone has been infected including Mr. Fantastic, and the infected superheroes retain their personalities but are fatally compromised by their ravenous hunger. And since they have run out of food on this Earth, Mr. Fantastic plans to open a portal to the Ultimate universe. While this framework provides a threat for the Ultimate Fantastic Four to defeat (like most superhero stories), it also portrays the original Marvel superhero universe as an abject corpse and therefore has the potential to undermine the Ultimate line's project.

Kirkman picks up the narrative and thematic threads in a limited series whose title is a colloquial term used to describe fans who automatically buy Marvel titles and no others. At the beginning, Kirkman kills Magneto, one of the only superpowered characters in Millar's story not compromised by the zombie virus, and crafts a story that revolves around the zombie superheroes. Defying expectations for superhero and zombie stories, the series is filled with gross depictions such the zombie version of Captain America losing half is head and saying, "I'd rethink that theory on the brain–I've got evidence to the contrary."[79] Since the humor is often broad (such as zombie versions of Spiderman and Power Man playing "Go Fish"), it's hard to believe Kirkman's claim about the series, "I don't consider it to be a humor book. The people who are sadistic and messed-up think it's a humor book but the people who are level-headed and straight-laced think it's serious."[80] If his claims are not made sarcastically, Kirkman must be taking the series' implicit critique of the superhero industry quite seriously.

In comics critic Michael Dean's review, this story is lined up with Marvel's problematic corporate strategy: "Not a creature walks upon the Earth that is not a corporate-owned Marvel superhero. And just as the comics-shop Direct Market has derived diminishing returns from the aging, condensing superhero-fan demographic on which it feeds, the Marvel zombies find they have eaten their way to a dead end."[81]

While Marvel seems to encourage a folktale-like proliferation of superhero stories with the Ultimate line, the company does not relinquish their control of their properties, trying to expand their audience through the limitations of the same formulas. In *Marvel Zombies*, the story of Galactus is retold, but in this version, the planet devourer is devoured by the zombie superheroes, and they use his godlike power to leave the Earth and devour the universe. It is interesting to note that *Marvel Zombies* was released just a few years before the establishment of Marvel Studios—just another way to use Marvel properties to reach a broader universe on which to feed.

Although the author of the long-running superhero series *Invincible*, Kirkman has long been critical of the genre that saved many companies in the wake of the Comics Code: "Superhero comics dominate the market. It's all male-power fantasy stuff."[82] In addition to finding fault with the power obsession of superhero stories, Kirkman sees a problem in stories like cross-over events told not for their own sake but for the promotion and management of properties: "'Oh my God! Sweeping change and nothing will ever be the same!' I know now that's not how things work. I know that Civil War being what it is, Captain America will be alive again soon and Iron Man and he will be best friends… and all the consequences of Civil War will be undone… That's how it works."[83]

In addition, he has complained about superhero publishers undermining the integrity of the medium by treating comic books as research and development for more profitable film, television, and video game projects. In Brian Crecente's overview of Kirkman's company Skybound, he explains that Kirkman believes "a new creation [doesn't have] to start out as a comic book. That's in part because Kirkman, who still values comics most, doesn't want to use the medium as a means to an end."[84] Above all, Kirkman wants stories to have meaning beyond corporate considerations,[85] an opinion that may be the luxury of an influential creator like himself. Nevertheless, the powerful appeal of zombies and his star status enabled him to write a story in the Marvel universe critical of Marvel's overgrown superstructure. With *Marvel Zombies*, Kirkman writes zombie fiction in an effort to block infectious and self-destructive business practices.

Of course, that would make no sense to Fredric Wertham, who put crime, horror, and superhero comics in the same category and understood them all (and their industry) as a problem. Based on his unilateral interpretation of their content, he judged comics to be unsuitable for general consumption and a cause of juvenile delinquency. While he criticized these types of comics in particular, he never recommended other types to encourage healthy psychological development and good citizenship.

However, if Wertham had, his most likely choice would have been teen comedy comics like those of Archie Comics, titles shaped by the vision of John Goldwater. Of course, the Comics Code was shaped by the vision of John Goldwater in an effort to appease the critics of comic books and save his corner of the comics industry.

The stories in Archie Comics were unblemished by things prohibited by the Code, taking place in a prelapsarian world where teenagers were morally upright and never had to deal with the real challenges of adulthood. Titles like *Life with Archie* featured Archie and his pal Jughead (among other high schoolers) and often revolved around Archie's frustrations over having two girls who loved him: Betty and Veronica. Archie's escapades continued longer than many predicted as their audience shrunk in a post-direct market era that dismantled the Comics Code, eventually read not only as straightforward teen humor but also (and moreover) as tongue-in-cheek kitsch. However, its relaunch in the 2010s moved Archie into more realistic territory with its narrative and art, even featuring storylines with a homosexual character whom Archie eventually sacrifices his life to save.[86] However, the aesthetics of the fallen world and the undeniable infection of popular culture are seen even more clearly in the Archie series beginning in 2013: *Afterlife with Archie*.

Drawn in a hyper-realistic style with a monochromatic and moody color palate by Francesco Francavilla, *Afterlife with Archie* has the appearance of a horror comic likely to feature zombies. And written with a subtlety and eloquence that builds drama by Roberto Aguirre-Sacasa, the series has the dark tone of a horror comic inclined to seriously present supernatural content. Deeply indebted to the genre, the series fully embraces horror conventions that allow the story to work for readers unfamiliar with the Archie world. And all of these things are woven together with an affection for Archie characters that makes this zombie story compelling for readers familiar with the Archie world. In Riverdale, the zombie pandemic starts when Sabrina, the teenage witch, brings Jughead's beloved Hot Dog back to life; this misguided act of compassion leads Jughead to discover something just isn't right with his resurrected dog. While the summary may seem to veer toward camp, the story is in fact terrifying, tragic, and especially moving for readers with an in-depth knowledge and love of Riverdale.

When Jughead is revealed as a zombie or when Archie is forced to kill his zombie father, the story is poignant not only due to Roberto Aguirre-Sacasa's storytelling but also due to the destruction of the perfect world that only ever existed in the fantasy that was Archie Comics.

Moreover, since horror is not parodied, the story represents the loss of *Life with Archie*'s good, clean fun—the last bulwark against the horror Wertham saw in comics. The horror was real in the horror comics of the 1950s comics scare but no more horrible than forces that failed to understand it and sought to censor comics. With Archie comics formerly part of the overgrown civilization that horror comics targeted, *Afterlife with Archie* demonstrates the enduring powers of horror and how much the public at large wants a close encounter with horror.

Horror has a long history, and Kirkman recognizes contemporary horror creators have long shadows cast over them (even within the incredibly new subgenre of the zombie story): "I'm a firm believer that, you know, Stephanie Meyer is to Bram Stoker as Robert Kirkman is to George Romero."[87] While the genre-specific connections between the practitioners of horror are understandable, the comparison between Meyer's embarrassingly bad *Twilight* and Kirkman's vitally important *The Walking Dead* is not. *Afterlife with Archie* demonstrates that we now live in Kirkman's world in comic books and beyond. According to *Afterlife with Archie*, we are not the good, clean Americans imagined by Fredric Wertham and John Goldwater; we are the walking dead. Such an awareness encourages us to confront the well-guarded self (rather than oppress the defenseless other), but people often lack awareness and infrequently examine the self. Through his work, Kirkman argues there is horror in not knowing but even greater horror in knowing and building a government, an industry, and a culture that hides that knowledge.

Chapter 6 Notes

1 Daniel Robert Epstein, "Robert Kirkman," Anderswolleck blog@SuicideGirls, last modified June 12, 2005, https://www.suicidegirls.com/girls/anderswolleck/blog/2679246/robert-kirkman/.

2 "Testimony of William M. Gaines, Publisher, Entertaining Comics Group, New York, NY," *TheComicbooks.Com*, last modified 2016, http://www.thecomicbooks.com/gaines.html.

3 Robert Kirkman and Tony Moore, *Walking Dead, Vol. 1: Days Gone Bye* (Berkeley: Image, 2103), 2.

4 Kyle William Bishop, *American Zombie Gothic: The Rise and Fall (and Rise) of the Walking Dead in Popular Culture* (Jefferson, NC: McFarland, 2010), 12.

5 Jeffrey Jerome Cohen, *Monster Theory: Reading Culture* (Minneapolis: U of Minnesota P, 1996), 4.

6 Ibid., 6.

7 W. Scott Poole, *Monsters in America: Our Historical Obsession with the Hideous and the Haunting* (Waco: Baylor UP, 2011), 197.

8 Eric Gary Anderson identifies "The Fall of the House of Usher" as this sort of historical starting point (Eric Gary Anderson, "The Fall of the House of Po' Sandy: Poe, Chesnutt, and Southern Undeadness," *Undead Souths: The Gothic and Beyond in Southern Literature and Culture*, ed., Eric Gary Anderson, Taylor Hagood, and Daniel Cross Turner [Baton Rouge: Louisiana State UP, 2015], 23).

9 Teresa A. Goddu, "Introduction to American Gothic," *The Horror Reader*, ed., Ken Gelder (London: Routledge, 2000), 270.

10 Flannery O'Connor, *Mystery and Manners: Occasional Prose* (New York: Farrar, Straus, and Giroux, 1970), 44.

11 Lorna Jowett and Stacey Abbott, *TV Horror: Investigating the Dark Side of the Small Screen* (London: I.B. Tauris, 2013), 113.

12 Ibid., 117, 119.

13 Ibid., 109.

14 Cynthia J. Miller and A. Bowdoin Van Riper, "Introduction," *Undead in the Old West II: They Just Keeping Coming*, ed., Cynthia J. Miller and A. Bowdoin Van Riper (Lanham, MD: Scarecrow, 2013), xx.

15 Kyle William Bishop, *American Zombie Gothic: The Rise and Fall (and Rise) of the Walking Dead in Popular Culture*, 32.

16 Ibid., 13.

17 Ibid., 76.

18 W. Scott Poole, *Monsters in America: Our Historical Obsession with the Hideous and the Haunting*, 202. Some connect the zombie narrative to the historical precedent of *Invasion of the Body Snatchers* (1956), a science fiction vision of the contemporary times overrun with pod people.

19 Kyle William Bishop, *American Zombie Gothic: The Rise and Fall (and Rise) of the Walking Dead in Popular Culture*, 124.

20 *Day of the Dead* was not a financial success, and this led to Romero's long break from zombie films. However, his pattern of critique continues with later sequels including *Land of the Dead* in 2005 (high-rise apartments, government, and civilization) and *Diary of the Dead* in 2008 (video recording and reality-shaping technology).

21 Wheeler Winston Dixon, *A History of Horror* (New Brunswick: Rutgers UP, 2010), 117.

22 Kyle William Bishop, "Battling Monsters and Becoming Monstrous: Human Devolution in *The Walking Dead*," ed., Marina Levina and Diem-My T. Bui, *Monster Culture in the 21st Century: A Reader* (London: Bloomsbury, 2013), 75.

23 David J. Skal, *The Monster Show: A Cultural History* (New York: Farrar, Straus, and Giroux, 1993), 311. "The legacy of the Vietnam War in particular became a silent partner in the birth of modern horror... the war itself became a kind of undead monster, one that overcame every attempt to keep it in the ground" (W. Scott Poole, *Monsters in America: Our Historical Obsession with the Hideous and the Haunting*, 197).

24 This change in the public's attitude may account for the failure of Romero's *Day of the Dead*, also released in 1985.

25 Kyle William Bishop, *American Zombie Gothic: The Rise and Fall (and Rise) of the Walking Dead in Popular Culture*, 29.

26 Julia Round, "The Horror of Humanity," *The Walking Dead and Philosophy: Zombie Apocalypse Now*, ed., Wayne Yuen (Chicago: Open Court, 2012), 166.

27 W. Scott Poole, *Monsters in America: Our Historical Obsession with the Hideous and the Haunting*, 201. Slavoj Žižek argues for the actual presence of the apocalypse with the four horsemen being ecological crisis, consequences of biogenetic revolution, imbalances in the system, and social divisions; Žižek believes the concept of the apocalypse is a default because it is easier to imagine an apocalypse than to realize actual cultural change (Sherryl Vint, "Abject Posthumanism: Neoliberalism, Biopolitics, and Zombies," *Monster Culture in the 21st Century: A Reader*, ed., Marine Levine and Diem-My T. Bui [London: Bloomsbury, 2013], 134).

28 Simon Abrams, "The Robert Kirkman Interview," *The Comics Journal* 289 (April, 2008): 48. Kirkman has the sense that Image improved in this regard: "As a company, I think it's stronger than it has been in a long time" (Simon Abrams, "The Robert Kirkman Interview," 69). However, Image's strategies haven't entirely changed as the toy line is still very profitable–especially with toys based on *The Walking Dead*. (Kirkman was made a partner at Image in 2008.)

29 Simon Abrams, "The Robert Kirkman Interview," 82.

30 Robert Kirkman and Tony Moore, *Walking Dead, Vol. 1: Days Gone Bye*, 2.

31 In my possibly faulty counting, the series has had only three flashbacks: two tied to memory and one to dream.

32 Simon Abrams, "The Robert Kirkman Interview," 68.
33 Simon Abrams, "Re-Animator: Focus on Robert Kirkman's *The Walking Dead*," *The Comics Journal* 289 (April, 2008): 101.
34 John Shelton Lawrence and Robert Jewett, *The Myth of the American Superhero* (Grand Rapids, MI: Eerdmans, 2002).
35 Rick's transformation into a cowboy by donning the iconic oversized hat is described by Michael J. Blouin in "Robert Kirkman and Tony Moore's *The Walking Dead*," *Critical Insights: The Graphic Novel*, ed., Gary Hoppenstand (Armenia, NY: Salem Press, 2014), 187.
36 Robert Kirkman, Tony Moore, Charlie Adlard, and Cliff Rathburn, *The Walking Dead, Book 1* (Berkeley: Image, 2008), 14.
37 Ibid., 20.
38 Ibid., 131–32.
39 Ibid., 264.
40 Robert Kirkman, Charlie Adlard, Cliff Rathburn, and Rus Wooton, *The Walking Dead, Book 2* (Berkeley: Image, 2008), 108–110.
41 Ibid., 108.
42 Robert Kirkman, Charlie Adlard, Cliff Rathburn, and Rus Wooton, *The Walking Dead, Book 6* (Berkeley: Image, 2010), 268.
43 Simon Abrams, "Re-Animator: Focus on Robert Kirkman's *The Walking Dead*," 103.
44 "He is anything but the clear-cut hero, and his actions do not always represent the correct choice–morally, ethically, or personally" (Jeffrey Sartain, "Days Gone Bye: Robert Kirkman's Reenvisioned Western *The Walking Dead*," Undead in the Old West II: They Just Keeping Coming, ed., Cynthia J. Miller and Bowdoin Van Riper (Lanham, MD: Scarecrow, 2013), 255).
45 Robert Kirkman, Charlie Adlard, Cliff Rathburn, and Rus Wooton, *The Walking Dead, Book 2*, 82.
46 Ibid., 47.
47 Jeffrey Sartain, "*Days Gone Bye*: Robert Kirkman's Reenvisioned Western *The Walking Dead*," 249–50.
48 David Fear, "Robert Kirkman: Inside 'Walking Dead' Creator's Twisted Mind, New Show," *Rolling Stone*, last modified May 31, 2016, http://www.rollingstone.com/tv/features/robert-kirkman-inside-walking-dead-creators-twisted-mind-new-show-20160531.
49 Jeffrey Sartain, "*Days Gone Bye*: Robert Kirkman's Reenvisioned Western *The Walking Dead*," 252.

50 Robert Kirkman, Charlie Adlard, Cliff Rathburn, and Rus Wooton, *The Walking Dead, Book 5* (Berkeley: Image, 2010), 220–25.

51 Robert Kirkman, Charlie Adlard, Cliff Rathburn, and Rus Wooton, *The Walking Dead, Book 4* (Berkeley: Image, 2009), 109–10.

52 Robert Kirkman, Tony Moore, Charlie Adlard, and Cliff Rathburn, *The Walking Dead, Book 1*, 224.

53 Robert Kirkman, Charlie Adlard, Cliff Rathburn, and Rus Wooton, *The Walking Dead, Book 5*, 147.

54 Taylor Hagood, "Going to Ground: The Undead in Contemporary Southern Popular Culture Media and Writing," *Undead Souths: The Gothic and Beyond in Southern Literature and Culture*, ed., Eric Gary Anderson, Taylor Hagood, and Daniel Cross Turner (Baton Rouge: Louisiana State UP, 2015), 256.

55 Eric Gary Anderson, Taylor Hagood, and Daniel Cross Turner, "Introduction," *Undead Souths: The Gothic and Beyond in Southern Literature and Culture*, ed., Eric Gary Anderson, Taylor Hagood, and Daniel Cross Turner (Baton Rouge: Louisiana State UP, 2015), 7.

56 Kyle William Bishop, *American Zombie Gothic: The Rise and Fall (and Rise) of the Walking Dead in Popular Culture*, 206. Acknowledging that the story is not really about zombies, fans often jokingly refer to the series as a "zoap opera."

57 Kyle William Bishop, "Battling Monsters and Becoming Monstrous: Human Devolution in The Walking Dead," 83.

58 Julia Round, *Gothic in Comics and Graphic Novels* (Jefferson, NC: McFarland, 2014), 214.

59 Robert Kirkman, Charlie Adlard, Cliff Rathburn, and Rus Wooton, *The Walking Dead, Book 2*, 267–68.

60 Robert Kirkman, Charlie Adlard, Stefano Gaudiano, Cliff Rathburn, and Rus Wooton, *The Walking Dead, Book 10* (Berkeley: Image, 2014), 200.

61 Kyle William Bishop, "Battling Monsters and Becoming Monstrous: Human Devolution in The Walking Dead," 77. "I think zombies were popular during the Cold War and zombies are popular again because of the threat of terrorism and how we all live in fear now" (Simon Abrams, "The Robert Kirkman Interview," 87).

62 Michael J. Blouin in "Robert Kirkman and Tony Moore's *The Walking Dead*," *Critical Insights: The Graphic Novel*, 185.

63 Robert Kirkman, Charlie Adlard, Stefano Gaudiano, Cliff Rathburn, and Rus Wooton, *The Walking Dead, Book 11* (Berkeley: Image, 2015), 107–109.

64 In *The Transparency of Evil: Essays in Extreme Phenomena*, Jean Baudrillard redefines evil as everywhere in the things that cause the exponential growth of meaninglessness (London: Verso, 2009).

65 Sherryl Vint, "Abject Posthumanism: Neoliberalism, Biopolitics, and Zombies," 140.

66 Robert Kirkman, Charlie Adlard, Stefano Gaudiano, Cliff Rathburn, and Rus Wooton, *The Walking Dead, Book 10*, 40–42.

67 Robert Kirkman, Charlie Adlard, Stefano Gaudiano, Cliff Rathburn, and Rus Wooton, *The Walking Dead, Book 12* (Berkeley: Image, 2015), 244–45, 250.

68 Ibid., 234.

69 Robert Kirkman, Charlie Adlard, Stefano Gaudiano, Cliff Rathburn, and Rus Wooton, *The Walking Dead, Book 13* (Berkeley: Image, 2016), 99–100.

70 Ibid., 221.

71 Cinematic versions of *The Sandman* and *The Goon* have been in development since the 1990s and the 2000s, respectively; Warner Bros. Studios (the parent company of DC and Vertigo) has worked on a live action version of *The Sandman,* and the director David Fincher and Blur Studio has worked on an animated version of *The Goon* (with the help of a Kickstarter campaign).

72 One of Romero's Living Dead sequels (*Diary of the Dead*) uses this first person film shooter approach.

73 Michelle Chalen, "'Walking Dead': Zombies Thrive on Weak Economy," *CNBC*, Last modified March 22, 2013, http://www.cnbc.com/id/100583639.

74 Critical approval of the television series isn't uniform, and the most frequent criticism concerns implicit sexism and racism, things that are not necessarily drawn from the comic book series: "The print version often features more complex notions of gender that are congruent with feminist deconstructions of binary stereotypes, while the television series tends to fall into affirmations of dualistic gender stereotypes that overvalue traditional masculinity" (Jeffrey A. Sartain, "Days Gone Bye: Robert Kirkman's Reenvisioned Western *The Walking Dead*," *Undead in the Old West II: They Just Keeping Coming*, ed., Cynthia J. Miller and Bowdoin Van Riper [Lanham, MD: Scarecrow, 2013], 250).

75 Julia Round, *Gothic in Comics and Graphic Novels*, 153. This is an early estimate, and the audience tripled in size before plateauing.

76 Brian Crecente, "The Kirkman Effect: How an Undead Army May Recreate Entertainment," *Polygon*, last modified March 30, 2015, https://www.polygon.com/features/2015/3/30/8311735/the-walking-dead-invincible-outcast-fear-the-walking-dead-interview-robert-kirkman.

77 Sometimes this dynamism is expressed intertextually but also within the television series itself. Episode 6.8, "Start to Finish," ends with a boy calling to his mother in a crowd of zombies and hearing a growl in response (implying that she is now a zombie). However, at the start of the episode 6.9, "No Way Out," the sequence is ignored, a bait-and-switch, and the episode follows an alternate route to the same conclusion.

78 In the Marvel universe, the Earth is labeled Earth-616 by Alan Moore.

79 Robert Kirkman, Sean Phillips, June Chung, and Randy Gentile, *Marvel Zombies* (New York: Marvel, 2006), 18.

80 Simon Abrams, "The Robert Kirkman Interview," 84. It is hard to not find dark humor in this, just as it is hard not to laugh at some of Neegan's commentary in *The Walking Dead*. However, the humor that humanizes Neegan is often revealed as another tool for manipulating characters (and possibly the reader).

81 Michael Dean, "Our Zombies, Ourselves," *The Comics Journal* 289 (April, 2008): 40.

82 Simon Abrams, "The Robert Kirkman Interview," 47.

83 Ibid., 76. However, Kirkman did produce a less-compelling sequel to Marvel Zombies that dealt with the resistance of B-list heroes.

84 Brian Crecente, "The Kirkman Effect: How an Undead Army May Recreate Entertainment"

85 "No one reads books or watches movies and only ever aspires to create sequels to those books or movies. People don't get into those creative jobs to make *Pulp Fiction 2* or write *Moby Dick 2*. But that's how the business of comic books works" (Brian Crecente, "The Kirkman Effect: How an Undead Army May Recreate Entertainment").

86 Archie's death is over-the-top and on-the-nose as a social statement but is more realistic than his hijinks in the previously perfect world of *Life with Archie*.

87 David Fear, "Robert Kirkman: Inside 'Walking Dead' Creator's Twisted Mind, New Show."

CONCLUSION

The Monstrous Infection: Horror Comics and the End of the World as We Know It

There was always a minority afraid of something, and a great majority afraid of the dark, afraid of the future, afraid of the past, afraid of the present, afraid of themselves and shadows of themselves.
Ray Bradbury[1]

The Death of All We Know: A Threat Less Femme and More Fatale

The Comics Code that essentially prohibited horror comics is like the Hayes film production code; through the depiction of a perfect world that has never existed, it prescribes a moral vision that reinforces the authority of those in power. This can be seen in America's nostalgia for small town life, the morally upright picket fence representation of everything for which the cowboy fought but in which the cowboy could never reside. One of Ray Bradbury's most famous and arguably most beloved works is *Dandelion Wine*, a short story collection loosely based on the WWI-era small town of Bradbury's youth; hardly a nostalgic indulgence, the work is bittersweet, suggesting things were never as good or morally upright as people remember them being. In fact, the consistent presence in the stories is the serial killer referred to as "the Lonely One" (and the one story wholly devoted to him easily falls into the category of horror).[2] While not claiming the past as an idyllic place to be maintained, Bradbury suggests that all his stories have a basis in the "reality" of his own life: "Was there a Lonely One? There was. And that was his name. And he moved around at night in my home town when I was six years old and he frightened everyone and was never captured.... Why and how? Because I say so."[3] With a wry tone that identifies the affinity of fact and fiction, his "why and how" statement undermines the author(ity) of his past and works interactively, offering the reader the ability to ultimately determine what is real.

Bradbury is also well-known as the author of the classic horror novel *Something Wicked This Way Comes* and the dystopic science fiction novel *Fahrenheit 451*, which depicts the government burning questionable print materials.

However, a more succinct statement about the actual burning of horror comics can be found in Bradbury's the *Martian Chronicles.* In the futuristic tale "April 2005: Usher II," the government has banned all references to "ghosts, vampires, faeries, and any creature of the imagination"[4] in order to produce a "moral climate." The protagonist, William Stendahl, interacts with an artist who has no awareness of "The Fall of the House of Usher" or even Edgar Allen Poe, and the artist believes "'the burning' [of prohibited materials] was a good thing."[5] But as Stendahl describes it, their unimaginative culture of repression is the result of people looking out for their own interests and ultimately fearing their misapprehensions of themselves: "Oh, it started very small. In 1950 and '60 it was a grain of sand. They began by controlling books of cartoons and then detective books and, of course, films, one way or another, one group or another, political bias, religious prejudice, union pressures; there was always a minority afraid of something, and a great majority afraid of the dark, afraid of the future, afraid of the past, afraid of the present, afraid of themselves and shadows of themselves."[6]

With this in mind, it is important to note that Bradbury is not only a genre writer who started his career in the pulps but also a respected author who won the National Book Award (also controversially given to Stephen King). More important to this volume, he has an important place in comic book history as a writer whose works were regularly adapted in EC horror comics and considered some of the finest work produced within those titles. The relationship between EC and Bradbury began when Bradbury's "The Emissary" was almost directly copied (in comic book form) in *The Vault of Horror* No. 22. While the pulps often inspired EC writers, this went beyond inspiration, and Bradbury wrote Bill Gaines, asking with good humor and his tongue in his cheek, why EC was "overlooking sending me my royalty payments."[7] After Gaines sent a check as well as a letter of apology, this incident led to an incredibly productive relationship (producing the string of aforementioned–and clearly credited–adaptations). Quite important to note, the relationship started because Gaines admitted EC's error, something that would not likely be done by an industrial representative well advised by lawyers concerned with the corporate interests in a highly developed civilized culture.

A code that governs content is a teleological plan for the civilized world that outlines a system producing a happy ending–but only for those who hold a specific ideological position. The Comics Code basically prohibits crime comics that show that the American dream's center does not hold and horror comics that show that the center may have been an illusion from the start.

According to Albert Einstein, possibly the twentieth century's foremost expert on how the center may have been an illusion from the start, "Unthinking respect for authority is the greatest enemy of the truth."[8] Gaines certainly didn't have "unthinking respect" as part of his ideology, and his desire to question authority drives the humor in his congressional testimony: "Our American children are for the most part normal children. They are bright children, but those that want to prohibit comic magazines seem to see dirty, sneaky, perverted monsters who use comics as a blueprint for action. Perverted little monsters are few and far between. They don't read comics."[9]

On one hand, Gaines implied that his accusers undeservedly consider children to be dirty, sneaky, perverted monsters. On the other hand, Gaines counted on the monsters who bought his horror comics and set themselves at odds with culture at large.[10] And in contemporary times, a readership monstrous in size, and presumably outlook, has returned to horror comics. Despite the long-standing compatibility of crime and horror in comic books, crime comics are more concerned with fighting against the aggressively humorless aftermath of Fredric Wertham, and horror comics are more concerned with carrying on the frighteningly witty legacy of Bill Gaines.[11] While the results may be similar, those differences are there in the nuances of the way Alan Moore and Neil Gaiman redefine comics as art and the way Mike Mignola, Eric Powell, and Robert Kirkman critique society as abject.

And yet before presenting acknowledgements specific to this volume's coverage of horror comics, I must mention one last example in regard to the results of the resurgence of crime and horror comics in the contemporary comics industry. Ed Brubaker[12] and Sean Phillips's *Fatale*, a disquieting synthesis of Raymond Chandler and H.P. Lovecraft, demonstrates how much things have changed since the beginning of the Comics Code's big business era. Subsequent to *Fatale*'s success, Image Comics made an unprecedented deal with Brubaker and Phillips[13] in full recognition of how many things have changed in a Code-defunct creator's rights era. In consequence, these comic book artists now work with an open-ended commitment to publish whatever they produce with complete editorial freedom and intellectual property ownership.

The Big Scare: The Monster Is Never Dead

My goal was to identify distinctive stages of the resurgence of horror comics as connected to horror fiction in other mediums as well as to numerous historical factors influencing the medium in particular and thought in general. My secondary goal was to represent these stages through the work of the most important, influential, and self-conscious creators of horror comics.

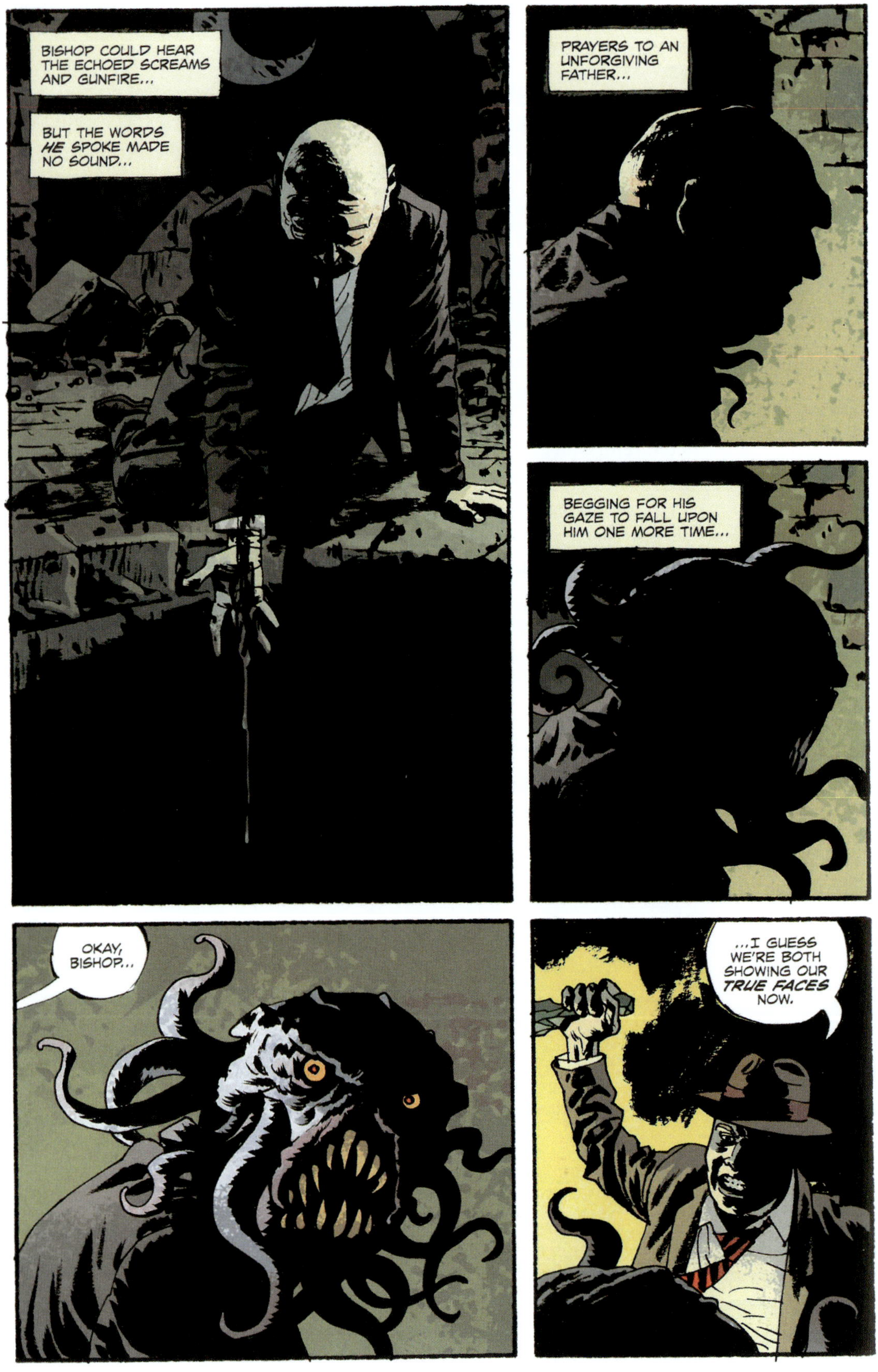
BISHOP COULD HEAR THE ECHOED SCREAMS AND GUNFIRE...
BUT THE WORDS HE SPOKE MADE NO SOUND...
PRAYERS TO AN UNFORGIVING FATHER...
BEGGING FOR HIS GAZE TO FALL UPON HIM ONE MORE TIME...
OKAY, BISHOP...
...I GUESS WE'RE BOTH SHOWING OUR TRUE FACES NOW.

As a consequence, many creators who are part of this new comics scare have not be mentioned (or were mentioned only in passing): Rafael Albuquerque, Charles Burns, Ben Catmull, Jamie Delano, Steve Dillon, Garth Ennis, Attila Futaki, Mike Henderson, Joe Hill, David Lloyd, Steve Niles, Gabriel Rodriguez, Scott Snyder, Ben Templesmith, and Joshua Williamson, among others.

Along those lines, I don't want to ignore that the creators I discussed continue to work beyond the eras profiled and produce other texts very much worth further study: Alan Moore's *Providence* and *Necronomicon*; Neil Gaiman's later *Sandman* texts (especially *Sandman: Overture*) and his fiction such as *Neverwhere* and *The Ocean at the End of the Lane*; Mike Mignola's extended Mignolaverse including *Hellboy in Hell*, *BPRD*, *Abe Sapien*, *Lobster Johnson*, and others; Eric Powell's *Hillbilly* and *Billy the Kid's Old Timey Oddities*; and Robert Kirkman's *Outcast*.

Fig. 7.1
Fatale No. 5, Image, 2012, © Basement Gang, Inc. Through the intersection of crime and horror in *Fatale*, Ed Brubaker and Sean Phillips find the deal of a lifetime for comics creators.

In connection to other horror fiction, I left out many classic and contemporary authors and filmmakers; this acknowledgement is made not to point out a weakness in my work but to highlight its selectivity and perhaps encourage continued work for research in this fertile area.[14] As Mike Benton has noted, horror comics have had a direct influence on major writers like Stephen King and filmmakers like George Romero,[15] and horror comics are the source material for excellent works of horror in other media forms like *Hellboy*, *The Walking Dead*, and *Preacher*. Among other things, adaptations by industries seeking a money-making product bring up the complicated continuing journey of stories inspired by folktales and folktale-like source material.

At this point, it makes sense to return to a definition of horror. In response to the question of "What is horror?" Charles Weigel wisely replies, "That is a dangerously misleading question. We should ask instead, what isn't."[16] While this acknowledges the multifaceted nature of horror, this statement doesn't provide a means to develop an effective analysis of horror comics, and therefore, the following definition was offered in this volume. Moving beyond the common definition of the horror story as a tale of the supernatural fundamentally focused on threats posed by one or more monsters, twentieth- and twenty-first-century comics horror represents the widespread anxieties of common people in ways that are excessive, sometimes gratuitous, and often resistant to the authority of the powers-that-be.

More particularly, this end is achieved through the experiences of fear and disgust achieved through contact with the monstrous that force the individual to lose a sense of distance between the self and the tale, having closer contact with both the individual and cultural unconscious. In this way, contemporary horror comics engage a practice that is specific to its genre, medium, and historical context but also engage a tradition that is much more general. For instance, ancient and medieval Christianity balanced the glories of heaven with the horrors of hell in the pictorial designs of churches meant for illiterate congregations, but that balance was lost in post-medieval and especially post-Enlightenment churches. As the church more clearly became a part of the hegemony of European civilization, the focus shifted to kingdom-building with civilization as the means to salvation. Rather than identify Halloween and All Saints Day as equal partners in representing the human experience,[17] the former became the pagan past and the latter became the pious future.

C.S. Lewis, a medieval scholar best known for his children's fantasy and Christian apologetics (and generally characterized as a conservative political and religious voice), reclaimed demons as part of church history with *The Screwtape Letters*. More importantly, he portrays demons as part of a corporate structure characteristic of overgrown civilization. The novel rejects civilization as the saving agent and shows how the church should be radically opposed to the corrupting influence of civilization. However, the portrayals of religion as an abject experience set in opposition to civilization are regularly deemed objectionable: something best represented in this volume by Rick Veitch's industry-censored *Swamp Thing* story about Jesus.

As Karl Marx and Louis Althusser argue, modern religion and industry are parts of a super-structural network that supports and extends its hegemonic control of civilization. In a phrase that almost perfectly describes a haunting, Marx states, "The dead weight of the past hangs like a nightmare in the brains of the living."[18] Horror comics resist civilization by resisting the Comics Code's tenet that the world is safe in the past, present, and future. The notion that safety is normal and should be our highest priority is something presented in comics approved by the Code; and ultimately, it is a recipe for sacrificing one's own rights and the rights of others to those in power. Protecting one's self from harm may be desirable, but it is impossible in absolute terms, and it is something that too often justifies the cruel oppression of others.

Civilization has a self-perpetuating nature that defines itself as the only means to secure the safety of one's body, mind, and soul: the ultimate reality against which everything else is proven false. In America, that reality is connected to democracy and capitalism but a democracy and a capitalism narrowly defined so that they look more like government despotism and corporate greed. In the comics industry, that leads to centralized power that satisfies a consumer's prescribed needs at the expense of comics creators, the artistry of the medium, and the larger culture's moral self-awareness. Luckily, the rumblings of the individual unconscious become the rumblings of the cultural unconscious and are something the industry can't indefinitely oppose.

In the case of the resurgence of horror comics, a mainstream publisher turned to an iconoclastic writer like Alan Moore to be more profitable, and through the genre of horror, Moore redefined comics as art.[19] As an anarchist and occultist, Moore represented the ultimate outsider in the version of the United States set forth by Fredric Wertham, Estes Kefauver, and John Goldwater.[20] Practically in opposition to their attempt to control, Moore states, "I don't want to impose my will on the universe. I'd rather the universe imposed its will on me."[21] Along those lines, it is important to no longer identify figures like Wertham, Kefauver, and Goldwater as ghosts against whom one must continue to fight for the greater good of contemporary comics. Instead, they should be regarded as essential parts of comics history that have shaped the unique contours of this outlaw medium.

Moore believes less in safety and more in vulnerability, and by depicting the monster within, he shows in his horror stories how radically unsafe people truly are. Although reprehensible to some, this anxiety leads to a destruction of the other as a concept and to something that radically enables human connection. "If you understood everybody, you'd love them… [T]he only way you could ever understand [even the most reprehensible people]… is to in some way love them or at least suspend judgment, at least not hate, at least not draw back in revulsion from the very idea of these people"–"these people"[22] likely referring to people like Wertham, Kefauver, and Goldwater.

Contemporary horror comics move beyond the limitations imposed by the Code, and their depiction of the monstrous demonstrates how corporate structures collapse under the weight of their supposed unity, built more on greed than truth. As something of a cynic, I'm not sure that horror can do more than dismantle the known, enabling people in the way described by Moore. (As Stephen King states, horror presents "a classic no-win situation.")[23] However, horror is undeniably a protest against a perspective based on shiny surfaces that prevents a culture from recognizing that people are as much dead as alive. In the process of identifying post-industrial civilization as a fiction that we can choose not to believe, the most recent wave of the comics scare just might enable the reader in that way. And the longer monsters lurk on the borders of my dream worlds, the more certain I become that the contemporary comics scare can. How and why? Because I say so.

Conclusion Notes

1 Ray Bradbury, *The Martian Chronicles* (New York: Simon and Schuster, 2012), 140.

2 When a would-be victim stabs and kills the Lonely One, the town's youngsters lament the fact that he looks so ordinary and not at all like a traditional monster–like the ordinary-looking human monsters in EC comics.

3 Ray Bradbury, *Dandelion Wine* (New York: Doubleday, 1990), xii–xiii. His experience differs from the Lonely One story in *Dandelion Wine* in some ways. In the short story, the plot ends at the height of terror with the intended victim hearing someone in another room. However, the subsequent story reveals that she stabbed the Lonely One and brought his killing spree to an end. Nevertheless, this gives birth to a more profound fear because the monster looks just like everyone else.

4 Ray Bradbury, *The Martian Chronicles* (New York: Simon and Schuster, 2012), 143.

5 Ibid., 142.

6 Ibid., 139–140. Ultimately, Stendahl seals the censor ("the Investigator of Moral Climates") in the wall, referencing Poe's "The Cask of Amontillado." Stendahl claims he does so not because the investigator destroyed books but because he refused to understand what he destroyed. This story makes a statement about repressing the imagination and thereby encouraging a desire to enact the repressed in terrible ways.

7 Quoted in Digby Diehl, *Tales from the Crypt: The Official Archives* (New York: St. Martin's Press, 1996), 44.

8 Quoted in Roger Highfield and Paul Carter, *The Private Lives of Albert Einstein* (New York: St. Martin's Press: 1994), 78–79.

9 "Testimony of William M. Gaines, Publisher, Entertaining Comics Group, New York, NY," *TheComicbooks.Com*, last modified 2016, http://www.thecomicbooks.com/gaines.html.

10 Gaines may genuinely have been trying to use their rhetoric against them and may not have been fully conscious of this undercurrent. Nevertheless, it's nearly inconceivable that he wasn't aware of the irony at some level.

11 By making this statement, I don't mean to argue that Gaines deserves status as a hero any more than Wertham deserves status as a villain. Some research has been biased in this direction (such as Diehl's in *Tales from the Crypt: The Official Archives*) but other research has given a well-rounded sense of Gaines's complex character (such as Hajdu's in *The Ten Cent Plague*).

12 Ed Brubaker is best known as a crime and superhero writer but made a foray into horror/crime earlier with the Sandman spin-off, *The Deadboy Detectives*.

13 The series ran 2012 to 2014, and the deal from Image was made in 2014.

14 Other things left out include video games (crime video games such as *L.A. Noire*, *Grand Theft Auto*, and *Mafia,* and horror video games such as *Resident Evil*, *Silent Hill*, and *Amnesia*).

15 Mike Benton, *Horror Comics: The Illustrated History* (Dallas: Taylor Publishing, 1991), 5.

16 Charles Weigel, "Introducing Horror," *Hop on Pop: The Politics of Popular Culture*, ed., Henry Jenkins, Tara McPherson, and Jane Shattuc (Durham: Duke UP, 2002), 717.

17 Neil Gaiman states, "There were days that changed everything: birthdays and New Years and First Days of School, days that showed us that there was an order to all things, and the creatures of the night and the imagination understood this, just as we did. All Hallows' Eve was their party, the night all their birthdays came at once. They had license–all the boundaries set between the living and the dead were breached" (Neil Gaiman, "Ghosts in the Machines," *The New York Times*, last modified Oct. 31, 2006, http://www.nytimes.com/2006/10/31/opinion/31gaiman.html).

18 Karl Marx, "The Eighteenth Brumaire of Louis Bonaparte. Karl Marx 1852," Marxists.org, last modified 2006, https://www.marxists.org/archive/marx/works/1852/18th-brumaire/ch01.htm.

19 "In the 1940s, the Frankfurt School put forth a monolithic theory of popular culture, according to which the 'culture industry' was seen as a homogenous, manipulative machine that molded individuals into mainstream capitalist ideology.... Later work on these topics tended to separate popular culture's participative and egalitarian potential from mass culture's manipulation, while the postmodern approach to popular culture often depicts media messages as a realm for the post-colonial expression of formerly subjugated minorities.... the influential work of Alan Moore is infused with an anarchist strand and an ongoing critical view of power structures and oppression. Moore's left-leaning comics post challenging theoretical questions, given that much of his work has been released by mainstream companies that publish superhero comics–a genre traditionally depicted as a vehicle for right-wing ideas" (Antonio Pineda and Jesus Jimenez-Varea, "Popular Culture, Ideology, and the Comics Industry: Steve Ditko's Objectivist Spiderman," *The Journal of Popular Culture* 46 [2013]: 1156–57).

20 Despite seemingly radical political and religious differences, Moore shared a vision of industrial age civilization directly in line with C.S. Lewis (and *The Screwtape Letters)*: "I love the comic medium. It is one that I shall never abandon. But the industry–in fact, increasingly all forms of industry–it's dark Satanic mills" (Alex Musson, "Alan Moore: Mustard Interview," *Mustard*, last modified Jan. 12, 2017, http://www.mustardweb.org/alanmoore/index.htm).

21 Matthew De Abaitua, "Alan Moore Interview," *Alan Moore: Conversations*, ed., Eric Berlatsky (Jackson: UP of Mississippi, 2012), 84.

22 Barry Kavanagh, "*From Hell*," *Blather.Net*, last modified Oct. 17, 2000. http://www.blather.net/projects/alan-moore-interview/from-hell/. This quote is related to *V for Vendetta* (and not specifically the works discussed in Chapter 3). However, the anxiety about culture is the same in this dystopic work even though it might not be classified as horror.

23 Stephen King, *Danse Macabre* (New York: Gallery, 1981), 117. This phrase refers to how the dread of something exceeds the horror of actually encountering it.

BIBLIOGRAPHY

Abaitua, Matthew De. "Alan Moore Interview." *Alan Moore: Conversations*. Edited by Eric Berlatsky, 61–94. Jackson: University Press of Mississippi, 2012.

Abbott and Costello Meet Frankenstein. Directed by Charles Barton. Hollywood: Universal, 1948.

Abrams, Simon. "Re-Animator: Focus on Robert Kirkman's *The Walking Dead*." *The Comics Journal* 289 (April 2008): 97–103.

———. "The Robert Kirkman Interview." *The Comics Journal* 289 (April 2008): 41–96.

Aguire-Scasa, Roberto, Francesco Francavilla, and Jack Morelli. *Afterlife with Archie*. New York: Archie Comics, 2014.

Alien vs. Predator. Directed by Paul W.S. Anderson. Hollywood: 20th Century Fox, 2004.

Al-Tabaa, Najwa. "Hell Can Be Good for You." *Neil Gaiman and Philosophy: Gods Gone Wild!* Edited by Tracy L. Bealer, Rachel Luria, and Wayne Yuen, 127–134. Chicago: Open Court, 2012.

American Gothic. CBS, 1995–1996.

American Werewolf in London. Directed by John Landis. Hollywood: Polygram, 1981.

Anderson, Eric Gary. "The Fall of the House of Po' Sandy: Poe, Chesnutt, and Southern Undeadness." *Undead Souths: The Gothic and Beyond in Southern Literature and Culture*. Edited by Eric Gary Anderson, Taylor Hagood, and Daniel Cross Turner, 23–35. Baton Rouge: Louisiana State University Press, 2015.

Anderson, Eric Gary, Taylor Hagood, and Daniel Cross Turner. "Introduction." *Undead Souths: The Gothic and Beyond in Southern Literature and Culture.* Edited by Eric Gary Anderson, Taylor Hagood, and Daniel Cross Turner, 1–9. Baton Rouge: Louisiana State University Press, 2015.

Anglo, Michael. *Penny Dreadfuls and Other Victorian Horrors.* London: Jupiter, 1977.

Arndt, Richard J. *Horror Comics in Black and White: A History and Catalogue, 1964–2004.* Jefferson, NC: McFarland, 2013.

Auerbach, Nina. *Our Vampires, Ourselves.* Chicago: University of Chicago Press, 1995.

Barber, Paul. *Vampires, Burial, and Death: Folklore and Reality.* New Haven: Yale University Press, 1988.

Barker, Clive. "Introduction." Neil Gaiman, Mike Dringenberg, Malcolm Jones III, Chris Bachalo, Michael Zulli, Steve Parkhouse, Robbie Busch, and Todd Klein. *The Sandman: The Doll's House.* 6–7. New York: DC, 1995.

Barrett, Rich. "Our Interview with *Hellboy* Creator Mike Mignola." *Mental Floss.* Last modified March 22, 2014. http://mentalfloss.com/article/55606/our-interview-hellboy-creator-mike-mignola.

Batman. Directed by Tim Burton. Hollywood: Warner Bros., 1989.

Baudrillard, Jean. *The Transparency of Evil: Essays in Extreme Phenomena.* London: Verso, 2009.

Beatty, Bart. *Fredric Wertham and the Critique of Mass Culture.* Jackson: University Press of Mississippi, 2005.

Beineke, Colin. "'Her Guardiner': Alan Moore's Swamp Thing as the Green Man." *ImageText: Interdisciplinary Comics Studies* 5. Last modified 2010. http://www.english.ufl.edu/imagetext/archives/v5_4/beineke/.

Benshoff, Harry M. *Monsters in the Closet: Homosexuality and the Horror Film.* Manchester: Manchester University Press, 1998.

Benton, Mike. *Horror Comics: The Illustrated History.* Dallas: Taylor Publishing, 1991.

Beowulf. Translated by Seamus Heaney. New York: Farrar, Straus, and Giroux, 2000.

Berlatsky, Eric L. "Introduction." *Alan Moore: Conversations.* Edited by Eric Berlatsky, vii–xx. Jackson: University Press of Mississippi, 2012.

Bettelheim, Bruno. *The Uses of Enchantment: The Meaning and Importance of Fairy Tales.* New York: Vintage, 2010.

Big Trouble in Little China. Directed by John Carpenter. Hollywood: 20th Century Fox, 1986.

Birke, Dorothee. "Challenging the Divide? Stephen King and the Problem of 'Popular Culture.'" *The Journal of Popular Culture* 47 (2014): 520–36.

Birkhead, Edith. *The Tale of Terror: A Study of the Gothic Romance.* London: Constable and Company, 2004.

Bishop, Kyle William. *American Zombie Gothic: The Rise and Fall (and Rise) of the Walking Dead in Popular Culture.* Jefferson, NC: McFarland, 2010.

——. "Battling Monsters and Becoming Monstrous: Human Devolution in *The Walking Dead.*" Edited by Marina Levina and Diem-My T. Bui. *Monster Culture in the 21st Century: A Reader.* London: Bloomsbury, 2013, 73–85.

Bissette, Stephen. "Taboo Is Taboo." *Taboo* 9. Northhampton, MA: Kitchen Sink, September 1995, 123–128.

Bloom, Harold. "For the World of Letters, It's a Horror." *Los Angeles Times.* Last modified September 19, 2003. http://articles.latimes.com/2003/sep/19/opinion/oe-bloom19.

Blouin, Michael J. "Robert Kirkman and Tony Moore's *The Walking Dead.*" *Critical Insights: The Graphic Novel.* Edited by Gary Hoppenstand, 183–94. Armenia, NY: Salem Press, 2014.

Botting, Fred. *Gothic.* London: Routledge, 2013.

Boucher, Geoff. "Dream a Little Dream: Neil Gaiman on the 20th Anniversary of 'The Sandman.'" *Hero Complex.* Last modified December 1, 2008. http://herocomplex.latimes.com/uncategorized/dream-a-little/.

———. "Neil Gaiman: 'Alan Moore got to be The Beatles.... I was Gerry and the Pacemakers.'" *Hero Complex*. Last modified December 2, 2008. http://herocomplex.latimes.com/uncategorized/neil-gaiman-ala/.

Bradbury, Ray. *Dandelion Wine*. New York: Bantam, [1946] 1990.

———. *Fahrenheit 451*. New York: Simon and Schuster, [1953] 2012.

———. *The Martian Chronicles*. New York: Simon and Schuster, [1950] 2012.

———. *Something Wicked This Way Comes*. New York: Avon, [1962] 2006.

Braidotti, Rosi. *The Posthuman*. Malden, MA: Polity, 2013.

Bratman, David. "A Game of You–Yes, You." *The Sandman Papers: An Exploration of the Sandman Mythology*. Edited by Joe Sanders, 41–54. Seattle: Fantagraphics, 2006.

Brayshaw, Christopher. "Between Two Worlds: The Mike Mignola Interview." *The Comics Journal* 189 (August 1996): 64–90.

Breton, Andre. *Anthology of Black Humor*. San Francisco: City Light Publishers, 2001.

Bride of the Monster. Directed by Edward Wood. Rolling M. Productions, 1955.

Briefer, Dick. "Three-Fold Horror and Revenge." *The Monster of Frankenstein* 31. New York: Prize, June–July 1954.

Brigley-Thompson, Zoe. "Theorizing Sexual Domination in *From Hell* and *Lost Girls*: Jack the Ripper versus Wonderlands of Desire." *Sexual Ideology in the Works of Alan Moore: Critical Essays on the Graphic Novels*. Edited by Todd A. Comer, 76–87. Jefferson, NC: McFarland, 2012.

Brisbin, Ally and Paul Booth. "The Sand/wo/man: The Unstable Worlds of Gender in Neil Gaiman's Sandman Series." *The Journal of Popular Culture* 46 (2013): 20–37.

Brownstein, Charles. *Eisner/Miller*. Milwaukie, OR: Dark Horse, 2005.

Brubaker, Ed, Bryan Talbot, Steve Leialoha. *Sandman Presents: Dead Boy Detectives*. New York: DC, 2008.

Brubaker, Ed, Bryan Talbot, Steve Leialoha, Daniel Vozzo, and Willie Schubert. *The Sandman Presents: The Dead Boy Detectives*. New York: DC, 2001.

Buell, Lawrence. *The Future of Environmental Criticism: Environmental Crisis and Literary Imagination*. Malden, MA: Blackwell, 2005.

Buffy the Vampire Slayer. Fox, 1997–2003.

Bukatman, Scott. *Hellboy's World: Comics and Monsters on the Margins*. Oakland: University of California Press, 2016.

Butler, Gary. "Mike Mignola on *Hellboy*." *The Hellboy Archive*. Last modified April 7, 2004. http//completehellboy.com/interviews/1996-2007/apr-7-2004/.

Cabinet of Dr. Caligari. Directed by Robert Wiene. Germany: Decia-Bioscop, 1920.

Campbell, Hayley. *The Art of Neil Gaiman*. New York: Harper Design, 2014.

Candelaria, Matthew. "Green Love, Red Sex: The Conflation of the Flora and the Flesh in Swamp Thing." *Sexual Ideology in the Works of Alan Moore: Critical Essays on the Graphic Novels*. Edited by Todd A. Comer. 28–39. Jefferson, NC: McFarland, 2012.

Candyman. Directed by Bernard Rose. Hollywood, Polygram, 1992.

Carrie. Directed by Brian De Palma. Hollywood: MGM, 1976.

Carter, Angela. *Angela Carter's Book of Fairy Tales*. London: Virago, 2007.

——. *The Bloody Chamber and Other Stories*. London, Vintage: 2006.

——. *Little Red Riding Hood, Cinderella, and Other Classic Fairy Tales of Charles Perrault*. New York: Penguin, 2008.

Casey, Dan. "Comic Book Day: Eric Powell's a Total 'Goon.'" *Nerdist*. Last modified April 25, 2012. http://nerdist.com/comic-book-day-eric-powells-a-total-goon/.

Castaldo, Annalisa. "'No More Yielding than a Dream': The Construction of Shakespeare in *The Sandman*." *College Literature* 31 (Fall 2004): 94–110.

Chalen, Michelle. "'Walking Dead': Zombies Thrive on Weak Economy." *CNBC*. Last modified March 22, 2013. http://www.cnbc.com/id/100583639.

Chaykin, Howard. *Black Kiss*. Runnemede, NJ: Dynamite, 2010.

Clarke, Graham. "Introduction." *Edgar Allen Poe: Critical Assessments*. Edited by Graham Clarke, 1–4. East Sussex: Helm Information, 1991.

Clover, Carol. *Men, Women, and Chain Saws: Gender in the Modern Horror Film*. Princeton: Princeton University Press, 2015.

Cohen, Jeffrey Jerome. "Monster Culture (Seven Theses)." *Monster Theory: Reading Culture*. Edited by Jeffrey Jerome Cohen, 3–25. Minneapolis: University of Minnesota Press, 1996.

Colan, Gene. "Escape to Nowhere." *Journey into Unknown Worlds* 37. New York: Marvel. November 1951.

Conrich, Ian. "Seducing the Subject: Freddy Krueger." *Horror Film Reader*. Edited by Alain Silver and James Ursini, 223–36. New York: Limelight, 2006.

Conway, Gerry, Robert Bloch, and Pablo Marcos. "The Man Who Cried Werewolf." *Monsters Unleashed* 1. New York: Marvel, March 1973.

Cotter, Robert Michael. *The Great Monster Magazines: A Critical Study of Black-and-White Publications of the 1950s, 1960s, and 1970s*. Jefferson, NC: McFarland, 2008.

Craig, Johnny, Marie Severin, and Jim Wroten. ". . . And All Through the House . . ." *Vault of Horror* 35. New York: EC, February–March 1954.

Craig, Johnny and Jim Wroten. "Curse of the Full Moon!" *The Crypt of Terror* 17. New York: EC, April–May 1950.

Crecente, Brian. "The Kirkman Effect: How an Undead Army May Recreate Entertainment." *Polygon*. Last modified March 30, 2015. https://www.polygon.com/features/2015/3/30/8311735/the-walking-dead-invincible-outcast-fear-the-walking-dead-interview-robert-kirkman.

Creepshow. Directed by George A. Romero. Hollywood: Laurel, 1982.

Dahlen, Chris. "Steve Bissette: Interview." *The Onion A.V. Club*. Last modified July 23, 2009. http://www.avclub.com/article/steve-bissette-30751.

Daniels, Les. *COMIX: A History of Comic Books in America*. New York: Outerbridge and Dienstfrey, 1971.

Darabont, Frank. "Introduction." Eric Powell, Robin Powell, Shaynne Corbett, Barry Gregory, and Ben Cocke. *The Goon: Heaps of Ruination*. Milwaukie, OR: Dark Horse, 2011, 1–4.

Dark Shadows. ABC, 1966–1971.

Dawn of the Dead. Directed by George A. Romero. Laurel Group, 1978.

Day of the Dead. Directed by Geroge A. Romero. Laurel Group, 1985.

The Dead Zone. Directed by David Cronenberg. Hollywood: Dino De Laurentiis, 1983.

Dean, Michael. "Our Zombies, Ourselves." *The Comics Journal* 289 (April 2008): 38–40.

———. "The Young Cannibals: How Phil Seuling and a Generation of Teenage Entrepreneurs Created the Direct Market and Changed the Face of Comics." *The Comics Journal* 277 (July 2006): 49–59.

DeFino, Dean. *The HBO Effect*. New York: Bloomsbury, 2013.

del Toro, Guillermo. "Mike Mignola Is a Genius: An Unapologetically Subjective Introduction." Mike Mignola, Dave Stewart, and Pat Brosseau. *Hellboy: Conqueror Worm* 1. Milwaukie, OR: Dark Horse, 2003.

Deliverance. Directed by John Boorman. Hollywood: Warner Bros., 1972.

Demott, Benjamin. "Darkness in the Mall: The 'New Wave' of Adult Comic Books Fetures Defeat, Cynicism, and Despair." *Psychology Today* (February 1984): 48–52.

Deppy, Dirk. "Suicide Club: How Greed and Stupidity Disemboweled the American Comic-Book Industry in the 1990s." *The Comics Journal* 277 (July 2006): 68–75.

Diary of the Dead. Directed by George A. Romero. Romero-Grunwald Productions, 2007.

Diehl, Digby. *Tales from the Crypt: The Official Archives*. New York: St. Martin's Press, 1996.

Di Liddo, Annalisa. *Alan Moore: Comics as Performance, Fiction as Scalpel*. Jackson: University Press of Mississippi, 2009.

Dixon, Thomas. *The Leopard's Spots*. New York: Doubleday, 1990.

Dixon, Wheeler Winston. *A History of Horror*. New Brunswick: Rutgers University Press, 2010.

Dracula. Directed by Tod Browning. Hollywood: Universal, 1931.

Dracula. Directed by Terrence Fisher. UK: Hammer, 1959.

Drucker, Aaron. "Empowering Voice and Refiguring Retribution: Neil Gaiman's Anti-Feminism Feminist Parable in The Sandman." *Feminism in the Worlds of Neil Gaiman: Essays on the Comics, Poetry, and Prose*. Edited by Tara Prescott and Aaron Drucker, 81–101. Jefferson, NC: McFarland, 2012.

Dubay, Bill and Richard Corben. "Bless Us Father…" *Creepy* 59. New York: Warren, January 1974.

Dueben, Alex. "The Goon Show: An Interview with Eric Powell." *Ninth Art*. Last modified October 18, 2004. https://www.ninthart.org/display.php?article=936.

Duncan, Randy and Matthew J. Smith. *The Power of Comics: History, Form, and Culture*. New York: Bloomsbury, 2009.

Durgnat, Raymond. "The Subconscious: From Pleasure Castle to Libido Hotel." *Horror Film Reader*. Edited by Alain Silver and James Ursini, 39–50. New York: Limelight, 2006.

Eaton, Lance. "The Horror Narrative and the Graphic Novel." *Critical Insights: The Graphic Novel*. Edited by Gary Hoppenstand, 17–28. Armenia, NY: Salem Press, 2014.

Edward Scissorhands. Directed by Tim Burton. Hollywood: 20th Century Fox, 1990.

Elder, Robert K. "Gods and Other Monsters: A Sandman Exit interview and Philosophical Omnibus." *The Neil Gaiman Reader*. Edited by Darrell Schweitzer, 54–78. Holicong, PA: Wildside, 2007.

Ellison, Harlan. "Introduction." In Neil Gaiman, Kelly Jones, Mike Dringenberg, Malcolm Jones III, Matt Wagner, Dick Giorgano, George Pratt, P. Craig Russell, Steve Oliff, Danile Vozzo, and Todd Klein. *The Sandman: Season of Mists.* New York: DC, 1992, 7–11.

Epstein, Daniel Robert. "Robert Kirkman." *Anderswolleck blog@SuicideGirls.* Last modified June 12, 2005. https://www.suicidegirls.com/girls/anderswolleck/blog/2679246/robert-kirkman/.

Ervin-Gore, Shawna. "Mike Mignola Interview." *Dark Horse Comics.* Last modified June 2002. http://www.darkhorse.com/Interviews/763/Mike-Mignola.

Evil Dead. Directed by Sam Raimi. Hollywood: Renaissance Pictures, 1981.

Evil Dead 2. Directed by Sam Raimi. Hollywood: Renaissance Pictures, 1987.

"Exclusive Interview: Neil Gaiman on the Weird." *Weird Fiction Review.* Last modified November 1, 2011. http://weirdfictionreview.com/2011/11/exclusive-interview-neil-gaiman-on-the-weird/.

The Exorcist. Directed by William Friedkin. Hollywood: Warner Bros., 1973.

Fassbender, Tom. "Mike Mignola Interview." *Ralf Hildebrandt.* Last modified January 17, 2007. https://www.arschkrebs.de/interviews/Mignola9704.shtml.

Fear, David. "Robert Kirkman: Inside 'Walking Dead' Creator's Twisted Mind, New Show." *Rolling Stone.* Last modified May 31, 2016. http://www.rollingstone.com/tv/features/robert-kirkman-inside-walking-dead-creators-twisted-mind-new-show-20160531.

Harry Harrison and Wally Wood. "Werewolf." *The Vault of Horror* 14. New York: EC, August–September 1950.

Feldstein, Al, Johnny Craig, Marie Severin, and Jim Wroten. "Midnight Snack." *Tales from the Crypt* 24. New York: EC, June–July 1951.

Feldstein, Al, Jack Davis, Marie Severin, and Jim Wroten. "Bats in My Belfry!" *Tales from the Crypt* 24. New York: EC, June–July 1951.

——. "Dead Right!" *Tales from the Crypt* 37. New York: EC, August–September 1953.

——. "Foul Play!" *Haunt of Fear* 19. New York: EC, May–June 1953.

Feldstein, Al, Jack Davis, and Jim Wroten. "Lower Berth!" *Tales from the Crypt* 33. New York: EC, December 1952–January 1953.

Feldstein, Al, Graham Ingels, Marie Severin, and Jim Wroten. "Horror under the Big Top!" *Crime SuspenStories* 7. New York: EC, October–November 1951.

——. "The Living Death!" *Tales from the Crypt* 24. New York: EC, June–July 1951.

——. "Wish You Were Here." *Haunt of Fear* 22. New York: EC, November–December 1953.

Feldstein, Al, Jack Kamen, Marie Severin, and Jim Wroten. "The Orphan." *Shock SuspenStories* 14. New York: EC, April–May 1954.

Feldstein, Al, Wally Wood, Marie Severin, and Jim Wroten. "The Whipping." *Shock SuspenStories* 14. New York: EC, April–May 1954.

Ferguson, Christine. "Victoria-Arcana and the Misogynistic Poetics of Resistance in Iain Sinclair's *White Chapel Scarlet Tracings* and Alan Moore's *From Hell.*" *Literature Interpretation Theory* 20 (2009): 45–64.

Fisher, Terrence. "Horror Is My Business." *Horror Film Reader*. Edited by Alain Silver and James Ursini, 67–76. New York: Limelight, 2006.

Fiske, John. *Understanding Popular Culture*. London: Routledge, 2011.

Foley, John Miles. *Pathways Project*. Last modified December 16, 2011. http://pathwaysproject.org/pathways/show/HomePage.

"For *Hellboy* Creator Mike Mignola, the Real Horror Is Hollywood." *Wired*. Last modified October 12, 2012. https://www.wired.com/2012/10/geeks-guide-mike-mignola/.

Fox, Gardner, Bob Kane, and Sheldon Moldoff, "Batman vs. the Vampire, Part 1." *Detective Comics* 31. New York: DC, September 1939.

——. "Batman vs. the Vampire, Part 2." *Detective Comics* 32. New York: DC, October 1939.

Frankenstein. Directed by J. Searle Dawley. New York: Edison, 1910.

Frankenstein. Directed by James Whale. Hollywood: Universal, 1931.

Frankenstein Meets the Wolfman. Directed by Roy William Neill. Hollywood: Universal, 1943.

Freaks. Directed by Tod Browning. Hollywood: MGM, 1932.

Freddy vs. Jason. Directed by Ronny Yu. Hollywood: New Line, 2003.

Freud, Sigmund. *Beyond the Pleasure Principle*. New York: W.W. Norton, 1990.

Friday the 13th. Directed by Sean Cunningham. Hollywood: Paramount, 1980.

Friedenthal, Andrew J. *Retcon Game: Retroactive Continuity and the Hyperlinking of America*. Jackson: University Press of Mississippi, 2017.

Friedrich, Mike, Gil Kane, Wally Wood, and Milt Snapinn. "His Name Is… Kane." *The House of Mystery* 180. New York: DC, May–June 1969.

From Hell. Directed by Albert Hughes and Allen Hughes. Hollywood: 20th Century Fox, 2001.

——. "Ghosts in the Machines." *The New York Times*. Last modified October 31, 2006. http://www.nytimes.com/2006/10/31/opinion/31gaiman.html.

——. *The Ocean at the End of the Lane*. New York: William Morrow, 2013.

———. "Popular Writers: A Stephen King Interview." *Neil Gaiman's Journal*. Last modified April 28, 2012. http://journal.neilgaiman.com/2012/04/popular-writers-stephen-king-interview.html.

———. "The Thing We Don't Talk About." *The Art of Horror*. Edited by Stephen Jones, 8. Milwaukee, WI: Applause, 2015.

Gaiman, Neil, Mike Dringenberg, Malcolm Jones III, Chris Bachalo, Michael Zulli, Steve Parkhouse, Robbie Busch, and Todd Klein. *The Sandman: The Doll's House*. New York: DC, 1995.

Gaiman, Neil, Kelly Jones, Mike Dringenberg, Malcolm Jones III, Matt Wagner, Dick Giorgano, George Pratt, P. Craig Russell, Steve Oliff, Daniel Vozzo, and Todd Klein. *The Sandman: Season of Mists*. New York: DC, 1992.

Gaiman, Neil, Kelly Jones, Charles Vess, Colleen Doran, Malcolm Jones III, Robbie Busch, Todd Klein. *The Sandman: Dream Country*. New York: DC, 1990.

Gaiman, Neil, Sam Keith, Mike Dringenberg, Malcolm Jones III, Robbie Busch, and Todd Klein. *The Sandman: Preludes and Nocturnes*. New York: DC, 1995.

Gaiman, Neil, Jill Thompson, Vince Locke, Dick Giordano, Danny Vozzo, and Todd Klein. *The Sandman: Brief Lives*. New York: DC, 1994.

Gaines, Bill, Al Feldstein, Jack Davis, and Jim Wroten. "Grounds… for Horror!" *Tales from the Crypt* 29. New York: EC, April–May 1952.

Gaines, Bill, Al Feldstein, Graham Ingels, Marie Severin, and Jim Wroten. "The Rug!" *Shock SuspenStories* 1. New York: EC. February–March 1952.

Germana, Monica. "Madness and the City: The Collapse of Reason and Sanity in Alan Moore's *From Hell*." *Alan Moore and the Gothic Tradition*. Edited by Matthew J.A. Green, 140–158. Manchester: Manchester University Press, 2013.

Glen or Glenda. Directed by Edward Wood. Hollywood: George Weiss, 1953.

Goddu, Teressa A. "Introduction to American Gothic." *The Horror Reader*. Edited by Ken Gelder, 265–70. London: Routledge, 2000.

Goldfarb, Edward. "The Vampire Puppet." *Witchcraft* 2. New York: Avon. May–June 1952.

Gonzalez, Jesus A. "'Living in the Funnies': Metafiction in American Comic Strips." *The Journal of Popular Culture* 47 (August 2014): 838–56.

Goodlad, Lauren M.E. and Michael Bibby. "Introduction." *Goth: Undead Subculture*. Edited by Lauren M.E. Goodlad and Michael Bibby, 1–40. Durham: Duke University Press, 2007.

Goodwin, Archie. "Who Serves the Cause of Chaos?" *Vampirella* 8. New York: Warren. November 1970.

Goodwin, Archie, Gene Colan, and Ben Oda. "Hatchet Man." *Creepy* 4. New York: Warren, July 1966.

Goodwin, Archie, Reed Crandall, and Ben Oda. "Tell-Tale Heart!" *Eerie* 13. New York: Warren, February 1968.

——. "Vampires Fly at Dusk!" *Creepy* 1. New York: Warren, November 1964.

Goodwin, Archie, Angelo Torres, and Ben Oda. "Monster Rally!" *Creepy* 4. New York: Warren, June 1965.

Grandenetti, Jerry and Milt Snapinn. "Boom!" *The House of Mystery* 185. New York: DC, March–April 1970.

Grannell, Craig. "An Interview with Mike Mignola, Part 6." *Revert To Saved*. Last modified August 17, 2008. http://reverttosaved.com/2008/08/17/an-interview-with-mike-mignola-part-six/.

"Grave Rehearsal." *Strange Fantasy* 7. New York: Farrell, August 1953.

Gray, Maggie. "A Gothic Politics: Alan Moore's *Swamp Thing* and Radical Ecology." *Alan Moore and the Gothic Tradition*. Edited by Matthew J.A. Green, 42–64. Manchester: Manchester University Press, 2013.

Green, Matthew J.A. "Alan Moore and the Gothic Tradition." *Alan Moore and the Gothic Tradition.* Edited by Matthew J.A. Green, 3–20. Manchester: Manchester University Press, 2013.

Griffin, Susan. *Pornography and Silence.* New York: Harpercollins, 1982.

Groth, Gary. "The Alan Moore Interview." *The Comics Journal.* Last modified June 13, 2012. http://www.tcj.com/the-alan-moore-interview-118/.

Hagood, Taylor. "Going to Ground: The Undead in Contemporary Southern Popular Culture Media and Writing." *Undead Souths: The Gothic and Beyond in Southern Literature and Culture.* Edited by Eric Gary Anderson, Taylor Hagood, and Daniel Cross Turner, 248–260. Baton Rouge: Louisiana State University Press, 2015.

Hajdu, David. *The Ten Cent Plague: The Great Comic-Book Scare and How It Changed America.* New York: Farrar, Straus, and Giroux, 2008.

Hallett, Martin and Barbara Karasek. "Introduction." *Folk and Fairy Tales.* Edited by Martin Hallett and Barbara Karasek, 15–26. Peterborough, Ontario: Broadview, 2009.

Halloween. Directed by John Carpetner. Hollywood: Compass, 1978.

Hand, Richard J. *Terror on the Air! Horror Radio in America, 1931–1952.* Jefferson, NC: McFarland, 2006.

Harper, David. "Artist August: Eric Powell (Interview)." *Multiversity Comics.* Last modified August 15, 2011. http://www.multiversitycomics.com/news-columns/artist-august-eric-powell-art-feature/.

Hauskeller, Michael. *Sex and the Posthuman Condition.* New York: Palgrave Macmillan, 2014.

Heater, Brian. "Interview: Eric Powell Pt. 1 [of 2]." *The Daily Cross Hatch.* Last modified February 24, 2009. http://thedailycrosshatch.com/2009/02/24/interview-eric-powell-pt-1-of-2/.

———. "Interview: Eric Powell Pt. 2 [of 2]" *The Daily Cross Hatch*. Last modified March 2, 2009. http://thedailycrosshatch.com/2009/031./02/interview-eric-powell-pt-2-of-2/.

Heath, Russ. "Mark of the Witch." *Suspense* 5. New York: Cornell, November 1950.

Hellboy. Directed by Guillermo Del Toro. Hollywood: Columbia Tristar, 2004.

Heller, Jason. "Interview: Mike Mignola." *The Onion A.V. Club*. Last modified July 24, 2008. http://www.avclub.com/article/mike-mignola-14279.

Hellraiser. Directed by Clive Barker. Hollywood: Cinemarque Entertainment, 1987.

Hess, Elizabeth. "Meet the Spiegelmans." *Village Voice*. January 14, 1992: 87.

Highfield, Roger and Paul Carter. *The Private Lives of Albert Einstein*. New York: St. Martin's Press: 1994.

Hocus Pocus. Directed by Kenny Ortega. Hollywood: Walt Disney, 1993.

Hodkinson, Paul. *Goth: Identity, Style, and Subculture*. Oxford: Berg, 2002.

House of Wax. Directed by André de Toth. Hollywood, Warner Bros., 1953.

Howlett, Mike. *The Weird World of Eerie Publications: Comic Gore that Warped Millions of Young Minds!* Port Townsend, WA: Feral House, 2010.

Huet, Marie-Helen. *Monstrous Imagination*. Cambridge: Harvard University Press, 1993.

Hume, Kathryn. "Neil Gaiman's *Sandman* as Mythic Romance." *Genre* 46 (Fall 2013): 345–65.

The Hunchback of Notre Dame. Directed by Wallace Worsley. Hollywood: Universal, 1923.

The Indian Fighter. Directed by André de Toth. Hollywood: United Artists, 1955.

"Interview–Neil Gaiman, Likely Stories." *The Dreamcage*. http://www.thedreamcage.com/2016/04/interview-neil-gaiman-likely-stories.html.

"An Interview with Neil Gaiman." *Gothic Beauty*. Last modified December 1, 2004. https://www.gothicbeauty.com/2004/12/an-interview-with-neil-gaiman/.

Invasion of the Body Snatchers. Directed by Don Siegel. Hollywood: Walter Wanger, 1956.

Irving, Christopher. "Raising Hellboy: Mike Mignola on the Development of *Hellboy* and His Work Past, Present, and Future." *The Hellboy Archive*. Last modified 2007. http://completehellboy.com/interviews/1996-2007/1998/.

Jackson, Shirley. *The Haunting of Hill House*. New York: Penguin, [1959] 2006.

Jahlmar, Joakim. "'Give the Devil His Due': Freedom, Damnation, and Milton's Paradise Lost in Neil Gaiman's *The Sandman: Season of Mists*." *Partial Answers: Journal of Literature and the History of Ideas* 13 (June 2015): 267–286.

Jaws. Directed by Steven Spielberg. New York: Universal, 1975.

Johnson, Brian. "Libidinal Ecologies: Eroticism and Environmentalism in Swamp Thing." *Sexual Ideology in the Works of Alan Moore: Critical Essays on the Graphic Novels*. Edited by Todd A. Comer, 16–27. Jefferson, NC: McFarland, 2012.

Jones, Gerard. *Killing Monsters: Why Children Need Fantasy, Super Heroes, and Make-Believe Violence*. New York: Basic, 2002.

Jones, Russ, Jack Davis, and Ben Oda. "Heh-Heh, Welcome–." *Creepy* 1. New York: Warren. November 1964.

Jones, Timothy. *Gothic and the Carnivalesque in American Culture*. Chicago: University of Chicago Press, 2015.

Jowett, Lorna and Stacey Abbott. *TV Horror: Investigating the Dark Side of the Small Screen*. London: I.B. Tauris, 2013.

Katsiadas, Nick. "Mytho-auto-bio: Neil Gaiman's *Sandman*, the Romantics, and Shakespeare's *The Tempest*." *Studies in Comics* 6 (2015): 61–84.

Kavanaugh, Barry. "*From Hell.*" *Blather.Net*. Last modified October 17, 2000. http://www.blather.net/projects/alan-moore-interview/from-hell/.

Khoury, George. *The Extraordinary Works of Alan Moore*. Raleigh, NC: TwoMorrows, 2008.

King, Stephen. *Carrie*. New York: Anchor, [1974] 2011.

——. *Cujo*. New York: Pocket, [1981] 2016.

——. *Danse Macabre*. New York: Gallery, 1981.

——. *The Dark Tower I: The Gunslinger*. New York: Scribner, [1982] 2016.

——. *The Dead Zone*. New York: Pocket, [1979] 2016.

——. *Desperation*. New York: Pocket, [1996] 2016.

——. *The Green Mile*. New York: Pocket, [1996] 1999.

——. "An Introduction." Neil Gaiman, Bryan Talbot, John Watkiss, Michael Allred, Michael Zulli, Shea Anton Pensa, Alec Stevens, Gary Amaro, and Todd Klein. *The Sandman: World's End*. New York: DC, 1994, 2–7.

——. *Misery*. New York: Pocket, [1987] 2017.

——. "National Book Award Acceptance Speech." *National Book Foundation*. Last modified 2003. http://www.nationalbook.org/nbaacceptspeech_sking.htmlNo. .WSSHRTOZMk8.

——. *Salem's Lot*. New York: Anchor, [1975] 2011.

——. *The Shining*. New York: Anchor, [1977] 2012.

——. *Thinner*. New York: Pocket, [1984] 2016.

Kirkman, Robert, Charlie Adlard, Stefano Gaudiano, Cliff Rathburn, and Rus Wooton. *The Walking Dead, Book 10*. Berkeley: Image, 2014.

——. *The Walking Dead, Book 11*. Berkeley: Image, 2015.

——. *The Walking Dead, Book 12*. Berkeley: Image, 2015.

——. *The Walking Dead, Book 13*. Berkeley: Image, 2016.

Kirkman, Robert, Charlie Adlard, Cliff Rathburn, and Rus Wooton. *The Walking Dead, Book 2*. Berkeley: Image, 2008.

——. *The Walking Dead, Book 4*. Berkeley: Image, 2008.

——. *The Walking Dead, Book 5*. Berkeley: Image, 2010.

——. *The Walking Dead, Book 6*. Berkeley: Image, 2010.

Kirkman, Robert and Tony Moore, *Walking Dead, Vol. 1: Days Gone Bye* (Berkeley: Image, 2013), 2.

Kirkman, Robert, Tony Moore, Charlie Adlard, and Cliff Rathburn. *The Walking Dead, Book 1*. Berkeley: Image, 2008.

Kirkman, Robert, Sean Phillips, June Chung, and Randy Gentile. *Marvel Zombies*. New York: Marvel, 2006.

Krewson, John. "Interview: Neil Gaiman." *The Onion A.V. Club*. Last modified February 3, 1999. http://www.avclub.com/article/neil-gaiman-13579.

Kristeva, Julia. *Powers of Horror: An Essay on Abjection*. Translated by Leon S. Roudiez. New York: Columbia University Press, 1982.

Landau, Ken. "There's a New Star Tonight." *Adventures into the Unknown* 62. New York: American Comics Group, November–December 1954.

Land of the Dead. Directed by George A. Romero. Hollywood: Universal, 2005.

Lawley, Guy and Steve Whitaker. "Alan Moore." *Alan Moore: Conversations*. Edited by Eric Berlatsky, 26–43. Jackson: University Press of Mississippi, 2012.

Lawrence, John Shelton and Robert Jewett, *The Myth of the American Superhero*. Grand Rapids, MI: Eerdmans, 2002.

Lewis, C.S. *The Screwtape Letters*. New York: HarperOne, [1942] 2015.

Lovecraft, H.P. *At the Mountains of Madness*. New York: Modern Library, [1936] 2005.

——. "The Picture in the House" *The Complete Fiction of H.P. Lovecraft.* New York: Chartwell, 2014, 103–09.

——. "Supernatural Horror in Literature," *The H.P. Lovecraft Archive.* Last modified October 20, 2009. http://www.hplovecraft.com/writings/texts/essays/shil.aspx.

Luthi, Max. "The Fairy Tale Hero: The Image of the Man in the Fairy Tale." *Folk and Fairy Tales.* Edited by Martin Hallett and Barbara Karasek, 315–22. Petersborough, Ontario: Broadview, 2009.

Mailer, Norman. *The Executioner's Song.* New York: Warner, [1979] 1980.

Marx, Karl. "The Eighteenth Brumaire of Louis Bonaparte. 1852." *Marxists.org.* Last modified 2006. https://www.marxists.org/archive/marx/works/1852/18th-brumaire/ch01.htm.

Matheson, Robert. *I Am Legend.* New York: ORB, [1954] 1995.

McCabe, Joseph. *Conversations with Neil Gaiman and His Collaborators: Hanging Out with the Dream King.* Seattle: Fantagraphics, 2004.

McCarthy, Bob. "When Sorcerers Meet." *Strange Tales* 47. New York: Marvel, June 1956.

McCarthy, Cormac. *The Road.* New York: Knopf, 2006.

McFarlane, Todd, Steve Oliff, Reuben Rude, and Tom Orzechowski. *Spawn, Book* 1. Fullerton, CA: Image, 1998.

Means-Shannon, Hannah. "It's a Battle for The Goon's Soul in 2015–Eric Powell in The Bleeding Cool Interview." *Bleeding Cool.* Last modified December 11, 2014. https://www.bleedingcool.com/2014/12/11/battle-goons-soul-2015-eric-powell-bleeding-cool-interview/.

Mesce, Bill. *Inside the Rise of HBO: A Personal History of the Company that Transformed Television.* Jefferson, NC: McFarland, 2015.

Meyer, Stephanie. *Twilight.* New York: Megan Tingley, [2005] 2006.

Miettinen, Mervi. "'Do You Understand How I Have Loved You?': Terrible Loves and Divine Visions in *From Hell*." *Sexual Ideology in the Works of Alan Moore: Critical Essays on the Graphic Novels.* Edited by Todd A. Comer, 88–99. Jefferson, NC: McFarland, 2012.

Mignola, Mike, John Byrne, Mark Chiarello, and Matthew Hollingsworth. *Hellboy: Seed of Destruction.* Milwaukie, OR: Dark Horse, 2003.

Millar, Mark, Greg Land, and Mitch Breitweiser. *Ultimate Fantastic Four, Vol. 3.* New York: Marvel, 2007.

Mignola, Mike, James Sinclair, Matthew Hollingsworth, Dave Stewart, and Pat Brosseau. *Hellboy: "The Chained Coffin" and Others.* Milwaukie, OR: Dark Horse, 2003.

Mignola, Mike, Dave Stewart, and Pat Brosseau. *Hellboy: The Right Hand of Doom.* Milwaukie, OR: Dark Horse, 2003.

Mignola, Mike, Dave Stewart, and Clem Robbins. *Hellboy: Strange Places.* Milwaukie, OR: Dark Horse, 2006.

Miller, Cynthia J. and Bowdoin Van Riper. "Introduction." *Undead in the Old West II: They Just Keeping Coming.* Edited by Cynthia J. Miller and Bowdoin Van Riper, xvii–xxviii. Lanham, MD: Scarecrow, 2013.

Miller, Frank. "Introduction." Todd McFarlane, Steve Oliff, Reuben Rude, and Tom Orzechowski. *Spawn, Book 1.* Fullerton, CA: Image, 1998, 2–3.

Mishkin, Dan, Gary Cohn, and Adrian Gonzales. "This Property Is Condemned." *The House of Mystery* 321. New York: DC, October 1983.

Mitchell, Margaret. *Gone with the Wind.* New York: Scribner, [1936] 2011.

Moore, Alan. "Ask the Author: Alan Moore." *Good Reads.* Last modified October 30, 2015. https://www.goodreads.com/author/3961.Alan_Moore/questions.

——. "Introduction." Mike Mignola, James Sinclair, and Pat Brosseau. *Hellboy: Wake the Devil.* Milwaukie OR: Dark Horse, 1997, 1.

Moore, Alan, Stephen Bissette, Rick Veitch, John Totleben, and Tatjana Wood, *Saga of the Swamp Thing, Vol. 1.* New York: DC, 1987.

—. *Saga of the Swamp Thing, Vol. 2.* New York: DC, 2009.

—. *Saga of the Swamp Thing, Vol. 3.* New York: DC, 2010.

Moore, Alan and Eddie Campbell. *From Hell.* Marietta, GA: Top Shelf, 2006.

Moore, Alan, John Totleben, Tatjana Wood, and John Costanza. *Swamp Thing* 53. New York: DC, October 1986.

Moore, Alan. Rick Veitch, Alfredo Alcala, Tatjana Wood, and John Costanza. *Swamp Thing* 52. New York: DC, September 1986.

Moore, Christopher. *Practical Demonkeeping.* New York: William Morrow, 2004.

Moore, Stuart. "Introduction." In Garth Ennis, Steve Dillon, Matt Hollingsworth, and Clem Robbins. *Preacher, Book 2.* New York: DC, 2013, 3–4.

Moritz, Edvard. "The Boy Who Cried Wolf." *Adventures into the Unknown* 10. New York: American Comics Group, April–May 1950.

The Munsters. CBS, 1964–1966.

Murphy, B. Keith. "The Origin of *The Sandman.*" *The Sandman Papers: An Exploration of the Sandman Mythology.* Edited by Joe Sanders, 3–24. Seattle: Fantagraphics, 2006.

Musson, Alex. "Alan Moore: Mustard Interview." *Mustard.* 2014. Last modified January 12, 2017. http://www.mustardweb.org/alanmoore/index.htm.

Near Dark. Directed by Kathryn Bigelow. Hollywood: De Laurentiis Entertainment, 1987.

Nebot, Joan. "Purification." *Vampirella* 16. New York: Warren, April 1972.

New Nightmare. Directed by Wes Craven. Hollywood: New Line, 1994.

"Newswatch: Rick Veitch Quits *Swamp Thing*: Scheduled Successors–Gaiman and Delano–Also Resign." *The Comics Journal* 129 (May 1989): 7–11.

Nightmare on Elm Street. Directed by Wes Craven. Hollywood: New Line, 1984.

Night of the Living Dead. Directed by George A. Romero. Laurel Group, 1968.

Night Stalker. ABC, 1972.

Nosferatu. Directed by F.W. Murnau. Germany: Prana-Film, 1922.

Nostrand, Howard and Joe Rosen. "The Rift of the Magis." *Tomb of Terror* 11. New York: Harvey Comics, September 1953.

Nyberg, Amy. *Seal of Approval: The History of the Comics Code*. Jackson: University Press of Mississippi, 1998.

O'Connor, Flannery. *Mystery and Manners: Occasional Prose*. New York: Farrar, Straus, and Giroux, 1970.

O'Connor, Laura. "The Corpse on Hellboy's Back: Translating a Graphic Image." *The Journal of Popular Culture* 43 (2010): 540–63.

Ogline, Tim E. "Myth, Magic, and the Mind of Neil Gaiman: A Conversation with the Dream King." *Wild River Review*. Last modified August 1, 2007. http://www.wildriverreview.com/4/worldvoices-neilgaiman.php.

Oleck, Jack, Alex Toth, and John Costanza. "The Devil's Doorway." *The House of Mystery* 182. New York: DC, September–October 1969.

O'Malley, Seamus. "Speculative History, Speculative Fiction: Alan Moore and Eddie Campbell's *From Hell*." *Graphic History: Essays on Graphic Novels and/as History*. Edited by Richard Iadonisi, 162–183. Newcastle: Cambridge Scholars Publishing, 2012.

Ong, Walter. *Orality and Literacy*. London: Routledge, 2002.

Parkin, Lance. *Magic Words: The Extraordinary Life of Alan Moore.* London: Aurum Press, 2013.

Pearson, Bill, Joe Orlando, and Ben Oda. "Image of Bluebeard!" *Creepy* 7. New York: Warren, February 1966.

Pepperell, Robert. *The Posthuman Condition: Consciousness Beyond the Brain.* Portland: Intellect, 2003.

The Phantom of the Opera. Directed by Rupert Julian. Hollywood: Universal, 1925.

Pietrzak-Franger, Monika. "Envisioning the Ripper's Visions: Adapting in Alan Moore and Eddie Campbell's *From Hell*." *Neo-Victorian Studies* 2 (Winter 2009/2010): 157–85.

Pineda, Antonio and Jesus Jimenez-Varea. "Popular Culture, Ideology, and the Comics Industry: Steve Ditko's Objectivist Spiderman." *The Journal of Popular Culture* 46 (2013): 1156–1176.

Pinkham, Jeremy. "The Rick Veitch Interview." *The Comics Journal*. Last modified May 24, 2013. http://www.tcj.com/the-rick-veitch-interview/.

Plan 9 from Outer Space. Directed by Ed Wood. Reynolds Pictures, 1956.

Poe, Edgar Allan. *Complete Stories and Poems of Edgar Allan Poe.* New York: Doubleday, 1984.

Polidori, John William. *The Vampyre and Other Tales of the Macabre*. Oxford: Oxford University Press, 2008.

Poole, W. Scott. *Monsters in America: Our Historical Obsession with the Hideous and the Haunting.* Waco: Baylor University Press, 2011.

Powell, Bob and Howard Nostrand. "Happy Anniversary." *Chamber of Chills* 19. New York: Harvey, September 1953.

Powell, Eric. *The Goon: Chinatown and the Mystery of Mr. Wicker.* Milwaukie, OR: Dark Horse, 2007.

——. *The Goon: Wicked Inclinations.* Milwaukie, OR: Dark Horse, 2006.

——. *Satan's Sodomy Baby* 1. Milwaukie, OR: Dark Horse. April 2007.

Powell, Eric and Robin Powell. *The Goon: Nothin' But Misery.* Milwaukie, OR: Dark Horse, 2010.

Powell, Eric, Robin Powell, Shaynne Corbett, Barry Gregory, and Ben Cocke. *The Goon: Heaps of Ruination.* Milwaukie, OR: Dark Horse, 2011.

Powell, Eric and Dave Stewart. *The Goon: Rough Stuff.* Milwaukie, OR: Dark Horse, 2010.

Powell, Eric, Dave Stewart, and Nate Piekos. *The Goon: Death's Greedy Comeuppance.* Milwaukie, OR: Dark Horse, 2011.

Psycho. Directed by Alfred Hitchcock. Hollywood: Paramount, 1960.

"Puddles of Blood." *Time.* March 29, 1948.

Pustz, Matthew J. *Comic Book Culture: Fanboys and True Believers.* Jackson: University Press of Mississippi, 1999.

Queenan, Joe. "Drawing on the Dark Side." *The New York Times.* Published April 30, 1989. No posting date. http://www.nytimes.com/1989/04/30/magazine/drawing-on-the-dark-side.html?pagewanted=all.

Quint. "Quint Talks with *The Goon* Creator Eric Powell about the Upcoming Animated Feature, David Fincher, Paul Giamatti, and Much More!!!" *AintItCool.com.* Last modified August 23, 2010. http://www.aintitcool.com/node/46242.

Radcliffe, Ann. *The Mysteries of Udolpho.* Oxford, Oxford University Press, [1794] 2008.

Rauch, Stephen. *Neil Gaiman's The Sandman and Joseph Campbell: In Search of the Modern Myth.* Holicong, PA: Wildside, 2003.

Return of the Living Dead. Directed by Dan O'Bannon. Hollywood, Fox Films, 1985.

Return of the Swamp Thing. Directed by Jim Wynorski. Lightyear Entertainment, 1989.

Reynolds, G.W.M. *Wagner the Wehr-Wolf.* Mineola, NY: Dover, [1846–1847] 1975.

Rice, Anne. *Interview with the Vampire.* New York: Knopf, [1976] 2007.

Roach, David A. and John B. Cooke. *The Warren Companion: The Definitive Compendium to the Great Comics of Warren Publishing*. Raleigh, NC: Twomorrows Publishing, 2001.

Roach, David, Andrew Jones, Simon Jowett, and Greg Hill. "Gary Leach and Alan Moore," *Alan Moore: Conversations*. Edited by Eric Berlatsky, 8–25. Jackson: University Press of Mississippi, 2012.

Robinson, Tasha. "Interview: Alan Moore." *The Onion A.V. Club*. Last modified October 24, 2001. http://www.avclub.com/article/alan-moore-13740.

——. "Interview: Alan Moore." *The Onion A.V. Club*. Last modified June 25, 2003. http://www.avclub.com/article/alan-moore-13821.

——. "Interview: Neil Gaiman." *The Onion A.V. Club*. Last modified September 28, 2005. http://www.avclub.com/article/neil-gaiman-13953.

Romer, Jean-Claude. "Bloody New Wave in the United States." *Horror Film Reader*. Edited by Alain Silver and James Ursini, 63–66. New York: Limelight, 2006.

Rose, Steve. "Moore's Murderer." *The Guardian*. Last modified February 1, 2002. https://www.theguardian.com/film/2002/feb/02/sciencefictionfantasyandhorror.books.

Rosemary's Baby. Directed by Roman Polanski. Hollywood: William Castle, 1968.

Rosenberger, John. "One Exciting Knight!" *Forbidden Worlds* 37. New York: American Comics Group, October 1955.

Round, Julia. "Embedded Metafiction: Cain and Abel in DC Comics." Paper presented at the PCA/ACA Conference, Seattle, WA, March 2016.

——. *Gothic in Comics and Graphic Novels*. Jefferson, NC: McFarland, 2014.

——. "The Horror of Humanity." *The Walking Dead and Philosophy: Zombie Apocalypse Now*. Edited by Wayne Yuen. 155–166. Chicago: Open Court, 2012.

——. "Transforming Shakespeare: Neil Gaiman and *The Sandman.*" *Beyond Adaptation: Essays on Radical Transformations of Original Works.* Edited by Phyllis Frus and Christy Williams, 95–110. Jefferson, NC: McFarland, 2010.

Russell, P. Craig. "Introduction." Mike Mignola, James Sinclair, Matthew Hollingsworth, Dave Stewart, and Pat Brosseau. *Hellboy: "The Chained Coffin" and Others.* 1. Milwaukie, OR: Dark Horse, 2003.

Rymer, James Malcolm. *Varney the Vampire or the Feast of Blood.* Mineola, NY: Dover, [1845–1847] 2015.

Sartain, Jeffrey A. "*Days Gone Bye*: Robert Kirkman's Reenvisioned Western *The Walking Dead.*" *Undead in the Old West II: They Just Keeping Coming.* Edited by Cynthia J. Miller and Bowdoin Van Riper, 249–268. Lanham, MD: Scarecrow, 2013.

Schatz, Thomas. *The Genius of the System: Hollywood Filmmaking in the Studio Era.* Minneapolis: University of Minnesota Press, 2010.

Schrotter, Gus. "The Pit and the Pendulum." *Yellowjacket Comics* 3. Derby, CT: Charlton, November 1944.

The Searchers. Directed by John Ford. Hollywood: Warner Bros., 1956.

Shelley, Mary. *Frankenstein.* New York: W.W. Norton, [1818] 2012.

The Shining. Directed by Stanley Kubrick. Hollywood: Warner Bros., 1980.

Sim, Dave and Alan Moore. "Correspondance: *From Hell*, Part 3: A Conversation Between Dave Sim and Alan Moore." *A Moment of Cerebus.* Last modified September 27, 2015. http://momentofcerebus.blogspot.co.uk/2015/09/correspondence-from-hell-part-3.html.

Simpson, Helen. "Introduction." Angela Carter. *The Bloody Chamber.* London: Vintage, 2006, vii–xix.

Sinclair, Upton. *The Jungle.* Mineola, NY: Dover, [1906] 2001.

Skal, David J. *Hollywood Gothic: The Tangled Web of Dracula from Novel to Stage to Screen.* New York: Farrar, Straus, and Giroux, 2004.

——. *The Monster Show: A Cultural History.* New York: Farrar, Straus, and Giroux, 1993.

Sommers, Joseph Michael. "Crooked Appalachia: The Laughter of the Melungeon Witches in Mike Mignola's Hellboy: The Crooked Man." *Comics and the U.S. South.* Edited by Brannon Costello and Qiana J. Whitted, 214–241. Jackson: University Press of Mississippi, 2012.

Stagecoach. Directed by John Ford. Hollywood: Walter Wanger, 1939.

Stevenson, Robert Louis. *The Strange Case of Dr. Jekyll and Mr. Hyde.* Mineola, NY: Dover, [1886] 1991.

Stoker, Bram. *Dracula.* New York: Penguin, [1897] 2004.

Strieber, Whitley. *The Hunger.* New York: Pocket, 1981.

Swamp Thing. Directed by Wes Craven. Hollywood: Embassy, 1982.

Tales from the Crypt. Directed by Freddie Francis. England: Metromedia, 1972.

Tales from the Crypt. HBO, 1989–1996.

Tartar, Maria. "Introduction." *The Classic Fairy Tales.* Edited by Maria Tartar, ix–xviii. New York: W.W. Norton, 1999.

"Testimony of William M. Gaines, Publisher, Entertaining Comics Group, New York, NY" *TheComicbooks.Com.* Last modified 2016. http://www.thecomicbooks.com/gaines.html.

Texas Chainsaw Massacre. Directed by Tobe Hooper. Vortex, 1974.

Them! Directed by Gordan Douglas. Hollywood: Warner Bros., 1954.

The Thing. Directed by John Carpenter. Hollywood: Universal, 1982.

Thomas, Roy. "Ghosties and Ghoulies and Things That Go Bump in the Brain..." *Monsters Unleashed* 1. New York: Marvel, March 1973.

Thriller. Directed by John Landis. Hollywood: Optimum, 1983.

Tilley, Carol L. "Seducing the Innocent: Fredric Wertham and the Falsifications That Helped Condemn Comics." *Information and Culture: A Journal of History* 47 (2012): 383–413.

Todorov, Tzvetan. "Definition of the Fantastic." *The Horror Reader*. Edited by Ken Gelder, 14–19. London: Routledge, 2000.

Trombetta, Jim. *The Horror! The Horror!: Comic Books the Government Didn't Want You to Read.* New York: Harry N. Abrams, 2010.

True Blood. HBO, 2008–2014.

Tuska, George. "The Kill-Crazy Fleagle Brothers." *Crime Does Not Pay* 50. New York: Lev Gleason Publications, March 1947.

28 Days Later. Directed by Danny Boyle. UK: DNA Films, 2002.

Twin Peaks. ABC, 1990–1991.

Twilight Zone. CBS, 1959–1964.

Veitch, Rick and Michael Zulli. Unpublished manuscript of *Swamp Thing* 88. *20th Century Danny Boy.* Last Modified October 22, 2011. http://ohdannyboy.blogspot.com/2011/10/morning-of-magician-swamp-thing-meets.html.

Vint, Sherryl. "Abject Posthumanism: Neoliberalism, Biopolitics, and Zombies." *Monster Culture in the 21st Century: A Reader*. Edited by Marine Levine and Diem-My T. Bui, 133–146. London: Bloomsbury, 2013.

Voger, Mark. *Monster Mash: The Creepy, Kooky Monster Craze in America 1957–1972*. Raleigh, NC: TwoMorrows, 2015.

Wagner, Hank, Christopher Golden, and Stephen R. Bissette. *Prince of Stories: The Many Worlds of Neil Gaiman.* New York: St. Martin's, 2008.

The Walking Dead. AMC, 2010–2018.

Walpole, Horace. *The Castle of Otranto.* Oxford: Oxford University Press, [1764] 2009.

Wandtke, Terrence. *The Dark Night Returns: The Contemporary Resurgence of Crime Comics*. New York: RIT Press, 2015.

——. *The Meaning of Superhero Comics*. Jefferson, NC: McFarland, 2012.

Webb, Charles. "Return of 'The Goon': An Interview with Eric Powell." *MTV.com*. Last modified March 11, 2011. http://www.mtv.com/news/2621595/return-of-the-goon-an-interview-with-eric-powell/.

Weigel, Charles. "Introducing Horror." *Hop on Pop: The Politics of Popular Culture*. Edited by Henry Jenkins. Tara McPherson, and Jane Shattuc, 700–20. Durham: Duke University Press, 2002.

Wein, Len, Berni Wrightson, Tatjana Wood, and Ben Oda. "Swamp Thing." *House of Secrets* 92. New York: DC, June–July 1971.

Weiner, Stephen, Jason Hall, and Victoria Blake. *Hellboy: The Companion*. Milwaukie, OR: Dark Horse, 2008.

Wessler, Carl, Graham Ingles, Marie Severin, and Jim Wroten. "The Prude." *The Haunt of Fear* 28. New York: EC, November–December 1954.

White, Claire E. "A Conversation with Neil Gaiman." *The Internet Writing Journal*. Last modified March 1999. http://www.writerswrite.com/journal/mar99/a-conversation-with-neil-gaiman-3991.

Whitted, Qiana J. "Of Slaves and Other Swamp Things: Black Southern History as Comic Book Horror." *Comics and the U.S. South*. Edited by Brannon Costello and Qiana J. Whitted, 187–213. Jackson: University Press of Mississippi, 2012.

Wilde, Oscar. *The Portrait of Dorian Grey*. Mineola, NY: Dover, [1890] 1993.

The Wolf Man. Directed by George Waggner. Hollywood: Universal, 1941.

Wolfman, Marv. "Speaking with… Len Wein, Part 1." Marv Wolfman.com. http://www.marvwolfman.com/marv/Speaking_With_Len_Wein_Part_One.html.

Wolfman, Marv, Gene Colan, Tom Palmer, Linda Lessmann, and John Costanza. "Night-Fire!" *Tomb of Dracula* 27. New York: Marvel, December 1974.

Wood, Robin. *Hollywood from Vietnam to Reagan... and Beyond.* New York: Columbia University Press, 2003.

Wright, Bradford. *Comic Book Nation: The Transformation of Youth Culture in America.* Baltimore: Johns Hopkins University Press, 2001.

The X-Files. Fox, 1993–2002.

Yoe, Craig. *Secret Identity: The Fetish Art of Superman's Co-Creator Joe Shuster*. State College, PA: Harvey Abrams, 2009.

Zipes, Jack. "Introduction: The Remaking of Charles Perrault and His Fairy Tales." *Little Red Riding Hood, Cinderella, and Other Classic Fairy Tales of Charles Perrault.* New York: Penguin, 2008, vi–xxxii.

Žižek, Slavoj. *Everything You Wanted to Know about Lacan... but Were Afraid to Ask Hitchcock.* New York: Verso, 1992.

INDEX

Page numbers in italics indicate illustrations

Page numbers in italics indicate illustrations

C

Page numbers in italics indicate illustrations

D

Page numbers in italics indicate illustrations

E

F

G

Page numbers in italics indicate illustrations

H

I

J

K

Page numbers in italics indicate illustrations

L

M

Page numbers in italics indicate illustrations

N

O

P

Q

Page numbers in italics indicate illustrations

R

S

Page numbers in italics indicate illustrations

W

Page numbers in italics indicate illustrations

X

Y

Z

COLOPHON

Molly Q. Cort
Editor

Bruce Ian Meader
Designer

Marnie Soom
Production

More Vang
Alexandria, Virginia
Printer
This book was made possible, in part, through the generosity of More Vang.

Blazer Silk
80 lb. text and 100 lb. cover
Inside and Cover Paper

Adobe Caslon Pro, Neutraface 2
Typefaces